Italian Drama in Shakespeare's Time

Mario Mazza, *L'Acamante, tragedia* (Bologna, 1642), frontispiece.
The original words on the sheepskin held by the figures of
Comedy, Tragedy, and Pastoral are "L'Acamante, Tragedia di Mario Mazza."
Courtesy of the Thomas Fisher Rare Book Library, University of Toronto.

Italian Drama in Shakespeare's Time

LOUISE GEORGE CLUBB

YALE UNIVERSITY PRESS
New Haven and London

Designed by Sonia L. Scanlon
and set in Sabon
type by G & S Typesetters, Inc., Austin, Texas.
Printed in the United States of America by Vail-Ballou Press,
Binghamton, New York.

Library of Congress Cataloging-in-Publication Data
Clubb, Louise George.
Italian drama in Shakespeare's time / Louise George Clubb.
p.   cm.
Bibliography: p.
Includes index.
ISBN 0-300-03712-0 (alk. paper)
1. Italian drama—To 1700—History and criticism.
2. Shakespeare, William, 1564–1616—Sources.   3. Litera-
ture, Comparative—Italian and English.   4. Literature,
Comparative—English and Italian.
I. Title.
PQ4139.C58   1989
852'.409—dc20   89-31963
CIP

The paper in this book meets the guidelines for permanence
and durability of the Committee on Production Guidelines for
Book Longevity of the Council on Library Resources.
10   9   8   7   6   5   4   3   2   1

For Will

What's in the braine that Inck may character,
Which hath not figur'd to thee my true Spirit?

Polonius. The best actors in the world, either for tragedy, comedy, history, pastoral, pastoral-comical, historical-pastoral, tragical-historical, tragical-comical-historical-pastoral; scene individable, or poem unlimited. Seneca cannot be too heavy, nor Plautus too light. For the law of writ and the liberty, these are the only men.

—*Hamlet*, II.2.387–92

Contents

TRAGEDY

Preface

his book was planned long ago to supply what I knew I could not be alone in needing—a picture of Italian drama as Shakespeare might have seen it. It was to open a view different from that of Italianists on the one hand and of traditional source studies on the other. Herrick and Lea implicitly had pursued a similar aim, in the process adding immeasurably to the knowledge heaped up by the grand old positivistic *Quellenstudien* and various successive accounts of "backgrounds" and "influences." But there was no body of readings nor literary geography of the structures of dramatic texts. On the whole the standard works were written from the distance established by modern decisions about achievements in Renaissance drama. How the theater of Italy appeared to the sixteenth and seventeenth centuries was at most a question incidental to defining Cinquecento Italian drama as a prelude to a greatness not its own. This much I had learned while studying Giambattista Della Porta, whose plays belong to Shakespeare's time and were the Italian dramatic works most often translated by Elizabethans and Jacobeans.

Investigating one aspect after another, I saw also how different Italian Renaissance drama looked when approached from contemporary Italy and England rather than from ancient Greece and Rome. The theatrical movement frequently depicted as mechanically imitative, deservedly neglected by Shakespeare, appeared instead as a dynamic foundry where instruments were forged for kinds of theatrical representation not attempted by the ancients but made possible by Renaissance imitation of them. The results established a practice of writing, reading, and acting plays and defined a tradition, in which Shakespeare claimed his place. These phenomena were not unknown but demanded presentation from new angles. As my work continued it took various forms, dioramic and microscopic, as papers and articles published in increasingly separate arenas of discussion.

In a field as vast as this one gradually revealed itself to be, only an encyclopedia of sorts could have accomplished what I had had in mind to begin with. But the idea of a less gargantuan book remained until, by redrafting the material from some of my essays into a unified historical account, I detected a falseness in imposing today's perceptions on yesterday's. Revision and updating of my work on this subject seemed an illusory attempt to remake the past, and I concluded that consolidating the results of this long communion with Italian Renaissance drama meant giving the present an excessive privilege, draining each essay of its own history and character.

On rereading the original versions, I found nevertheless that something of constancy had emerged naturally from early to late. Aside from a few *pentimenti,* there was a core of conviction confirmed by time about the common ground of Renaissance drama: the principles of construction, the repertory of movable parts, the theoretical and ideological forces at work in avant-garde Italian drama, and the general notion of it shared in an international culture. If only to bring conveniently together my relevant studies issued in diverse Italian and American publications, there seemed reason to gather selected essays, the earliest printed twenty-five years ago, the latest published here for the first time. They now appear not in the order of writing but with their individual identities preserved, the published ones essentially intact, except in two chapters where portions of early material have been transplanted.

Research for chapters 2, 4, and 5 was supported by the John Simon Guggenheim Foundation; chapters 1 and 3 and part of chapter 6 were completed with the help of a grant from the American Philosophical Society; chapters 7 and 9, as well as the second part of chapter 6, were funded by the American Council of Learned Societies; fellowships at three different times from the Berkeley Humanities Research Council contributed to my work on chapters 1, 3, and 7 and enabled me to write the Prologue.

The choice and order of the essays were determined by the illustration each offered of characteristic aspects of the genres by which Italian dramatists and Shakespeare (or at least Polonius) conceived of plays and classified them. These are epitomized by the classical trio of feminine personifications mingling on the title page of Mazza's *Acamante:* sandaled Comedy and satyr-hooved Pastoral flanking crowned and sceptered Tragedy. Two of the essays treat of tragedies written after Shakespeare's lifetime but representative of Italian drama at the close of the same era. They attest identifying strains of Renaissance theater and certain constants in my thinking about it. The opening essay, on theory and structure, and the last, on practice and the *commedia dell'arte,* are disposed as prologue and epilogue to the others because both of them touch on all three genres. None represents my last word on the subject. But from this end of a span in time, certain views glimpsed early remain clear to me although the light has changed.

Given the history of this book, the number of those who have shared in its making is necessarily greater than my power to thank each by name, but I am thankful to them all. Long debts have accumulated to the Bancroft Library of the University of California, Berkeley, to the Folger Shakespeare Library, the Newberry Library, and the Joseph Regenstein Library of the University of Chicago, the Biblioteca Nazionale of Florence, the Biblioteca Marciana of Venice, the Biblioteca del Vaticano, and in Padua the Biblioteca Universitaria and the Biblioteca del Museo Civico. In the last stages, I was wonderfully aided by the staff at I Tatti, the Harvard University Center for Italian Renaissance Studies, in Florence. Susan Bates triumphed over word processors and photocopiers with skill and taste. Fiorella Superbi Gioffredi's fast magic produced essential microfilms when they were most needed. Julian Kliemann supplied erudite counsel, computer-wise first aid, and photographs with equal ease. The generous intercession of other colleagues, Vittore Branca, Paolo Trovato, and Marianna Shreve Simpson, helped to complete the illustrations. I was blessed in having Elisabeth Giansiracusa, most keen-eyed and knowledgeable of research assistants, at my side throughout the preparation of the final manuscript. I am grateful to Edward Tripp of the Yale University Press for carrying on the tradition of the scholarly bookman who both hunts and harvests, and am greatly obliged as well for the editorial finesse and judgment of Fred Kameny. The last and most inadequate thanks go to my husband, William Graham Clubb, for whom I wrote every word, revised some, and excised many others.

Curzio Gonzaga, *Gli inganni, comedia*
(Venice, 1592), 27.
Courtesy of the Folger Shakespeare Library.

Cristoforo Castelletti, *I torti amorosi, comedia*
(Venice, 1591), 203.
Courtesy of the Folger Shakespeare Library.

Gonzaga, *Gli inganni* [26v].

Prologue

Theatergrams

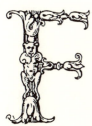or historians, the relation between the Renaissance drama of Italy and that of England is a hardy perennial, never prevented by radical skepticism from sending up new interrogative shoots. According to one line of scholarship, stretching back before E. K. Chambers, W. W. Greg, and T. W. Baldwin, analogues, common sources, and numerous instances of borrowing do not add up to evidence that the Italian Renaissance theater had a significant "influence" on the Elizabethan. This negative conclusion follows logically from standard methods of source study and from the premise that in critical comparisons differences are more revealing than similarities. Paradoxically, the denial also mirrors the dissatisfaction of addicted readers of Italian and English plays who meet in the contrary conviction that there existed what is better conceived of as a common system than as an influence; for them too, the constantly rising number of discrete, apparently unrelated connections between Italian and English drama discovered by *Quellenstudien* is not enough to account for the broader kinship insistently suggested by the collective testimony of theatrical texts.

Nowhere is the suggestion stronger than in relation to Shakespeare's comedies, and nowhere does the conspicuous position of the classical sources that he shared with Italian drama more obstruct a comprehensive view of the cultivation of comic genres in the Renaissance. Source studies that acknowledge the pretextuality of Plautus and Terence to Shakespeare necessarily, if sometimes unintentionally, raise the question of how the nonpareil of the English Renaissance is related to the powerfully fashionable Continental genres that were also rooted in Attic-Roman New Comedy. Ruth Nevo's demonstration that the "stratagems

This chapter appeared in slightly different form in *Comparative Critical Approaches to Renaissance Comedy*, ed. Donald Beecher and Massimo Ciavolella (Ottawa: Dovehouse, 1986), 15–33. The illustrations used here and in chapters 3 and 4 are described in my "Pictures for the Reader: A Series of Illustrations to Comedy, 1591–1592," *Renaissance Drama*, o.s. 9 (1966): 265–77, with corrigenda in *Renaissance Drama*, n.s. 1 (1968): 340–41.

of the New Comedy supplied Europe with its comic fictions for two millennia and Shakespeare with his plots from *The Comedy of Errors* to *The Tempest*" is sound genealogy.[1] Certainly, from Menander to Dustin Hoffman is a long span in Western culture, and doubtless something of the dynamics of culture in general can be learned from observing that the complications of Menander's *Sikyonios* and those of the television play-within-the-play in Hoffman's *Tootsie* are dismissed by the device of identifying one of the major characters as the long-lost brother of another. Something more particular can be learned, however, from the fact that *Tootsie* is punctuated by allusions to Shakespeare, the principal one being that the title character is a transvestite male whose motives and actions reconstitute those of Viola in *Twelfth Night,* but with the sexes reversed; and that although this familiar theatrical phenomenon can be traced to numbers of Cinquecento Italian comedies, its genealogy does not go back as far as Plautus, notwithstanding his much imitated boy-bride in *Casina,* for the Renaissance stratagems of Viola and the modern ones of Tootsie are altogether different from classical identity shifts in both components and consequences.

   Twelfth Night, which Nevo treats as the summit of the peculiarly Shakespearean genre romantic comedy, is emblematic of the current state of our question. A play permeated by unequivocally Cinquecento theatrical structures, signally by those adapted from medieval romance and contingent on the exploitation of the combinatory possibilities of the transvestite heroine in an Italianized New Comedy framework, *Twelfth Night* testifies to an English-Italian relationship the more pervasive for being unspecific, although Shakespeare's contemporaries could see that *Twelfth Night* was closer to *Inganni* than to its distant Plautine source.[2] It has proved impossible to fix the relationship by

   1. Ruth Nevo, "Shakespeare's Comic Remedies," *Shakespearean Comedy,* ed. Maurice Charney (New York, 1980), 4. For comparison of Shakespeare's comedy with the Terentian model see Nevo's *Comic Transformations in Shakespeare* (London and New York, 1980). In "Towards a 'Philosophy' of Renaissance Theatre," an essay from the volume for which my prologue "Theatergrams" was written, Riccardo Scrivano admirably displays other aspects of the generative inheritance and "storeroom" of Renaissance comedy. See also Scrivano's "Spazio e teatro nella Ferrara del Cinquecento," *Finzioni teatrali da Ariosto a Pirandello* (Messina and Florence, 1982), 51–117.

   2. John Manningham's diary note on a performance in 1602 surely refers not to Secchi's or Gonzaga's *Inganni* but to the much imitated, adapted, and translated *Gl'ingannati,* the collective work of the Sienese Accademia degli In-

old-fashioned source studies, resistant as they are to historicizing synthesis. On the other hand, the undeniable existence of a relationship has been conducive to metahistorical contrasts, as well as to diachronic demonstrations of Shakespeare's drama as the apex of an evolution in genre or even as its final cause.

Incorporating some of the best of such teleological theory into his admirable comparative analysis, Leo Salingar has made it impossible ever again to doubt that Shakespeare's use of Italian elements was "not mere imitation of New Comedy of Italian plots, but application of Italian methods to new purposes." And by adding a voice to Coghill's and Doran's perceptions of Shakespeare's participation in the classicism of his time ("Jonson associated classical comedy with . . . satire, following a sixteenth century tradition, while Shakespeare, also, however, following tradition, associated it with romance"),[3] Salingar helps to return Shakespeare to the central community of Renaissance theater from which he is often still barred by the disposition to order cultural history toward a previewed end by means of polar oppositions.

Most polarizations divide European theater into regular, "Aristotelian," theoretical Italian and French on one hand and irregular, pragmatic Spanish and English on the other, whether the antipodal concepts are labeled classical and romantic, or have been further dehistoricized as learned and spontaneous, or artificial and natural, or evolved politically into conservative and progressive or elite and popular. In local contexts, they line up Jonson against Shakespeare and *commedia erudita* against *commedia dell'arte*, as well as "pure" genres against mixed ones. The oppositions are not historically unfounded, of course. Jonson himself provided a view of two camps: he was in one and the colleague he loved "on this side idolatry" in the other.[4] Lope de Vega paraded his acquaintance with the road not taken in his "new art."[5] Italian *trattatisti*

---

tronati performed in 1531 and printed in 1537: "At our feast wee had a play called "Twelve Night, or What You Will", much like the *Commedy of Errores,* or *Menechmi* in Plautus, but most like and neere to that in Italian called *Inganni*." I quote from Geoffrey Bullough, *Narrative and Dramatic Sources of Shakespeare*, vol. 2 (London and New York, 1958): 269.

3. Leo Salingar, *Shakespeare and the Traditions of Comedy* (Cambridge, England, 1974), 77, 225.

4. *Timber; or, Discoveries,* in C. H. Herford and P. E. Simpson, eds., *Ben Jonson*, vol. 8 (Oxford, 1947): 584.

5. Lope de Vega, *El arte nuevo de hacer comedias* (1609).

warred over the permissibility of mixing tragedy and comedy. But positions destined to become the right and left banks of the Great Divide of cultural history may in the late Cinquecento and early Seicento have appeared rather as hypotheses about issues internal to the new institution of the theater. Ordering of the past according to such contrasting pairs of timeless concepts as classical and romantic has obscured the common premises of Renaissance drama and skewed modern perceptions of Italian theater.

Italian scholarship long tended to apologize for Cinquecento theater, even in the act of discovering its remarkable achievement. Romantic and post-Romantic criticism generally shied away from the imitative principle at the humanistic core of a literarily transmitted theater, and instead praised whatever in it could be called "unclassical," as if only by a deracinating self-assertion could the identity of Italian drama be maintained against its Latin and Greek antecedents.

The Shakespeare revered in Italy, moreover, is still a Schlegelian one, a version of Coleridge's bard of truth to Nature and knowledge of the human heart, his comedy admired for being so much farther from Plautus and Terence than the Italian genre, which is reproached by the comparison. The political implications of such metahistorical polarization appear in Gramsci's rebuke to Sanesi for observing that the anonymous author of the extraordinary but structurally old-fashioned *La venexiana* had not followed the avant-garde model of humanistic comedy produced by Ariosto, Bibbiena, and Machiavelli. For Gramsci, theater was ideally a vox populi and neoclassicism at all times of Italian history an exhalation of authority, a conservative enemy to innovation, costumed in his imagination as a *codino,* or pigtailed aristocrat, target of the French Revolution.[6] The late Ludovico Zorzi, too good a historian to let stand this anachronism, acknowledged the accuracy of Sanesi's view of the commedia erudita as innovative and the linear medieval play model as old-fashioned, but he residually shared Gramsci's conventional anticlassicism. Zorzi therefore felt it necessary to isolate Ruzante from the standard idea of Italian Renaissance comedy, and in so doing subscribed for Marx and for himself to a cliché opposition of commedia erudita to the comedy of Shakespeare. In *La moscheta* and the dialogues, wrote Zorzi, Ruzante

> per dirla con Marx, scopre veramente sé stesso e shakespeareggia: se shakespeareggia significa, secondo il concorde giudizio, rappresentare la genuina natura umana contro gli schemi convenzionali,

6. Antonio Gramsci, *Letteratura e vita nazionale* (Turin, 1955), 4: 70–71.

e la costruzione di personaggi secondo idee preconcette e modelli moralistici.[7]

as Marx says, discovers himself and Shakespearizes, if by Shakespearize is meant, as is generally agreed, to represent true human nature, as opposed to conventional patterns and character construction according to preconceived ideas and moralistic models.

Here the character of commedia erudita is obliterated in the polarization of romantic and classical reinvoked long past its usefulness, and Shakespeare's greatness is used to shut out the light that would show him standing in the theater of his time, instead of merely towering over it. Here another sort of *idea preconcetta* obscures what a mass of fragmentary and disorderly but substantial evidence points to: that the same theatrical movement that promulgated the imitation of classical models produced romantic comedy and mixed genres, in Italy as well as England, and did so through a common process based on the principle of contamination of sources, genres, and accumulated stage-structures, or theatergrams.

If we look synchronically at Shakespearean and Italian theater, we find the latter in a state of broad development and diversification. The century that had begun with Ariosto's *Nova comedia* fostered a self-consciously modern system of imitating reality by means of a contract between spectators and play makers for forming an alternative physical space, a place for controlled play within the uncontrollable play of life around them, in which kinds, means, and goals of representation and things represented could both reflect and exclude aspects of the encompassing outer world. The idea that distinct genres were necessary to such representation and were available in ancient models was a strong determinant established well before theoretical debate was sparked by commentaries on Aristotle. The premise was one underlying the Renaissance practice of *imitatio* in general, and rested on a choice as deliberately calculated as were the choices of forms and materials from antiquity that Quattrocento humanists had made to achieve some independent definition of their present, in resistance to the undifferentiating and massive pressure of their immediate past.[8]

7. Ruzante, *Teatro, prima edizione completa: Testo, traduzione a fronte e note,* ed. Ludovico Zorzi (Milan, 1967; repr. 1969), lxvi n. 64. Zorzi refers to Marx's letter to Lassalle, 19 April 1859, on the subject of revolutionary tragedy.

8. Particularly valuable among numerous works on the subject, though not concerned with the theater, are Nancy S. Struever, *The Language of History in*

The prospect of wielding power over perceptions of reality by using as an instrument of selection the luminous clue of ancient comedy promised ideological, political, and economic gain; it also provided technological motivation that led inevitably to comic excursions into tragedy and to more far-reaching experiments in crossbreeding of genres. By the late Cinquecento innumerable conjunctions had been tried, and there had proliferated various kinds of plays, of audiences, of auspices, and, most consequential, of actors, private and professional, male and female. The difference within the range of drama could be as great as that between a five-act academic, Sophoclean pastoral tragicomedy in verse prepared for a royal wedding, such as Guarini's *Pastor fido,* and a three-act prose *zannata* improvised in a piazza by a hat-passing, traveling troupe; nevertheless, viewed from the measured distance that permits historical periodization, such representations were but separate branches of a common enterprise.

Constant as a principle from the time of Ariosto on was construction by contamination, the meditated and usually explicit combination of pre-texts. But in addition to the mere fusion of borrowed plots, this demanded the interchange and transformation of units, figures, relationships, actions, *topoi,* and framing patterns, gradually building a combinatory of theatergrams that were at once streamlined structures for svelte play making and elements of high specific density, weighty with significance from previous incarnations. The *elementi drammaturgici* that Ferruccio Marotti identifies as common building blocks of the commedia dell'arte that often frustrate attempts to make precise historical connections and attributions constitute a class of these resources.[9] When the work Zorzi bequeathed to his Florentine circle is finished and all the scenarios in extant collections have been cross-referenced, we shall see more of theatergrams at work in the professional theater. But the process of transformational theater from the common repertory was immensely larger than the commedia dell'arte branch of Renaissance drama can suggest. Whatever the primary sources of any comedy, literary or improvised, may have been, the ubiquitous and unceasing activation of the

the Renaissance: Rhetoric and Historical Consciousness in Florentine Humanism (Princeton, 1970) and Thomas M. Greene, *The Light in Troy: Imitation and Discovery in Renaissance Poetry* (New Haven, 1982).

9. Ferruccio Marotti, "La figura di Flaminio Scala," in *Alle origini del teatro moderno: La commedia dell'arte,* ed. Luciano Mariti (Rome, 1980), 23–24.

essential principles of Cinquecento comedy, contamination and complication, illustrates how theater came from theater, self-nourishing, self-reproducing, and evolving.

The practice of several generations of playwrights in a century of testing their principles and expanding their process stretched combinatory structures to new lengths, made new reverberations, sometimes generating philosophical overtones in unexpected settings, and brought to Italian theater an inwardness that only critical commonplaces about "conventional patterns," "preconceived ideas," and forced contrasts with Shakespeare can prevent us from recognizing as effects characteristic of much of his work too. Construction by contamination of plots and theatergrams was soon extended to produce contamination of genres. From the cultivation of comedy and tragedy arose a movement toward a third genre, a predictable next step in the long humanistic competition with antiquity. It coincided with a response to the challenge thrown down by the dissemination of the *Poetics,* with an answering attempt to make perfect plots in Aristotle's sense, adapting to comic structure the acclaimed Sophoclean peripety by displacing the dynamics of fate and predestination with a theatrical expression of the essential Counter-Reformation tenets of divine providence and free will. The results were mutations of the comic repertorial structures to allow for imitation of kinds of reality previously unattempted in Renaissance drama, but without abandoning the controllable, alternative, represented space that had been achieved by Cinquecento play making and without returning to the linear "illustrated narration" technique of medieval drama.

Nova comedia, which had been called *commedia grave* to denote the high theoretical claim of its neoclassical form, became grave in content too as playwrights increasingly weighted the genre with loans from tragedy. There appeared more kinds and levels of action, higher-ranking or more exotic characters, integrating designs in aid of polysemous representation: a comedy that was more romantic, more serious, and a pastoral drama that was tragicomic. These take shape by fission and fusion of theatergrams under pressure from new materials and directions. I propose to illustrate this phase of expansion and diversification by following the fortunes of one particular theatergram, one of the humbler ones, through the century: or, more precisely, by pursuing a complex of specific elements, for to speak of one alone is to reduce it to the abstraction of stock character or situation. (Of the latter a superrational analyst once claimed there were only thirty-six.) My aim is the opposite, to show the unlimited fertility and transformational capability implicit in each configuration. Any of these demonstrates the core process: permutation and declension by recombination with compatible units, whether of person, association, action, or design.

The choice of a sexual center differentiating Renaissance New Comedy from its Roman model (in which a bound-for-bed action was optional only, and marriageable female characters could easily be dispensed with as stage presences) directed the mainstream of the Cinquecento genre toward the figure of the woman desired and desiring, a requisite datum of plot that with usage would become the staple *giovane innamorata*. This theatergram of person called for and partly defined itself by another, with which to form a theatergram of association; in turn it motivated certain stageworthy actions. The young woman in love requires specifically a confidant, encourager, agent, messenger, or perhaps all of these, so that from the association there may arise expository scenes and plot-forwarding motions toward the lovers' unions and toward connections with other characters whose own associations and actions may further or oppose such ends.

In the cornerstone comedy of the genre, Ariosto's prose *Cassaria*, which his prologue introduces as "nova comedia . . . piena / di vari giochi, che né mai latine / né greche lingue recitarno in scena" (new comedy . . . full of diverse play never put on stage in either Latin or Greek),[10] the women in love are mere merchandise, assigned to wait for their respective Greek and Turkish lovers to buy them and set them up as mistresses. When Ariosto revised the comedy into verse he made important changes, transferring the action closer to the spectators' world, from the Greek Metellino to Sibari in the Italian Magna Grecia, and turning the lovers into an Italian and a Spaniard and the girls into sisters, but still slaves. As before, they function as confidants to each other and receive assurances and Petrarchan compliments directly from their lovers, without intermediaries. Ariosto adds the character of an old *fantesca*, by status eligible to act in a variety of associations (as the theatergram of the maidservant would later do), including that of confidant and go-between to the innamorata, but he does not put her into communication with the sisters nor engage her in the intrigue, reserving her for the purely ethical function of showing the procurer's bad character

10. *La cassaria* (prose version, 1508), in Ludovico Ariosto, *Opere minori*, ed. Cesare Segre (Milan and Naples, 1954), 242.

and contrasting the advantages of pretty girls with the condition of used up old servants whom love will not liberate (III.4).

With his second comedy, *I suppositi,* Ariosto confirmed the inclination of the Italian genre toward a looking-glass perspective that distanced it increasingly from Plautine and Terentian hellenizing by bringing the plot home to Ferrara; the woman in love is now marriageable, and her lover is a Sicilian student who has reached her bed by changing identities with his servant and obtaining work in her father's house. Polimnesta's associate is her nurse (anonymously "Nutrice" in the prose version, "Balia" in the verse revision); the expository scene reveals that when Polimnesta was smitten by love at first sight the nurse encouraged her to sleep with Erostrato, by praising him to Polimnesta and then leading him to her bedroom (I.1). It is also established that the Nutrice, later called an old whore ("puttana vecchia" III.3) and a bawd ("ruffiana" III.4), has accepted money for this aid; but she claims hypocritically to have acted simply out of pity and now advises Polimnesta to forget the lackey ("famiglio") and turn her mind to a more advantageous match ("onorevole amore"). In her status and significant stances the nurse has taken on shades of the *ānus* from Roman comedy, as in *Hecyra* and *Mostellaria,* as well as of *La Celestina* and her antecedents, and the resulting cluster of traits and deeds fits her to represent the first of the false "suppositions" forming the comedy's warp. Polimnesta, moreover, defines her own character by contrast with the nurse, revealing that she and Erostrato aim at marriage, that she does not share the nurse's comfortable acceptance of a plurality of lovers, and that she has been keeping her own counsel as to the true identity of her future husband.

From a cultural accretion of clues to the variability of two contrasting feminine personae, triggering separately and in associations an even more variable series of actions and attitudes, a theatrical combination has been worked to answer the demands of plot plausibly and dramatically (that is, representably on stage) within the urban domestic space that commedia claimed as its site. While Polimnesta and her nurse declare and supersede their own history, they authorize the recombinations to come, of theatergrams of association (specific pairings in the *serva padrona* range) that would generate theatergrams of motion: actions and reactions with apposite speeches, kinds of encounters, use of props and parts of the set for hiding, meeting, attack, defense, seduction, deceit, and so forth. All these produce variations of plot and character united in theatergrams of design, patterns of meaning expressed by

the disposition of material reciprocally organizing the whole comedy
and the spectators' perception of its form.[11] Ariosto's great reputation
with later connoisseurs and playwrights for bringing coherent structure
to the genre may owe something to his success in patterning this second
comedy by permuting substitutions and suppositions,[12] or, as Gascoigne
would translate, of "supposes" of one thing for another,[13] clinched with
porno-puns on suppository acts at the beginning of the prologue and
the end of the last act, intensified and doubled in the verse revision.

Though relegated to a single scene, Polimnesta and her nurse demonstrate at the outset of Cinquecento comedy a relationship and attendant
points of behavior perpetually useful and variable. In countless plots
these theatergrams of action recombinable for new structures reappear,

11. Good examples and demonstration of the multiple dramatic functioning
of typical theatergrams of action are in Pamela D. Stewart, "Il giuoco scenico
dei 'begli scambiamenti' nella *Calandria*" and "Il travestimento come teatro nel
teatro," both in *Retorica e mimica nel "Decameron" e nella commedia del Cinquecento* (Florence, 1986), 125–40, 161–248.

12. Gianmaria Cecchi, for one, praised Ariosto on Horatian critical grounds,
especially for setting up standards for the logic of successive action: "Cede a te
nella comica palestra / Ogni Greco e Latin perche tu solo / Hai veramente di-
monstrato come / Esser deve il principio, il mezzo e'l fine / Delle comedie"
(Every Greek and Roman must give way to you in the comic arena, for only you
have truly demonstrated the proper beginning, middle, and end of comedies).
Intermedio 6, *Le pellegrine*, quoted in Ludovico Ariosto, *Commedie e satire*,
annotated by Giovanni Tortoli (Florence, 1856), lxii. Ariosto's other devices for
structural coherence also moved Cecchi to imitation in more than one of his
own comedies. On the linguistic coherence offered by Ariosto's "lingua comica
unitaria" to the inherently plurilingual Italian comic theater, see Gianfranco
Folena, "Le lingue della commedia e la commedia delle lingue," *Scritti lin-
guistici in onore di Giovan Battista Pellegrini* (Pisa, 1983), 1498–99.

13. Ariosto announces in the prologue to *I suppositi* (prose version, 1509),
"El nome è li *Suppositi*, perché di supposizioni è tutta piena" (Its name is *Suppositions* because it is completely filled with them). See *Opere minori*, ed. Segre,
298. Gascoigne: "Our Suppose is nothing else but a mistaking, or imagination
of one thing for another . . . I suppose that euen already you suppose me very
fonde that have so simply disclosed unto you the subtilties of these our Supposes; where, otherwise, in-deede, I Suppose you shoulde have heard almoste
the laste of our Supposes before you could haue supposed anye of them aright."
Supposes . . . Englished by George Gascoygne . . . 1556, Prologue, in *Chief Pre-
Shakespearean Dramas*, ed. Joseph Quincy Adams (Cambridge, Mass., 1924),
537.

often reassigned to alternative personae. In Bibbiena's *Calandria* the in-namorata is a *malmaritata,* an unhappy wife old enough to have a grown son, but the variation impedes none of the standard operations: messages are carried, disguises put on, and clandestine meetings arranged, and the character of the innamorata is thrown into relief by that of the serva. In Francesco D'Ambra's *Furto* many but not all of these functions are performed, with a different final effect, by a professional, free-lance *mezzana,* or procuress. In *Mandragola,* a comedy launched by the mainstream but not quite in it, the young wife Lucrezia is not an innamorata, or not at first: that she becomes one at all is a triumph of the lover's machinations, requiring several persuaders and confidants. Within a decade of Ariosto's first comedy, Machiavelli's corrosive satire of corrupt institutions—the Church in the person of Fra' Timoteo and the family in those of Messer Nicia and Sostrata—is already testing the limits of what is generically possible in the nova comedia by recombining person, association, and action, dividing the pimping action of a mezzana between a priest and a mother who urges her daughter to adultery for economic and social security, but also for fun, having herself been easygoing, a "buona compagna" (I.1) in her youth. By this shuffling of associations, Machiavelli confirms Lucrezia as the only reluctant party to the hilariously vicious fraud by which her husband cuckolds himself. The equally famous and still more influential *Gl'ingannati* contains two innamorate: one has a *balia* and the other a *fante,* between whom portions of the theatergrams of association and action subsisting among such personae are divided or shared.

In *Twelfth Night,* the play supposed to prove that Shakespeare imitated *Ingannati,* there is no balia for Viola; and though the lady Olivia has in Maria a variety of the fantesca, their relationship does not run to confidential chat or plans in aid of Olivia's love for Cesario/Sebastian. Shakespeare uses the balia for such actions in *Romeo and Juliet* (only some of which are found in Arthur Brooke's *Romeus and Juliet,* the source of which was, nota bene, a play) as he uses the maid in *Two Gentlemen of Verona,* or, with still other variations, in *The Merchant of Venice.* His not involving either persona in the same associations and actions as are used in *Gl'ingannati* is another demonstration of his working on the principles of nova comedia, not by borrowing plots from sources but by *contaminatio* of structures, recombining in novel ways theatergrams that had become part of a large common repertory, discarding those that were not to the purpose of the highly individual structure of each of his plays. In *Twelfth Night* even the noble Illyrian

milieu is a new version of an Italian commonplace: the coastal city of
Ragusa, the Dalmatian Venice, that was the setting of some *commedie*
and the provenance of the figure of the *raguseo*, usually a seafarer,
recurrent in Italian comedy and represented in Shakespeare's by the
"Ragozine" of *Measure for Measure*.

In Shakespeare's time many other actions were used of course in
cross-combinations with those attributed to Ariosto's *Nutrice*: the balia,
old fante, or mezzana may natter earthily about maidenheads and marriage and invite reprimand, like Bernardino Pino's Frosina [14] or Juliet's
nurse; perhaps her nattering is joined to a manipulative opportunism,
like Pasquella's in *Gl'ingannati* or Mistress Quickly's in *The Merry
Wives of Windsor;* she can be a flirt, old or young, encouraged or rejected; or, rather than flirt, she may indulge in slanging matches with
insulting boys; there is name calling between the old *ancilla* and the
ragazzino in *I suppositi*, a theatergram that by the time of *Gl'ingannati*
had ripened into the sexually flavored mockery with which the transvestite innamorata accosts her balia before revealing herself; and the
flavor is still riper in Shakespeare's recombination, in the dialogue of
Mercutio and the Nurse.

Pursuit of signifying form in the Italian theater eventually attached
the power of abstract representation to the design of comedy. The radical
contaminatio of genres that enriched the second half of the Cinquecento
with comic structures and possibilities of unprecedented expressive
scope touched even the homely little theatergram of the innamorata's
abettor. In *La balia*, as in *La Cecca*, [15] Girolamo Razzi gives the title role
and a great manipulative power to the earthy succorer of lovers. By their
dexterity in sneaking suitors into their young mistresses' bedrooms,
both the Balia and Cecca (identified as "serva") continue the tradition
of this particular relationship between servant and mistress, but whereas
Cecca counsels carpe diem and the more the merrier, *La balia* attests
Razzi's shift toward serious comedy, a move that earned him condemna-
tion from Sanesi and Herrick in our century, [16] but put him in the van of
a kind of tragicomedy that is a major clue to the constitution of the Re-

14. Bernardino Pino, *Gli ingiusti sdegni, comedia* (Rome, 1553), II.1.

15. Girolamo Razzi, *La balia, comedia* (Florence, 1560); *La Cecca, comedia* (Florence, 1563).

16. Marvin T. Herrick, *Italian Comedy in the Renaissance* (Urbana, Ill.,
1960), 178; Ireneo Sanesi, *La commedia*, 2d ed. (Milan, 1954), 344.

naissance theater and to its claims in that period of cultural history. The melodramatic and almost tragic matter itself is less interesting than the form that the choice of such matter entailed. The Balia engineers a quadruple bed trick of mistaken identity, a darkroom substitution that causes the innamorata to think she has committed incest with her half-brother (Herrick emphasizes the resemblance to Tasso's Sophoclean tragedy *Torrismondo*). Of course she has not done so; such violent transgression of the genre's limits would lose the name of commedia. But the manipulation of familiar theatergrams of association and action to weave a potentially tragic nexus, subsequently untied by a dénouement of revealed changes of identity and substitution of children, shows Razzi participating in the theatrical movement toward a third genre, thus undertaking what the ancients had not achieved, and doing so in the only way it was imagined they would have approved: by adhering to Aristotle and imitating in comedy the form of tragedy that he had ranked highest, that of Sophocles' *Oedipus rex*. By temporarily investing the title character of *La balia* with an unaccustomed semiotic weight (as the designer, unwittingly providential, of this intrigue plot with pretensions to tragic formal gravity), Razzi joined his otherwise undistinguished play to the many commedie, *tragicommedie,* and *favole pastorali* that variously attempted the ultimate imitation of classical models—one that would be at once transmission and exploratory transgression.[17]

The pastoral play was swept into fashion by a confluence of the movement toward the third genre with attempts to adapt the "perfect" Sophoclean plot to comedy, and with an ideological hope of replacing the representation of fate (in which pagan concept Catholic Counter-Reformers descried a perilous correspondence to Calvinistic predestination) by an image of providence, guaranteeing the will's freedom while foreseeing its choice. A providential pattern emerged in some commedie gravi, a theatergram of design by which an intrigue plot could become a metaphor for the labyrinth of life and invoke the timely analogy of the *theatrum mundi:* the world as a stage where God is both spectator and

---

17. The semitragic thrust of the late commedie gravi naturally led also to assigning moral speeches to nurses and maids; but though it is not uncommon to hear virtuous resolutions from balie, as in Sforza Oddi's *Prigione d'amore* (Florence, 1590) and Raffaello Borghini's *Donna costante* (Florence, 1578) even in very grave romantic comedies it often suited the design to keep the balie to the usual coarse or commonsensical actions in their associations with the innamorate.

dramatist. The reverse corollary, expressed in ritual quotation from Aelius Donatus, is that the play is a mirror of the world in which a human audience may see not only the *imitatio vitae* of physical reality but also its meaning, the *imago veritatis* of a transcendent order.

As a setting Arcadia was better suited than the city of comedy or the court of tragedy to represent immaterial reality and universal psychological or spiritual experience, by virtue of being a mental space, natural, private, and oneiric, the inner side of the civilized public and waking scene of city and court. And yet, when the pastoral world took to the stage and play makers reached for theatrical instrumentation for the ancient abundance of pastoral situations, characters, topoi, attitudes, and stories, the repertory of tried and proven structures of the established genres was at hand, and theatergrams, of comedy especially, were put to work in Arcadia.

The experience of love, self-knowledge, and the vision of harmony that could be felt straining against the limits of commedia grave committed to urban economic realities could be approached directly and expressionistically in pastoral drama. Change of heart and self-discovery could be acted out more freely there than in a comic genre still oriented to love primarily as the winning force in a conflict of domestic interests. Even in the most romantic commedie the loves of the young couples to be mated by the victory are relatively static: when love changes, it is usually because of an absolute impediment, such as consanguinity, or because a prior claim is filed, usually a first attachment renewed when rationally presented as the alliance best suited to the social resolution of the intrigue. In the pastoral, on the contrary, there are always psychological mutations and developments, and the irrationality together with the experience of gradually falling in love is a centerpiece of the action, which taken as a whole, is simply the action of love's motions dramatized. But whether the theatrical image of love in its varieties made possible by the Arcadian Elsewhere is mounted as a comedy of mistakes, errors produced when love is blocked by circumstances, or rather as an elevated Sophoclean action of dramatic irony modulated into a happy major key, with courtly or even regal characters threatened by the blindness of their passions, by tragic *antefatti* and portentous oracles revealing through the motions of their loves the benignity of providence, the theatergrams of comedy repeatedly declare themselves as the process for giving stage presence and form to the pastoral matter.

The action of persuasion to love becomes more essential in pastoral drama than in comedy, because the gradual education of the virgin heart is a principal motif of the developing genre, a design of conversion, in this instance of the devotee of Diana to the service of Venus. The action of the practical go-between, with its subsidiary actions assignable to the range of balia-serva-mezzana characters in associations with innamorate and innamorati, shows up in the pastoral all the more prominently because it is almost indispensable to plots in which psychological movement toward true love is paramount; but it relies for stage presence on redirections of familiar relationships and actions. The persuader is commonly a *ninfa attempata*, a middle-aged nymph, whose experience in love, carpe diem advice, propensity to flirt, and practical impatience with idealistic scruples or ascetic notions define her relationships and function within the pattern made by the total range of positions on love in a given play. Even if she is on an equal footing with the innamorata in a classless or one-class Arcadian society, the old nymph inevitably suggests to an audience wise in the ways of commedia both the function and aims of the balia-serva type, while at the same time her presence measures how far from that theatergram of person a variation moves when tuned to the inner world of the heart that is the venue of the third genre.

Even in Tasso's atypical but persistently imitated *Aminta*, with its severely economical offstage action and distance from the ethos of commedia, there transpires the useful comic model. Dafne, the aging persuader who dominates much of the play, moves on the invisible wheels of comic theatergrams as she reminisces about the joys of love in her youth, chides Silvia in the famous "Cangia, cangia consiglio / pazzarella che sei: / che 'l pentirsi da sezzo nulla giova" (I.1.121–31: Change, oh change your counsel, foolish girl that you are: for late repentance is useless),[18] flirts cautiously with Tirsi and is as delicately mocked by him, laughs knowingly at signs of Silvia's awakening to love, and hints with a vestige of the coarseness of a typical balia or serva that a little force from Aminta might be more effective than respectful adoration (II.2.933–39).

Diana pietosa, comedia pastorale by Raffaello Borghini,[19] already an established author of commedie gravi, furnishes an example of how after *Aminta* a playwright more openly incorporates pastoral matter into theater by fusing and redistributing comedy's associations, persons, and actions. Here the function of Tasso's Dafne is performed by Cariclea,

18. *Aminta, favola boschereccia* (1573), in Torquato Tasso, *Opere*, ed. Bruno Maier (Milan, 1963), 1: 95.

19. Raffaello Borghini, *Diana pietosa, comedia pastorale* (Florence, 1585).

a *vecchia* with a distant origin in Greek romance and an immediate
presence keyed to balia-serva models. Her behavior and attachments
contribute to a commedia design of deception and error, but they are
here redirected toward pastoral revelation of love's blindness and its
cure and of hope crowned with joy by a sympathetic, providential goddess. To this benign purpose the power of Fortune, traditionally supreme in comedy, is geared and subordinated.

In such a calculated contaminatio, functioning as in comedy but
without its socioeconomic context, old Cariclea is essentially a woodland balia, an accomplice to Silveria's disguise and to the tricking of
Ismenio into marriage, the "dolce inganno" (V.8) approved by the
oracle of Diana. Like the balia or serva of comedy who carries messages
and beseeches the reluctant giovane, Cariclea solicits Ismenio for Silveria, but she does so with a pastoral topos that echoes, with the gen-
ders reversed, the words Tasso's Dafne uses to Silvia: "Cangia, cangia
voglia / Semplicetto che sei" (III.1: Change, oh change your desire,
simple boy that you are).

Cristoforo Castelletti's *Amarilli, pastorale*[20] illustrates the Ovidian
magical pastoral that comprises country clowns in servo-padrone associations with refined *pastori* and ninfe, and theatergrams of metamorphosis, of which Shakespeare's Bottom with his ass's head would be the
supreme version. Castelletti's bumptious *capraio* is turned into a tree by
a naiad whose waters he has profaned. His master obtains his release
and scolds, like a jollier Prospero to a grosser Ariel: "havresti meritato,
ch'io t'havessi / Lasciato star nel tronco eternamente" (IV.4: You would
have deserved it had I left you in the tree trunk forever). To the design
formed by this combination of rustic farce and fantasy with poetic revelation of love's providence, an experienced, older ninfa brings an analogous psychological and conceptual amalgam of mezzana, serva, and
classically learned initiate in love's mysteries. She carries messages and
urges several shepherds and nymphs to love, employing a curiously
mixed battery of familiar arguments: carpe diem, the material advantage of marriage to prosperous sheepowners, regret for beauty's loss and
missed opportunities, and such divine examples as Jupiter's transformations for the sake of love, with which Terence's "Eunuch" had egged
himself on to rape (III.584–91) and which Falstaff remembers when he
awaits his assignation with one of the merry wives in Windsor Forest,
disguised as Herne the hunter wearing a buck's head (V.5.1–15).

20. Cristoforo Castelletti, *Amarilli, pastorale* (Venice, 1582).

Another recombination of *Aminta* with the magical pastoral and its repertorial actions and associations produces Pietro Cresci's *Tirena, favola pastorale*,[21] in which the title figure is an old nymph, a nagging nanny who preaches carpe diem to the Arcadian *jeunesse dorée* but angrily rejects the clown's gross advances and manipulates the plot toward a providential pattern linked to the idea of Time in its flight and fullness.

With *Il pastor fido, tragicomedia pastorale*,[22] Guarini brought into definitive integration the pastoral play, the movement toward the third genre, and the adaptation of theatrical form to ideological representation. Only deconstruction or refraction can identify vestiges of the theatrical microstructures that Guarini reassembled for his ambitious transformation. The human manipulator of a plot that is Sophoclean tragedy in design and intrigue comedy in the disposition of its theatergrams (Guarini termed it "l'ordine comico")[23] is Corisca, a character who seems so distant from the nurse-servant figure that to allege the antecedent makes a point only in an analysis of theatrical recombination and contamination. Corisca is not quite a ninfa attempata, although she is somewhat older and vastly more experienced than the other nymphs. Her function by association with this family of characters and actions would expectedly be that of a subordinate well-wisher to the young lovers, like Cresci's manipulative Tirena or Tasso's Dafne, but on the contrary Corisca is not benign. She wants to contrive the death of the innamorata Amarilli in order to have the faithful shepherd Mirtillo for her own. To deceive the lovers, she adopts the role of conventional well-wishing confidant and go-between: she exhorts Amarilli to love, urges Mirtillo to boldness, and arranges a rendezvous for the two. All this Guarini fuses with another staple of comic action, the compromising discovery of lovers in a dark room. Because the scene is Arcadia, the function of the comic *camera terrena* is assigned to a grotto, appropriately dark. Corisca's strategy of deception and her pragmatic dismissal of moral ideals bear the stamp of long use by comic servants, and the scene of violent encounter with the *satiro* whom she has loved and cast aside, and who grabs her by the hair but is left with only a wig in his hands and taunts in his ears, evokes the city street-corner of comedy.

21. Pietro Cresci, *Tirena, favola pastorale* (Venice, 1584).

22. *Il pastor fido, tragicommedia pastorale* (1589), in Battista Guarini, *Il pastor fido e Il compendio della poesia tragicomica*, ed. Gioacchino Brognoligo (Bari, 1914).

23. Ibid., 231.

In the cursed and tragic Arcadia of *Il pastor fido,* city noises, the physical clashes, and the verbal wrangling of servi and *cortigiane* strike the mind's ear as a faint but distinct tone in the measured discord that Guarini composes.

His redistribution and reversal of elements of action and association make of Corisca as wicked a variation on the clever manipulator of comedy as that constituted by Iago in the ultimate distortion of commedia achieved by Shakespeare in *Othello.* The comprehensive theatergram of design in *Il pastor fido* moves as in *Othello* or *Oedipus Rex,* but toward a happy rather than a tragic ending, and it draws new significance from the old patterns: the tragic inescapability of fate becomes by a providential reversal a comic image of blind human pursuit of error, which takes good for evil and vice versa, misinterprets divine oracles, and in unwitting self-enmity works against the ineffable plan for men's happiness that heaven implements by the least expected means. In *Othello* the design of the tricker tricked, of mischief hoist by its own petard (which in comedy works to the benefit of the good), is horribly turned inside out, and innocence as well as guilt works its own downfall. The function of "improvising manipulator" assigned to the complex character of Iago is both adapted to this design and contributes to its formation, interacting with the credulity of Othello and naiveté of Desdemona, who helps to do herself in by her inability even to imagine of what she is suspected. Corisca's machinations throughout *Il pastor fido* surprisingly become the means whereby truth is at last discovered and the oracle fulfilled. The fusion and reversal in her of attitudes and actions shared with the serve, balie, and ninfe attempate in comedies and other pastorals are appropriate and necessary to an ironic final peripety that includes her in the universal and divinely foreseen happiness against which the Arcadians have blindly struggled. In short, there is a structural kinship between the designs of *Othello* and the *Pastor fido:* both are reversals of the tricker tricked and as such add to the technical and conceptual range of the mixed genres under exploration by a theatrical movement that had become international. *Othello* is made by its new contaminatio of genres into unrelieved tragedy and *Il pastor fido* by an evenhanded blending into tragicomedy, both ventures in genre conducted by the recombination of persons, associations, and actions from the repertory of commedia.

Il pastor fido was to become the single most influential example of pastoral drama and of the calculated mixture of comedy and tragedy, but contamination of theatergrams in all declensions, effecting contamination of the two classical dramatic kinds, continued to propose other versions of a third genre.

When professionals of the *arte* began using the combinatory process for improvisation from scenarios, they tailored their mixtures of comedy, pastoral, and tragedy to the semifixed roles assumed as specialties by given actors and to the compact size of an acting company. The result has repeatedly been cast as the antithesis of regular theater, but when it is reattached to the cultural system to which it belonged originally the commedia dell'arte appears rather as an alternative style of participation in the accretive repertory begun in commedia erudita, polished by constant contaminatio into an arsenal of classical play making, and then directed afield to the dialectical modern triumph of a third genre. By the late sixteenth century the great theatrical enterprise belonged not exclusively to a primarily private and festival drama but to Italian commercial show business and, more or less, to all the players and playwrights of Europe.

Although the acting troupes who developed the commedia dell'arte took part in more than one kind of pastoral play, to judge by extant scenarios the variety of the third genre that they preferred for their characteristic improvisational mode was the mixture of magic and romance in which exiled nobles, raucous peasants, and servants mingled in Arcadia with shepherds, sorcerers, satyrs, tutelary deities, and other supernatural beings. With limitations on the size of the cast and with emphasis on the potential for spectacle and physical action of the fantasy that was permissible in this Ovidian kind of pastoral, the role of innamorata's confidant was more dispensable than in psychologizing literary versions; such functions that the plot left room for as persuading to love, remembering lost love, and juxtaposing experience to naiveté, were redistributed among the necessary stock types.

The scenarios of Arcadia unearthed by Ferdinando Neri and Flaminio Scala's *Arbore incantato,* together with related pastoral elements in other *giornate* of his *Favole rappresentative,* document a preference among Italian professional players for the same ingredients of the magical pastoral that Shakespeare chose for *A Midsummer Night's Dream* and *The Tempest.*[24] As usual, Shakespeare pitched his variations at new

24. Ferdinando Neri, *Scenari delle maschere in Arcadia* (Città di Castello, 1913; repr. Turin, 1961); Flaminio Scala, *Il teatro delle favole rappresentative* (1611), ed. Ferruccio Marotti, 2 vols. (Milan, 1976).

frequencies and went so far as to leave out the shepherds, but the familiar features identify the genre. The magician with rod and book, the spirits, the urban refugees, wandering lost and hallucinated, the transformations into animal, vegetable, or mineral forms, the boisterousness of self-infatuated clowns with their minds on drink and license jarring with the arcane or spiritually rarefied ethos of the wood or island to which they wander—these are repertorial features of literary *favole pastorali* like those of Cresci, Castelletti, Pasqualigo, or Guazzoni[25] that the *comici dell'arte* and Shakespeare took up for some of their excursions from the city and court.

It illustrates the way the common fund of theatrical coin was drawn on that a theatergram suppressed or subdivided beyond recognition by the exigencies of one generic formation, such as the magical pastoral, might in another remain indefinitely in use in all its varieties. Of Scala's fifty model scenarios the first forty are labeled *commedia* and display the credentials of the genre in their contemporary urban settings and actions of a stock cluster of variable characters, whose individual functions could be increased in inverse proportion to the size of the troupe (the frequent double duty of Capitano Spavento as both braggart comic butt and worthy innamorato being an example).

In the comedy scenarios the figure of Franceschina is the most mature as well as the most essential of the various female servants. Ricciolina, Olivetta, and others come and go, but Franceschina is always on hand and comes into play as confidant, balia, mezzana, innkeeper, and sexy serva as the permutations and redistributions of theatergrams continually form new plays. Her range includes actions of the balia as a repository of the innamorata's secrets (*La finta pazza,* giornata 8) and associations that had been acclimatized to the stage a century earlier when Ariosto wrote the scene between Polimnesta and her Nutrice. Franceschina is a buxom, bawdy foil to her lovesick padrona in *Li tragici successi* (giornata 18), which was Scala's version for improvisational purposes of the plot of Borghini's *Donna costante*. But in *Il marito* (giornata 9) Franceschina becomes the nutrice and not only is an inciter to virtue, confidant of the innamorata, and manipulator of the plot, but also is singularly enterprising: assuming the transvestite disguise that is more commonly the prerogative of the innamorata herself, Franceschina poses as the jealous husband of her young padrona, whom she thus

25. Luigi Pasqualigo, *Gl'intricati, pastorale* (Venice, 1581); Diomisso Guazzoni, *Andromeda, tragicomedia boscareccia* (Venice, 1587).

saves from an unwanted marriage.[26] When Scala expanded his scenario into a complete five-act text, *Il finto marito,* with the characters renamed, his additions and changes were all further recombinations from the repertory of theatergrams.[27]

Neither the commedia dell'arte nor Shakespeare's plays as we know them would have been conceivable except at this moment in a movement that had acquired great formal variety and geographical extension (but not so great as to have shifted its center of intelligibility),[28] and that rested on basic developmental principles, codes, vocabularies, and the memory of a common beginning in the specifically Renaissance Will to Genre that Shakespeare recapitulates in the advance publicity of the players in *Hamlet,* where he underlines the choice of Latin models, the transgressive creation of new genres from the fusion of old, and the equal function of "writ" and the "liberty," that is, of literary dramatic text and actor's improvisation.[29] Polonius's famous description of the players sums up a large and mature dramaturgical system in which both the commedia dell'arte and Shakespeare worked.

When Shakespeare dramatized the tale of Romeo and Juliet he did not do what Borghini in literary comedy or Scala in scenarios did with similar combination of theatergrams, but instead kept the dark outcome of da Porto's, Bandello's, and Brooke's narrative versions to make a "la-

26. That Franceschina was often played by a male actor, unlike other serve in commedia dell'arte, adds another digit to the multiplier by which the action theatergram of disguise within disguise could be readapted inexhaustibly. The possibilities were still being exploited in the 1970s in Jean Poiret's *Cage aux folles,* when Albin tries to conceal his being a drag queen by posing as conventional Uncle Al, and, that failing, as "Maman."

27. Flaminio Scala, *Il finto marito, commedia* (Venice, 1619), repr. in *Commedie dei comici dell'arte,* ed. Laura Falavolti (Turin, 1982).

28. The resemblances that justly have persuaded comparatists from Allardyce Nicoll, O. J. Campbell, Winifred Smith, and Kathleen M. Lea to Ninian Mellamphy of the importance to Shakespeare of commedia dell'arte, and led Walter L. Barker to credit itinerant comici with the "eruption" of Elizabethan drama (*Three English Pantalones: A Study in Relations between the Commedia dell'arte and Elizabethan Drama* [diss., University of Connecticut, 1966, p. 204]) in most cases point back to features that originated in earlier Cinquecento literary theater and continued there, often modified by the reciprocal pressure of the art of the comici. See also n. 13 to the Epilogue.

29. See the quotation on p. vi.

mentable tragedy." The code of its construction, however, places Shakespeare's play squarely in the experimental theater of mixed genres as a
comitragedy. At any moment *Romeo and Juliet* could be turned by an
accident of good fortune or simply by the failure of one of the accidents
of bad fortune into a romantic comedy. Even Tybalt's death could be
assimilated by the commedia grave, as is that of the innamorata's cousin
in the analogous *Donna costante*.

The perception of Shakespeare's use of the world of romantic comedy
as the matrix of tragedy which Susan Snyder comes to by comprehensive genre theory with psychological underpinnings and global premises
about comedy as a "rejection of singleness" and tragedy as an isolation
in a unique fate, is arrived at without reference to the Italian forays into
genre combinations.[30] Salingar brings the specificity of cultural history
to his study of comic traditions and recognizes Shakespeare's mastery
of Italian techniques. But he sees this primarily as a mechanical feat,
learned from Italian comedies of the early sixteenth century and most
clearly illustrated by *The Merry Wives of Windsor,* one of Shakespeare's
least romantic comedies; he points to the doubling of plots, the use of a
repertoire of casts and situations from joint narrative and stage traditions, and the construction of comic actions as networks of tricks and
vicissitudes of Fortune. It is rather to an ulterior addition of elements
from Ovid and medieval romance that Salingar attributes the motif of
transformation, the changes within characters, the poetic and moving
spectacles of restoration, reconciliation, and illusion opening the way to
self-knowledge. These are the essence of Shakespeare's romantic comedy and have caused the late plays especially to be commonly called "romances," "comedies of forgiveness" (by Robert G. Hunter), and "pastorals" (by Thomas McFarland).[31]

Absent from these views of Renaissance drama (an omission that di-
minishes both Italian theater and Shakespeare) is the middle term between distant sources and individual achievement, that is, the resources
of the theatrical movement that in Italy produced neat intrigue comedies
in the early Cinquecento and later romantic comedy, and experiments

30. Susan Snyder, *The Comic Matrix of Shakespeare's Tragedies* (Princeton,
1979), 4ff.

31. Robert G. Hunter, *Shakespeare and the Comedy of Forgiveness* (New
York and London, 1965); Thomas McFarland, *Shakespeare's Pastoral Comedy*
(Chapel Hill, 1972).

with tragedy, as well as a pastoral drama that was cultivated with an intent to stage the kinds of visions at which Shakespeare eventually excelled.

Evidence that Shakespeare used Arthur Brooke's verse narrative as a source for *Romeo and Juliet* suggests how complex the relationship was among source, dramatization, and contemporary dramaturgy, but it need conflict neither with Snyder's conclusion that Shakespeare made tragedy out of romantic comedy nor with Salingar's that he deployed Italian techniques. Brooke said that he "saw the same argument lately set forth on stage,"[32] and even without his statement it could be deduced from the figure of the "noorse" alone, whose character and behavior he establishes by a cluster of associational attitudes and actions from the lexicon of the stage. The "noorse's" tantalizing of the impatient innamorata by dragging out the lover's message, her ancient, earthy reminiscence of the pleasure of losing a maidenhead, encouraging and contrasting with Juliet's high passion, her practical, unprincipled and uncomprehending advice to Juliet to commit adultery (that is, bigamy with Paris), her taking Romeo's money and glossing it with silence—such moves, long familiar in various combinations of the balia or serva in Italian comedy, are not essential to the tragic narrative, as we have seen. They confirm Brooke's statement that he saw the story in a play, and tell us that the play's theatergrams were comic ones. Shakespeare accepts this generic placement and intensifies it. He adds more bawdy nattering for the Nurse, a rebuke from her padrona, Lady Capulet, and taunts and sexual slurs from Mercutio on the street (who here assumes the action most commonly assigned to the impudent *ragazzo* in association with an old serva, or often with a *pedante*), thus supplementing the current coin of the genre commedia with more of the same. Simultaneously he employs the principle of dramatizing specific narrative sources by contaminations of theatergrams pointed toward contamination of genres. But instead of bringing comedy to the verge of tragedy and then reversing it into a happy ending, as his Italian contemporaries were doing, he pushes it all the way.

In the process he disposes the units in an integrating comic theatergram of design redirected; the Nurse's function as messenger, for ex-

32. Arthur Brooke, Preface "To the Reader," *The Tragicall Historye of Romeus and Juliet* (1562), in Shakespeare, *Romeo and Juliet*, ed. Brian Gibbons (London and New York, 1980), 240.

ample, takes its place in the pattern of missed messages, disastrous gaps in understanding, and crossed stars that finally illuminates the tragic nature of the play. The same elements had long been intrinsic to the *ordine comico* that Guarini adduced in his construction, as even the titles of many comedies announce. Just as the label *Comedy of Errors* names a pattern of mistakings and *Much Ado about Nothing* an intricate figure of overreactions to misinterpreted "noting" or ocular impressions, so *Gl'ingannati* and *I suppositi* had described earlier designs of deceits and impersonations, while later *La cangiaria* (the play of identity changes), *Gl'intrichi d'amore, Gl'ingiusti sdegni, La furiosa,* and such pastoral titles as *I sospetti, Gl'intricati,* and *Danza di Venere* point to the theatergrams of design constantly being formed from recombinations of smaller parts.

Juliet's Nurse, although she is Shakespeare's only balia proper, shares functions with other characters whose individual differences illustrate Shakespeare's inventiveness as much as their partial similarities do his mastery of theatergrams. Margaret of *Much Ado,* Lucetta of *Two Gentlemen of Verona,* and Nerissa of *The Merchant of Venice* all are identified in the First Folio as waiting-women, but of different social rank, and all have assignments appropriate to the serva in association with the innamorata, though not the same ones: Margaret is not a confidant but a mildly bawdy foil to Hero closely involved in the shaping design of misconstrued seen things about which there is so much ado; Lucetta is not bawdy, only teasing and more blasé than her lovesick mistress: Nerissa is the most intimate with the innamorata, Portia, and also shadows her in other associations and actions, falling in love, putting on male disguise, and participating in the merciful deceit that saves the merchant's pound of flesh. Mistress Quickly of *The Merry Wives of Windsor* is listed as Caius's servant but functions primarily as a freelance mezzana.

In *Othello* Emilia is identified only as Iago's wife, but as Barbara Heliodora De Mendonça is not alone in observing, she plays the *servetta* to the "innamorata" Desdemona.[33] Earthy, practical, and outspoken, a spinoff in the mold of serva, ninfa attempata, and balia more than the ensign's wife she is labeled, Emilia represents the kind of acute distortion of models that was one of Shakespeare's characteristic skills.

---

33. Barbara Heliodora De Mendonça, "*Othello:* A Tragedy Built on a Comic Structure," *Shakespeare Survey* 21 (1968): 35.

She and Juliet's Nurse are related through comic theatergrams and both belong to tragedies, but they and the tragedies are each a unique recombination of parts and kinds. In *Othello* Shakespeare contaminates the same two genres, but this time he does not make a commedia grave with an unfortunate end as he does in *Romeo and Juliet;* rather he begins with comic commonplaces and allows their farthest imaginable psychological weight and consequence to overpower the scenario and subvert all the theatergrams. The design of the adulterous trickery plot, with jealous cuckold, malmaritata, young innamorato, and the rest, is transferred to Othello's mind, evoked by Iago. To deny the obscene farce in which he imagines himself he turns it to tragedy, with his own hands killing Desdemona and himself. (These are tragic theatergrams of action, incidentally, with visual and semiotic substance radically differentiating them from the ways in which "Disdemona" and the Moor meet their deaths in Shakespeare's Giraldian narrative source.) Othello thinks in theatergrams; Shakespeare reveals the distance between them and reality. But to do so he uses them as signs that can be joined with other signs, carrying over old meanings against which the result defines itself as new.

Positivistic Quellenstudien, concentrating on a precise sequence of linear transmission, contribute little to our perception of movement by continual recombination and variation, but many of the other roads of historical criticism do lead to Rome, or at least to Italy and its theater. Modern editors' accounts of Shakespeare's handling of materials, and individual analyses such as the one Salingar makes of Italian techniques in what Jeanne Roberts defines as Shakespeare's "English" comedy,[34] *The Merry Wives of Windsor,* in synthesis testify to a layer of dramaturgy called into action somewhere between the choice of specific sources and the finished play, to a central process comprising contaminatio, patterned complication, and variation of theatergrams.[35] Unlike most Italian playwrights and all the scenario-smiths, Shakespeare never repeats

34. Jeanne Addison Roberts, *Shakespeare's English Comedy: The Merry Wives of Windsor in Context* (Lincoln, Neb., and London, 1979).
35. For further discussion of the process and for comparison of *Much Ado about Nothing* with a contemporary commedia grave on the same source plot see the introduction to my edition and translation of Giambattista Della Porta, *Gli duoi fratelli rivali/The Two Rival Brothers* (Berkeley, Los Angeles, and London, 1980).

himself; each play, distinct even from those of his other plays nearest it, is like a solution to a problem in theatrical genre. The system that generated such problems and concomitantly offered terms and a process for their solutions was one made in Italy, but enlarged and used wherever in Europe Renaissance drama flourished.

Comedy

Serlio's "Scena Comica"
"Le Second livre de Perspective"
Il Primo Libro d'Architettura di Sebastiano Serlio, Bolognese (Paris, 1545).
By permission of the National Gallery of Art, Mark J. Millard Architectural
Collection (1983.49.106).

CHAPTER ONE

Italian Renaissance Comedy

talian Renaissance comedy: a phrase to open a debate about genre. It could be argued that the comic novella or Folengo's mock heroics or the smiling narrative cosmos of the *Orlando furioso* are no less comedy than the commedia that preempted the name at the first performance of Ariosto's *Cassaria* in 1508 and was still flourishing when Della Porta died in 1615. Even if limited by Northrop Frye's "radical of presentation," Cinquecento comedy in a liberal definition comprehends many theatrical kinds, including *farse,* moral and otherwise, various secular outgrowths of rhymed *sacre rappresentazioni,* Ruzante's peasant plays, and the improvisations of the professional *comici.* Distinct from all of these is the vernacular five-act drama with intrigue plot employing characters and situations developed from Attic New Comedy and from the Boccaccian novella tradition, regulated by unity of time and place according to principles of generalized realism, representing a contemporary urban middle class as festival entertainment for an élite audience. So run the rough specifications of the model that emerged early and determined an enormous production in the sixteenth century alone, from the definitive examples set in Ferrara, Florence, Urbino, and Rome by Ariosto, Machiavelli, and Bibbiena, through comedies of Piccolomini, D'Ambra, Firenzuola, Grazzini, Cecchi, Caro, Aretino, Gelli, Pino, Razzi, Bargagli, Oddi, Calderari, Parabosco, Loredano the elder, Borghini, and Della Porta.[1] The genre was published as well as performed, discussed

This chapter appeared in slightly different form in *Genre* 9, no. 4 (Winter 1976–77; special issue, *Versions of Medieval Comedy,* ed. and with an introduction by Paul G. Ruggiers). Copyright © 1977 by University of Oklahoma Press.

1. These are the general boundaries of commedia erudita not disputed by recent Italian scholarship, for significant examples of which see Mario Baratto, *La commedia del cinquecento* (Vicenza, 1975); Nino Borsellino, *Rozzi e Intronati: Esperienze e forme di teatro dal Decameron al Candelaio* (Rome, 1974); Nino Borsellino and Roberto Mercuri, *Il teatro del Cinquecento* (Bari, 1973), 10–72; Ettore Paratore, "Nuove prospettive sull'influsso del teatro classico nel '500," *Il teatro classico nel'500"* (Rome, 1971), 9–95; Gianfranco

by theoreticians, and soon illustrated by its own classics. Modern taste
on the whole confirms the opinion entrenched by 1554, when Girolamo
Ruscelli edited a collection of "elect" comedies already long in print:
Bibbiena's *Calandra* (or *Calandria*), Machiavelli's *Mandragola, Gl'ingannati* of the Accademia degli Intronati, and Piccolomini's *Amor costante* and *Alessandro*.[2]

Treatises on drama and prologues to comedies of the time bear witness to continuing agreement about tradition and the status of the new
classics. Bernardino Pino, spokesman for the serious commedia admired
later in the sixteenth century, addresses his "Brief Consideration on the
Composition of Comedy in Our Times" to Sforza Oddi, with whose
Erofilomachia, overo Il duello d'amore, et d'amicizia it was published
six years after its drafting:[3] predictably, Pino refers with admiration to

---

Folena, ed., *Lingua e struttura del teatro italiano del rinascimento: Machiavelli,
Ruzzante, Aretino, Guarini, commedia dell'arte* (Padua, 1970); Giulio Ferroni,
*"Mutazione" e "riscontro" nel teatro di Machiavelli, e altri saggi sulla comme-
dia del Cinquecento* (Rome, 1972); Aulo Greco, *L'istituzione del teatro comico
nel rinascimento* (Naples, 1976). Discussions in English include Marvin T. Herrick, *Italian Comedy in the Renaissance* (Urbana, Ill., 1960); Douglas Radcliff-
Umstead, *The Birth of Modern Comedy in Renaissance Italy* (Chicago, 1969);
Beatrice Corrigan, "Italian Renaissance Comedy and Its Critics: A Survey of Recent Studies," *Renaissance Drama*, n.s. 5 (1972): 191–211; Franco Fido, "Reflections on Comedy by Some Italian Renaissance Playwrights," *Medieval Epic
to the "Epic Theater" of Brecht*, ed. Rosario P. Armato and John M. Spalek
(Los Angeles, 1968), 1:85–95; Louise George Clubb, *Italian Plays
(1500–1700) in the Folger Library* (Florence, 1968), Introduction; Leo Salingar, "Shakespeare and Italian Comedy," *Shakespeare and the Traditions of
Comedy* (Cambridge, England, 1974), 175–242. For neo-Latin predecessors
see Antonio Staüble, *La commedia umanistica del Quattrocento* (Florence,
1968). In addition to editions of works by individual authors are the following
collections: Ireneo Sanesi, ed., *Commedie del Cinquecento*, 2 vols. (Bari, 1912),
repr. ed. Maria Luisa Doglio (1975); Nino Borsellino, ed., *Commedie del Cinquecento*, 2 vols. (Milan, 1962–67); Aldo Borlenghi, ed., *Commedie del Cinquecento*, 2 vols. (Milan, 1959); and Guido Davico Bonino, ed., *La commedia
del Cinquecento*, 3 vols. (Turin, 1977–78).

2. *Delle comedie elette novamente raccolte insieme, con le correttioni, et
annotationi di Girolamo Ruscelli* (Venice, 1554).

3. Bernardino Pino da Cagli, *Breve considerazione intorno al componimento de la comedia de' nostri tempi* (Venice, 1578), repr. in Bernard Weinberg,
ed., *Trattati di poetica e retorica del Cinquecento* (Bari, 1970), 2:629–49.

Oddi, as to Plautus and Terence, but with pointed discrimination he also names Piccolomini's comedies as models and pays homage to Bibbiena. He forbears to observe, however, that *La Calandria* was composed on moral grounds very different from those he was urging for the genre in his own time.

The comici dell'arte exhibited a kindred taste in choosing plays to borrow. The actor and manager Fabrizio de' Fornaris was given the comedy he published in 1585 under the title *Angelica* by "a most accomplished Neapolitan gentleman,"[4] probably the author himself, Giovanni Battista Della Porta, whose *Olimpia* is clearly the original version. In an "Amorous Debate on Comedy," one of the *contrasti scenici* culled from her repertory of scenes for improvisation and published posthumously, the foremost actress of the century, Isabella Andreini, speaks authoritatively of Aristotle's *Poetics* and of peripety and recognition in comedy, and recommends imitating Plautus, Terence, Piccolomini, Trissino, Calderari, Pino, and Aristophanes.[5] What the literary dramatists and professional actors agreed on as the model of the genre is the subject of this essay.

For the High Renaissance, genre was not solely a hypothetical instrument of analysis; it was a fact of art and a prescription. The commedia determined by this view is called *erudita* or *grave* because it was deliberately developed from a learned tradition after centuries of hiatus, *osservata* or *regolare* because linked with nascent theory in search of rules for literary and dramatic criticism, *letteraria* because written with attention to classical and Trecento linguistic precepts or in polemic against them, *classica* for these reasons and because it was cultivated by an avant-garde to whom neoclassicism was still an innovation.

4. Fabrizio de' Fornaris, *Angelica, comedia* (Paris, 1585), Dedication, "Gl'anni adietro mi fu da un gentil-homo Napolitano virtuosissimo spirto, donata questa comedia" (Some years ago this comedy was given me by a most accomplished Neapolitan gentleman).

5. "Amoroso contrasto sopra la comedia," *Fragmenti di alcune scritture della Signora Isabella Andreini Comica Gelosa, et Academica Intenta: Raccolti da Francesco Andreini Comico Geloso detto il Capitano Spavento, e dati in luce da Flamminio Scala Comico* (Venice, 1620), 60; in the preface Isabella's husband, Francesco, states that the volume contains his compositions also, but does not say which they are. Aristophanic airs were put on early and late: see Alessandro Vellutello, Preface to Agostino Ricchi's *I tre tiranni* (Venice, 1533) and Melchiore Zoppio, *Il Diogene accusato* (Venice, 1598). Perhaps Machiavelli's lost *Le maschere* was more genuinely in the spirit of Aristophanes.

Theorizing through their prologues in the spirit of *serio ludere* that
so often governed humanists in the first half of the Cinquecento, playwrights could apologize slyly with Ariosto for the inevitable inferiority
of modern vernacular comedy to its Greek and Latin prototypes,[6] explain with Donato Giannotti that one could improve on a Plautine plot
to make a comedy both new and old,[7] or boast with Francesco D'Ambra of not having written a *comedia grave* with sententious speeches
like any of Terence;[8] the differences in the attitudes struck in these prologues and the forty years separating the first from the last obscure neither the kinship of the comedies they introduce nor that the three *commediografi* were at one in identifying the context of their genre. They
saw themselves as heirs and above all as competitors of Menander, Plautus, and Terence.

Scholarly attention has often singled out the departures from the generic norm and the challenges to it presented by individual comedies.
Probably the most original achievement in Italian comedy, however,
was the collective one of setting that norm. It took a considerable time
to do, more than three decades merely to cast the first mold, and the
emergence of a definitive shape did not end the experimentation with
genre. If the construction of a generic model in the early Cinquecento is
interesting, moreover, so is the reaffirmation and testing that simultaneously occupied comic dramatists after the 1540s. The form of the commedia was continually tried for flexibility and balance, its limits prod-
ded, its capacity for meaning stretched. An unremitting concern for
genre is attested by what remained constant, from the most representative, most often performed, and most prophetic of commedie, the
Calandria of 1513, to the atypical *jeu d'esprit*, Giordano Bruno's anti-
commedia *Candelaio* of 1582. Even the changes that bear the comedies
of Oddi, Borghini, and Della Porta far away from *La Calandria* and
Mandragola are motivated by curiosity about the genre and vigilance
about its fundamental principles.

First among these was the principle of contaminatio. Defending his

6. *La cassaria* (prose version), Prologue, in *Commedie e satire di Lodovico
Ariosto*, ed. Giovanni Tortoli (Florence, 1856). Further references to Ariosto are
to this edition.

7. Donato Giannotti, *Il vecchio amoroso* (1533–36), Prologue, in Nino
Borsellino, ed. *Commedie del Cinquecento*, vol. 1. Further references to Giannotti are to this edition.

8. Francesco D'Ambra, *I Bernardi* (1547), Prologue, in Aldo Borlenghi,
ed., *Commedie del Cinquecento*, vol. 2.

Andria from the critics who objected to contamination of one plot with another,[9] Terence had owned to mixing the two Menandrian comedies *Perinthia* and *Andria*. What Terence defended Ariosto boasted of in the prologue to the prose *Suppositi*, pointing out his mixture of Terence's *Eunuchus* with Plautus's *Captivi*. What had been simply a convenient practice of the ancients determined a formal goal for generations of Italian *commediografi:* a fusion of increasingly numerous and disparate sources, displaying sure technique of construction. Ironically, Montaigne criticized this kind of composition and its exaggerated emphasis on story in contrast with the Terentian comedy he admired (*Essais* II.10).

Corollary to the principle of contamination was that of complication, proceeding from an early preoccupation with structure and plot that would be reenforced by the later vogue of Aristotle's *Poetics*. The standard of form demanded not only unity of action, aided by the strictures on time and place that were supposed to guarantee to the plot the tension of crisis, but multiple intrigue as well. The specific flaw in his Plautine source, *Mercator,* that Giannotti aimed to remedy in *Il vecchio amoroso* was that "molto semplicemento fusse tessuto" (Prologue: it was very simply woven).

Even in the first three decades of experimentation, exceptions to the principle of complication were rare and not persuasive. After the first *Cortigiana* of 1525, Aretino set about building intrigue structures; the plots of his *Talanta* and *Ipocrito* even overcompensate for an initial lack of complexity. *L'anconitana* (1534–1535?) shows Ruzante's willingness to sacrifice his best gifts on the altar of structural principle. *La mandragola,* numbered among the *comedie elette* that Ruscelli edited as monuments in the history of the genre, was not admired for its structure. Although he praises the language and even the disposition of scenes, and excuses the simple plot as a consequence of Machiavelli's wanting to make all the action arise from Messer Nicia's stupidity, Ruscelli nevertheless recommends against imitation, for "la Comedia dal primo atto fino al quarto, et ancor molte volte sino al principio o mezo del quinto, ha da andar sempre crescendo in disturbi, in difficoltà, in intrighi" (From the first act through the fourth and often midway through the fifth, Comedy should proceed by ever-increasing upheavals, differences, intrigues), whereas in *Mandragola*, "La onde il quarto e il

---

9. *Andria,* Prologue, "Disputant contaminari, non decere fabulas," in *Terence,* with trans. by John Sargeaunt, vol. 1 (1912; repr. Cambridge, Mass., and London, 1959).

principio del quinto, ne' quali suole essere la maggiore intentione de gl'intrichi, procedono tutti quietamente, e di bene in meglio; che per certo in quanto al soggetto è cosa da fuggirsi in una Comedia" (The fourth and the beginning of the fifth acts, in which usually occurs the greatest complication, proceed quietly from good to better; which certainly, as far as plot is concerned, is something to be avoided in a comedy).[10]

If form was the primary aspect under which Italian comedy was seen as a reemerging genre, content also required an ideal formulation. A spacious one with excellent credentials was at hand in the phrase that Aelius Donatus had attributed to Cicero and applied to the comedies of Terence: "comoediam esse Cicero ait imitationem vitae, speculum consuetudinis, imaginem veritatis" (Cicero said that comedy is an imitation of life, a mirror of custom, an image of truth).[11] This was translated into early Cinquecento comedy as an exhortation to realistic, that is, verisimilar, imitation of contemporary middle-class life. However stylized the human relationships or overcharged with coincidence the commedia seems to an audience familiar with nineteenth-century drama and twentieth-century film, Renaissance playwrights' pride in their truth to reality is caught in Giovanni Battista Gelli's boast that his clever contemporaries were not to be taken in by the unbelievable stuff of saints' lives,[12] which were standard fare in medieval *rappresentazioni* combining religious and local folk legend in modes at brief remove from pageant and ritual. Modern commedia seemed closer to real life because it reduced the strain on the spectators' credulity. The physical and temporal confines of the action dispensed the audience from having to imagine more than that the events of one day in one city could be reflected in a few hours on one piazza. At the same time new demands were made. Ruscelli was not alone in emphasizing that the function of

10. Ruscelli, *Delle comedie elette* (Venice, 1554), "Annotationi," 182–83.

11. *Aeli Donati quod fertur Commentum Terenti,* ed. P. Wessner (Leipzig, 1902), 1:22.

12. *La sporta,* 1st ed. (1543). I quote from the prologue to the edition published in 1550 Florence: "Le genti sono diventate tanto astute che Santa Anfrosina non istarebbe più cinque anni frate, che quei padri non si fossero accorti s'ella fossi maschio, o femina: ne Santo Alessio dieci anni sotto una scala senza essere da suo padre e da sua madre riconosciuto" (People have become so shrewd that Saint Anfrosina could no longer remain a monk for five years without those holy fathers' discovering whether she was male or female, nor Saint Alexis under the stairs for ten years unrecognized by his father and mother).

modern audiences was to see.[13] As spectators, observing rather than participating, they were invited to engage in an unaccustomed exercise of conscious detachment from the immediate reality of life in the street outside the palace in which they were gathered for the performance, a reality reproduced inside by a *prospettiva* (or *perspettiva* in Serlio's edition of 1560) of canvas, paint, wood, and costumed friends or familiars. This aping of quotidian reality seems to have been exhilarating in itself; the act of counterfeiting was often drawn to the spectator's attention in prologues. Reality was treated as an object and the act of assuming a position apart from it, so as to compare its substance with its theatrical reflection, was a stimulating game. The game was still being played, or played on, in Duke Orsino's theatrical metaphor for the amazing resemblance between the twins in *Twelfth Night:*

> One face, one voice, one habit, and two persons—
> A natural perspective that is and is not.
>
> (V.1.208–09)

The fictional time in the commedia was the present, the place a specific Italian city; and although the scenery was often general, an ideal model of Cinquecento urban architecture, reusable for a comedy set in another city (and therefore conducive to jesting in the prologue about the evanescence and arbitrariness of the theatrical illusion), it was the realism of the scene in perspective that was valued. Vasari's praise of Baldessare Peruzzi's scene for *La Calandria* does not dwell on its resemblance to any particular quarter of Rome, where the action is supposed to take place, but makes much of the success of the trompe l'œil; it was the more original, adds Vasari, in that in Baldessare's day comedy had been out of use for a very long time and *feste* or rappresentazioni were undertaken instead.[14]

Whether the setting is courtly Ferrara, papal Rome, or nominally bourgeois Florence, the characters of the street scene at doorways, alleys, windows, loggias, and church porches are for the most part burghers, and their economic dependents—those to whom they are employers, relatives, clients, and gulls. Their concerns are domestic, turning on money and love and the conflict of generations, parents against children in the manner of New Comedy, old husbands against young wives and lovers in the Decameronian style.

13. Ruscelli, "Annotationi," 170–72.

14. Giorgio Vasari, *Delle vite de' piu eccellenti pittori scultori et architettori,* vol. 3 (Florence, 1568): 141.

Typically, a denouement may work in two ways: to conceal and to reveal. The plots lifted from novellas about cuckolds and dissatisfied young wives accommodate adultery and the deceits accompanying it, potentially antisocial actions that are kept secret when the order disturbed at the beginning is restored at the end. *Mandragola* is entirely a comedy of concealment: the revelation made to the audience is not fully shared with the society of the fiction, which remains split into the deceived (Messer Nicia) and the deceivers (everyone else). On the other hand, plots from New Comedy, with its inheritance from romance, are resolved by marriages and new beginnings, correction of old errors, forgiveness of past deceits, recognitions and reidentifications of kin. Both sorts of denouement would persist in the late Cinquecento. *Candelaio* is essentially a comedy of concealment: the old order is not overthrown by the demonstration that its only realities are sex, violence, deceit, and words. But comedy of concealment, if hardy, lost some ground as the century unfolded. The spirit of carnival gave way to the celebration of social order. The conclusion of the commedia became increasingly a tour de force of denouement culminating in a revelation, or series of revelations, sweeping all complexities into a neat design of marriages, family reunion, economic recovery, and neighborhood pacification, extending in some late plays even to municipal concord. The comic Oedipus situation that Frye descries behind New Comedy underlies the triumph of the younger generation in comedy of revelation; the reintegration achieved at the end is one that continues the old order, but that by shifting power to those who are next in line to become parents makes the society new.

Both concealment and revelation are the ends of Bibbiena's *Calandria*. This play has so often been cited as containing what Baratto calls the "dramaturgical matrix" of Cinquecento comedy that any other example of generic principle in practice would be less hackneyed. But no other example is so apt. The early date, unique comprehensiveness, and waxing prestige of *La Calandria* throughout the sixteenth century give it a primacy in the genre that must still be acknowledged, as it was by Ruscelli.[15]

Bibbiena's contaminatio merges two sources, Boccaccio and Plautus, but more than two plots. Several novelle of the *Decameron* are fused in the dramatic action involving Calandro, the feeble-minded cuckold in love with the transvestite lover of his wife, and Fulvia, the malmaritata

15. Ruscelli, "Annotationi," 166.

who employs a fake magician to further her love affair and is enabled by luck to conceal her adultery from Calandro and regain the domestic upper hand by discovering his. Simultaneously, other novelle and Plautine sources in addition to *Menaechmi* are tapped for the plot of Santilla and Lidio, twins from the Greek city of Modone (Methone) whom fortune reunites in Rome. The mistakes inadvertently provoked by her disguise as a boy, for the sake of safety, and his as a girl, for the sake of love, are compounded by the deliberate deceits practiced for fun and gain by a manipulating servant, Fessenio, and a charlatan, Ruffo. The revelation of the twins' identity and the betrothals arranged for them with the son of Fulvia and Calandro and the daughter of another rich Roman family restore the Greeks to wealth and to each other, creating a new order in the Italian community, while the suppression of the truth about Fulvia keeps up the appearance of the old one. The total gain is appraised by the arch-trickster Fessenio, the character most nearly in control of the intrigue, who caps Lidio's jubilant "Staremo meglio che a Modon!" (We shall be better off here than we were in Methone!) with words that are as applicable to the principles of the new genre of commedia founded on and surpassing Attic New Comedy as they are to the happy conclusion of the drama: "Tanto meglio quanto Italia è più degno della Grecia, quanto Roma è più nobil che Modon e quanto vaglion più due ricchezze che una. E tutti trionferemo" (V.12: By just so much as Italy is worthier than Greece, by so much is Rome nobler than Methone and two fortunes are more valuable than one. And all of us are winners).[16] Rounding off the play, the ringing humanistic boast echoes the first prologue, attributed until recently to Castiglione,[17] in which the superiority of new Italian comedy and its inheritance from Boccaccio and Plautus are simultaneously proclaimed. The claim is confirmed by the five acts that lie in between, a synthesis of characters and episodes displayed in prose that is at once modern and timelessly Boccaccian, held in dramatic tension by contraction of the time to a day and the space to a street scene.

The complication that Bibbiena practices in the disposition of his multiple contaminatio of raw materials creates a network of actions, a working model and probably the original inspiration of Ruscelli's for-

16. Bernardo Dovizi, Cardinal Bibbiena, *La Calandria*, in Nino Borsellino, ed., *Commedie del Cinquecento*, vol. 1. All quotations are from this edition.

17. The prologue is shown to be Bibbiena's own composition by Giorgio Padoan in his edition of *Calandria* (Verona, 1970), 139–79.

mula for the ideal plot. Lidio's intrigue with Fulvia gives rise to Calandro's attempt at intrigue with Lidio; fleeing one labyrinth, Santilla is
drawn into another by the charlatan's plan to dupe Fulvia. The confusion reaches such a pitch by the end of the fourth act that even Fessenio,
who has previously taken a detached artistic pleasure in the ironic pattern of the intrigue, begins to believe that Lidio's feminine disguise has
become a genuine metamorphosis. As Ruscelli recommended, the intrigue continues well into the fifth act, and Santilla's wail "In che la-
berinto mi trovo io!" (V.2: In what a labyrinth I find myself!) is both a
description of the plot and the vaunt of the playwright, shortly preceding the sudden revelation and concealment of the denouement.

The principle of complication implies not only some degree of causal
interdependence of action but also multiplication of details and reflections of one pose or episode in another: a prostitute takes Lidio's place
in the dark to fool Calandro about his mistress, Santilla takes Lidio's
place with Fulvia to fool Calandro about his wife, and Fannio plans to
take Santilla's place to fool Fulvia about her lover; the pivotal disguise
in the comedy is that of Santilla as a boy, and Bibbiena multiplies it by
four, decreeing transvestitism for Lidio, Fulvia, and Fannio as well; in
addition to the crazy image created by Calandro's coupling with the
prostitute of the affair between Fulvia and Lidio, there is another brief
reflection of it in the quick, behind-the-door tumble of the servants
Samia and Lusco.

As an imitation of life, mirror of custom, and image of truth *La Calandria* represents the prevailing, but not unanimous, sixteenth-century
view of the proper subject of the genre. The reality Bibbiena brings on
stage is not the Cinquecento Florence evoked by the language of Machiavelli or Grazzini, not Annibal Caro's slice of Piazza Farnese or the
contemporary Roman customs satirically surveyed by Aretino, still less
the brutal postwar Veneto of the deracinated peasant Ruzante. Rather,
the reality of *La Calandria* is generalized, an updated Decameronian
holiday world, tangible and plausible, a territory of common cultural
ownership that was speedily accepted in the Cinquecento as the realm of
life to be imitated by commedia. The coincidences permitted here by
fortune are as unlikely and exaggerated as the gullibility of Calandro,
the tricks of Fessenio, or the indiscretion of Fulvia, but they are nevertheless selections from real life, artistically heightened and related. It is
not only in fiction that old men can be stupid and lustful, dissatisfied
wives run wild for love, con men make people believe almost anything,
families can be separated in wartime, impecunious foreigners cast about

for means to financial security, and fortune plays a disconcerting role in life; indeed, the dramatic force of the coincidences and of the extraordinary effects of love's tyranny depends on the context of an ordinary, if generalized, reality and requires it. In its own time even the racy but literary prose of *La Calandria* required and received warrant from objective, extraliterary experience: although the dialogue is thick with stylized epigrams from Boccaccio, Ruscelli explains that the natural syntax has been twisted to imitate the way Greeks speak Italian.[18]

The units with which Bibbiena constructed his simulacrum of physically perceptible reality are not only generally prophetic of the materials of the genre for more than a century but also specifically identical with the primordial movable parts of theme, situation, and character, of which comedy after comedy would be put together. Fortune, the force that moves and baffles the plots, now seconding the power of love, now allying itself with wit, now indiscriminately threatening all with its caprices, also figures throughout *La Calandria* as a topos, beginning with Fessenio's opening words, "Bene è vero che l'uomo mai un disegno non fa che la Fortuna un altro non ne faccia" (I.1: How true it is that for every design man makes, Fortune makes another). "Le femmine sono mutabili" (I.2: Women are fickle) is another of the topoi that would be handed down from one play to another, here introduced as a preface to some joking about homosexuality. Patterns of verbal encounters are set in scenes like the one in which the serva Samia, breathless from running an errand, answers her mistress's anxious questions with gasps, irrelevancies, and malapropisms (III.5). Such exchanges, like the give-and-take of sententiae or the deceiving fragments of eavesdropped dialogues, are units of drama adapted from Boccaccio for the stage, or from Plautus to exploit Italian vocabulary and allusions. In synchrony with a cross fire of Tuscan proverbs, they emerged in *La Calandria* as sections of a new vernacular structure that could be reassembled into other compositions in the genre, like the scenery for most productions of comedy.

The same holds true for the theatergrams of situation and nonverbal action first organized in *La Calandria:* the repeated substitutions of lovers in the dark; the slippings in and out of that useful portion of the set, the camera terrena; the optical illusions created deliberately by costume changes and accidentally by family resemblances. So too the relationships that would be the human staple of the commedia are already well developed in *La Calandria*. There is a considerable range of com-

18. Ruscelli, "Annotationi," 170.

binations of serva (or servo) and padrona (or padrone), and calculated
contrasts between the association of sex and madness in Fulvia's sympa-
thetically presented love with that of sex and food in Calandro's ridiculed cravings. Had it been written forty years later as a compendium of
generic structures, *La Calandria* could not be more representative than
it is of the commedia in its first half-century.

By attaching so much value to the principle of contaminatio even in
the early Cinquecento, when they were trying to free the ideal modern
genre from its Latin swaddling clothes, Italian dramatists acted on that
impulse to mix things that throbs beneath most movements in Renaissance art. Although Annibal Caro could claim as late as 1543 that the
law of comedy had not yet been entirely established,[19] fundamental
principles were no longer at issue, as is clear from the nature of the "innovation" he defended; rather a matter of quantity than of quality, a
triple plot instead of a double one. In the decades that followed, curiosity to know how much the structure of commedia would bear led to
combining not only individual sources but also the newly defined genres
themselves. The results would be diverse hybrids of matter and tone,
displays of thematic chiaroscuro and variations on structural units in
the superstructure of the *intreccio* plot, with its prescribed denouement.
It is an axiom of criticism that Cinquecento commedia began in unity
and ended in pieces, having produced a pathetic and sentimental strain
that nourished the music drama and baroque tragicomedy of the Seicento, and a miscellany of comic turns and techniques that would be
maintained by the commedia dell'arte. The second half of the Cinquecento, coinciding with the phase of Italian comedy closest to Shakespeare's time, witnessed developments in the genre that prepared for the
ultimate disintegration. A modern preference for the pioneers of the
genre sometimes obscures the fact that these developments also produced sophisticated theatrical instruments and demonstrated potentialities of comedy previously unrealized.

The impulse to mix was encouraged no less by an interest in the capabilities of form than by appetite for varied content. An intense critical
activity following the publication of Robortelli's translation and explication of the *Poetics* in 1548 fostered attempts to extrapolate what Aristotle must have thought about comedy from what he had said about
tragedy. Although writers of commedia had learned much earlier from

19. Annibal Caro, *Gli straccioni*, Prologue, in Borsellino, *Commedie del
Cinquecento*, vol. 2.

Plautus and Terence to accomplish recognition and reversal in their plots, Aristotle's praise of Sophocles' use of these means of resolution led to the competition of comedy with tragedy and to such claims as that which Guido Decani made for Flaminio Maleguzzi's *Theodora, commedia* in 1568: that the peripety employed in it is "l'istessa con quella d'Edipode Tiranno, tanto celebrata da Aristotele; se ben quella è di felicità in infelicità; ove questa è tutt' all'opposito" (the same as that in Oedipus Tyrant, so much celebrated by Aristotle; although that moves from happiness to woe, whereas this is exactly the opposite).[20]

Imitating *Oedipus rex* in comedy also meant transposing somber dramatic irony into a happy key: unavoidable fate was replaced by unhoped-for providence. As a consequence, the peripety, heretofore functional primarily as a mechanism, became in itself a content-structure full of meaning for the times. An important goal of the Counter-Reformation's campaign against fortune-telling and belief in fate, or predestination, was the reaffirmation of the doctrine defined by Aquinas and the church fathers before him: of the sovereignty of divine providence, limiting fortune's power and guaranteeing man's free will. The idea of a peripety that is not merely another turn of fortune's wheel but the revelation and unexpected result of a plan for human happiness made by a power greater than luck was perfectly formed to serve a Catholic indoctrination program. It was a case of dramatic criticism effortlessly seconding theological orthodoxy and responding to the Counter Reformation's appeal for an engaged art.

The abstract quality of much late Renaissance drama, often blamed on an Inquisitional censorship that made representation of social reality dangerous and satire nearly impossible, may be discerned even in external details. One need think only of the ideonyms that Borghini fastens on the leading innamorati in *L'amante furioso* (1583), Filarete and Aretafila. What can be described as escapism, however, can also be attributed to receptivity on the part of playwrights to critical theory and to the spirit of the Counter-Reformation. The tendency toward abstraction paralleled the universalizing trend in drama that was furthered by Horace's principle of decorum and Aristotle's preference of ideal fiction over real history as a subject for tragedy. At the same time, general moral and cultural currents were influenced by the hope of a return to a universal church, away from the particularities of schism and heresy and

20. Flaminio Maleguzzi, *La Theodora, comedia,* written before 1564 (Venice, 1572); Guido Decani's dedication is dated 1568.

from the moral empiricism associated with such earlier Renaissance writers as the banned Machiavelli. In comedy, one of the results was an intermittent symbolism that looked back to the allegory of medieval drama, but without sacrifice of the structural refinements developed by the experiments of Renaissance humanism in the genre. The abstractness of late commedie originated in a meeting of neoclassicism with neomedievalism, of the form of New Comedy enriched by supercharged Aristotelian peripety with allegorical and didactic possibilities as strong as those of Quattrocento rappresentazioni and farse morali, if not as direct.

Like other charter principles of regular comedy, its ideal definition as imitation of life, mirror of custom, and image of truth remained in force but suffered an expansion. The delight in reproducing the appearance of concrete reality that had attended the début of vernacular comedy gave way in Tridentine times to an impatience with merely sensible objects of imitation and a manneristic scrutiny of the ironies and inadequacies of appearance. The challenge to make a theatrical image of a truth above custom and not susceptible of being reflected by a mirror was taken up in the line of sentimental comedies springing from the first efforts of Piccolomini and the other members of the Sienese Accademia degli Intronati of the 1530s, in which the invisible inner reality of the heart was brought onstage in pathetic situations and emotional scenes, often dominated by articulate women with strong feelings.

Extension of the idea of dramatically imitable reality was directed not only inward, to the hidden motions of the heart, but outward, to the invisible workings of an eternal world in which the day's span of a comedy was a brief but possibly significant moment, even an emblematic one. The concept of providence, central to the tradition of romance, inherent in New Comedy and indispensable to Christian doctrine, was one such reality toward which the generic structures of the commedia gravitated. The intreccio plot itself, so carefully perfected by practice of contaminatio and complication, could be used not only as a dramatic mechanism for rational organization of a selected reality but as the vehicle for a complex of ideas or as a metaphor for the twisted, fortune-ridden, temporal appearance of human life, which is in reality an orderly design eternally present to the eye of providence.

Representation of such truths had to be achieved without loss of verisimilitude; the effect of wonder demanded from commedia by the neo-Aristotelians depended no less than before on strict plausibility. Although Castelvetro's insistence on pleasure and credibility and on limiting fictional time and place to performance time and single scene suggests an audience weak of imagination,[21] the spectators of the comedies with an expanded field of reality were in fact being invited to perform the dual mental action of observing the pleasing fiction and perceiving the truth for which it was a sign.

In the later Cinquecento private drama flourished at universities and petty courts, in the country as well as in the centers of Venice, Ferrara, Florence, Rome, and Naples, and the public professional troupes traveled everywhere. One of the least-examined results of experiments with genre in this very active period was the mutation of the grave comedy. The adjective that D'Ambra had used to distinguish Terence's tone from his own, more playful, Florentine one became a means of relating the best modern comedy to a tradition that included both D'Ambra and Terence, while simultaneously opposing it to the ill-constructed improvisations of the poorer sort of commedia dell'arte zanies. Girolamo Razzi was proud to record that *La Cecca* had been considered by some to be "troppo grave e severa, e per dir così poco alla Zannesca" (too grave and severe, and, as you might say, too little *alla Zannesca*).[22] Commedia grave, as the term was used by Castelletti and Oddi for their own works and by Pompeo Barbarito to describe Della Porta's *L'Olimpia,* could refer on one side to firm, interlocking structure and variety of substance fused by contaminatio (as forecast by *La Calandria*) and on the other to a seriousness that made comedy resemble its sister, tragedy, as Tasso put it in a sonnet praising Pino.[23] The admired *gravità* could include actions and characters fit for tragedy, the effects of "meraviglia, dolore e compassione" (wonder, sorrow and pity) of which Castelletti boasted in *I torti amorosi,* or the symbolism of dramatic structure indicated by Luigi Pasqualigo's claim that the love plot of his *Fedele* makes manifest

21. Lodovico Castelvetro, *Poetica d'Aristotele vulgarizzata, et sposta* (Basilea, 1576), quoted in H. B. Charlton, *Castelvetro's Theory of Poetry* (Manchester, 1913), 84–85 n. 2.

22. Girolamo Razzi, Dedication (1560) to the 2d ed. of *La balia* (Florence, 1564).

23. Cristoforo Castelletti, *I torti amorosi,* 1581 (Venice, 1591), Prologue, and *Le stravaganze d'amore,* 1584 (Venice, 1613), I.5; Sforza Oddi, *Prigione d'amore,* 1570? (Florence, 1592), Prologue; Giambattista Della Porta, *L'Olimpia* (Naples, 1589), Dedication; Torquato Tasso, *Le rime,* ed. A. Solerti (Bologna, 1902), 190.

gli affanni e le miserie passate a chi in sicuro porto condotto per benignità de i cieli più non teme la malignità della fortuna, perche essendo così disposte le cose di qua giù dal Sommo fattore, che stanno sempre in continuo moto, non è persona, che molto o poco non sia agitata da questo continuo flusso, e reflusso.

Prologue: the ordeals and deprivations suffered by him who, guided to safe harbor by the heavens' goodness, no longer fears fortune's evil power, because all things here below having been so disposed by the Great Maker that they are forever in continual motion, there is no one who is not more or less moved by the constant flow back and forth.[24]

Fortune's subordination to providence, briefly acknowledged in comedy by Ariosto in the prose *Suppositi* (V.8) and elaborated by Aretino in *La Talanta* (V.1) as the Counter-Reformation began, had become a commonplace of structure by 1589, when Calderari called the peripety of *La schiava* an "essempio a ciascuno: che non è giamai l'huom cosi perturbato dalla avversa Fortuna, che in un punto, in un'attimo Dio non lo renda felice, e contento" (V.9: example to all that no man is ever so harried by adverse Fortune that in a moment, in a second, God may not make him happy and contented).[25]

When Della Porta announced in a prologue that a new, wonder-arousing and well-balanced plot was the soul of comedy and that in his work peripety would be born of peripety and recognition of recognition, causing the ghosts of Menander, Epicharmus, and Plautus to rejoice at being surpassed by the moderns, he was attesting the longevity of the first principles of commedia as well as boasting of progress. The comedy with which one version of this prologue appeared was *Gli duoi fratelli rivali*, a well-developed specimen of late Cinquecento commedia grave written ten or more years before its publication in 1601.[26] Its New Comedy ancestors and recent Italian antecedents are declared at every turn: by the verisimilitude, the Salerno street setting, the time span (limited to a Tuesday and a Wednesday), the two innamorati with a clever servant apiece, the parasite, the braggart captain, the contaminatio of borrowings from *Mercator*, *Andria*, and other Plautine and Terentian

24. Luigi (Alvise) Pasqualigo, *Il fedele* (Venice, 1576), Prologue.
25. Giovanni Battista Calderari, *La schiava* (Vicenza, 1589), V.9.
26. *Gli duoi fratelli rivali, comedia nuovamente data in luce, dal Signor Gio. Bat. Della Porta gentilhuomo Napolitano* (Venice, 1601).

sources, with a primary plot from the tale by Bandello that Shakespeare also used in *Much Ado about Nothing.*[27]

The choice of a romantic and nearly tragic novella with echoes of Ariosto's courtly tale of Ariodante and Genevra (*Orlando furioso* V), and Della Porta's inclusion of scrambled facts from Salernitan history and his own family records, however, illustrate the more comprehensive use of contamination in late commedia. The result is an intreccio of contrasting genres, a theatrical story of the rivalry of the nephews of the Spanish viceroy of Salerno for the love of Carizia Della Porta, one of two daughters of an impoverished nobleman. With the help of a clever servant, a venal glutton, a bawdy maidservant, and a gullible braggart, the disappointed suitor tricks his more fortunate brother into accusing Carizia of wantonness. Her apparent death elicits the truth, her return pacifies the new rivalry ignited by the viceroy's order that one brother marry her sister, and a double wedding averts the last threat of tragedy.

Details of characterization in *Fratelli rivali* reveal the reciprocity between commedia grave and the commedia dell'arte that coexisted with dramatists' attacks on the actors' often shapeless zannate. For example, Della Porta's *miles gloriosus,* Martebellonio, produces comic cadenzas that would be suitable for any braggart captain and may have been borrowed by actors for use in other comedies. Many of them, in fact, resemble the tirades for the mask of Capitano Spavento published by Andreini on his retirement from the stage in 1607.[28] The heroic passion and peril that are juxtaposed with broad foolery in *Fratelli rivali* likewise seem intended to exploit the range of the comici's professional skill, and they explain something of Della Porta's popularity with the actors. These darker elements also demonstrate the lengths to which contaminatio could be carried in comedy. Units developed when the genre was being defined and differentiated from others are loaded in this late play with noncomic weights. The grouping of servo and padrone, young lovers and old opponents, innamorata and balia, and their encounters in the street and at windows belong to the familiar bourgeois reality. But the major characters have been promoted to a social rank as high as that demanded for tragedy by Italian theorists. The long-established generic

27. Matteo Bandello, *Novelle,* 1.22. See Giambattista Della Porta, *Gli duoi fratelli rivali/The Two Rival Brothers,* ed. and trans. L. G. Clubb (Berkeley, Los Angeles, and London, 1980), Introduction.

28. Francesco Andreini, *Le bravure del Capitano Spavento divise in molti ragionamenti in forma di dialogo* (Venice, 1607).

relation of nurse to girl decrees the confidence that Madonna Angiola
enjoys and the part she plays in the courtship; but Della Porta makes her
Carizia's aunt, thereby establishing Angiola as a duenna instead of a
balia and emphasizing the family's place in an aristocratic ambience
equal to that inhabited by the analogous characters of Bandello and
Ariosto. With the character of the viceroy, Della Porta goes not only beyond earlier commedia but also beyond Bandello, by adding to the novella plot from the tradition of comedy the figure of a guardian, but turning him from a foolish or menacing blocker of youth's desire into a
potentially tragic ruler with an almost Shakespearean mission as a re-
storer of order and arbiter of peace.

In disposing and entwining the multiple threads of this fabric, Della
Porta fulfills the promise of his prologue and upholds his predecessor's
principle of complication. His means are the generic topoi and movable
parts of commedia, but like many writers of late commedia grave he employs them both for achieving greater complexity of pattern and for representing feelings, moral example, or some other incorporeal object.
Many of the units observed in *La Calandria* appear in *Fratelli rivali:* the
originally Plautine scenes of questions and irrelevant answers (II.9) and
of eavesdropping (II.4), the topos of woman's frailty (II.2), the exchange
of proverbs (III.1), the substitution of partners at a rendez-vous in a
dark camera terrena (II.11), and the deflating comparison of love and
food obsessions (I.3), among others. But the old structural units have
become means to new ends. The hoary, misogynistic saw leads into a
scene in which Carizia's grace and virtue shine out so wonderfully as to
convert even her detractor, an example of the spiritual embellishment of
the innamorata that was undertaken in many commedie gravi and that
is continued in *Fratelli rivali* by further vicissitudes of the plot, including false accusation, apparent death, resurrection, and triumph. The exchange of contradictory proverbs is used to sum up the pros and cons of
the deceit perpetrated by the brother associated with shifty, Machiavellian ideas about fortune and efficiency that are condemned by the explicit moral of the play. The deception in the dark is played for laughs,
but also for pathos and echoes of the theme of false appearance and the
unreliability of human means of cognition, which resonates somewhat
spasmodically throughout the comedy.

Revelation rather than concealment is the natural end of such commedia grave. In *Fratelli rivali* the venerable device of discovery of kinship is not needed as a literal passage to the idea revealed; the distance
between what appears to be and what is, played on with every deceit

and misunderstanding at every turn of the intrigue, itself becomes the final revelation. Death, violence, and disorder, the represented "facts," are proved at last to be unreal or transitory, dissolved by the real and the permanent: love, virtue, and the supernatural power in whose plan of order chaos is merely a phase. The ways of the heart and of providence are given as much theatrical substance as the limitations of the genre allow.

The late Cinquecento preoccupation with hybrid genre and perfect peripety facilitated imitation of the invisible realities. Spectators long accustomed to appraise comedy according to generic conventions of content and form could be brought not only to see that all ends well but to observe the ending as a peripety, to eye the design as connoisseurs, and to recognize it as the image of a truth not confined by the fiction. Signs posted at turnings in the labyrinth of *Fratelli rivali* (V.3: "God . . . alone has decreed in Heaven that events so difficult and impossible to resolve be brought to so happy and end") are officially sanctioned by the concluding words of the civil and domestic authority, the viceroy, who casts himself as a spectator of the events that are real to him and thus economically instructs the spectators offstage in how to see the play:

> Veramente mi son assai meravigliato, essendo spettatore d'un crudel abbattimento di dui per altro valorosi e degni cavalieri; ma or che veggio tanta bellezza in Carizia, e così ancor stimo la sorella, gli escuso e non gl'incolpo; e giudico che l'immenso Iddio governi queste cose con secreta e certa legge de' fati, e che molto prima abbi ordinato che succedano questi gravi disordini, accioché così degna coppia di sorelle si accoppiono con sì degno paro di fratelli, che par l'abbi fatti nascere per congiungerli insieme.

> V.4: In truth, as spectator, I greatly wondered at the cruel battle between two otherwise valorous and worthy noblemen; but now that I see so much beauty in Carizia—and likewise in his sister—I excuse and do not blame them, and I judge that God in his vastness governs these matters with secret and sure laws of the fates, and that long ago He ordained these grave disorders for that so worthy a pair of sisters might be matched with so worthy a pair of brothers, for it seems that by His will they were born to be joined together.[29]

29. Della Porta, *Gli duoi fratelli rivali*, ed. L. G. Clubb, V.4 (pp. 280–81).

Early and late, Cinquecento comedy was full of life. If its vitality is no longer self-evident, the commedia remains immeasurably valuable for the study of genre, being principled, fertile of structures, and evolutionary. Ultimately it was a genre inhibited by its principles. The commitments to a nominally specific setting in a contemporary urban place and to a verisimilitude that obviated the use of some means that would have been useful for imitating intangible objects decreed that other genres or subgenres would preempt the goal. The Italian genre that most programmatically did so was the pastoral tragicomedy, the history of which is properly a chapter in the larger history of the comedy. Even Guarini's *Pastor fido,* which defined the new genre in 1590 and was proffered as an even blend of tragedy and comedy, owes more to the comedy on which experiments with Sophoclean form and content were tried than it does to tragedy directly. As for the preliminary pastoral plays, from Beccari's *Sacrificio* of 1555 onward, in them the example of commedia is still more obvious, in the units of character and grouping, of verbal encounter, and of plot device, as it is likewise in the intreccio structure that was the choice of almost all pastoral dramatists but Tasso. Escaping from the residual realism of commedia grave into the new third genre, comic types and actions moved farther toward the abstract, shedding specificity to become theatrical shapes of feeling or idea, while the plots in which they figured became images of providential transformation of sorrow into joy or, as Thomas McFarland calls Shakespeare's pastoral comedies, "structures of hope."[30] Neither the wish to mix genres in a manner acceptable to neo-Aristotelian theory nor the desire to invent theatrical means of imitating invisible realities of emotion and universal order could be fully satisfied by the commedia grave, but when the hybrid genre was finally established in the form of the pastoral play and theorists warned over its aesthetic propriety, there spoke decades of experimentation with comic principles: *et in Arcadia comoedia gravis.*

30. Thomas McFarland, *Shakespeare's Pastoral Comedy* (Chapel Hill, 1972), 38.

CHAPTER TWO

Commedia Grave and *The Comedy of Errors*

aldwin's *On the Compositional Genetics of "The Comedy of Errors"* accounts exhaustively for every gene of Shakespeare's play, and not one is Italian. Nevertheless, Baldwin states that this comedy is "probably the most fundamentally Italianate play of the English lot, and yet there is not a specific element which can be traced to direct borrowing from the Italian," adding in a note: "It must be evident to anyone who has grasped this development of the type in England that so skillfully complicated a play as *Errors* could not have been constructed before the end of the 'eighties. Even so, it is as remarkable a personal accomplishment for the late 'eighties as Udall's *Ralph Roister Doister* was for the early 'fifties. I have the impression that this point of evolution would be stronger if it were put on the background of the development in Italy of this more complicated form from the simpler form of Plautus and Terence."[1]

Whether this impression, with its apparently subversive effect on the rest of his book, was inserted merely as a protective clause to appease Italianists, only Baldwin knows. But his suggestion is still very much worth taking, though it touches on the sore old question of whether or not Italian Renaissance comedy exercised any significant influence on the Elizabethan drama, especially Shakespeare's.

There are only a few proved connections to support Stephen Gosson's famous complaint that Italian comedies were "ransackt to furnish the Playe houses in London."[2] Some comedies of Ariosto, Grazzini, Aretino, the Intronati, Salviati, Piccolomini, Pasqualigo, Della Porta, and Oddi were translated or adapted in England.[3] From the late 1570s

This chapter appeared in slightly different form as "Italian Comedy and *The Comedy of Errors*," *Comparative Literature* 19, no. 3 (Summer 1967): 240–51. Reprinted by permission of *Comparative Literature*.

1. T. W. Baldwin, *On the Compositional Genetics of The Comedy of Errors* (Urbana, Ill., 1965), 208.

2. Stephen Gosson, *Playes Confuted in Five Actions* (London, 1582), D6v.

3. Ariosto's *Suppositi* in Gascoigne's *Supposes*; Grazzini's *Spiritata* in John Jeffere's (Jefferay's) *Buggbears*; Aretino's *Marescalco* in Jonson's *Epicoene*;

Italian comedy was decidedly chic at Cambridge, where Latin versions
were frequently performed.[4] Both of Machiavelli's comedies and four of
Aretino's were printed in London in 1588.[5] Royal interest in "comedia
italiana" is proved by Queen Elizabeth's request that her courtiers orga-
nize a performance of one. There are records of seven visits to England
by Italian players between 1546 and 1578, and by 1591 the traffic
seems to have been brisk enough to make disguise as Italian entertainers
desirable to foreign spies.[6]

But although a handful of facts have been established and analogues
have been recorded by several generations of scholars, the investigation
of the Elizabethan debt to Italian comedy has been stymied: by the scar-
city of documentary proof that there was physical contact or direct borrowing, and by the distractions of the common raw materials, notably
Latin comedy and *novelle*.

With regard to Shakespeare the question is especially tantalizing, for
half his plays smack of Italian drama, none more than *The Comedy of
Errors*. It is generally agreed that the sources of *The Comedy of Errors*
are a combination of *Menaechmi* and *Amphitruo*, Gower's version of
Apollonius of Tyre, and the account of St. Paul's travels in the Acts of
the Apostles; that Shakespeare's handling is more complex than Plautus's; and that the whole is given a serious turn, a touch of spirituality
and of horror. It is customary to add that Shakespeare raised the moral

---

the Intronati's *Ingannati* in the anonymous *Laelia*, a Cambridge Latin play;
Salviati's *Granchio* in the anonymous *Cancer,* also a Cambridge Latin play; Piccolomini's *Alessandro* in Chapman's *May Day;* Pasqualigo's *Fedele* in Fraunce's
Latin *Victoria* and Munday's *Fedele and Fortunio, the Two Italian Gentlemen;*
Della Porta's *Cintia* in Hawkesworth's Latin *Labyrinthus,* his *Trappolaria* in
Ruggle's Latin *Ignoramus,* his *Sorella* in Brooke's Latin *Adelphe* and Middle-
ton's *No Wit, No Help Like a Woman's,* and his *Astrologo* in Tomkis's *Al-
bumazar;* Oddi's *Erofilomachia* in Hawkesworth's Latin *Leander* and his *Morti
vivi* in Marston's *What You Will.*

4. See F. S. Boas, *University Drama in the Tudor Age* (Oxford, 1914).

5. By John Wolfe (STC 17158 and STC 19911), who three years later published Guarini's *Pastor fido* and Tasso's *Aminta*. Mere anti-Catholic spirit may
have created an English market for the only two well-known writers of comedy
banned by the Inquisition, but on the other hand, the plays of Machiavelli and
Aretino may have been printed in England because there was a general demand
for Italian drama, in the case of these two not to be satisfied by Italian printers.

6. K. M. Lea, *Italian Popular Comedy* (Oxford, 1934), 2:362–63, 352ff.

Sforza Oddi, *Prigione d'amore, commedia*
(Venice, 1591) [55v].
Courtesy of the Thomas Fisher Rare Book
Library, University of Toronto.

Oddi, *Prigione d'amore* [51v].

Gonzaga, *Gli inganni*, 45.
Courtesy of the Folger Shakespeare Library.

tone, cleaned up the meretrix, introduced topics of marriage, courtship, and providence, and developed the themes of madness and sorcery—indeed, Baldwin calls the latter the "chief structural thread."[7]

The Italianate quality of *The Comedy of Errors* has never been met head on. K. M. Lea does not commit herself beyond the suggestion that Shakespeare "seems to have been acquainted with the way the comedy of mistaken identity was exploited on the Italian stage"[8] and points to parallels between the devices for moving and complicating action in *The Comedy of Errors* and those in commedia dell'arte scenarios. Other scholars consider the style of *The Comedy of Errors* a derivation of Gascoigne's and Lyly's ventures into Italianate comedy, attributing the leftover differences to Shakespeare's desire to outcomplicate *Mother Bombie*.[9] Even M. C. Bradbrook, who distinguishes between the "English Plautine" *Mother Bombie* and the "Italian Plautine" *Comedy of Errors*,[10] does not come to grips with the Italian tradition or with the way in which *The Comedy of Errors* is linked to it.

From the time of its definition by Ariosto and his contemporaries, the regular Italian commedia, somewhat misleadingly dubbed *erudita*, was Roman in situation and structure. The Italian way of using the Latin material, however, was never that of simple imitation and expansion, but proceeded rather "by a reasoned synthesis based upon a close analysis of the structure of [Plautus] . . . analogous materials from other sources . . . [were] woven into this resulting plan to fill it out. The resultant structure . . . [was] in general consistent with itself." These words, which could accurately characterize the method instituted in Italy in the first decade of the sixteenth century, come from Baldwin's description of Shakespeare's procedure in constructing *The Comedy of Errors* from *Menaechmi*.[11] For the most part, "other sources" of the Italian playwrights were medieval and contemporary narratives, which exercised on Renaissance comedy an influence equal to that of Plautus and Terence.

Certain features became commonplaces almost at once: the cast of middle-class families and their servants, pedants, soldiers, innkeepers,

7. Baldwin, *Compositional Genetics,* 57.

8. Lea, *Italian Comedy,* 2 : 438.

9. William Shakespeare, *The Comedy of Errors,* Arden ed., ed. R. A. Foakes (London, 1962), Introduction, xxxiv; Baldwin, *Compositional Genetics,* 208, 356.

10. M. C. Bradbrook, *The Growth and Structure of Elizabethan Comedy* (London, 1955), 66.

11. Baldwin, *Compositional Genetics,* 201.

friars, and courtesans, joined in a series of encounters on the street, in doorways, and at windows; the combination of spatially and temporally restricted farcical intrigue with a potentially romantic antecedent history; the pattern of misunderstanding, disguise, and mistaken identity, kept moving and finally solved by peripeties and recognition. Although the playwrights customarily boasted in their prologues of debts to Plautus, Terence, and Boccaccio, the pieces they borrowed were reassembled to create a total different from the sum of its parts. In the process, they systematically outcomplicated the ancients and strained to do as much to one another.

After professional entertainers came into contact with this regular comedy, the commedia dell'arte appeared, whereupon literary dramatists in their turn began to borrow masks and mannerisms. The relationship was close but not altogether amicable, and by mid-century war had broken out—not, as is sometimes supposed, between amateurs and professionals, but between the regular five-act comedy written along the lines laid down by the generation of Ariosto, and one of the professionals' specialties, the loosely constructed, improvised farce described by Lodovico Dolce as *sciochezze ridicole,* consisting of "Buffoni sciocchi, et confusione vana di lingue, et di attioni poco honeste, nelle scene" (ridiculous inanities . . . silly buffoons, empty confusion of tongues and indecent actions in the scenes).[12]

In the second half of the century, with Counter-Reformation in the air, the terms of the quarrel were better defined. The shapeless, bawdy *zannata* ("clownpiece") was challenged by the comedy of reform issuing from such dramatists as Bernardino Pino, Luigi Pasqualigo, Girolamo Bargagli, Raffaello Borghini, Cristoforo Castelletti, Giovanfrancesco Loredano, Giambattista Della Porta, Sforza Oddi, and Giambattista Calderari, to name only those writing before 1589, the earliest likely date for *The Comedy of Errors.* Although historians have usually either ignored the type as such or labeled it, inadequately, "tearful" or "serious" comedy, the practitioners themselves called it *commedia grave,* choosing a term once applied to humanistic comedy in general and recharging it with particular reference to the new seriousness. Castelletti deplored flaccid audiences unable to appreciate *meraviglia, dolore,* and *compassione:* "stimano più una chiacchierata all'improviso . . . d'un vecchio Vinitiano, & d'un servitor Bergamasco, accompagnata da quattro attioni disoneste . . . che una Comedia Grave, che vi si serà stentato

12. Lodovico Dolce, *Fabritia* (n.p. [Venice], 1549), Dedication.

tre anni a comporla, e sei mesi a recitarla" (they esteem more highly some improvised chatter . . . between an old Venetian and a Bergomask servant, seasoned with four indecent gestures, than a Grave Comedy that took three years of hard work to compose and six months to rehearse and stage).[13] The gravity being advocated was aesthetic as well as moral and emotional, and the resulting standards of form and matter represented the farthest advances of the sixteenth century in the development of Italian regular comedy.

While writers of commedia grave held one of their purposes to be the defense of regular comedy against the zannate, they were equally determined to improve the regular comedy itself. They preserved the basic situations, characters, and structures of the earlier commediografi, and although there were repudiations like Pino's of "recognoscersi genti incognite, scambiamenti de panni, somiglianza de visi" (recognitions of unknown strangers, exchanging of clothes for disguises, identical facial resemblances),[14] these commonplaces lost none of their currency. Nevertheless, the changes were considerable. The didactic note of Terence, echoed intermittently and without conviction in earlier regular comedy, sounded insistently in late commedia grave, and Pino could advertise on the title page that his *Falsi sospetti* was "Per instruttione de' prudenti Padri di famiglia, d'ubidienti figliuoli, et di fedeli servitori."[15] Dirty jokes were still a necessity, but marriage and the church were treated with new respect. The figure of the corrupt friar disappeared, adultery was cut to a minimum, and even fornication was reduced.

A direct result of the didactic force was discourse on a moral topic growing out of the plot and presented as debate or soliloquy. Not only the time-honored discussions of parental and filial duties but also the questions raised in countless Cinquecento treatises became fashionable matter for set pieces in commedia grave. Along with the debate of love and honor (love usually wins) and that of love and friendship (friendship wins), the nature of feminine honor and the requirements of marriage were favorite subjects. The conclusions were both serious and funny. In *I falsi sospetti* the neglected Bellisaria tots up the score of her marriage and informs her confidante that as the wife of the studious Doctor of Law she has become learned but would much rather have become pregnant (I.1). On the oft-invoked principle of "giovare e dilet-

13. Cristoforo Castelletti, *I torti amorosi* (Venice, 1581), Prologue.
14. Bernardino Pino, *Gli ingiusti sdegni* (Rome, 1553), Prologue.
15. Bernardino Pino, *I falsi sospetti*, 1st ed. 1579.

tare" (to be useful and to delight) such scenes were handled with as much wit as their authors possessed, and technically owe more than a little to the practice of the professional actors who memorized passages from various *ragionamenti* and *dialoghi* and used them in improvisation.

As usual in the long history of intimate relationship between regular comedy and commedia dell'arte, the influence was reciprocal. The better professional companies included written plays of all genres in their repertories, and they found already built into commedie gravi the kind of moral, emotional, and intellectual arias that they were wont to introduce into scenarios. Isabella Andreini offers a view of the relationship in her dialogue on comedy, half critical discourse and half love scene, when she echoes the prologues of commedie gravi, emphasizing the dignity of writing comedy and citing as models Piccolomini, Calderari, and Pino.[16] It is noteworthy that the last two wrote very grave comedies, and Piccolomini may be called their precursor by virtue of his occasional romantic and moral themes.

The gravity of the commedia grave was also evident in the increased emotional tensions, the fuller characterization and articulateness of the lovers (another reflection of professional practice), and the sad or sinister direction of the action. The seriousness might consist in additions of flowery love scenes and tender family reconciliations to basic farce, as in Della Porta's *Olimpia,* or in main plots built on nearly tragic contests of love and friendship, with threats of suicide and execution, as in Oddi's three comedies. Whatever the proportions, there was always a mixture of sentiment, pathos, and danger with lively comic action. There was now explicit development of the romantic potential in clichés of exile, conspiracy, trade wars, shipwreck, and kidnaping, and other remembered causes of separation of families. The resemblance of commedia grave to tragedy was pointed out both internally and externally. Hearing of her husband's safe return from a shipwreck, Castelletti's Clarice says: "comincio a prender augurio che la mia lagrimosa tragedia habbia ad haver comico fine" (I begin to see signs that my tearful tragedy is to have a comedy ending).[17] In the opening scene of Oddi's *Prigione d'amore,* Odoardo hopes that the "raro esempio d'amorosa prigione" provided by Flaminio's going to prison to save his friend will

16. *Fragmenti di alcune scritture della Signora Isabella Andreini Comica Gelosa, et Academica Intenta* (Venice, 1620), 60.

17. Cristoforo Castelletti, *Le stravaganze d'amore,* 1st ed. 1584 (Venice, 1613), V. 7.

prove to be comedy rather than tragedy.[18] The first of two prologues to
this play defines it as commedia grave, and the second presents a debate
in which the personified figure of Comedia is accused of usurping Tragedia's function and answers, "Nell'amarezza delle lagrime ancora stà
nascosta la dolcezza del diletto" (In the bitterness of tears there ever lies
hidden the sweetness of delight). Tasso's praise of Pino's *Ingiusti sdegni*
takes this form:

> Pino, il vostro leggiadro e vago stile
>   ha fatta in guisa la commedia adorna,
>   che fra duci ed eroi talor soggiorna
> lunge dal riso de la plebe umile.
> Arde e fiammeggia in lei sdegno gentile,
>   e pur bella vergogna in lei s'adorna;
>   e casto amor s'accende, e 'n lei si scorna
> avaro cor talvolta e scherne il vile.
> E veggendosi tal, ch'ella somiglia
>   l'alta sorella, ha certo il socco a sdegno,
>   e 'l coturno da voi prender vorrebbe.
> E dice:—Io già non feci il Pino indegno,
>   ma gloria nei teatri ei già m'accrebbe
>   ed or move pietate or maraviglia.

Pino, your graceful and pleasing style has so adorned comedy that
she dwells betimes with rulers and heroes far from the laughter
of humble folk. In her burns and flames noble anger and lovely
modesty shines too; and chaste love is kindled in her and oft the
miserly heart is ridiculed and baseness is mocked. And seeing herself such that she resembles her loftier sister, surely she disdains
the sock and from you would take the buskin. And she says:—I
did no dishonor to Pino heretofore [comedy was a creditable genre
even before Pino added elements from tragedy] but he has increased my glory and stature in the theaters and moves audiences
both to pity and to wonder.[19]

A minor effect of the new principles was visible in the manner of presenting the traditional figure of the courtesan. Although she could trace
her origin back to the Roman meretrix, the courtesan of Italian regular
comedy had always more closely resembled the ladies of the night in the

---

18. Sforza Oddi, *Prigione d'amore* (Florence, 1589), I.1.
19. *Le rime di Torquato Tasso,* ed. Angelo Solerti (Bologna, 1902), 4:190.

Decameron. It might be expected that the overhauled standards of sexual morality would cause the figure of the courtesan either to appear less frequently or to be treated with greater harshness. Some commedie gravi satisfy these expectations, but in others the courtesan becomes a strikingly more sympathetic figure than she was before. Often, surpassing even Terence's sweetest-natured meretrix, she is shown as an unmercenary, loving girl with an inclination toward fidelity. Sometimes she is nobler of mind than the innamorate. Benedetto Croce admired Oddi's Ardelia for her eloquent loyalty and high concept of love.[20] The most extreme example is Aurelia of *Gli ingiusti sdegni,* who offers to put her lover through school, provide him with room, board, clothing, pocket money, and the company of the most learned men in Rome, to live only with him but in continence, if he prefers, and at the end of a year to retire to a convent and leave him all her wealth. The lover and his avaricious father accept this offer gladly, for different reasons (V.3). For all the dubious morality here, this change in the courtesan is in keeping with the other developments toward general ennoblement and complication, of character as of plot. The commedia grave is romantic in comparison with earlier comedy and with farce, and so is the myth of the good-hearted whore.

But late commedia grave was not defined by content alone; in fact, it was on gravity of structure that the greatest artistry was expended. By mid-Cinquecento the pattern of protasis, epitasis, and catastrophe formed of multiple dramatic and narrative lines had been thoroughly worked over, and writers of commedia grave, inheriting structural aim as well as pattern, found that outcomplicating their predecessors called for intricate complications indeed. They strove to tie still more knots and to untie them with a still greater display of ease. As Ruscelli advised, they avoided imitating the simple plot of the otherwise admired *Mandragola* and made comedies progress from the first act well into the fifth, "sempre crescendo in disturbi, in difficoltà, in intrighi."[21] Crying up the superiority of modern comedy, specifically his own, Della Porta notes that the peripety occurs as if naturally in the course of the fourth act, and that a close observer may also see peripety born of peripety and recognition of recognition.[22]

20. Benedetto Croce, "Le commedie patetiche di Sforza Oddi," *Poeti e scrittori del pieno e del tardo rinascimento,* vol. 2 (Bari, 1958).

21. Girolamo Ruscelli, *Delle comedie elette novamente raccolte insieme, con le correttioni, et annotationi* (Venice, 1554), "Annotationi," 182.

22. Giambattista Della Porta, *Gli duoi fratelli rivali* written ca. 1590 (Venice, 1601), Prologue.

One way to increase complications was to double characters and misunderstandings, but as Bibbiena and his immediate successors had been no mean hands at the doubling trick, writers of commedia grave had to resort to double doubling. It is common to see several sets of lovers, parents, servants, and comic hangers-on, with as many encounters at cross-purposes as the size of the group makes possible and as may be straightened out with a few well-planned adjustments and revelations. The celebrated *Intrichi d'amore*,[23] a good example of the type's complexity if not of its quality, includes five couples and an extra man, all loving in the wrong place, half of them in disguises, all standing in unsuspected blood or legal relation to one another; this tangled mess is *meravigliosamente* ordered at the end so that each case is settled satisfactorily, and occasions conceited moralizing in the *congedo*.

More original than the doubling and recomplicating, which simply extended earlier methods of perfecting the form of regular comedy, was the increased use in commedie gravi of governing themes and motifs. Oddi, especially in *L'erofilomachia* and *Prigione d'amore*, uses the conflict of love and friendship as a controlling force working not only on the lovers but on the entire cast of characters, binding them in a web of consistent fiber, as Della Porta does to varying degrees with sibling rivalry in *Gli duoi fratelli rivali*, with love, friendship, and honor in *Il moro*, and with jealousy in *La fantesca*. Everyone in Pino's *Ingiusti sdegni* is unjustly angry with at least one other person at some time in the course of the play. Lovers quarrel over misunderstandings, parents are angry with children for imaginary faults, children blame parents with as little justification, masters erroneously accuse servants, honorable men are suspected of dishonorable dealing, the pedant hates the courtesan as a bad influence on his pupil (when in fact it turns out that her influence is better than anyone else's), and the same pupil's father is violently anti-intellectual, which last injustice calls forth the learned playwright's sharpest style of caricature. Thus the complex pattern of intrigue traditionally built on mistakes gains greater unity by corresponding to an abstract theme, on which variations occur, not consecu-

23. *Intrichi d'amore, comedia del Sig. Torquato Tasso. Rappresentata in Caprarola* (Venice, 1604), sometimes considered the joint work of members of the Accademia di Caprarola. Tasso's authorship has been defended by Enrico Malato, "Una commedia poco nota di Torquato Tasso," *Nuova Antologia* 482 (1961): 487–516. Malato has since edited and republished the comedy as Tasso's (Rome, 1976).

tively but intertwined, so that the audience may see several variations in action at once. The playwrights' expectation of applause presupposed the kind of courtly and academic audience that supported the regular drama in Italy, made up of the "attenti et avvertiti ascoltatori" (attentive and informed listeners) described by Pino in his *Breve consideratione.* These were spectators who demanded that comedy have "tutte le sue parti soavemente insieme corrispondenti" (all its parts smoothly fitted together), and for whom even the *intermedii* or *moresche* (Morris dances) must therefore be "di materia non molto lontana, ma in guisa del choro molto bene corrispondente et convenevole con l'argomento della favola" (of materials not very distant, but like a chorus closely corresponding and appropriate to the plot).[24] Their taste for a meaning manifested in pattern of action more than in development of individual characterization would be little regarded by later centuries, when comedy of situation seemed merely a mechanical prelude to a superior comedy of character. Our own century, receptive to signifying structure and mistrustful of simple distinctions between form and content, is better prepared to appreciate the grave formal aim of late Italian intrigue comedy.

The motif of supposed magic, specifically sorcery, alchemy, and astrology, which appeared early in Ariosto's *Il negromante* and earlier still in neo-Latin comedy, is tied in late commedia grave more closely than before to language, as well as to whatever happens to be the theme for the variations. Sometimes magic itself is the theme, as in Della Porta's *L'astrologo;* more often it is one of the variations.[25] Belief in sorcery and the powers of divination and transformation associated with it, which had long provided a target for the satire of regular comedy, became in the Counter-Reformation a matter for serious, concentrated attack.[26]

24. Bernardino Pino, *Breve consideratione intorno al componimento de la comedia de' nostri tempi,* 1572, first printed with Oddi's *Erofilomachia* (Venice, 1578), B3. Some integration of intermedio madrigals and plot could be seen in earlier comedies, for example in Giannotti's *Vecchio amoroso,* written between 1533 and 1536.

25. Only false magic is intended. Real magic, black or white, was reserved in written drama for sacre rappresentazioni, for irregular plays like those of the Congrega dei Rozzi, or for pastoral plays.

26. In the definitive Roman Index of 1559, for example, Pope Paul IV added magic arts to the list of practices condemned in local indices of 1554 (Venice, Milan), and the decree of Pope Sixtus V in January 1586 condemned judiciary astrology and other forms of divination. See Lynn Thorndike, *A History of Magic and Experimental Science* (New York, 1941), 6:147, 156.

The church's campaign against such arts as judiciary astrology underlies the comic playwright's newly biting and deliberate ridicule of charlatan sorcerers, alchemists, astrologers, and their gulls, but it is the dramatists' campaign to crush amorphous zannate and improve regular comedy that underlies the use of sorcery as a unifying structural motif.

The theme of sorcery was frequently used in conjunction with the theme of madness or as a variation on it; this was a favorite with writers of commedia grave. Real madness, supposed madness, assumed madness, fear of madness, and obsessions bordering on madness were familiar both as phenomena and as structural key signatures. The most obvious cause of alienation, in comedy as in epic and lyric poetry, was of course love. Alone, it supported several kinds of insanity, but often other causes were joined to it to create a set of mixed variations on the theme, as in Castelletti's *Stravaganze d'amore.* Here the madness, softened to *stravaganza,* or bizarre eccentricity, consists of several obsessions, and despite the title not all have to do with love. The prologue is a catalogue of stravaganze—of the courtier, the merchant, the alchemist, the miser, the lover. The characters regularly analyze the stravaganze around them, beginning with their own. Orinthia, who for love of Ostilio is disguised as her rival's maid, muses: "Che donne habbiano per amor preso habito d'huomini si è udito infinite volte, & le Comedie ne sono piene. Ma non si è mai inteso, nè letto, che donna nobile, & ricca, habbia tolto forma di vil fante, se non Orinthia . . . [è da] porgere a Comedie, novo, et Stravagante soggetto" (I.2: That women have put on men's clothes for love has been heard and seen repeatedly in comedies. But it has never been heard of or read that a noble and rich lady has put on the aspect of a lowly maidservant, except Orinthia . . . this is something to provide comedies with a new and bizarre subject).[27]

In such scenes Castelletti simultaneously links the particular situation to the general theme and mocks the clichés of the genre. Another cliché is ridiculed in the person of Rinuccio, the Platonic lover, whose recommendation of devotion to the lady's mind exclusively is mocked for its stravaganza by Ostilio, a suitor with broader aims (II.1). A third lover, Alessandro, is so *stravagante* in his passion that he has let his family think him dead and roams disguised as "Dottore Gratian atteggiando, e chiacchierando per questa piazza, come fanno i Gratiani nelle zannate con grandissimo dishonor" (I.1: Doctor Gratian attitudinizing and chattering in the square, as do the Gratiani with the greatest disrepute,

27. Castelletti, *Le stravaganze d'amore,* I.2.

in their clownish farces), as his servant puts it. Again Castelletti has a double aim, sketching another variation on the theme while attacking the zannate, as a writer of commedia grave should do. His use of the commedia dell'arte mask of Doctor Graziano, however, shows the interpenetration of the improvised and literary forms at the very moment when they seemed farthest apart. Alessandro's father suffers from a stravaganza on the subject of magic, imagines that malevolent spirits lie in ambush everywhere, and wastes his fortune in hopes of transmuting base metal into gold. The theme is illustrated also by the master plan that brings them together in encounters providing opportunities for other stravaganze. The structure is further tightened by reiteration of the word *stravaganza* and related imagery, and by the intermedio madrigals, each containing the title of the comedy analyzed from a different point of view.

An especially complex and intimate relationship obtained between the theme of Divine Providence and both structure and content of the commedia grave. Earlier regular comedy, like much of the Renaissance literature influencing it, had sometimes included the idea of Fortuna, operating independently of celestial control. But in the second half of the sixteenth century the Counter-Reformers found it necessary to remind Christians of the supremacy of God's providence. In tragedy it became common practice to attach a disclaimer explaining that the use by pagan characters of such words as *fortuna, fato,* and *sorte* does not represent the views of the author, a good Christian who knows that the only real Fortuna is the providence of the Prime Mover.[28]

In comedy there appeared frequent references to Divine Providence, sometimes explicit denials of fortune or stellar influence. More important, the ideas of fortune and providence were used structurally to create meaning, producing a variation on the medieval concept of comedy as metaphor of human life. Borghini's *La donna costante* provides an example of extensive development of the theme.[29] The innumerable peripeties, accidents, and chance encounters in this intrigue plot, based in part on the tale of Juliet and Romeo, are constantly attributed to fortune, the mutability of which is commented on and discussed at every opportunity. The characters invoke Fortuna, bless Fortuna, curse Fortuna, enumerate classical examples of Fortuna's fickleness in the good old medieval way. The intermedi include panoramas of the triumph and

28. See chapter 9.
29. Raffaello Borghini, *La donna costante* (Florence, 1578).

decline of the Roman Empire with comments on fortune's constantly changing style. Yet against the idea of fickle fortune is set the title of the play and the characterization of its heroine, Elfenice, whose constancy is firm in all vicissitudes. When at last the difficulties are resolved, she puts the quietus on Fortuna by thanking the "Motore di Cielo" (V.14), and the concluding intermedio neoplatonically praises love, the source of Elfenice's constancy, and defines it as a gift of the "Sommo Motore" (6th *intermedio*). Fortune only seems powerful; Providence reigns supreme, rewards constancy, and plans happy endings.

In few other commedie gravi is the pattern of intrigue governed so relentlessly by the theme of providence. But in play after play, like Castelletti's *Furbo* and Gonzaga's *Inganni*,[30] it is expressly stated that the seeming chaos and confusion of the intrigue are in fact part of a plan above change, a divine pattern, implicitly or explicitly Christian, guiding characters through innumerable *intrichi, inganni, labirinti,* and *errori* to perfect order. The very pattern of seemingly unresolvable complexities worked out to an unexpectedly simple and satisfying conclusion, the structural ideal of the writers of commedia grave, was held to be a reflection of the working of Divine Providence. And just as the theological virtue of hope depends on faith in God's providence, so the meaning of the design was tied back into the tissue of moral lesson. As Oddi says in the second prologue to *Prigione d'amore,* commedia grave teaches people, especially lovers, not to despair, by showing that in times of darkest confusion the pattern of their happiness is taking shape.

It will be noticed that except for certain commonplaces of situation, the plots of the plays used as examples of commedia grave do not resemble that of *The Comedy of Errors.* The time of searching for Shakespeare's immediate sources is past. Many Italian regular comedies are based on *Menaechmi,* but there is no reason to suppose that Shakespeare used any of them or to doubt that his sources were Plautus, Gower, and St. Paul. His choice of elements and his way of blending them, however, give pause. The addition of pathos and a hint of tragedy; the moral de-emphasizing of the courtesan's role to play up the wife Adriana and her sister; the dialogue of these two on the topos of jealousy in marriage; the weaving of multiple sources into a newly complicated pattern of errors with something like a unifying theme in the thread of feared madness and sorcery; Aegeon's evaluation of "the

30. Cristoforo Castelletti, *Il furbo* (Venice, 1584); Curzio Gonzaga, *Gli inganni* (Venice, 1592).

gods" at the beginning, proved false at the end, when the maddening errors and nearly fatal sentence become instruments to reunite families and confirm loves—the combination of these elements, characteristic of late Cinquecento commedia grave, could not have been suggested by Lyly or Gascoigne, for both *Mother Bombie* and *Supposes* belong to the earlier type of regular comedy.

Although Geoffrey Bullough recognizes that Shakespeare's addition of pathos and tragic import to his source was anticipated by "some of the Italians," he still accepts E. K. Chambers's statement that Shakespeare was "consciously experimenting with an archaistic form," and he adds, "The remarkable thing is the complexity he wove within the simple outline provided by Plautus' *Menaechmi*." [31] But examining *The Comedy of Errors* against the background of the Italian tradition, as Baldwin suggests, reveals that the form is anything but archaistic. The complexity answers the demands of Italian regular comedy in general, and the character of its unity reflects the late commedia grave in particular. As for the pathos and tragic import, they are not fortuitously anticipated by "some" Italians, but were deliberately developed by a sizable group of theorizing playwrights representing the avant-garde of the day.

It cannot be proved that Shakespeare read Italian plays, or saw commedia dell'arte troupes or Italian amateurs perform commedie gravi at Elizabeth's court, or heard about them from a friend. Nor can *The Comedy of Errors* simply be labeled *commedia grave*, for Shakespeare's Italianate play is still an English one. It is next to certain, however, that the brilliant young upstart crow knew something about the latest Continental fashion in comedy.

31. Geoffrey Bullough, *Narrative and Dramatic Sources of Shakespeare*, vol. 1 (London, 1957): 10, 3, 5.

Castelletti, *I torti amorosi*, 17.
Courtesy of the Folger Shakespeare Library.

Gonzaga, *Gli inganni* [17v].
Courtesy of the Folger Shakespeare Library.

Gonzaga, *Gli inganni* [77v].
Courtesy of the Folger Shakespeare Library.

CHAPTER THREE

Woman as Wonder: Theatergram of Italian and Shakespearean Comedy

he method inherited from the old positivists of studying the Continental background of Elizabethan and Jacobean drama by tracing units of specific content to ultimate sources has constructed a Shakespeare conversant with learning of many kinds and ages. Recent refinements in the study of genre promise at last to relate him also to leading movements in the theater of his own time. Evidence that Shakespeare knew something of Italian drama, literary and improvised, has long lain about casually acknowledged in the positivistic manner as paired analogies (*Twelfth Night* with *Gl'ingannati, The Tempest* with Arcadian scenarios, and so on); it has not been organized into needed conclusions about kind, principles, commonplaces, movable units, and recurrent patterns, despite many such exhortations as R. C. Melzi's to seek Shakespeare's frame of reference for *Twelfth Night* not only in *Ingannati* but in "the *Ingannati* family."[1] To search so is to find that Shakespeare often seems to be playing the game developed in Italian drama, with the customary pieces and principles but not by the usual rules, and always with original outcomes. A small portion of a rapport, probably irrecoverable in toto even by detailed reconstructions of the historical context in which fashions crossed the Channel, may be glimpsed by scrutinizing some generic features of *All's Well That Ends Well* and *Measure for Measure*, the comedies that G. K. Hunter calls "obvious twins" by virtue of the centrality to both of young women with divine missions and of the emphasis on

This chapter appeared in slightly different form as "Woman as Wonder: A Generic Figure in Italian and Shakespearean Comedy," in Dale B. J. Randall and George Walton Williams, *Studies in the Continental Background of Renaissance English Literature: Essays Presented to John L. Lievsay* (Durham, 1977). Copyright © 1977 by Duke University Press.

1. Robert C. Melzi, "From Lelia to Viola," *Renaissance Drama* 9 (1966): 69.

forgiveness that allies them with the symbolic romances of Shakespeare's last period.[2]

The perception that the vital principles of *All's Well* and *Measure for Measure* are to be found in ideas about the genre of tragicomedy, and the direct linking of the plays with Guarini, respectively by Arthur Kirsch and J. W. Lever,[3] properly direct attention to Italian drama, for which tragicomedy was an incendiary critical issue. But they seal off Shakespeare from pertinent forces in a movement of which Guarini was only a part. Kirsch finds in *Il pastor fido* the germ of the providential plotting in *All's Well* and the idea of tragicomedy behind it, as Lever finds the formal cause of *Measure for Measure* in *Il compendio della poesia tragicomica*. But whereas Guarini's practice and theory would bestow authority on the tragicommedia pastorale for the future, behind both lay decades of Italian tinkering with theatrical means of representing such ideas as providence and of mixing tragedy with comedy. The hybrids produced earlier were various, including Giraldi Cinzio's *tragedia di fin lieto*.[4] The most significant for comparison with Shakespearean comedy in general—and an important contributor to the development of the pastoral tragicomedy as finally established by Guarini—was the commedia grave of the stamp fostered by Bernardino Pino and praised by Tasso. Exponents of this serious comedy claimed "gravità" of form in the disposition, complexity, and thematic unity of their intrecci, and gravità of content in the morality, tragic emotion, fear, and *maraviglia* that they mixed with comic conventions. It was by retaining the lineaments and language of comedy, especially low comic types and bawdry and the prohibition of bloodshed, that commedia grave differed from the tragicomic mixture in *tragedia di fin lieto;* and it was by the jux-

---

2. William Shakespeare, *All's Well That Ends Well*, Arden ed., ed. G. K. Hunter, (London, 1959), Introduction, xxiii–xxiv, liv–lv. My quotations are from this edition.

3. Arthur Kirsch, *Jacobean Dramatic Perspectives* (Charlottesville, 1972), 7–15, 52–64; William Shakespeare, *Measure for Measure*, Arden ed., ed. J. W. Lever (London, 1965; repr. 1966), Introduction, lix–lxiii. My quotations are from Lever's edition.

4. The "tragedy with a happy ending" uses the complex plot of love intrigue characteristic of comic structure and illustrates justice by meting out rewards and punishments in the last act. See Giovanni Battista Giraldi Cinzio, *Discorsi . . . intorno al comporre de i romanzi, delle comedie, e delle tragedie, e di altre maniere di poesie*, 1554, repr. in Giraldi Cinzio, *Scritti critici*, ed. Camillo Guerrieri Crocetti (Milan, 1973).

taposition of extremes, high and low, serious and hilarious, and by its urban setting that it differed from Guarini's kind of tragicomedy, a studiedly mild third genre created by the fusion and tempering of the extremes of the two others. The concern for theme or controlling idea, which appeared in commedia grave before it reached a fuller development in pastoral tragicomedy, signals the expansion of Donatus's *imitatio vitae* and *imago veritatis,* an expansion long aimed at by Italian comic playwrights so as to include more of the inner reality of emotion and the outer cosmic reality of forces beyond human sight or comprehension, encircling human life in benign surveillance. The enlarged range of comic vision also accommodated timely instruction in a new sensibility and in the spirit of civil and religious obedience to authority deemed necessary to revitalize the Roman Church.[5]

Among the Counter-Reformation *commedie gravi* are a considerable number in which the tendency toward abstraction is definitive and the major theme is invested in a feminine figure developed from the generic commonplace of the *giovane innamorata.* Although I think that Shakespeare used fashionable developments in both commedia grave and pastoral plays from the beginning of his career, the particular type of commedia grave in which the figure of the woman functions as a vehicle for idea has a unique kinship with the "twin" comedies of his middle period.

The figure is to be distinguished from the merely enterprising innamorata whose energy and charm arouse a wonder belonging to "ordinary" life rather than to any transcendent truth: Julia of *Love's Labour's Lost,* Rosalind of *As You Like It,* and Viola of *Twelfth Night* are Shakespearean variations on this theatergram. The more spiritually specialized version of the innamorata, to whom Helena of *All's Well* and Isabella of *Measure for Measure* bear a family resemblance, directs the

5. The move toward abstraction in Italian theater of this period is examined, with specific reference to the drama as a vehicle of Counter-Reformation social propaganda, in Giulio Ferroni's valuable essays on Annibal Caro and Raffaello Borghini in his *"Mutazione" e "Riscontro" nel teatro di Machiavelli e altri saggi sulla commedia del Cinquecento* (Rome, 1972), and in Guido Baldi, "Le commedie di Sforza Oddi e l'ideologia della Controriforma," *Lettere Italiane* 23 (January–March 1971): 43–62. The depressing images of persuasion to conformity and passivity that emerge would seem to be the price paid on the side of content for the gains in dramatic form achieved when the concomitant trend toward religious propaganda began developing means to free comedy from a narrowly realistic interpretation of the principle of *imitatio vitae* and *imago veritatis.*

spectator's attention to a wonder beyond the plot or fable. The figure is distinguished by a remarkable intrinsic worth, established by her effect on other characters and by structurally disposed contrasts with them as foils. She functions as an example of virtue for imitation and admiration, and is associated now more, now less, with an extra-fabular reality that is invoked not by an obvious allegory but as an image of a truth physically unseen yet naturally related to the prima facie story. At her full development the figure is known by a hush that falls about her, a sense of her being a thing enskied and sainted.

Antecedent to this theatergram of person is the dramatized topos of love in action, but the distance from love's wonder to woman's, from rueful amazement to respectful admiration, may be measured by the difference between the relation of love's power to woman's in Bibbiena's *Calandria,* cornerstone of Italian literary comedy in general, and that in Piccolomini's *Amor costante,*[6] which points forward to late commedia grave in particular. In *La Calandria* the transvestite Santilla is a mechanical figure. Whatever wonder at feminine behavior the comedy proffers is reserved for Fulvia the malmaritata, also briefly transvestite and driven thereto by her passionate pursuit of Santilla's twin brother. Love's galvanic effect on her is repeatedly observed as a marvel, but in the same state of moral suspension as that obtaining in the *Decameron* stories, of which *La Calandria* is a parade of quotations. Fulvia's wonder at her own bravery—"Nulla è, certo, che Amore altri a fare non costringa. Io, che già sanza compagnia a gran pena di camera uscita non sarei, or, da amor spinta, vestita da uomo fuor di casa me ne vo sola" (III.7: There is nothing, certainly, that Love may not force one to. I, who would hardly leave my room without company, now, moved by love, leave my house alone, dressed as a man")[7]—confirmed by the servants Samia (III.6) and Fessenio (III.11), remains comment on a mood, neither statement of theme nor didactic injunction. The event that occasions the musings is not edifying: an adultery to be concealed at the end, celebrating at most a triumph of wit over stupidity in the execution of a fervid but somewhat one-sided and joyless affair that promises only to become more so in the future.

6. Alessandro Piccolomini, *L'amor costante, comedia . . . composta per la venuta dell'Imperatore in Sienna l'anno del XXXVI* (Venice, 1540), written in 1531 and perhaps performed in 1536; see Florindo Cerreta, *Alessandro Piccolomini, letterato filosofo senese del Cinquecento* (Siena, 1960), 14.

7. Bernardo Dovizi, Cardinal Bibbiena, *La Calandria,* in Nino Borsellino, ed., *Commedie del Cinquecento,* vol. 2 (Milan, 1967): 63.

Lucrezia of *L'amor costante,* on the other hand, appears onstage only once (V.4) but embodies a theme that has taken on moral connotations. Love is given structural status by the prologue:

Vi ammaestraremo, con la nostra comedia, quanto un amor costante (donde piglia il nome la comedia) abbia sempre buon fine and quanto manifesto error sia abbandonarsi nelle aversità amorose: perché quel pietosissimo dio che si chiama Amore non abbandona mai chi che con fermezza lo serve.

We shall teach you with our comedy how a constant love [whence the comedy takes its name] always wins through and how manifestly mistaken it is to give up at setbacks in love: for that most compassionate god called Love never deserts anyone who serves him with perseverance.[8]

And, as illustrated by Ferrante and Lucrezia, separated by pirates after their secret marriage and elopement, each left in doubt for seven years of the other's survival, the emphasis has shifted from love's power over nature to the virtue displayed by noble natures in love. Lucrezia's virtue in general is underscored in references to her "santimonia e bontà maravigliosa" (II.3: holiness and wonderful goodness), but it is ancillary to the particular virtue of constancy spelled out again in Corsetto's reaction to the lovers' trials and reconciliation: "Oh felicissima coppia d'amanti! oh amor costante! oh bellissimo caso da farci sopra una comedia eccellentissima!" (II.3: Oh most happy pair of lovers! oh constant love! oh most beautiful coincidence worthy to be the subject of a most excellent comedy!)

Other characters contribute variously to the theme: some voice their low opinion of woman's constancy (II.5), and the serva Agnoletta exhibits her unsentimental sexual greed in direct contrast to the idealizing devotion of Margarita to Giannino, who in turn is indifferent to Margarita but thinks himself a unique exemplar of constant love for Lucrezia (I.9). When Lucrezia is proved to be his sister, Giannino easily turns to Margarita, whom Agnoletta thereupon apostrophizes as the true exemplar: "Ora il tuo amor costante sarà esempio a tutto il mondo. Imparate, donne, da costei a esser costanti nei pensier vostri" (V.9: Now

8. Quotations from *L'amor costante* in this paragraph and the following one are from Borsellino, ed., *Commedie del Cinquecento,* vol. 1 (Milan, 1962): 307, 348, 349, 423, 412, 414.

your constant love will be an example to all the world. Learn, ladies, from her to be constant in your thoughts). Ferrante also vies with Lucrezia in a display of constancy, but she crowns the thematic spectacle. Fra Cherubino likens them both to Christian martyrs, describing how they contend for the first draught of the supposed poison they are forced to take: "Non credo che martire mai si conducesse a la morte con tanta costanzıa e fervore con quanto hanno fatto l'uno e l'altro di costoro" (V.3: I don't believe that any martyr ever went to death with so much constancy and fervor as those two). But it is Lucrezia who snatches the poison and tries to drink it all. Her refusal under pressure to marry, her devotion to a secret husband never enjoyed and presumed dead, make her seem nunlike, a saint (III.7), until she is discovered in bed with Ferrante. Her accuser, Guglielmo, rejects her explanation but declares that if it were true, then there never was any woman more chaste or any love more constant: "Se gli è così, non fu mai donna più casta di te né amor più costante." (V.4) The truth established, Lucrezia emerges hallowed by the encomium, a vowed saint in the religion of love. The love in question has no philosophical or theological overtones, but accords with general Cinquecento notions of domestic virtue, and is conceived as an ideal verity, of which Piccolomini's comedy undertakes to give a theatrical image.

In the later sixteenth century the pedagogical use of art encouraged by Counter-Reformation policy was bound to exploit the capacity inherent in the uniquely social art of drama to express the discrepancy between appearance and reality. In keeping with the universalist and neomedieval trend in official Catholic thought, Italian drama therefore began to shimmer with reflections of this discrepancy glimpsed as a contrast between human limitation and divine omniscience. As the preceding essays in this book suggest, contemporary critical polemics over genres and over the interpretation of Aristotle's *Poetics* also contributed to dramatization of the contrast. Aristotle's comments on the form of *Oedipus rex* spurred experimenters in generic hybridization to adapt the principle of Sophocles' tragedy to comedy. The results make ironic peripeties teach quietistic trust in a divine plan, for to apply the structure of *Oedipus* to comedy in a Christian era was to make comedy of providence from tragedy of fate. The idea of fortune traditional to comedy was presented in the early Cinquecento as an unforeseeable and all-powerful adversary or ally, with only an occasional passing reference to providence. This idea was subjected in post-Tridentine comedy to an orthodox, though hardly searching, scrutiny and demoted to the only place it could properly claim in a Christian world, the place firmly assigned it by Dante (*Inferno*, VII.73) as subordinate to "Colui lo cui saver tutto trascende" (Him whose knowledge transcends all). Overestimating fortune's power was seen by practical theologians to be dangerous not only to a right conception of providence but also to a proper belief in free will.[9] Dramatists did not turn into theologians bent on combating heresies of predestination or the inefficacy of good works, but, without returning to the literal miracles and allegories of medieval drama, many responded to the widening of the theatrical spectrum to include abstract significance by expanding their dramaturgy to develop appropriate means of expression. Consciousness of the doctrinal implications of a comedy cliché like that of fortune led to the association with the wonders of providence of other conventional elements of the genre, notably the figure of the innamorata, and to the cooperation with providence of active virtue.

Earlier I cited Raffaello Borghini's *Donna costante* as a theatrical metaphor of providential action.[10] Here I would reelucidate his alliance of the theme of love with the transcendent idea of providence in the person of the title character, and his invocation of wonder through the chief figure of the design visible in the intreccio: the constant woman central to the plot and embodying the divine permanence on which rests the providence that denies the supremacy of fortune. The abstracting tendency that Ferroni rightly sees in this comedy is in fact the hallmark of Counter-Reformation theater,[11] which although it did not in Italy culminate in a Calderón, nevertheless produced the experimental models for putting ideas onstage as a symbolic process, distinct from the more direct allegories of medieval drama. The justice of Ferroni's view of Borghini, as a jobber of merely serviceable abstraction confirming a

9. See chapter 9.

10. Raffaello Borghini, *La donna costante, commedia* (Florence, 1578). See chapter 2.

11. Giulio Ferroni, *"Mutazione" e "Riscontro,"* 260: "Non si tratta di un'astratezza congelata e contraddittoria, segno di un rifugio nell'introversione, e nell''idea' come salvezza dall'attacco di una realtá ostile e nemica. Il Borghini non è un artista dell'introversione (la sua scarsa intelligenza critica glielo avrebbe in ogni caso vietato), è invece un artigiano di un'astrazione tendente all'esterno, alla formulazione di norme sociali, alla organizzazione repressiva della realtà entro un circolo di dati vagliati e riconosciuti socialmente, nell'aspirazione alla conferma di un finale 'ordine' immobile e senza alternative" (It is not a fixed and contradicting kind of abstracting, the sign of a retreat inward

fixed order and repressive social norms, need not impede extending the aim of the abstracting tendency and the sphere of the fixed order to include theological doctrines from which the would-be monolithic society took its sanctions. When Borghini added the operations of divine providence to his objects of imitation, he did not do so alone. He was rather an exponent of an engaged dramaturgy that is historically relevant to Shakespeare as well. Shakespeare's abstractions have been called allegorical and liturgical in consonance with the prevailing tenets of the state religion under Elizabeth and James,[12] but he possessed along with the inwardness lacking in Borghini a genius, sometimes troubling to critics, for representing an experience simultaneously as an unforgettable individual datum and as a universal truth, verifiable by the workings of the spectator's own consciousness and even partially capable of abstraction from the context and of summation as a *sententia*.

The figure of wonder in *La donna costante,* a mosaic of dramatic commonplaces and novella situations (among which that of Romeo and Juliet is eminent), turgid with pathos and heroism, is the transvestite Elfenice, whose name seals her extreme proof of constancy in avoiding a second marriage by allowing herself to be buried for dead, a phoenix in the uniqueness of her virtue and in her resurrection. Her love for Aristide, banished slayer of her cousin, is paralleled by the love between her brother and Aristide's sister, who engage in a secondary display of self-sacrificing constancy. As in *L'amor costante,* auxiliary characters are used to enhance the wonder of the heroine's persevering fidelity with negative comments confuted by the facts (I.1) or with positive ones supported by them (I.3).

The topos of fortune is put through standard comic permutations with an unwonted insistence, to illustrate "come fortuna va cangiando stile"

---

and of taking refuge in "idea" as a defense against a hostile and inimical reality. Borghini is not an artist of introversion (his limited critical intelligence obviated that possibility); he is, rather, the artisan of an abstraction tending outward, toward the formulation of social norms, toward the repressive organization of reality within a body of socially examined and recognized data, all aiming at confirming a final immutable "order" to which there is no alternative).

12. Some of the best-known statements of such views are found in G. Wilson Knight, *The Wheel of Fire* (London, 1930) and *The Sovereign Flower* (London, 1958); Roy W. Battenhouse, "*Measure for Measure* and the Christian Doctrine of the Atonement," *PMLA* 61 (1946): 1029–59; Nevill Coghill, "Comic Form in *Measure for Measure,*" *Shakespeare Survey* 8 (1955): 14–27.

(*Intermedio* 5: how fortune constantly changes its aspect): from the glutton's parodic garble on the reverses of fortune (I.1), through a servo's conclusion that fortune is powerful despite the (Counter-Reformation?) sages (II.1), a serva's comic lament on fortune (III.10), the hero's recital of classical examples of fortune's shifts (IV.4), his friend's brooding on the subject (IV.4; IV.6), and the heroine's discourse (III.1) and solo aria "O Fortuna crudele" (IV.8), to the fourth and fifth intermedi representing the triumph and the downfall of Rome. By such elaboration fortune is set up to be duly knocked down, and it is Elfenice who emerges as the embodiment of the subduing power. Throughout the apparent reign of fickle fortune, Elfenice's eleven-year-long constancy is unswerving; like the miraculous bird for which she is named, she seems to surmount even death. The fifth-act reversal shows all the musings on fortune to have been mistaken: the capricious play of chance is not allowed responsibility for the happy peripety. Nor is fortune's defeat just another novelistic triumph of love. Elfenice thanks the "Motore di Cielo" (V.14) in the formulaic phrase by which sovereignty of providence over chance and fate was recognized in scholastically worded prefaces to tragedy. After this endorsement of providence by a title character whose constancy works miracles, there follows a final intermedio in which a neoplatonic identification of love with the action of the "Sommo Motor" is made: love is announced as the first cause of all good sent by the Prime Mover, and pagan gods descend from heaven in a spectacle of love's universal triumph. This decorative neoplatonizing would find more scope in the pastoral drama; here, in serious comedy, it shows the degree to which love as a wonder illustrated in the action of a singular woman could be associated with idea and, as the generic figure becomes more abstract, with Christian doctrine. Love is promoted to the rank of grace and providence, and the commonplace of feigned death and burial is used as more than an example of cleverness: it is a wonder of steadfastness signifying the right human action that cooperates through love in the stability of the Unmoved Mover, who is the source of love and of the providence that controls the mutability of fortune.

The woman who carries more than her own spiritual weight appears with a difference in Della Porta's *Gli duoi fratelli rivali*.[13] Carizia, the heroine, is not called on to perform miracles of constancy but to be the

---

13. Giambattista Della Porta, *Gli duoi fratelli rivali* (Venice, 1601). Quotations are from my edition and translation, *Gli duoi fratelli rivali/The Two Rival Brothers* (Berkeley, Los Angeles, and London, 1980).

occasion and victim of the principal psychological action, the conflict of two brothers who love her, one maligning and the other repudiating her, causing her apparent death. The character of incarnate marvel is first established for her by conventional hyperbolic compliment and by the familiar device of using a paler image as a foil; in Don Ignazio's description of Carizia and her sister as angels, the former is presented as incomparably superior, nature's very model of beauty in all its works (I.1).[14] At next sight Don Ignazio hails Carizia with a Petrarchan commonplace identifying her with the source of light and life, as they engage in the theatergram of action constituted by the window (or balcony) scene (II.2; II.3).[15] Carizia's responses are exemplary Counter-Reformation displays of chastity, generous love, concern for family

14. Della Porta, *Fratelli rivali*, I.1: "La maggiore avea non so che di reale e di maraviglioso: parea che la natura avesse fatto l'estremo suo forzo in lei per serbarla per modello de tutte l'altre opre sue, per non errar più mai" (The elder had an inexpressible air of majesty and of wondrousness: it seemed that nature's utmost exertion had gone into creating her, so as to keep a model for all her other works and never err again).

15. Ignazio's outburst at Carizia's appearance from above—"Già fuggono le tenebre dell'aria, ecco l'aurora che precede la chiarezza del mio bel sole, già spuntano i raggi intorno" (II.2)—has antecedents in other commedie gravi: for example, Pino's *Ingiusti sdegni* (Rome, 1553), in which the window scene between Licinio and Delia (I.5) includes this and other commonplaces of speech and gesture used by Della Porta; and comedies from the first half of the century, such as Ercole Bentivoglio's *Il geloso* (Venice, 1544), in which Fausto complains that Livia does *not* appear and apostrophizes her house as the dwelling of the sun (II.1). The association of the lady with the sun, and her abode and place of appearance with the east, was a well-established lyric trope; the Neapolitan poetaster in Castelletti's *Stravaganze d'amore* (Venice, 1584) gives as a sample of Tuscan love poetry, "La vostra fenestra è il mio Oriente, e'l lume de l'occhi vostri è il mio Parnaso" (II.5). The lady as sunlight and dawn was part of the Petrarchan tradition; commenting on Sonnet 219 in *Le rime di Francesco Petrarca*, ed. Giosuè Carducci and Severino Ferrari (1899; repr. Florence, 1943), Carducci notes Latin antecedents and Renaissance variations (p. 313). In comedy the conceit was adapted to the physical place and to plot conventions governing lovers' encounters, so that it became a movable part of the genre. Romeo's "What light through yonder window breaks? / It is the east, and Juliet is the sun!" (II.2) testifies to the international dissemination of the commonplace and the heights to which it could be carried. On the theatergram of the balcony scene see also Della Porta, *Gli duoi fratelli rivali*, ed. L. G. Clubb, Introduction, 35–38.

honor, filial duty, and ceremonial tact, expressed in words and gestures drawing further on the repertory of comic conventions to add moral perfection to superhuman beauty.

It is by association with Christian ideas, however, that Carizia becomes something more than a model young lady. The commonplace of fortune appears in this comedy not only in the usual exclamations but also in expanded discussions of how to bend fortune to one's ends, assigned conspicuously to the "wrong" side, Don Flaminio and his servant Panimbolo. Although less wicked than Don John and his henchmen in the similar plot of *Much Ado About Nothing,* these two are cast as the villains of the piece. In contrast to Don Ignazio and Simbolo, Don Flaminio and Panimbolo swear by self-interest, have dishonorable intentions toward Carizia, attempt to justify using bad means for their ends, and entertain Machiavellian opinions of fortune (II.9; III.1). Their views are shown to be as incorrect by orthodox standards as their machinations are morally wrong. The local shifts of fortune lead to a catastrophe, but the general motion and happy peripety that make all right are attributed explicitly to providence. The existence of fortune is not denied, but its place is defined as subordinate to providence and its power limited downward as well: although it can influence human impulse, it cannot overpower the freedom to act virtuously. The character in whom the ideas of free will and providence are invested is not Ignazio, who reveals himself as the "good" brother only by his matrimonial intentions and relative silence on the subject of fortune, but Carizia, in whose actions the exercise of positive, non-Machiavellian *virtù* is linked in orthodox paradox with the idea of providence. The connection is established in a scene of parental rejoicing at the engagement that will restore the family's prosperity. Her mother associates Carizia's virtue with providential planning and recounts how an impulse from heaven made the usually retiring girl insist on attending the festival where Ignazio first saw her.

> *Eufranone.* Chi può penetrar gli occulti secreti di Dio?
> *Polisena.* O Iddio, che mai vien meno a chi pone in te solo le sue speranze, ella si è sempre raccomandata a te, e tu li hai esaudite le sue preghiere, rimunerata la sua bontà e l'ubidienza estraordinaria che porta al suo padre e sua madre.

> *Eufranone.* Who can penetrate the hidden secrets of God?
> *Polisena.* Oh God, Thou who never failest him who puts his

> hopes only in Thee, she has always relied on Thee, and Thou hast heard and answered her prayers, rewarded her goodness and the extraordinary obedience she pays her father and her mother.

This trust in providence that places the parents also on the right side is not yet to be fulfilled, there being another ordeal ahead when Flaminio's deceit results in Carizia's supposed death. As she rises again, miraculously produced by her mother just as the brothers are about to kill each other, and even the griefstricken Ignazio abandons hope and blames all on fortune, Polisena hammers home the orthodox lesson: this is not merely another caprice of mutable fortune, nor even an accomplishment of unaided human volition, but the conclusion of a complex plan of providence: "Rendete le grazie a Dio, non a me indegna serva. Egli solo ha ordinato nel Cielo che i fatti così difficili ed impossibili ad accommodarsi siano ridotti a così lieto fine" (V.3: Give thanks to God, not to me his unworthy servant! He alone has decreed in heaven that events so difficult and impossible to resolve be brought to so happy an end).

The free exercise of virtue and the work of providence are definitively brought together in a final didactic crescendo when Carizia formally forgives everyone, sealing the bloodless reconciliation that distinguished commedia grave from the tragicomic mixture in tragedia di fin lieto, and her father says: "La tua bontà, o figlia, ha commosso Iddio ad aiutarti: egli ne' secreti del tuo fato aveva ordinato che per te ogni cosa si fusse pacificato, e perciò di tutto si ringrazii Iddio, che ha fatto che le disaventure diventino venture, e le pene allegrezze" (V.4: Your goodness, oh daughter, moved God to aid you; he had ordered in the secrets of your fate that all be made serene for you; therefore, thanks for all be to God, who has so wrought that misfortunes become good fortune and sorrows become joys). Meanwhile, the brothers' uncle, Viceroy of Salerno, figure of civil authority and by definition upholder of Tridentine orthodoxy, declares that seeing Carizia convinces him that God has planned the whole thing.

The analogous *Much Ado* is Italianate in story and in the dramatic articulation that uses labyrinthine structure to reveal invisible reality in contrast to visible appearance, another form of the pattern by which a providential plan is revealed at the expense of fortune; but it was not until *All's Well* and *Measure for Measure* that Shakespeare employed the figure of the woman to suggest the working of grace, investing her with the fairy-tale luminousness that looks toward his late romances.

Although Carizia's situation is that of Hero, and she shares more than one stage commonplace with Juliet, she belongs to the series of women, quivering with transcendent significance, that includes Elfenice, Helena, and Isabella and points forward to Imogen.

The necessarily multilateral approach through theatergrams to Shakespeare's Helena and Isabella must include Girolamo Bargagli's celebrated *Pellegrina,* written earlier than either *La donna costante* or *Fratelli rivali,*[16] and recommended to English readers in 1598 by its inclusion among the listed sources in John Florio's *Worlde of Wordes.* The title character, although not identified with providence, is a well-developed specimen of woman as wonder and bears a strong generic resemblance to Helena.

In the story of Drusilla, who arrives in Pisa (from Spain in the first version, from France in the revision) disguised as a pilgrim seeking Lucrezio, to whom she has been secretly married for some three years, appear the most characteristic elements of commedia grave: juxtaposed extremes of laughter and tears, careful complexity, thematic unity, Counter-Reformation didacticism, and effects of surprise, irony, pathos, and heroism calculated to arouse wonder. The plot combines a great variety of recognized narrative and dramatic sources, examined by Cerreta, to which should be added Boccaccio's tale of Giletta of Narbonne (*Decameron,* III.9), analogous in such details as the combination of the lady's pilgrim disguise, inherited medical knowledge, choice of two chaperones (male and female), status as a married virgin, and sense of rejection (in Drusilla's case unfounded). Moreover, by examining the construction of *La pellegrina* with an eye to the flourishing dramatic practice of shuffling theatergrams of person, association, and action, rather than to the specific provenance of each plot datum, we find that greater weight should be attached to the influence of *L'amor costante*— even more than is allowed by Cerreta, an authority on *Intronati* drama. *L'amor costante* is the distinguished precursor in the Intronati tradition

16. Written in 1567–68 and first printed in a revision by Girolamo Bargagli's brother, Scipione, as *La pellegrina, commedia . . . rappresentata nelle felicissime nozze del Sereniss. Don Ferdinando de' Medici Granduca di Toscana, e della Serenissima Madama Christiana di Loreno* (Siena, 1589). It is in this version that the play was long known, but the original version has been published from the authorial manuscript by Florindo Cerreta (Florence, 1971). I quote from Cerreta's edition, the speeches in question being substantially the same in both versions.

to which *La pellegrina* belongs, and the model for representing a heroine of constancy through an intrigue plot turning on a theme illustrated
by comparisons and contrasts of action and characters.

As in the plot of *L'amor costante,* there is a danger that one of the
lovers will be contracted to someone else, in this case Lucrezio to Lepida, already pregnant by her secret husband, Terenzio, and feigning
madness to avoid the new match. Also as in *L'amor costante,* the secondary example of constancy, Lepida again, is pursued by still another
suitor and attended by an affectionate servant, her balia, whose easygoing sexual and moral standards are a foil to the girl's ideal of constancy.
Like Piccolomini's Lucrezia, the nunlike Drusilla lacks the symbolic
bond with the stable power of heavenly providence and love controlling
mutable fortune that Elfenice of *La donna costante* would exhibit a decade later. Whereas Lucrezia is only a saint of constancy, however, the
more active and articulate Drusilla is elevated to a broader patronage,
dispensing wisdom, blessing, and scrupulous example. Her refusal to be
bedded or even kissed after her secret wedding or to enjoy its privileges
until it is publicly sanctioned (I.4) distinguishes her from other participants in the action theatergram of clandestine marriage, including the
secondary heroine Lepida, whose pregnancy enhances by contrast the
saintly Counter-Reformation rigor of Drusilla's chaste and law-abiding
self-denial. It is explicitly pointed out that marriages such as Lepida's
have been forbidden by the Council of Trent (V.4),[17] but in comedy this
stock device continued to meet with indulgence, so that Drusilla's strict
observance of the Tridentine spirit and letter appears the more wonderful. Her further practices of self-denial are more pleasing to modern
taste. On learning of Lucrezio's new engagement, without realizing that
he thinks her dead, Drusilla plans to go away quietly instead of urging
her prior claim, even while admitting that she would rather have Lucrezio "ingrato ed infedele che un altro leale" (II.1: ungrateful and
faithless than another loyal). She decides to stay because Lepida's madness throws the engagement in doubt and because there is need for her
own medical knowledge, which she says she always uses freely for the
good of others (II.7). Although he does not penetrate her disguise, Lucrezio is struck almost dumb by her noble aspect, not because of a sub-
conscious memory but as further evidence of Drusilla's intimidating su-

17. Cerreta notes that the conciliar decree "de clandestinis matrimoniis"
went into effect on 1 May 1564 (*La pellegrina,* Introduction, 193 n. 117).

periority. Her landlady, Violante,[18] an aging prostitute and additional foil to the figure of ideal constancy, is at first not sympathetic to the *donna tanto mirabile,* but even her irritation at Drusilla's inviolability is expressed by a classification of the pilgrim as something different from the rest of mankind (II.3). Seen from any angle, Drusilla is a thing apart: all impressions of her testify to a combination of enterprising independence with moral and intellectual superiority not originating in the individual sources of the play but developing in the commedia grave figure of the woman as an embodiment of spiritual values.

Bargagli does not incorporate doctrinal issues in his comedy, but he disposes the denouement so as to define Drusilla's pilgrimage of love as more than a holy simile, as in itself holy, by emphasizing her efficacy as a benefactress and conscience to all the other characters and as a resurrected saint to Lucrezio. Although only indirectly concerned in it, she presides over the climactic recognition scene of Lepida's and Terenzio's plot. Lepida's father, Cassandro, still adamant after Terenzio is proved to be a good matrimonial catch, demands punishment for the seduction: "Non sa quanto dolce cosa sia la vendetta né quanto ardentemente si desideri se non chi ha ricevuta l'offesa" (V.4: No one but the one offended can know how sweet vengeance is and how fierce the craving for it). Terenzio pleads, as does his brother, but the final plea and the one that moves Cassandro is Drusilla's: "Non è cosa nella quale l'uomo si faccia più simile a Dio che nel perdonare" (V.4: In nothing man does is he more like God than when he forgives). The following and final scenes are reserved entirely for Drusilla and the fulfillment of her heart's desire, dragged out for dramatic effect and emotional impact by her soliloquy and the scene of reconciliation with Lucrezio, who speaks of his supposedly dead wife as a saint and greets her on recognition as "Drusilla mia divina" (V.6). In this exalted mood Bargagli chooses to end, assign-

18. Although my purpose is to suggest generic similarities rather than specific debts, it is tempting to speculate on the First Folio stage direction to the scene in *All's Well* in which Helena as a pilgrim meets her landlady, the widow, and the daughter Diana, accompanied by "Violenta, and Mariana" (III.5). Violante, a name not uncommon but not associated with landladies except in *La pellegrina,* was metathesized in French translation and taken over twice by Painter in tales 37 and 42 of *The Palace of Pleasure,* though not in his tale of Giletta (38), Shakespeare's source. The introduction of the name by Shakespeare or by the scribe of the Folio copy into a situation generically similar to that in *La pellegrina* is at any rate a teasing coincidence.

ing the envoi not to a clown, as is more usual, but to Drusilla herself, and the play is concluded by a serious character, in the manner of some grave late Cinquecento comedies and of Shakespeare in *All's Well, Measure for Measure,* and the romances. Drusilla reasserts the thematic unity of her story, ending on a metaphor: "Ora è finito il pellegrinaggio, ora è ottenuta la grazia, ora sono adempiuti i voti" (V.6: Now the pilgrimage is ended, now grace has been obtained, now all vows are fulfilled). Placed as the finishing touch to a portrayal of the innamorata as an emblem of Counter-Reformation virtue, however, the metaphor is no simple expression of the quest, reward, and promises of love through the vocabulary of religion. Heaven has not been demoted to a vehicle for an amatory or at best temporal tenor. A pilgrimage of love that culminates in conventional tableaux of reconciliation made to radiate suggestions of ritual Christian forgiveness, miraculous resurrection, and eternal salvation offers a theatrical image integrating the secular and the religious.

To measure precisely the extent of the vogue for this variety of commedia grave, the use in it of the woman to arouse moral and religious wonder, and the range of theatergrams employed for didactic and symbolic ends and constituting the particular tragicomic mixture in which Shakespeare might have found a starting place for his more intellectual and symbolic casting of the formulas, it would be necessary to survey many other literary comedies, including two by Oddi.[19] Erminia of *Prigione d'amore,* who substitutes herself for her brother and undergoes apparent execution in prison, is a primary illustration of the Counter-Reformation injunction to quietism and trust in the powers that be, here embodied in the Duke of Ferrara, who is never present onstage but is continually referred to and given an effect on the action so as to associate him with the idea of providence and make him an example of the unitary civil and religious concept of power in post-Tridentine Italy. By means of a denouement in which the commonplace of supposed death takes the form of execution in a prison less grotesque than that of *Measure for Measure* but likewise frequented by clowns, the characters of *Prigione d'amore* learn and teach the lesson of submission to divine and ducal laws in their hierarchical relationship, and are brought to realize

19. Sforza Oddi, *Prigione d'amore,* written ca. 1570 (Florence, 1590); *I morti vivi* (Perugia, 1576). Baldi analyzes the civil aspect of Oddi's three comedies as a "modello di comportamento conformistico, bassato sulla passività e la rinuncia" in "Le commedie di Sforza Oddi," 45.

that the conflict between love and law is a false appearance, the reality being the benign providence of a paternalistic government. More directly concerned with providence is Oddi's *I morti vivi,* in which the Greek romance of Clitophon and Leucippe (also used by Annibal Caro in *Gli straccioni*) is refashioned to create a pattern of miraculous resurrection, with the baptized Egyptian heroine, Alessandra, functioning centrally as visible proof of God's miraculous providence and as an example of the virtues of faith, hope, and charity, which she illustrates by resignation on the one hand, perseverance on the other, and forgiveness to crown all. The diction throughout is weighted with allusions to heaven's will, providence, and miracles, and the characters exist in a state of collective wonder, especially with regard to Alessandra. Oddi alters his source by eliminating adultery, bringing the dead to life in a general reconciliation of families illuminated by Counter-Reformation zeal (a vow to make a pilgrimage to Loreto is part of the final rejoicing); and in the baptism of Alessandra and her father, Abraim, born again of water and the Holy Ghost, he attaches an original and ponderous Christian symbolism to the theme of returning from death that he employs as an organizing theatergram of design.

Although Shakespeare's strong reliance on Boccaccio's tale of Giletta of Narbonne makes the action of *All's Well That Ends Well* a contaminatio less eclectic than some of his other comic plots, the result nevertheless is more like commedia erudita than like any other form of dramatized novella, more like late commedia grave than any other species of commedia erudita, and more like the whole genre than like any particular specimen of it. Although Helena inevitably has something in common with Giletta and with the heroine of Bernardo Accolti's fifteenth-century dramatization of the tale, *La Virginia,* she is by quality and function distant from them—and also from such Shakespearean innamorate as Rosalind and Viola—much as Elfenice, Drusilla, and their kind are distant from the many enterprising Italian heroines whose significance stops short of transcendent symbolism. The plane of meaning on which Helena rather uncomfortably moves is the one attained by the feminine example and idea carriers, and Shakespeare's modifications of the novella bring the story closer to the theatrical genre in which they appear. Shakespeare magnifies Helena's intrinsic worth by enlarging on the wisdom, character, and beauty found in his source and by eliminating the external supports of relatives and wealth, so that Helena's native merit stands alone. He increases her power to arouse admiration by inventing the dowager Countess, who calls Helena "the most virtuous gentlewoman that ever nature had praise for creating" (IV.5.9–10), and by introducing, in contrast to Bertram, young nobles very willing to marry her. The use of the Clown, cynical about goodness in women (I.3.79), and of Parolles as foils to Helena's goodness and benign influence on Bertram also heightens her value and reflects the practice of Italian comic dramaturgy. In keeping with the theme of industry and perseverance proclaimed for the Third Day of the *Decameron*, Giletta is fixed unswervingly on her goal, but Helena, rejected by Bertram, at first decides to go away and spend her life in pilgrimage rather than block his return to Rossillion. It is not perseverance or ingenuity that Shakespeare is offering for our admiration at this juncture but the spirit of sacrifice common to the Drusillas, Erminias, and Alessandras of commedia grave.

Like Drusilla, Helena resumes the initiative when circumstances change, and with a still more altruistic incentive to add to that of self-interest, in that Bertram is falling into bad ways and needs the help he spurns. The form her help takes, the substitution of herself for Diana in a dark bedroom, that well-gnawed bone of Shakespearean controversy, was essential to the story and had been developed in Italy as a theater-gram of action almost a century earlier.[20] Distasteful or not, this action is the principal occasion for the figure of Helena to take on, in addition to the meanings she shares with Giletta and Drusilla, the identification with providence convincingly argued in Kirsch's analysis of the providential pattern in *All's Well*.[21] The dramatic conventions expressing the plan and Helena's role in it correspond more directly to the kind of commedia grave in which Counter-Reformation orthodoxy is taught or Sophoclean peripety adapted to comedy and made to function as a metaphor for providence, than to the Guarinian pastoral drama, incorporating the same idea and structural pattern, with which Kirsch links *All's Well*. Shakespeare's knowledge of this species of grave comedy and his creative awareness of its potential are apparent in his investment of idea in the figure of the woman, leading to a concluding secular miracle that produces secondary religious overtones for audiences attuned to everyday Christian interpretations of life.

20. A list of instances would be a catalogue of hundreds of Italian comedies. In Marcantonio Raimondi's *L'erotodynastia, over Potenza d'amore*, performed in 1614 (Venice, 1626), obviously too late to be a direct source of *All's Well* and offered as an example of the frequency with which the commonplaces and their details repeat each other, a landlady named Diana arranges for a girl to sleep with her future husband in Diana's house and in place of Diana herself (IV.4).

21. Arthur Kirsch, *Jacobean Dramatic Perspectives*, 59–60.

The brief acknowledgments of divine auspices in the source novella are expanded in Helena's urging:

> It is not so with Him that all things knows
> As 'tis with us that square our guess by shows;
> But most it is presumption in us when
> The help of heaven we count the act of men.
> Dear sir, to my endeavours give consent;
> Of heaven, not me, make an experiment.
>
> (II.1.148–53)

This statement appears in contrast with her earlier one:

> Our remedies oft in ourselves do lie,
> Which we ascribe to heaven; the fated sky
> Gives us free scope; only doth backward pull
> Our slow designs when we ourselves are dull.
>
> (I.1.212–15)

The contrast has been used to support the conclusion that Helena moves from an unjustified sense of self-sufficiency expressed in her first appearance to a reliance on God's power and providence. Richard Stensgaard argues that Helena's method of cure was the Paracelsian chemical system, based on the theory of contraries, which challenged the orthodox Galenic herbal system, based on the theory of humors and endorsed by the College of Physicians. He relates the Paracelsian reformers' sense of divine intervention, in opposition to the Galenists' "pagan atheistic" naturalism, to the theological controversy then alive over the roles in curing the plague of supernatural agencies as opposed to natural ones. He concludes that Helena, like the reformers, comes to know the error of the doctrine of human self-sufficiency.[22]

Stensgaard's presentation of the medical issues illuminates Helena's principles as a physician (and Shakespeare's interest in the controversy), but it does not follow that her views of human action and of providence are mutually exclusive. In the speech last quoted, Helena does not oppose self-sufficiency to dependence on God, but free will to astral influences. Limiting the power of the stars to influences and tendencies, she assigns the responsibility for actions to free will. This is like Aquinas's or Dante's pronouncements on the same subject, and also like those of neomedieval Counter-Reformation orthodoxy in its campaign against

22. Richard K. Stensgaard, "*All's Well That Ends Well* and the Galenico-Paracelsian Controversy," *Renaissance Quarterly* 25 (1972): 173–88.

the judiciary arts of astrology and fortune-telling.[23] The context in
which Helena makes this statement is that of her domestic and social
situation, of her love for Bertram and its seeming impossibility, of her
determination to do for herself what she can. Her expression of faith in
a power above herself, however, refers not to fate or the stars but to
divine providence, to which fortune is subordinate and which is the only
kind of destiny admitted to a Christian universe, on the broadest basis
of Renaissance Christianity, Catholic or Protestant, providence guaranteed freedom to choose the good.[24] The bed trick demands initiative action—not to say acting—like that of Giletta, but Helena sees it addi-
tionally as cooperation with providence, assuring the Widow:

> Doubt not but heaven
> Hath brought me up to be your daughter's dower,
> As it hath fated her to be my motive
> And helper to a husband.
>
> (IV.4.18–21)

Helena's actions and her awareness of their meaning do not chart a conversion—that is left to Bertram—but they metaphorically clarify the relation of invisible forces: providence encircles all, permitting some
scope to fortune and the stars, but protecting free will and guiding human affairs to a good end, most happily reached when human will par-
ticipates in God's plan.

Shakespeare's annexing of a ritual religious dimension to his secular
drama surpasses in integrity any Italian representation in comedy of
spiritual reality, and his doing so realizes the potential and transforms
the theatergrams of an Italian genre. Even the added detail of Helena's
spreading word of her own death at Saint Jaques le Grand, making her
reappearance seem a miraculous resurrection, shows her affinity with
the figure of the woman as wonder. It is no accident that every Italian

23. *Purgatorio*, XVI.73–84. Della Porta's defensive attempt to prove his orthodoxy in this regard is a comparable statement; *De humana physiognomonia
libri IIII* (Vici Aequensis, 1586), Dedication.

24. Roland Mushat Frye, *Shakespeare and Christian Doctrine* (Princeton,
1963), quotes Calvin's affirmation of the antiastrological commonplace (p. 160)
and relates it to *All's Well* (p. 162). In connection with *Hamlet* he cites Calvin's
pronouncement that "chances as well of prosperity as of adversity the reason of
the flesh doth ascribe to fortune," while the Christian mind "will firmly believe
that all chances are governed by the secret counsel of God" (p. 232).

heroine of commedia grave named above, whatever else she may omit, goes through the formulaic action of apparent death.

Shakespeare's treatment of the culminating act of forgiveness is also more elaborate and extra-fabular in applicability than in any commedia grave. By blackening Bertram's character beyond anything in his sources, Shakespeare creates a need of forgiveness, paralleling but intensifying a facet of reconciliation scenes in Italian comedy; whatever the effect on the psychological verisimilitude of the resolution, the alteration strengthens the symbolic charge of the finale, in which Helena's climactic appearance seems a benediction and miracle of grace to the remission of sin. Although her Italian generic analogues are even less suited than Helena herself to bear the mystical weight that G. Wilson Knight attached to the figure,[25] it is their centrality, exemplary goodness, and identification with concepts of active virtue, forgiveness, and resignation to providence that indicate the species of tragicomedy to which Shakespeare adapted the tale of Giletta. His intensification of the sense of wonder, in particular his emphasis in speeches like Lafew's (II.3.1–6) on the miraculous aspect of Helena's progress, places *All's Well* in an accelerated Shakespearean phase of a movement toward symbolic drama begun by fits and starts in the commedia grave, as does the prelude to the late romances that Hunter hears in this play, especially in the actions of the "magical" heroine.

In *Measure for Measure* the seriousness that Lever compares to the tone of Giraldi's *tragedia di fin lieto, Epitia,*[26] and the concerted attempt at tragicomedy that he links with Guarini's theory in the *Compendio della poesia tragicomica,* are still more clearly associated with the Italian generic structures I have proposed as antecedent and analogous to *All's Well.* "Measure," as Lever demonstrates it to be thematically at work in Shakespeare's play, is different from "measure," as Guarini made it a principle of constructing tragicomedy, dictating that mitigation of extremes, blending instead of juxtaposing, that produced *Il pastor fido.* The sharp contrasts, moral, tonal, structural, social, even ontological, in *Measure for Measure* distinguish it from Guarini's version of tragicomedy, just as the low comic elements and the eschewing of deaths—even deserved ones like that intended for Barnardine—distinguish it from Giraldi's tragedy with a happy ending. *Measure for Measure* does not correspond exactly to any Italian genre, nor to any En-

25. Knight, *The Sovereign Flower,* 100–102.
26. J. W. Lever, ed., *Measure for Measure,* Introduction, xl–xli.

glish one, certainly not to the "mongrel tragicomedy" deplored by
Sidney or the didactic "Historye" represented by Whetstone's *Promos
and Cassandra,* which was probably one of Shakespeare's sources. As
the commedia grave in range and decorum is the genre closest to Shakespearean comedy, so the kind of commedia grave in which the figure of
the woman is used to create wonder is the tragicomic mixture closest to
Measure for Measure.

As in *All's Well,* Shakespeare's modifications of his sources move toward Italian theatergrams. Claudio and Juliet become privately plighted
expectant parents, like Lepida and Terenzio in *La pellegrina.* The plot
involving Marianna depends on the commonplace of substitution in a
dark bedroom, ratifying as marriage the betrothal that constituted *de
futuro* spousal. These unions add up in time to marriage but in the early
stages fall short of the fully sanctioned sacrament insisted on by a Drusilla. They are interpolated and used by Shakespeare as foils, and as
measuring marks on a thematic scale that runs from Mistress Over-
done's prostitution and Angelo's blackmailing proposition, to Isabella's
proposal to become the Bride of Christ at the beginning and the Duke's
"motion" that she become a Duchess at the end. Like the structured alternation of appearances of Isabella and of characters from the underworld, these uses and interpolations are part of the "systematized contrasts" Lever descries in the first half of Shakespeare's tragicomic
structure.[27]

Isabella herself is the strongest argument for Shakespeare's acquaintance with the Italian genre and for his interest in testing further the dramatic capabilities of the feminine figure. Except in the preservation of
her virginity made possible by Shakespeare's overthrowing his sources,
Isabella strictly performs few of the formulaic functions of the *donna
mirabile.* She does not return from the dead (except by leaving the convent, where she would have become dead to the world); she is neither
agent nor emblem of providence, only an unwitting participant in its design. She is not even in love. By this last, radical change Shakespeare
takes a figure that was nunlike even in its unfledged state and more so in
the post-Tridentine innamorate with their pious garb or vocabulary and
their auras as of saints performing miracles, and he makes her a real nun
(at least a novice),

> enskied and sainted
> By your renouncement, an immortal spirit,

27. Ibid., xliv.

And to be talk'd with in sincerity,
As with a saint.

(I.4.34–37)

The test she leaves her convent in order to face is not one of constancy in love or of power to unite love with goodness, charity, or faith in providence, but a stark trial of virtue and principle, unsupported by exalted passion.

The theatergram of the woman as wonder began as a dramatic representation in which religion was only a metaphor: in *L'amor costante* Lucrezia is a votaress and saint in the religion of love. In late *commedie gravi*, religious law and ecclesiastical law are extra-fabular realities that also form the secular context in which the heroine may demonstrate the wonder of love's power and of her nature by conscious virtue and unconscious harmony with providence in her altarbound action. We need not identify Isabella as the soul of man, elected to be the Bride of Christ in an allegory of the Divine Atonement, to recognize that she is a vehicle for idea and that her personal, visible action may incarnate onstage, in the realm of the particular and local, a human possibility that had another existence in that of the general and the universal. If we set aside questions of whether Isabella can be likable to any audience, whether she must appear prudish and uncharitable in her zeal for salvation, or whether she is ignorant of the true nature of chastity, and confine the inquiry to the frame of reference composed of women who act as wonders in the kind of play that this one most resembles, we find that there remains one idea that Isabella consistently demonstrates through her ordeals, which involve her in a set of Italian theatrical commonplaces and conclude in a final test that she passes by an act of forgiveness.

From the moment Lucio begs her to leave her convent, Isabella has to make painful choices to do what she believes is right. Standing by Christian principles in a conventional order of importance (duty to kin, chastity, charity), she acts out the principle of free will. The analogy with the chaste heroine of *The Rape of Lucrece* by which Lever supports his view that Isabella's conception of chastity is tinged with pagan error rests on the assumption that the issue is the same in both cases.[28] The action for which Lucrece could be held responsible, however, was suicide. Isabella, on the contrary, is not threatened with rape. Although Angelo sophistically suggests that compliance would be but a "compell'd" sin (II.4.57), Isabella sees that she has a choice. The drama re-

---

28. Ibid., lxxx–lxxxi.

quires that her will be free. Just as in one test she is without the excuse of physical force, so in the other she is deprived of any tie with Angelo to motivate a plea for mercy toward him. The Duke refuses to remove her just cause for hatred; by letting her think Angelo her brother's murderer, he makes her choice of Christian forgiveness harder and therefore more illustrative of the will's freedom. The double function of Helena in *All's Well*—as the human will to good, working like a miracle within a providential plan, and as an emblem of providence itself—is divided in *Measure for Measure* between the Duke and Isabella: he identifying himself with providence and partaking of its omnipotence, confirmed by his status as civil authority; she lacking full knowledge but cooperating in a design that offers her a part to be freely improvised in a miracle of forgiveness that seems superhuman only because, as Drusilla says, it is the human action nearest the divine. Isabella cooperates with providence, as do Helena and the forgiving women of commedie gravi, but she is more forgiving than they need be. Having gone to some pains to underscore the freedom of her prayer for Angelo, Shakespeare puts only compassion and mercy in the balance against the good reasons for Angelo's death. The more difficult the exercise of free will for good, the greater the wonder; this aim, achieved, confirms the radical rightness of Shakespeare's removing from Isabella the principal motive of the innamorata.

The commedia grave characterized by the confluence of the exemplary heroine, generic mixture through contrast, and Counter-Reformation principles of active virtue and providence is a kind of romantic comedy in which the originally neoclassical structures of the Italian theater are developed into forms prophetic of the comedy of forgiveness defined by Robert G. Hunter and illustrated to different degrees by *All's Well* and *Measure for Measure*.[29] Italian attempts at symbolic drama were limited, however, and were dictated by the Counter-Reformation preoccupation with achieving doctrinal, civil, and social homogeneity. Shakespeare's variations were neither so limited nor so dictated, and he had the benefit of the tradition of English medieval and Tudor drama. But the latest Italian drama in his day, its neomedieval abstractions symbolic rather than allegorical, representing spiritual truths incidentally and pragmatically, was no secret outside of Italy. The sophistication of Shakespeare's technique, the commonplaces of form

29. Robert G. Hunter, *Shakespeare and the Comedy of Forgiveness* (New York, 1965), 106–31, 204–26.

and substance he chose, and the generic mixtures he made suggest more than a glancing knowledge of the polished, stageworthy, contemporary drama that had already developed structures and instruments to accommodate a neomedieval symbolizing impulse not unlike his own. The technical finish and formal capacity of these plays made them appeal to discerning dramatists—Christians, of course, but not theologians, Catholic or Protestant—and Shakespeare probably helped himself to what he liked with characteristic ease and discrimination.

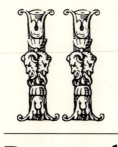

Pastoral

Serlio's "Scena Satirica"
"Le second livre de Perspective"
Il Primo Libro d'Architettura di Sebastiano Serlio, Bolognese (Paris, 1545).
By permission of the National Gallery of Art, Mark J. Millard Architectural
Collection (1983.49.106).

CHAPTER FOUR

The Making of the Pastoral Play:
Italian Experiments between 1573 and 1590

Una Maga prudente con liquori
Farà dormir ciascun, e de la notte
L'ombre faran sognar con finte larve:
E diverran tre bestie, tre animali:
Nel mezo, quattro miseri Pastori,
E quattro Ninfe, vi faran vedere
Come mal corrispondino i voleri
De gl'infelici, che son tutti Amanti
Ma l'una à l'altro di contraria voglia,
E come ragionando, di speranza
Vengon ripieni da la dolent'Echo;
Come fan sacrificio, e qual risposta
Hanno d'Amor nel Sacro Tempio havuta:
In fine, nel principio sentirete
Lunghe historie di pianti, e di martiri
Strane mutation, diversi casi,
Molte volubilità d'huomini e donne
E dal principio al fin burle vedrete
Assai nuove, e piacevoli: & io credo
Che non vi spiacerà d'haver il tempo
Speso in udir questa Intricata Selva
D'Amor, che porta d'Intricati il nome.
(Pasqualigo, *Gl'intricati,* Proemio)

A wise sorceress with liquors will put all to sleep, and the shades of night will cause dreams of false spectres; and three "animals" will become three beasts: midst which four unhappy shepherds and four nymphs will show you how ill-sorted are the desires of the unfortunate, for all are lovers, but no two in requited love; and

This chapter appeared in slightly different form as "The Making of the Pastoral Play: Some Italian Experiments between 1573 and 1590," in *Petrarch to Pirandello: Studies in Italian Literature in Honour of Beatrice Corrigan,* ed. Julius A. Molinaro (Toronto, 1973), 45–72.

how, discoursing, they are filled with hope by sorrowing Echo; how they perform a sacrifice, and what answer they have from Love in the sacred temple: in all, at first you will hear long histories of laments and sufferings, strange transformations, various cases, great inconstancy of men and women, and from beginning to end you will see very new and pleasing tricks: and I believe that it will not displease you to have spent the time in listening to this tangled wood of Love, that bears the name of *Intricati*.

his argument introduces a five-act verse play in which there occurs, as promised, a constructive redirection of affections among four pairs of shepherds and nymphs, whose names and concerns recall Montemayor's *Diana*. Caught in a maze of emotion complicated by a transvestite joke, they hold forth in various meters, singly, in duets, trios, and a final octet, on love, nature, illusion, the love of nature, the nature of love, the illusion of love, the nature of illusion, and so forth. They are encouraged and deceived by the voice of Echo. The sorceress who puts them to sleep and sets matters right with her magic liquor and therapeutic dreams employs an infernal spirit, one Lucifero, functioning invisibly or in human form, as needed. He summons shadows of the night to make images, cracks Boccaccian jokes at the expense of the mortals, and generally enjoys his work.

Also wandering the woods, bent on love, brawling with each other and ambushing nymphs, are a blustering Spaniard, Calabaza, a *villano* from the Maremma, and a Bolognese self-styled Doctor, predictably named Graciano. They join the refined shepherds for supper and singing, to which they contribute a clownish entertainment of their own. In parody of the shepherds' complaints, Graciano sings an insult to love, likened by the villano to the braying of lovesick asses in May in the Maremma. The villano then offers a song about money, followed by Calabaza's Spanish "Vellianico" (IV.4). These are the *animali* who become beasts by being fitted magically with the heads of a ram, a bull, and an ass:

Gracian.	O cha ne i ved ben, ò cha un gran bech
	Spagnol ti è deventà, e ti Villan,
	A sidi un gran cornut, un gran boaz:
	Mo pian un poch, che quest nè al mie mustaz.
Villano.	Asino Gracian sei diventato. (V.5)

Gracian. Either I can't see straight, or you've become a big buck goat, Spaniard, and you, peasant, are a great horned thing, a big ugly bull: now wait a bit, this is not my face.

Peasant. Gracian, you've turned into an ass.

When the Maga restores and dismisses them with a condescending order to leave love to their betters, they depart muttering but with unimpaired self-confidence.

Gl'intricati is remarkable neither for its quality nor for the *commedia dell'arte* mask of Graziano, nor even for its resemblance to *A Midsummer Night's Dream*. It is remarkable, in fact, only for being so unremarkable an example of Renaissance Italian pastoral drama, a genre too often defined exclusively by Tasso's and Guarini's treatments of it.

Many of the pastoral ingredients used in *Aminta* reappear in *Gl'intricati,* as they do in countless other pastoral plays: the arguments for and against love, in various meters and from several points of view, the *dubbi* posed in the spirit of courtly pastime, the attempted suicide, the oppression of nymphs by figures of lust (here the three clowns replace the more common satyr), the musing on time and mutability, the praise or abuse of the court, the appreciations of rural landscape of the Petrarchan stamp, the outbursts about the blindness of Cupid and of the human mind, the Ovidian reminiscences, and the hymeneal ending symbolizing reconciliations between Diana and Venus.

But *Gl'intricati* moves at a considerable distance from *Aminta* by virtue of the shape and substance of its action, including the element attributed in another example of the genre to the inspiration of Apollo, which moves the poet:

> mescer fra 'l pianto un breve riso
> Di semplici Villan sciocchezze, e scherzi
> Innestar anco fra dogliosi accenti
> (Castelletti, *Amarilli,* Prologo)

to mix with the tears the brief laughter of simpleminded peasants' foolishness, and also to include jests among the sorrowful accents.

Castelletti's *sciocchezze* include a goatherd who tries to make love to a friend's wife and is turned into a tree and back again by a naiad into whose fountain he falls, and a third peasant, who like Shakespeare's Caliban gets drunk in a tempest and imagines that he sees:

Cert'huomin, c'han l'orecchie lunghe, lunghe,
Giungon da terra in fin sopra le stelle,
Io non sò se sien asini, ò castroni.   (II.6)

Certain men with long long ears. They reach from earth up beyond the stars. I don't know if they are asses or geldings.

The *pianto* and *dogliosi accenti* arise from the stock troubles that the
god of Love, fleeing the court, visits upon Amarilli, her two suitors, and
her lovesick friend. As in Pasqualigo's play and in contrast to Tasso's,
the action is complex and the coexistence of laughter and tears, as well
as that of fantasy and the plausible, is established by the simple juxtaposition of unmodified opposites. As for *Il pastor fido,* which bears
out its author's claim to have diluted the extremes of two strains to
produce a milder third, it would seem on surface comparison that only
its complication of plot makes for a resemblance to pastoral plays of
comic intrigue, buffoonery, and Ovidian magic.

For all that contemporary criticism has revealed about the range of
correspondences between Arcadia and interior worlds of spirit, emotion, and imagination, about the serviceability of the pastoral in polar
tension with epic heroism as with urban mundanity, and about the
subtleties of the amatory fixation distinguishing the Renaissance pastoral from the classical, knowledge of the dramatization of the literary
pastoral has been left for the most part in nineteenth-century formula-
tions. Neither Empsonian soundings of the pastoral mode in its most
inclusive sense nor close analyses of a few exceptional plays show how
the pastoral tropes and types took the stage.

The undramatic character of *Aminta,* "the most beautiful madrigal
in Italian literature,"[1] has been remarked often. Compared with later
pastoral plays, for which it was a model of excellence and a quarry for
song, sentiment, and situation, it seems a lyrical pageant of love, symbolic and stylized into hieroglyph, more tenor than vehicle. Insofar as it
may be described as a dramatic genre, *Aminta* is a tragedy. More precisely, it is a series of eclogues grouped around a single situation, leading
to a simple, tragic denouement on which a happy ending is superim-
posed. Italian pastoral drama in the mass is essentially a comic genre,
however, as appears not only in the inherent happiness of the pastoral

1. "Il più bel madrigale della letteratura italiana"; Umberto Bosco, "Tasso,
Torquato," *Enciclopedia italiana di scienze, lettere ed arti* (Rome, 1937),
33:313.

world observed by Rousset,[2] but also in the theatrical articulation of the pastoral attitudes. This is true of *Il pastor fido* as well, despite Guarini's intention of raising the pastoral drama to Aristotelian dignity with supports borrowed from tragedy.

Were the commonly projected image of Italian pastoral drama to be enlarged, the variety of contributing detail thus made visible might encourage further comparison with English drama. Richard Cody's study of *Aminta* as a reenactment of Orphic rite and neoplatonic key to three Shakespearean comedies should be welcomed even by those hesitant to accept the rigorous hermeticism it imposes on the comedies, because Cody has understood that the effects of Italian pastoral drama may exist independent of Italy or of *pastori*.[3] A clearer picture of the original genre would show that even the members of Shakespeare's audience with no head for esoteric neoplatonism could have recognized the pastoral inspiration of *A Midsummer Night's Dream* and *The Tempest*. The mere dilettante of literary fashion would have known at least by hearsay the more obvious features of a few kinds of pastoral plays being produced at Italian courts and academies. If modern scholars neglect some of the features and most of the kinds, it is because certain received ideas have long obstructed our views of the pastoral play.

The first of these is that *Aminta* and *Il pastor fido* represent all there is to know about the genre. Long after the contributions of Carrara and Violet Jeffrey, this extraordinarily hardy simplification of Greg's conclusion has endured, explicitly in Gerhardt and in Orr,[4] implicitly even in Cody, although his thesis profoundly contradicts Greg in the large claim it makes for the importance to Elizabethan drama of the Italian pastoral play. Indeed, Cody dismisses Guarini with a few words, regarding *Aminta* as a sufficient example of orthodox Italian pastoral.

2. Jean Rousset, *La littérature de l'âge baroque en France: Circé et le paon* (Paris, 1953), 33.

3. Richard Cody, *The Landscape of the Mind: Pastoralism and Platonic Theory in Tasso's "Aminta" and Shakespeare's Early Comedies* (Oxford, 1969).

4. Enrico Carrara, *La poesia pastorale* (Milan, n.d. [1909]); Violet M. Jeffery, *John Lyly and the Italian Renaissance* (Paris, 1929); W. W. Greg, *Pastoral Poetry and Pastoral Drama: A Literary Inquiry, with Special Reference to the Pre-Restoration Stage in England* (London, 1906), 176, 210; Mia I. Gerhardt, *Essai d'analyse littéraire de la pastorale dans les littératures italienne, espagnole et française* (Leiden, 1950), 94:124–26; David Orr, *Italian Renaissance Drama in England before 1625: The Influence of Erudite Tragedy, Comedy, and Pastoral on Elizabethan and Jacobean Drama* (Chapel Hill, 1970), 74–75.

The second idea to discard is that experimentation in pastoral drama ended with *Aminta*. No one doubts that long and deliberate cultivation produced the pastoral play, but although scholars from Carrara to Bàrberi Squarotti have recognized that the simple tragic form of *Aminta* was not the structure used by Guarini,[5] not to mention the intervening lesser dramatists, certain assumptions are often contradictorily and mysteriously made: that Tasso's pastoral marked the end of the trials, if not of the errors, that it determined the genre's shape in addition to its vogue and much of its matter, and that later pastoral playwrights aimed no farther than at imitation or expansion of the kind supposed to have produced *Il pastor fido*. Had Greg closely read the plays of the 1570s and 1580s that he mentions only to discount as not forming a link in a chain of organic development,[6] he would have observed in them a re-doubled effort of experimentation with the same aims as those in pastorals that predate *Aminta*, with the added challenge of assimilating and rivaling Tasso's achievement.

Neither of these ideas should need refutation at this late date, for Carrara's encyclopedic work has long since supplied the information needed for an accurately revised view of the pastoral play. But Carrara himself, in the act of discarding such misleading simplifications, clouded the issue with his own categories, the "satirico" of Giraldi, the "comico" of Beccari and Lollio, the "tragico" of Tasso, and the "tragicomico" of Guarini, finally suggesting the possibility of a fifth type lost with the original version of Groto's *Calisto*.[7]

By way of a corrective I propose to survey a body of pastoral plays large enough to constitute a fair sampling, published between 1573, the year *Aminta* was composed and performed, and 1590, the year of *Il pastor fido*'s first printing (it was actually issued in December 1589), five years after its completion. As far as can be determined, these plays were also written or at least rewritten between these dates. They are the works of writers of the academies and courts, at the center of Italian

---

5. Tasso, *Aminta*, ed. Giorgio Bàrberi Squarotti (Padua, 1968). Bàrberi Squarotti speaks of Guarini's imitation of "punti strutturalmente fondamentali" (Introduction, p. 6), referring to the Golden Age chorus as an example, but his discussion of the plot and its "preteso 'lieto fine'" (p. 18) states the essential tragedy of *Aminta*. On theories of origins see Emilio Bigi, "Il dramma pastorale del '500," *Il teatro classico italiano nel '500* (Rome, 1971), 101–20.

6. Greg, *Pastoral Poetry*, 210ff.

7. Carrara, *La poesia pastorale*, 334.

literary life. The plays range in quality from deserving to undeserving of their common neglect, but in their time two-thirds of them went into more than one edition. Most of the authors wrote in other genres as well, some, like Groto, in many. Pasqualigo, Pino, Castelletti, and Borghini were highly regarded for comedy, and, fortuitously but significantly, the kind of commedia they cultivated was the weighty, emotional, and intricately plotted commedia grave with which many playwrights of academy or coterie in the second half of the sixteenth century hoped to give new aesthetic and moral seriousness to the genre.[8]

What is to be gained from the proposed reclassification of these twenty plays (for although Carrara mentions only about half of them, that half falls into his classifications given above) is not any permanent ordering system but a set of coordinates by which the path of the genre after Tasso may be traced, leading though a variety of experiments by writers who continued to search literary nature (which is how they conceived the world of literary forms) for the true shape of the pastoral play. Classifying the kinds with regard to mixtures of elements from diverse sources reveals something of the mutual attraction, largely underestimated by criticism, of courtly and popular traditions in Italian drama, and opens a new perspective on the distance between *Aminta* and *Il pastor fido* and on some of the developments in drama that contribute to this distance. Also, certain likenesses between the two, especially the commitment to verisimilitude and the tempered single style, avoiding clashes between high and low, appear less inevitable and more deliberate in the light of dissimilar combinations being made by contemporary rivals. Moreover, classifying these combinations in the pastoral play during its phase of definition incidentally throws into relief some elements that are significant for the English theater.

A   Antonio Ongaro, *Alceo, favola pescatoria* (Venice, 1582 [dedicated 1581]), 14 eds. to 1722.[9]

8. See chapters 1, 2, and 3.

9. See my *Italian Plays (1500–1700) in the Folger Library* (Florence, 1968), for further bibliographical details of the editions listed here, with the exception of Pescetti's *Regia pastorella*, which I have consulted at the Vatican Library and have included as the best-defined example of its particular and relatively rare type. The number of editions is taken from Lione Allacci, *Drammaturgia di Lione Allacci accresciuta e continuata fino all'anno MDCCLV* (Venice, 1755; facsimile repr. Turin, 1961). The plays by Della Valle, Pino, Gualterotti, Vida, Lupi, and Pescetti are not mentioned by Carrara.

B   Camillo Della Valle, *Fillide, egloga pastorale* (Ferrara, 1584 [per-
    haps written much earlier]), 1 ed.

C   Luigi Pasqualigo, *Gl'intricati, pastorale* (Venice, 1581 [published
    posthumously, probably written in the late 1570s]), 1 ed.

    Cristoforo Castelletti, *L'Amarilli, pastorale* (Venice, 1582 [first
    printed 1580, rev. 1582]), 9 eds., including original and 2 revised
    versions.

    Pietro Cresci, *Tirena, favola pastorale* (Venice, 1584 [written
    1584]), 2 eds.

    Cesare Simonetti, *Amaranta, favola boscareccia* (Padua, 1588), 1
    ed.

D   Luigi Groto, *La Calisto, nova favola pastorale* (Venice, 1583 [writ-
    ten 1561, rev. 1582]), 3 eds., 2 in Allacci.

    ———, *Il pentimento amoroso, nuova favola pastorale* (Venice,
    1585 [performed 1575]), 6 eds.

    Diomisso Guazzoni, *Andromeda, tragicomedia boscareccia* (Ven-
    ice, 1587 [possibly first printed 1574?]), perhaps 3 eds., 2 in
    Allacci.

    Gieronimo Vida, *Filliria, favola boscareccia* (Venice, 1587 [first
    printed 1585]), 4 eds.

    Pietro Lupi, *I sospetti, favola boschereccia* (Florence, 1589 [dedi-
    cated 1588]), 1 ed., 2 issues.

    Bernardino Percivallo, *L'Orsilia, boscareccia sdrucciola* (Bologna,
    1589), 1 ed.

E   Bernardino Pino, *L'Eunia, ragionamenti pastorali* (Venice, 1582
    [composed early, date unknown]), 1 ed.

    Raffaello Gualterotti, *La Verginia, rappresentazione amorosa*
    (Florence, 1584 [performed 1581, rev. 1582]), 1 ed.

    Camillo Della Valle, *Gelosi amanti, favola pastorale* (Ferrara,
    1585), 1 ed.

F   Orlando Pescetti, *La regia pastorella, favola boschereccia* (Verona,
    1589), 2 eds.

G   Giovanni Donato Cucchetti, *La pazzia, favola pastorale* (Venice,
    1597 [first printed 1581]), 5 eds.

    Gabriele Zinano, *Il Caride, favola pastorale* (Reggio, 1590? [first
    printed 1582, rev. 1590]), probably 3 eds., 2 in Allacci.

    Angelo Ingegneri, *Danza di Venere, pastorale* (Vicenza, 1584 [dedi-
    cated 1583]), 3 eds.

    Raffaello Borghini, *Diana pietosa, comedia pastorale* (Florence,
    1586 [first printed 1585]), 2 eds.

The features common to these plays reveal the conventions already accepted for the genre, with the sense thereby achieved of its being distinct from, if sometimes indebted to, other dramatic kinds in which pastoral and rustic elements also figure. No matter what the generic subtitle, they all have five acts and enjoy a fairly high degree of unity of time and place. Eight are set in Arcadia (Greece or Magna Graecia not specified), two elsewhere in Greece, and the rest in Italy. Lyly's Lincolnshire and Shakespeare's Arden are in the latter line of transplanted and rechristened Arcadias. All but Pino's are in verse, basically *endecadillabi, piani,* except for Groto's and Percivallo's *sdruccioli,* but with considerable metrical variation. Pastoral figures, names, song contests, love laments, praises of landscape, musing on the Golden Age, and comparisons of the country with the court are ubiquitous, usually in the style of Tasso and Sannazaro, often with evidence of direct recourse to the classical models of both. Montemayor also seems to be part of the common material, but his debt to Sannazaro makes for uncertainty in most cases. The following divisions are warranted by differences in organization of the common material, and by the introduction of other elements in combinations reminiscent of dissimilar pastorals that preceded *Aminta:*

A   Ongaro's *Alceo,* famed as "l' *Aminta* bagnato," is alone in a group reserved for pastorals in which the imitation of Tasso is carried out almost to the letter, in simple plot, single level of lyric style, and the absence of low humor and unverisimilar elements, other than the unexpendable figure of the satyr, who need not be represented more implausibly than as a hairy man, or, in *Alceo,* as a scaly one. He is another antecedent of Caliban.

B   Della Valle's *Fillide* illustrates the continuation of the court entertainment of the static, recited eclogue accompanied by mythological tableaux. Cases of love, here set in slight motion with minor complications stated as problems in the manner of court games, are demonstrated by a range of effects from tears to nymphs' practical jokes on an amorous old shepherd, which result in Ovidian transformations into trees and streams and require the personal intervention of deities. As in *Aminta,* the sense of elegant pastime and probably of neoplatonic rite is strong, but both these aspects are displayed in *Fillide* with uninhibitedly unverisimilar mythological representations. The play's direct predecessors include Poliziano's *Orfeo,* Sabba da Castiglione's *(La barona) Lamento del disgraziato Clonico pastore* (1528), and Epicuro's *Mirzia,* which, significantly, passed for new when published pseudonymously long after its author's death.[10]

C   A combination of broad clowning along rustic lines as a foil to the ideal manners and emotions of two or more pairs of shepherds and nymphs, with free use of unverisimilar elements, including Ovidian transformations and magic from the *romanzo* tradition, the distinguishing characteristic of this kind. Its forebears are less structured mixtures of coterie and folk types, such as Andrea Calmo's *Egloghe pastorali*, the rare *grottesca pastorale* occasionally cultivated by Mariano il Maniscalco in the early days of the Sienese artisan plays,[11] and Iacomo Contrini's *Lite amorosa, comedia nova pastorale* (1568), in which nymphs, shepherds, a comic peasant, and two raucous Spaniards are entangled until a magician-hermit decrees a double wedding. Inevitably the combination suggests Lyly's *Gallathea*, his *Love's Metamorphosis*, and even more *A Midsummer Night's Dream*.

D   Plays in this group are differentiated from those in group C by the absence of the clown. Not that comedy is lacking in this kind—the lascivious cavorting of a transvestite Jove and Mercury in Groto's *Calisto*, for example, is as broad as anything in the preceding group—but the peculiarly sharp contrast obtained by juxtaposition of the extremes, the farcical peasant or mechanical, whose language, manners, and grasp of life crazily reflect and comment on the shepherds, is missing. All the possibilities of magic and the supernatural are however left. Carrara classes Lollio's *Aretusa* (1564) and Beccari's *Sacrificio* (1555) together as simply comic, but Beccari's resolution of a love problem by transforming the blocking character into a wolf differentiates his view of the pastoral drama from Lollio's and links him with the later trials repre-

10. Selvaggio de' Selvaggii, *La Martia, pastoral comedia* (Parma, 1582). The attribution of *Mirzia* to Epicuro, as well as its relation to *La Martia* and to a still later version, *Trebazia*, are discussed by Parente in Marc'Antonio Epicuro, *I drammi e le poesie italiane e latine*, ed. Alfredo Parente (Bari, 1942), 233–52.

11. Andrea Calmo, *Le giocose moderne et facetissime egloghe pastorali* (Vinegia, 1553). For pastoral elements in the works of the Sienese Rozzi and their precursors see Roberto Alonge, *Il teatro dei Rozzi di Siena* (Florence, 1967), esp. 47ff. Ruzante's *La pastoral*, in Ruzante, *Teatro*, ed. Ludovico Zorzi (Milan, 1967), is related by its dialect and loose structure to this kind of pastoral entertainment, as is the later *Egloga pastorale di Morel*, ed. G. B. Pellegrini (Trieste, 1964).

sented by this group. Lollio tailored the pastoral to meet the demands of commedia regolare, whereas Beccari borrowed comic structure to support some classic pastoral actions alien to regular comedy.

E   Some pastoralists tried to draw nearer to the plausibility expected of urban commedia erudita by banishing magic and the supernatural. The result is city comedy in the country. When Gualterotti decided to revise for publication and add verisimilitude to his *Verginia*, first performed as a pastoral the preceding year, he had only to change the setting to Florence. The most powerful immediate example for dramatists pursuing this line was Lollio's *Aretusa*, in which the conventional attempted suicide of the lovelorn shepherd leads to a Terentian resolution of what turns out in retrospect to have been a New Comedy situation. Casalio's *Amaranta* (1538) and the *commedie villanesche* of the prime period of the Rozzi have a less direct but still visible kinship with the type. The strongly comic flavor is not confined to a single social level. Della Valle's pranksters are refined shepherds, but Pino uses rustics who are less like the abysmally crude villani of farces by the Rozzi than like the trim countryfolk of Lorenzo il Magnifico's *Nencia da Barberino*, closer to Jacquenetta of *Love's Labour's Lost* than to Audrey of *As You Like It*. Still, they are unconditionally rustic, designed not only in function but also in character as foils for the *pastori*.

F   Rare but not unknown to Italian literary drama is the pastoral in which characters of a rank fit for epic and tragedy mingle with the lowest of clowns, and in which the country is not a closed world to be measured against the spectator's extra-theatrical reality but a place to visit and to leave within the fiction, if not actually within the represented action. The type owes something to Giraldi Cinzio's earlier *tragedia di fin lieto*, and more to the commedia grave, but its true analogues are *As You Like It*, *Two Gentlemen of Verona*, and above all *The Winter's Tale*, which Pescetti's play also resembles not only in kind but in several details.

G   Were the *Pastor fido* included in my proposed classification it would belong here, although none of these plays is labeled *tragicommedia* or depends on the material of classical tragedy, as Guarini's play partly does. As in groups A and E, the supernatural element is rationalized as far as possible, and the worship of pagan deities conducted by priests with oracles is the fictive veil for late Renaissance Catholicism of the quietistic sort. The didactic possibilities of the pastoral are more fully developed in this type than in any other; the dialogue tends to the overtly metaphysical and the action to the psychologically complicated. The impression of weightiness and of attention to Aristotle, with a pointed concern for decorum and verisimilitude, is confirmed by the absence of clowns and magic. The plots are all elaborate syntheses disguising the extremes of which they are formed. In the complexity of structure and the numerous vestiges of comic characterization and relationships lies the major difference between plays of this group and *Aminta*. These playwrights, like Guarini, used and modified results of other pastoralists' experiments with comedy, whereas Tasso sidestepped the genre almost entirely. The famous "sorriso di Tasso" is only the mild light in which, as Toffanin has it, the favola pastorale looks into the mirror of Greek tragedy to see if there is a resemblance.[12]

Despite the differences represented by the above categories, these plays with one exception have more in common with each other than they have with *Aminta*. The point obscured by Carrara's divisions is that all of them but *Alceo*, including the "tragicomico" *Pastor fido*, depend on the intrigue structure of regular comedy and are therefore separated from Tasso by their first principle. True, all twenty of them testify by some borrowing or reference to admiration for Tasso, and the generic subtitle most in evidence among them is his *favola boscareccia*, which had the virtue of being the least committing to an established form, the most hospitable to experiment. For the structural means of dramatizing the borrowed material, however, only Ongaro followed the master's lead, and even his watery copy is more dramatic than the original, in that Alceo and his Eurilla are brought face to face at least once (III.4). Tasso's purpose in avoiding a confrontation may well have been part of a neoplatonic design, as Cody asserts, but the omission increases his singularity among pastoral dramatists.

The authors of the other nineteen plays turn back before Tasso to the example of the pastoral experimenters who were in one way or another tapping the resources of the regular comedy, rooted in society, involving a larger number of people and their various concerns. They reached toward drama in which love is not only divine furor, epiphany, or tragic obsession but also a motive in human relations adding to the complexity of ordinary life, where money, marriage, and family figure in an in-

12. Giuseppe Toffanin, *Il Tasso e l'età che fu sua* (Naples, 1949), 88.

terplay of personalities, generations, and classes. The relations among the characters in most of these plays betray exposure to comic practices. Earlier, in both courtly eclogue tableau and popular, semipastoral farce, there usually obtained a Saturnalian equality among mortals in common subjection to the sylvan deities, or a temporary juxtaposition of members of separate worlds, an extraordinary encounter of literary shepherds with local rustics and witches and gods, perhaps with burghers and princesses too. But attempts to make pastoral a regular dramatic genre brought a sense of society into the play, a suggestion of the social distinctions necessary to comedy and, under Guarini's influence, of the courtly hierarchy of tragedy. Pasqualigo's clowns represent a position of compromise. They are footloose on vacation in Arcadia, but they are snobbishly aware of social levels, urban ones at that, and Graciano claims a rank to which the *maga* declares him not entitled (V.5).

Guazzoni's Panfila is identified as a servant in the dramatis personae, and although she comes in for her share of the amorous unrest suffered by the loftier nymphs, her task is to fetch and carry: she is, in short, a fantesca from commedia erudita. The distance that Guarini's Amarilli perceives between herself and the enviably simple Arcadian shepherdess of her wistful imagination (II.5.627) is the semitragic version of the same social distinction.

Of the theatergrams of person drawn from the comic stable for the making of the pastoral play the most versatile and catalytic is the servo, who in commedia regolare may be a dynamic element, acting as an intriguer or go-between, or an ethical one, providing wit or absurdity, often borrowing characteristics from his fellows, the parasite and the braggart. Either way he functions in opposition to the sons, husbands, and fathers whose domestic conflicts constitute the intreccio—not in opposition to their plans, which he abets and often originates, but to their image of life. In the Arcadian social scale he is at the bottom, and his tag in the dramatis personae is usually capraio, *percoraio* (distinct from pastore), or villano. Occasionally, however, he is labeled *pastore* and only his behavior identifies him as an underling. Sometimes he performs lustful acts associated with satyrs and sometimes, on the contrary, a satyr is assigned some aspect of a comic servo role. In the plays in group G the servo exists only vestigially, as in the *Pastor fido,* where traces of him are visible in the Satiro, especially in his scenes with Corisca, echoing the exchanges in commedia erudita between servo and fantesca, and servo and *cortigiana.* The existence of such traces testifies to the history of this figure in the dramatization of the pastoral by

Guarini's time, whereas Tasso's Satiro is not comic, and although his view of love is different from Aminta's and inferior to it, it is not complementary in any of the ways that the servo's is to the padrone's.[13]

The lumpishness of the clowns' lechery, incomprehension of love, or devotion to some gross object—edible, potable, or bestial—may simultaneously show off and show up the delicacy and intensity of the courtly shepherds.

In a single scene (II.3) Cresci's Orsacchio runs through a repertory of comic commonplaces proper to the villano. He begins with Terentian complaints about servitude, refers to his own love for the indifferent "Smartilla," in its brevity and infidelity a travesty of the pastoral ideal, likens himself to an ass who carries wine but drinks water,[14] gets drunk, and has a song contest with his friend Corbaccio. They stagger off together, ending with a mock-platonic reference to blindness, whereupon the Chorus with bland violence juxtaposes a serious observation on the timidity of true lovers and the coldness of beautiful women.

Guazzoni uses Montano, a capraio, or goatherd, as a busy manipulating and tangling agent bored by love, interested in food and drink, and given to swearing by Mercury, the god of thieves (and also, to Cinquecento audiences, the god of servi by dint of his masquerade as Sosia in *Amphitruo* and its adaptations in commedia erudita). Speaking good Tuscan and never descending to slapstick, however, Montano also testifies to the gradual refinement of the rustic servo to fit him for the complex but homogenized pastoral drama of Guarini and the playwrights of group G.

13. In his *Compendio,* on the subject of mixing the social ranks, "persone grandi" and "persone vilissime," Guarini offers justifications that nullify each other; that is, that humble characters are introduced only as instruments, not so that their manners may be depicted, and that the confidants and *nudrici* of noble persons are not really humble, but only less noble than the persons to whom they are attached. See *Il pastor fido e Il compendio della poesia tragicomica,* ed. Gioachino Brognoligo (Bari, 1914), 256. In practice Guarini's Satiro is a restrained delineation fit for the middle genre, but his ambiguous sharpness reflects the conventional presentation of the *servo scaltro.*

14. Images of asses and hallucinations are common in clown scenes, although only Pasqualigo amalgamates and expands them into a transformation like Bottom's. The deformation of the name Amarilli into "Smartilla" is also used by Castelletti's Zampilla (I.4); mispronunciation of difficult words by the unlettered servo had by mid-century been used nearly to the point of exhaustion in commedia erudita and passed on to improvised comedy.

Intrigue structure, as a means of translating matter into motion, was definitive in making the pastoral play and is the characteristic shared by the greatest number of these samples. As a critical term in this connection, intrigue structure must be allowed no more than its literal meaning of "complex pattern" involving a substantial number of characters with individual aims, whether or not their actions contribute severally to dramatic conflicts and resolutions. Dynamic use of intrigue structure was a comic ideal characteristic of many of these pastorals, including those of Castelletti, Lupi, Cucchetti, and Guarini, but static or expository handling of an intrigue situation also occurs. Instead of the single case of love proceeding along an episodic line to its end, as in *Aminta* and *Alceo*, all the plays in groups B through G contain multiple love affairs. In *Fillide* Della Valle presents love affairs with three different obstacles, and tries to avoid simple parallelism by slightly intertwining the cases, using the comic devices of misunderstanding and mistaken identity. In his next pastoral, *Gelosi amanti*, he enlarges and twists his plot further in the direction of comedy and employs the trick of transvestism.

When Bibbiena established transvestism onstage in *La Calandria* by merging the disguise of sex from medieval narrative with mistaken identity as used in New Comedy, he set the theatrical precedent for a device that would flourish also in Arcadian nondramatic genres (as it did in Montemayor's much-imitated *Diana*). By the time the dramatization of pastoral had become a serious concern, transvestism was an old theatergram of action. Pino denounced the device in comedy as worn-out and absurd,[15] but his pastoral *ragionamenti* include a shepherd disguised as a nymph and a nymph disguised as her own brother, with results familiar to audiences of both *La Calandria* and *Twelfth Night*. Either Pino wrote his pastoral play before tiring of the commonplace or he had different standards for verisimilitude in the pastoral, perhaps sharing Guarini's conception of the mode as the image of virginal human nature rather than as a mirror of custom and daily life. The other pastoral dramatists who used the disguise of sex in the 1570s and 1580s apparently did not hold its familiarity against it. Characteristically, Guarini accepts this comic theatergram, but tones it down by keeping it offstage, while making it the foundation of Mirtillo's narration of falling in love (II.1.59).

With or without transvestites, static or dynamic, nineteen of the twenty plays under consideration reveal attempts to make multiple

15. Bernardino Pino, *Gli ingiusti sdegni, comedia* (Rome, 1553), Prologo.

cases of love intertwine, depend on, or otherwise affect one another, and to achieve that integrated complexity in demand by writers and theorists of commedia grave. In addition to the tangle of misplaced affections that Beccari had borrowed earlier for *Il sacrificio,* most of the commonplaces of situation and action known to Italian comedy are annexed by these pastoralists: long-lost relatives whose recognition brings about the general resolution, disappearances, presumed deaths, vows taken or broken, mistakes in identity growing out of these past events, perpetuated and multiplied by disguises.

The roots of the action in Castelletti's *Amarilli* lie in a ten-year-old scandal involving supposed murder, madness, and the heroine's flight under an alias. Della Valle's Celio searches for his runaway sister, who masquerades as her brother. In Gualterotti's singularly inept play, Beatrice, disguised as Isabella, wants Verginia to be magically changed into a boy, until Verginia turns out to be her missing husband in disguise. Pescetti's shepherdess is enabled to marry the prince of Lidia by the discovery that she is the long-lost daughter of the king of Caria. Such pressures from the past not only touch off individual actions at different moments in a play but also contribute to the tension of its action in a five-act present as a whole. A similar framing effect is sometimes achieved, as in comedy, through a motive more immediate in time, such as the determination of Guazzoni's Cupid to subjugate the elusive Andromeda, a purpose that agitates and unifies all parts of the play. Guazzoni's work, like Lyly's *Gallathea,* suggests the interest of dramatists in making internal action, involving specific characters in a comic movement of pursuit and evasion, out of Tasso's less dramatic use in prologue and epilogue of the ancient motif of the errant Cupid.

The complexity is great even in plays where the stories seem to exist primarily in support of the kind of neoplatonism that Cody finds in *Aminta.* Ingegneri's *Danza di Venere,* short on low comic elements but full of the sort of Terentian echoes dear to regular comedy, inherits from Boccaccio's tale of Cimone (*Decameron* V.1) its theme of love's power to refine and the lover's consequent power to act. The time setting is May Day, Venus is in the ascendant, and her power is centrally dramatized: a dance is performed in the middle of the play (III.3), not as part of choral intermezzo but in the action proper, and is immediately followed by the abduction (a literal *raptio*) of the heroine. But for all the symbolism, the pattern of action is not that of *Aminta* but that of commedia erudita and its New Comedy heritage, its continual quarrying of novelle, its peripeties, recognitions, and large-scale final reunions. Although Groto's *Pentimento amoroso* also seems designed primarily to run a neoplatonic gamut of loves, its aim is achieved by employing a large number of characters in a complex design of cross-purposes and motives typical of the comic structure most admired in the author's day.

All the standard comic features absent from *Aminta* are present, though blunted, in Guarini's *Pastor fido*. His use of tragedy, specifically of Sophocles', was not a violent mutation in the comic evolution of pastoral drama. *Il pastor fido* is undoubtedly a result of the confluence of comedy with tragedy characteristic of the period, but so is commedia grave. Although Guarini associates his *antefatto* (the curse on Arcadia and the oracle) with *Oedipus rex*, the use of a framework story giving dramatic action a past and a relation to time and futurity was a practice of comedy also used by pastoralists more obviously comic than Guarini. Commonplaces of situation and action found both in New Comedy and in *Oedipus rex* (lost children, mistakes, and linked recognitions) were developed in Cinquecento comedy with consciousness of both sources. The foundations for Guarini's claim to the invention of the third genre were laid by those writers of commedia grave who boasted of closing the gap between comedy and tragedy and invoked Sophocles without any apparent sense of inconguity, as Maleguzzi's editor had claimed the pattern of *Oedipus rex* for *Theodora,* or as Della Porta was said to have done for *La sorella.*[16] The phenomenon brings to mind, with due reservations, Northrop Frye's identification of New Comedy as a concealed "comic Oedipus situation."[17]

In the pastoral also it was possible to use intrigue structure as an expression of the ubiquitous late sixteenth-century theme of the discrepancy between appearance and reality, by making metaphor of highly developed intreccio. With the precedent of occasional references in early Cinquecento comedies to the existence of a power higher than human foresight,[18] which arranges denouements while human beings think

16. See chapter 1, and the printer's dedication to G. B. Della Porta, *La sorella, comedia* (Naples, 1604).

17. Northrop Frye, "The Argument of Comedy," *English Institute Essays,* ed. D. A. Robertson (New York, 1948), 59.

18. An example is the exclamation of Ariosto's Cleandro, "E tu credi, Filogono, che così dal cielo ordinato era; che per altra che per questa via non era possibile che del mio Carino avessi mai ricognizione" (V.8: And you must believe, Filogono, that it was so ordained by Heaven; that in no other way could I have known my Carino again). *I suppositi,* prose version in Ludovico Ariosto, *Opere minori,* ed. Cesare Segre (Milan and Naples, 1954). Comments on un-

their entanglements hopeless, writers of commedia grave were using their complex plots as illustration of the happily ironic truth that when mortals, especially lovers, think themselves in unresolvable difficulties, they are in reality merely traversing the dark phase of a providential plan for their happiness. Commentaries placed in the last act as pointers to this truth, and the use of labyrinthine intrigue as structural metaphor of Divine Providence, attended by ironic peripeties and musings on human blindness to the ways of heaven were the hallmarks of the most elaborate and self-conscious kind of literary comedy during and preceding the decade in which *Aminta* appeared. Underlying the tendency was a general distrust of overconfidence in human reason, action, and ability to perceive truth. This Counter-Reformation quietistic moralism, by which Matteo Cerini would distinguish Guarini from the "Renaissance" Tasso, is in fact endemic in Italian drama of all genres after 1550,[19] whether articulated in detail or merely gestured at in exclamations on the providential efficacy of love or some other benign, suprahuman force.

The metaphoric use of intrigue plot was a practice ripe for exploitation in conjunction with such pastoral tropes and figures as the blind Cupid, the labyrinth of love, and love-death (symbolized in attempted suicide, or apparently fatal disappearance or transformation) causing changes or awakenings of heart. Tasso turns the commonplace of the shepherd's suicidal leap into a literally fortunate fall,[20] and his chorus comments on the discrepancy in knowledge that separates Love from his mortal victims on the "ignote strade" to happiness (V.1.1839–47). But Tasso limits application of this perception to the power of Love, platonic without the Christian overtones it would have in *Il pastor fido*, and uses it as simple declaration without benefit of support from a complex intrigue plot.

When Cresci paraphrases Tasso, however, he does so with specific

---

foreseen resolutions in Latin comedy are on the whole more casual and refer to chance rather than providence. See for example Plautus, *Captivi*, Prologue, and Terence, *Phormio* (V.757).

19. Matteo Cerini, "L'ombra di un capolavoro: Il *Pastor Fido* del Guarini," *Letterature Moderne* 7, no. 4 (1957): 459.

20. V.1.1877: "Fu felice il precipizio." Quotations from *Aminta* are from Bàrberi Squarotti's edition. In this speech Elpino goes on to say that under the sad image of death the fall brought life and joy to Aminta.

reference to the resolution of the entanglement, and extends the range of his observation with philosophical generalization:

> Certamente la legge, onde governa
> Amore 'l mondo è cosi giusta, e retta,
> Che quando men si spera nel suo regno
> Haver del suo servire il guiderdone;
> All'hor piu si consegue, *ma l'humana*
> *Natura, ch'è imperfetta non discerne*
> *L'arti celesti sue,* e le maniere
> E gli incogniti modi, ond'egli pone
> I suoi seguaci in non sperata gioia.
>
> (V.2 [italics mine])

Truly the law by which Love rules the world is so just and right that in his kingdom when one least hopes for reward of his service, the more he then receives, but human nature, which is imperfect, does not discern his celestial arts and manners and the unknown ways by which he places his followers in unhoped-for joy.

Ingeneri's Coridone, resolved on abduction but unwilling to presume enough on Venus's goodwill to seek sanctuary in her temple, marks the transitional phase in the gradual recognition of the pattern of his action when he recognizes that

> Non lece à noi d'interpretar la mente
> De gli alti Dei. Ciò forse ad alcun fine
> Venere volle, il qual è à noi celato.
>
> (III.1)

It is forbidden us to interpret the mind of the high gods. That which is hidden to us is perhaps willed to some purpose by Venus.

Cucchetti's *Pazzia,* still closer to *Il pastor fido* in this respect, is dominated by an emphasis on the worship of Jove, greater than other gods, to whom are addressed prayers with a Christian flavor (IV.5). Livia's bad advice to Alteria not to trust Fileno is based on the principle that one should never trust unless "l'esperienza unica madre / Della ra-gion, non se ne faccia certa" (experience, sole mother of reason, verifies it), to which Alteria answers that it is foolish to test basic things ordered by "sommo Dio de gl'altri Dei" (II.7: the highest God of gods), and the unfolding of the plot proves her antiempirical Counter-Reformation orthodoxy to have been right. At the end the character of Branco, a deceiver much like Corsica, is forgiven for his machinations because the actions he did for ill turned out to be for good, as heaven intended: he was the unwitting instrument, the others the surprised beneficiaries (V.3).

Pasqualigo's prologue emphasizes his play's need for explanation because of its being *intricato;* his Selvaggia observes that the lovers have been set at cross-purposes by the "disegni fallaci" (fallacious designs) of the "cieche menti nostre" (I.2: our blind minds) and to the joint prayer "O mostrane la via, ch' uscir possiamo / Fuori di così oscuro labirinto" (IV.1: Oh show us the way out of so dark a labyrinth) a heavenly voice assents. The assent always comes, the conclusion is always hymeneal combination and pacification, a *discordia concors* that reveals love's providence (in plays of group G extending in the direction of Christian Providence), and the power of the providence and the wonder it arouses are in direct ratio to the complexity of the knot that it unties.

Guarini's view is still more clearly Counter-Reformation Christian, allowing for the veil of pagan terms. The paean in *Il pastor fido* at the moment of recognition includes a rehashing of the misunderstandings and confusions, all owed to the

> cecità de le terrene menti!
> In qual profonda notte,
> In qual fosca caligine d'errore
> Son le nostr' alme immerse,
> Quando tu non le illustri, o sommo Sole!
> (V.6.1039–43)

blindness of earthly minds! In what deep night, in what dark fog of error are our souls immersed, unless you illuminate them, oh highest Sun!

Later in the same speech Tirenio apostrophizes heaven directly: "O alta providenza, o sommi dei" (1117: Oh, high providence, oh lofty gods).[21]

Although the image of blindness is probably the one most often used by Italian pastoralists to express the general difference between appearance and reality, especially in love, the image of the labyrinth also un-

---

21. Quotations from *Il pastor fido* are from the edition of Luigi Fassò in *Teatro del Seicento* (Milan and Naples, 1956).

derscores frequently and specifically the function of the intrigue structure as the metaphor of human error. It was a theatergram of design often employed in comedy, but one that pastoral drama could use more searchingly because of the half-articulated understanding that the subject of the pastoral in general was the mind or heart, and because the scene of the pastoral drama in particular included a wood. The *selva* and *prato* ordinarily specified in stage directions are part of one set, but they are two different places. As the writer of comedy could make his characters wander the maze of a city represented by a few houses and three or four streets converging on a piazza, still more dramatically could the pastoral playwright render visible the erring of love by developing emotionally contrasting atmospheres for meadow and forest, without stretching the unity of place any more than it was stretched by the comedy set in which a neighborhood stands for a whole city.

The dark wood confirmed by Dante as a landscape for human error had also for the late Cinquecento poet the specific aspect of labyrinth of love, reminiscent of Horace and Petrarch but primarily identified with *Orlando furioso,* in which it is fictional "fact," principle of plotting, and, continually simile.[22] Mario Praz's intuition of a spiritual affinity between *Orlando furioso* and *A Midsummer Night's Dream* merely omits the middle term in the process of transmission,[23] the pastoral play in which the woods, and the love errantry and its amazing effects, take on the solidity of stage place, stage persons, and stage action. The playwrights' recognition of Ariosto's importance to the genre is expressed in their including him in prefatory genealogies and in their plundering of *Orlando furioso.* Della Valle places Ariosto with Petrarch in the first rank of pastoral authority by using both to make his plays partial centos—his rule in *Fillide* is as follows "E sempre obligo di chiudere il terzetto, e le stanze delle canzoni con un verso del Petrarca" (Each tercet [in *terza rima*] and each stanza of the *canzoni* must end with a line from Petrarch" [title-page]); and in *Gelosi amanti* he quotes Ariosto by the

22. The most telling is the famous "Gli [amor] è come una gran selva, ove la via conviene a forza, a chi vi va fallire: chi su, chi giù, chi qua, chi là travia" ([Love] is like a great forest, in which whoever goes must lose his way: all go astray, one up, another down, one here, another there). Ludovico Ariosto, *Orlando furioso,* ed. Lanfranco Caretti (Milan and Naples, 1954), XXXIV.2.3–5.

23. Mario Praz, "Ariosto in England," *The Flaming Heart: Essays on Crashaw, Machiavelli, and Other Studies in the Relations between Italian and English Literature from Chaucer to T. S. Eliot* (Garden City, N.Y., 1958) 301–05.

same rule in acts 1 and 3, Petrarch in 2 and 4, and both, alternately, in act 5.

Even when not directly quoted, *Orlando furioso* is often evoked by the presence of didactic sorcerers resembling Atlante or Melissa, and by pastoral transformations, especially those of the loquacious arboreal variety, in which Ariosto's particular blend of the amorous cause from Ovid and Petrarch with the monitory effect from Vergil is dominant.[24] The Ariostean atmosphere is as natural to the pastorals of Pasqualigo, Guazzoni, and all the others in which magic or love madness occur as it is alien to *Aminta*. Like Beccari and Giraldi Cinzio before him, however, Tasso uses the forest in sinister contrast to the meadow or pleasance. The satyr's (narrated) attack on Silvia takes place in the woods, but not as part of labyrinthine action. Many of Tasso's successors, on the other hand, use the woods for visual demonstration of tragic error and complex action. In Groto's *Pentimento amoroso*, for example, tangled in love's deceits, Filovevia is lured to the woods by a potential murderer (IV.3), while Dieromena wanders in another part of the forest (IV.3), beset with Dantesque thoughts of the many shepherds who have committed suicide there (IV.4).

As it was not forbidden by rationalizing theory, Guarini also uses the forest in opposition to the pleasance by making it the chosen ambience of Silvio, the opposer of love, the place where he kills the boar and ironically where he wounds himself with love by wounding Dorinda, who wears her wolf's disguise (IV.8). But Guarini does not develop the wood as a place of error, because he has no need to limit this kind of movement to a single locus. His Arcadia does not include error but is itself in error, and not only about love. When the oracle's truth is finally understood, providence recognized, the general redemption is expressed in a metaphor reminiscent of Tasso's "ignote strade":

> Eterni numi, oh come son diversi
> Quegli alti, inaccessibili sentieri,
> Onde scendono a noi le vostre grazie,
> Da que' fallaci e torti,
> Onde i nostri pensier salgono al cielo!
> (V.6.1207–11)

---

24. In *Orlando furioso*, VI.27–53, the voice of Astolfo speaks from a tree, describing his seduction and transformation by the Circean Alcina as a warning to Ruggero, a hero still more susceptible than Aeneas to distraction from his dynastic mission.

Eternal gods, oh, how different are those high, inaccessible paths by which your grace descends to us from the erring and wrong ones by which our thoughts ascend to heaven!

But this perception of the common experience is preceded by individual recognitions of mistaken directions and providential actions in the separate cases that make up the complex plot.[25] The metaphor of twisted paths in fact describes what the spectator has witnessed in the entanglements of the multiple plot.

Certain pastoral actions that were impossible to represent on the street set prescribed for commedia erudita without losing the verisimilitude prized by its practitioners were nevertheless naturally suited to articulation within the comic intrigue structure of misunderstandings, cross-purposes, misplaced affections, recognitions, and reversals. One of these actions is sleeping, which occurs in ten of the twenty plays; another is dreaming, which occurs in eight. For authorized pastoral sleep, Italian dramatists needed to look no farther afield than to Sannazaro's *Arcadia*. Uranio's sleep in the second eclogue, and Sincero's sleep and allegorical dream in the twelfth prose episode, demonstrate the utility of these actions for contrast between the real and the apparent, the inner life and the outer. In the theater, Beccari had used sleep in combination with the truth drug administered by the Satiro to Turico to discover the name of his love (*Il sacrificio*, I.5). Among early rustic plays, the whole of *La pastoral* is projected by the dream of Ruzante, who unlike Shakespeare's Christopher Sly is also an actor in his own dream. Still earlier, semidramatic use of the dream is recorded among the mimes and clowns before the flourishing of the proto-Rozzi, to trace back no farther the path of a very old topos. The dreams are often compliments to patrons, like Glauca's panegyric of the Estes in Percivallo's *Orsilia* (II.4), and even when not so locally applicable are flexibly symbolic, providing the playwright with one more way to represent the effects of love. There was no rule against recounting dreams in commedia erudita. The phenomenon is rare, however, because in comedy the dream cannot be connected with sleep in the same organic way as in the pastoral, for simple lack of a locus, the comic street set affording no closer equivalent to places of rest than uncomfortable balconies and open loggias.

25. See Coridone's recognition that his loss of Corisca was really a gain (IV.7). His case is a minor eddy that repeats the major movement while contributing to it, an example of the functional complexity Guarini boasts of in the *Compendio*.

In the pastoral setting, on the contrary, falling asleep on grassy banks is a natural action that almost effortlessly makes for misunderstandings, deceits, and reversals desirable to the plot. It can be the occasion for attempted rape abridged into the stealing of a kiss, as in Guazzoni's *Andromeda* (I.8) or in Groto's *Pentimento amoroso* (III.1), where Menfestio finds Panurgia asleep and, acting on his impulse to kiss her, changes her love for him to a fury that begets further action. Or the rape may not be abridged, as in Groto's *Calisto,* in which case both the sleeping and its consequences occur offstage and are only narrated (V.1). The sleep of Ingegneri's Amarilli cures madness and engenders love in Coridone (I.1), converts Amarilli herself by means of a dream (II.5), and sets off several complications. Sometimes, as in *Gl'intricati,* sleep is induced by magicians to pierce through illusion to reality, truth, and self-knowledge. Lyly's *Endymion,* as well as *A Midsummer Night's Dream* and *The Tempest,* suggest the range of variations this pastoral convention could support.

Il pastor fido contains the distilled result of continued variation on the topos of sleep-dream in Montano's prophetic dream (I.4.790–819), which Guarini uses in the oracular manner more common in tragedy and at the end dignifies with redefinition as "sogno non già, ma vision celeste!" (V.6.1160: no dream indeed but a heavenly vision); in Tirenio's imagery; and in Mirtillo's concluding speech describing the realization of his happiness as dreamlike (V.10.1591–97). In none of the Italian plays are sleep and dream used so insistently or made so encompassing as by Shakespeare and Calderón, but the convention inviting such use owed its existence in considerable part to pastoral drama.

The pastoral device best suited to dramatic demonstration of the nature of love was one utterly forbidden even to the most romantic commedia grave. The magicians, alchemists, astrologers, and necromancers who turn up often in regular comedy, claiming many powers including that of transforming people into other forms, invariably turn out to be charlatans. But as several of these twenty pastoral plays demonstrate, real magic and Ovidian metamorphosis were stock elements of the third genre. The transformations of clowns into animals and fountains constitute one example, and metamorphoses of the nobler characters are more common still.

The preferred sources include the episode of Circe in the *Odyssey,* that of Polydorus in the *Aeneid,* many stories of the *Metamorphoses,* and the Renaissance epic amalgams of them all, especially Ariosto's. In drama, on the courtly academic side, was the precedent of mythological pageants and plays in which kaleidoscopic spectacles were standard features. Epicuro had turned a shepherd into a fountain and a nymph into a tree and had restored the nymph onstage. The dominant Ferrarese line of pastoral drama produced examples running the gamut from prayers for metamorphosis in Lollio's realistic *Aretusa,* through Beccari's offstage transformation of a troublesome character into a wolf, to Giraldi's transformation, also offstage, of his entire female cast into woodland properties.[26] On the rustic side, the Rozzi also turned nymphs into fountains and trees,[27] and in his more academic but not much more dramatic *Egloghe pastorali* Calmo mixed Ovid with medieval magic: old Fondolo, for example, becomes a talking stone statue onstage (III.1), Clonico turns into a tree (III.2), and both are restored by the arts of the Maga and her familiar devil (III.3).

Cresci transforms Dafne both into a fountain (III.1) and back again (V.1), whereas Vida merely restores (V.7) a nymph who has been a fountain since before the beginning of the play. Like Lyly's Fidelia in *Love's Metamorphosis,* Della Valle's Fillide appears first as a talking tree, but, more fortunate than Fidelia, she is restored by Cupid and bestowed on a shepherd (V.7, 8). A less spectacular kind of metamorphosis, one closer to the practice of regular comedy although hardly verisimilar, is the transformation of one nymph into another by Venus and Cupid in Della Valle's *Gelosi amanti* (IV.1). Groto has Jove and Mercury take on and put off the forms of Diana and her nymph Isse. These exchanges of identity and sex are radically different from those in comedy, in that they are real instead of feigned. Although mere disguise became common in pastoral drama under the influence of comic practice, genuine transformation was never permitted in regular comedy.

Like stage sleeping and dreaming, stage metamorphosis can lead to and express perceptions of illusion, including love, and perceptions of truth, also including love. In pastoral drama, which by its nature is a means to such insights, metamorphosis can have the effect of a play within a play. Both the genre and the particular action belong to an inward movement in late Renaissance theater, and metamorphosis was an action peculiarly effective for gaining distance from the external world of physical law and historical fact. It was part of continued experimen-

26. [Epicuro] *Selvaggio de' Selvaggi, Martia,* III.2, II.9, III.3; Lollio, *Aretusa,* IV.4; Beccari, *Il sacrificio,* V.6; G. B. Giraldi Cinzio, *Egle, satira* (n.p. [Ferrana], n.d. [1545–50?]), V.5.

27. Alonge, *Il teatro dei Rozzi,* 53, 56.

tation toward the unverisimilar, the opposite direction from that which the Italian pastoral play would ultimately be made to take. In *Aminta,* as in *Pastor fido,* magic and metamorphosis are not admitted into the play proper except as psychological change. The supernatural and implausible are banished to the intermezzi. Only Tasso's lyrics for the intermezzi to *Aminta* are extant, without descriptions of the action, but it is safe to assume that the spectacle accompanying Proteo's verses included transformation. Guarini's stage directions omit no technical possibility of metamorphosis: he specifies appearances of nymphs from trees and streams, satyrs from stones, and so forth, with admonitions to "imitare il verisimile." [28]

The nonmagical Ovidian incident of Silvia's bloody veil and apparent death is imitated from Tasso by playwrights in different groups: Ingegneri, Pino, Lupi, Vida, for example. Apparently a reminder of Ovid seemed essential to some pastoralists, together with an action symbolizing death or radical change, but an equally strong need for verisimilitude caused them to prefer his story of Pyramus and Thisbe to those involving metamorphosis. Vida uses both actions, although without the Shakespearean irony in *A Midsummer Night's Dream* of presenting the magical metamorphosis as real and the episode of Pyramus and Thisbe as a play. Guarini, as usual, assimilates the experiments and rationalizes the results into verisimilitude. Dorinda's neardeath in *Il pastor fido* occurs while she is *disguised* as a beast.

Guazzoni combines supernatural effects of many sorts: a magician, a dragon, Cupid roaming in human form (female, then male), Florido petrified into a statue (III.7) and restored (IV.4). But the eventual triumph of verisimilitude is unexpectedly forecast in this play: Florido's discussion of his transformation with Fillide reveals that it was effected by hypnosis (IV.4)—in short that it was apparent, a deceit of the senses, pointing to the conclusion that human perception and human art are defective. The mago is benevolent and powerful, but his art operates only to create illusion and change Florido's exaggeratedly high opinion of human power. Like the magic rite in Lupi's *Sospetti,* which takes place offstage and though effective is strongly doubted by one of the characters, Guazzoni's use of metamorphosis is an approach to the plausible and natural, or at least to the debunking of magic, which together with the judiciary arts was under Inquisitional ban. The skep-

28. Guarini, "Intermezzi per una rappresentazione del *Pastor fido,*" in *Teatro del Seicento,* ed. Fassò, 319–22.

ticism of Lupi's doubter is an additional *sospetto*, working out the central theme of mistrust but like Guazzoni's treatment of metamorphosis, it also points toward Guarini's use of the pastoral to make orthodox comments about magic and divination, without altogether losing the attendant theatrical benefit. Guarini follows Tasso in neutralizing magic as medicine and goes beyond him in making pagan superstition a counter for true faith, the Arcadian oracle a veil for Divine Providence. At the moment of recognition, when blind Tirenio exclaims,

> O Montano, di mente assai più cieco
> Che non son io di vista,
> Qual prestigio, qual démone t'abbaglia
> (V.6.1049–51)

Oh Montano, more blind of mind than I of sight, what artifice, what demon dazzles you.

Guarini glosses the word *prestigio* as follows: "Voce latina, che secondo i teologi è un inganno che non ha la sua causa dalla parte della cosa che si trasforma, ma da quella di colui che vede o in quanto all'organo o in quanto alla potenza" (A Latin word which, according to theologians, means a deceit which takes its cause not from the thing transformed but from the person who observes it, with reference either to his organ of sight or to the power).[29] The idea of a demon, here merely part of a metaphor but in broader pastoral practice a member of the dramatis personae, and the careful explanation of the term *prestigio* as a defect in the eye of the beholder (the kind of hallucination, in fact, by which Guazzoni's magician accomplishes a metamorphosis), are a key to Guarini's realistic adaptation of elements that elsewhere were used externally but to express the same inner states of blindness and confusion.

When the pastoral play was finally established by Guarini as a genre that could be defended in Aristotelian terms against stricter Aristotelians, all that was really left of metamorphosis was change of heart and maturing under the pressures of love. Development in character was uncommon in other regular genres of Italian drama, owing to the demands of unity of time and of the decorum regulating fixed types. It is rare in commedia erudita for characters to fall out of love or change their objects, except when death, discovery of consanguinity, or some

---

29. Guarini, "Annotazioni al *Pastor fido*," quoted by Fassò, *Teatro del Seicento*, 301 n. 1051.

similarly external event intervenes to rearrange the situation. The countless shifts and conversions of pastoral lovers, however, with or without magic and metamorphosis, opened new possibilities of characterization. And when magic and metamorphosis are subsumed under this more verisimilar psychological alternation, the impression of something like growth or at least mutability in characters is heightened.

What happened to the Italian pastoral play is ironic. It seems to have been cultivated out of need for a genre that unlike the other dramatic genres in the sixteenth century could deal with "virgin human nature,"[30] with love and change, a genre that in its stylized way would probe reality rather than mirror it. Serious playwrights were committed by their critical bias to imitate life, however, and in seeking to make the needed third genre respectable in terms of current theory, many of them tried to restrict the pastoral, characterized by a vision for the mind's eye, to action that could not be rejected by the testimony of the senses.

The homogeneity of tone and style and the verisimilitude common to *Aminta* and *Il pastor fido* gradually dominated the genre, without ever becoming a rule. When Castelletti revised *Amarilli* for the last time,[31] he cut his clownish rustics from four to one and did away entirely with the naiad and the Ovidian transformation. As a result, the comic discord of styles is reduced, plausibility is gained at the expense of charm, and *Amarilli* moves from group C into group E. Although even after *Il pastor fido* was in print there appeared pastoral plays containing magic, gods, and combinations of high style with low, clowning with idealized love,[32] such mixtures were more likely to be found in intermezzi, commedia dell'arte scenarios, or music drama derived from pastoral.[33] As the seventeenth century began, the literary pastoral play had years of life ahead, but in those years the imitations of *Il pastor fido* would out-

30. Battista Guarini, *Il Verato ovvero difesa di quanto ha scritto M. Giason Denores contra le tragicomedie, e le pastorali, in un suo discorso di poesia* (Ferrara, 1588), 11v. Guarini's omission of the phrase when he revised *Il Verato* and *Il Verato secondo* as *Il compendio della poesia tragicomica* may indicate belated recognition of how far from the simple eclogue and how near to the "artifices of the city" his tragicomedy had taken the pastoral mode.

31. Cristoforo Castelletti, *L'Amarilli, pastorale. Nuovamente dall'istesso auttore accresciuta, emendata, e quasi formata di nuovo* (Venice, 1587).

32. See for example Carrara, *La poesia pastorale*, 367ff.

33. For examples of special uses of pastoral elements in seventeenth-century intermezzi and melodrammi see Beatrice Corrigan, "Tasso's Erminia in the Italian Theater of the Seicento," *Renaissance Drama* 7 (1964): 127–50.

number other types of pastoral, and the imitation would be closer to their original than *Il pastor fido* had been to *Aminta*.

Tasso had rejected not only magic, metamorphosis, and clowns but also intrigue structure and other accoutrements of comedy. Guarini, on the contrary, expanded Tasso's speeches and situations, maintaining his verisimilitude and unified tone in a dramatic action that carried forward the series of attempts to match the pastoral milieu with the form of comedy, and vice versa. Guarini's baroque aim, to establish a middle genre fusing tragedy and comedy, distinct from both, had certain requirements:

> dall'una [tragedia] . . . le persone grandi e non l'azione; la favola verisimile ma non vera; gli affetti mossi, ma rintuzzati; il diletto, non la mestizia; il pericolo, non la morte; dall'altra [commedia] il riso non dissoluto, le piacevolezze modeste, il nodo finto, il rivolgimento felice, & sopratutto l'ordine comico.

> from the one [tragedy] . . . high characters but not high action; the plot verisimilar but not true; the passions moved, but tempered; not sadness, but pleasure; danger, not death; from the other [comedy] laughter not dissolute, seemly pleasantries, the fictional intrigue, the happy reversal, and above all the order of comedy [from trouble to joy].[34]

But even the "high" characters of *Il pastor fido* bear the marks of comic ancestry, the verisimilar action was a demand of comedy as much as of tragedy, and both passions and danger had long been essential to the intrecci of commedia grave. The experiments in pastoral drama that continued until Guarini's synthesis finally established an orthodoxy for the genre help to identify and weigh the constituent elements of the orthodoxy. Prime among them is the regular comedy, a source of structure and character types for the overwhelming majority of experiments and for Guarini as well.

When Jonard contrasts the play of love and chance in traditional comedy, by which he means Attic New Comedy and its Renaissance continuation, with that of love and destiny in *Il pastor fido*,[35] he makes a distinction that could as well serve to distinguish the regular commedia

---

34. Guarini, *Compendio della poesia tragicomica*, in Brognoligo, ed., *Il pastor fido*, 231.

35. Norbert Jonard, "Le baroquisme du *Pastor Fido*," *Studi secenteschi* 9 (1969): 7.

grave of the first half of the sixteenth century from the intensification of its gravity in the second half. Guarini's synthesis of comedy and tragedy was made at a time when comedy was already imbued with certain tragic principles and practices, so that the division between his debts to the one genre or the other is not as sharp or the balance as equal as his own analysis would make them.

The elements that faded from the orthodox pastoral play, especially fantasy and the contrast between high and low styles as they appear in the experiments of the 1570s and 1580s, also help to explain the difference between *Aminta*, where they are quite absent, and *Il pastor fido*, where they exist vestigially. Moreover, these elements are to be found in English plays that give off pastoral vibrations but are rarely studied in connection with Italian drama, because they are not like *Aminta* and *Il pastor fido*. The odd play of Fletcher or Daniel clearly inspired by Guarini is justifiably regarded as exceptional. The conviction that the works of Shakespeare and some of his contemporaries are more closely related to Italian drama than has yet been established awaits confirmation through increased knowledge of what that drama was. The range of comic possibilities, the mixtures of tones, ranks, and of the plausible with the fantastic displayed by the twenty plays examined here show that for a long time Italian dramatists entertained a very liberal idea of what a stage pastoral could be and do.

It is the effect of multiplicity achieved by juxtaposition of contrasting elements and levels of style that makes the many Elizabethan plays in which pastoral elements are used without declarations of form seem alien to the Italian genre as represented by *Aminta* and *Il pastor fido*. Shakespeare's green world, in particular, seems to belong entirely to the immemorial English countryside, with its local folk customs, far from the literary Arcadia evoked for the court of Ferrara. Yet even C. L. Barber, without breaking a neoplatonic code, has sensed the aura of Arcadia in Shakespeare's "wood outside Athens."[36] Although native festivals and submerged memories of the primitive wild of romance, as they have been revealed in this context by Barber and by Frye,[37] doubtless provided Shakespeare with the manner of variation he would make

36. C. L. Barber, *Shakespeare's Festive Comedy: A Study of Dramatic Form and Its Relation to Social Custom* (Princeton, 1959), 145.

37. Northrop Frye, "The Argument of Comedy," and *A Natural Perspective: The Development of Shakespearean Comedy and Romance* (New York, 1965).

on the conventions he chose, the conventions themselves belong to a more self-conscious and sophisticated art. *Aminta* and *Il pastor fido* alone cannot tell the story of that art, nor yield up that sense of the capacity of the pastoral dramatic genre shared by its Italian practitioners before Guarini and, I think, by many Englishmen, of whom Shakespeare was only the greatest.

Vincenzo Panciatichi, *Gli amorosi affanni, favola pastorale*, V (Venice, 1606).
Courtesy of the Folger Shakespeare Library.

CHAPTER FIVE

Pastoral Nature and the Happy Ending

dward Tayler has contributed to the recovery of the philosophical meaning inherent in the paired terms Nature and Art by examining their use in one species of the genus bucolic literature—the symbolic pastoral that flourished intensely into the seventeenth century and then disappeared so effectively as to leave Dr. Johnson without a clue to *Lycidas*. Tayler's record of the "interaction of a philosophical idea with a literary genre"[1] recognizes that the division of Nature and Art was in the Renaissance a habitual way of classifying human experience, and that in the literary convention equivalent to this philosophical commonplace, the shepherd had for the sixteenth century a value like that of the pilgrim Everyman for the Middle Ages. The possibilities of moral and philosophical debate employing the categories represented by Nature and Art varied according to the kinds of experience under discussion, to the specific subject, and to each writer's conviction. The division might be applied to man alone, in which case Nature stood for instinct, Art for reason and will; or to the entire temporal world, with Nature standing for the works of God, Art for those of man. Subjects on which the paired terms were commonly invoked ranged from cosmetics and gardening to genetics, education, the good life, and the human condition.

The orthodox Renaissance view subordinated Art to Nature, but as a complement: in the realm of morality as in that of poetry, Art was conceived as "erected wit" and thought to perfect Nature, a view lent authority by Aristotle, Horace, and Seneca, and one that accommodated both the Christian estimate of postlapsarian human nature and the dominant Renaissance respect for reason as man's highest faculty. The main alternative was the view taken by the minority composed of primitivists,

---

Parts of this chapter appeared in slightly different form as "The Moralist in Arcadia: England and Italy," *Romance Philology* 19, no. 2 (November 1965): 340–52; and "The Tragicomic Bear," *Comparative Literature Studies* 9, no. 1 (March 1972): 17–30.

1. Edward William Tayler, *Nature and Art in Renaissance Literature* (New York and London, 1964), 7–8.

fideists, and naturalists, that of "counterfeit" Art in opposition to "true" nature. With the first view Tayler associates, for example, Christian humanism, Milton, and the literary depiction of courtly society; with the second, libertine naturalism, Montaigne, and Arcadia. It is the second view, which denigrates Art, that most engages Tayler's attention, but only as it is united to the pastoral genre to produce a trope able to impart orthodoxy to a moral preference for Nature. In the way the relationship between genre and idea was accepted by the Renaissance as a donnée, he finds a key to the moral and philosophical content of Spenser's Legend of Courtesy, the pastoral sequences in Shakespeare's late romances, especially *The Winter's Tale,* and Marvell's "Mower" poems.

Despite ambivalence in Plato and traces in Cicero of grist for the mill of naturalism, there was a general bias among the ancients toward the examined life, the examination requiring conscious Art, regarded as complementary to Nature. To the Middle Ages the division of Nature and Art had less importance, so much greater was the concern then for the division of Nature and Grace. Those who did not condemn Nature as devilish generally accepted the Christianized Aristotelian dictum: Nature is God's Art. Such ideas were passed on automatically to the Renaissance, ready for use when interest in the philosophical controversy would be rekindled by the recovery of ancient texts and the discoveries of the primitive societies in the New World. The Renaissance uses in pastoral literature of the controversy over Nature and Art are first anticipated in Longus's *Daphnis and Chloe.* Its fusion of Arcadia with the Golden Age into a healthy world of Nature contrasting with the sickly, urban world of Art is hailed by Tayler as the moment at which philosophical ideas have become literary ideas.[2] From medieval writers who purged the genre of pagan implications by means of allegory the Renaissance inherited the kind of pastoral in which Arcadia is a metaphor for Eden. One of the two traditions of Renaissance pastoral was therefore that which employed a "Christian landscape" and provided Spenser, Shakespeare, and Marvell with an ideal world against which to measure the real one, with a green world implicitly prelapsarian, where Nature needed no Art.

On the subject of late Shakespearean comedy Tayler agrees with mythic or symbolic interpretations, suggesting that any of these, or perhaps all of them, can mesh with his own explication of the conceptual patterns of pastoral Nature and Art. It is apparent, however, that he

2. Ibid., 68.

thinks the mythic critics of *The Winter's Tale* have rather missed the Renaissance point by not looking seriously at the meaning of the pastoral genre itself. Using it to deepen the significance of the cycle of experience of Polixenes and Leontes—childhood harmony followed by alienation, ending in reconciliation proceeding from the pastoral world—and pitting the two major Renaissance opinions in the controversy over Nature and Art against each other in Polixenes' debate with Perdita, so as to comment on the larger action of the play, Shakespeare is as orthodox as Spenser, though less committed.

Tayler's thesis sheds its strongest light on Marvell. After a glance at the early pastoral poems in which naturalism and Christian faith are successively expressed, Tayler shows how the Mower (Marvell's variation on the traditional shepherd), alienated from Nature by Juliana's coming, reveals the poet's Christian sense of the Fall as a change in the way man's mind regarded Nature, resulting in a corruption of Nature by Art. Marvell avoids allegory but uses the Arcadia-Eden trope as a foundation for a complex system of allusions, both personal and traditional. To the cure offered in *The Garden*, a rejection of the corrupted outer world for the creation of an inner world of Nature preceding a higher illumination of the soul, Tayler likens the Miltonic "Paradise within thee, happier far." His juxtaposition of Marvell's progressive use of the pastoral with the Renaissance association of the genre and the philosophical controversy makes of that moment of human reintegration with Nature something more than what Renato Poggioli calls the "pastoral of solitude," something more like Dante's hard-won and brief sojourn in the equally green world of the Paradiso Terrestre.[3]

Renaissance uses of the terms Nature and Art being what they were, contradictions or at least confusions lurk in the subject itself. The distinction between kinds of human reason that Tayler makes with regard to the *ratio recta* of Cicero, Aristotle, Aquinas, and Spenser, especially deserves more attention and broader application. The Art that perfects Nature is an Art associated with reasons and with law, according to what Tayler characterizes as the dominant and humanistic Renaissance view of the matter. By the same orthodox view, reason was identified with Nature. This identification, says Tayler, was attacked by primi-

3. Renato Poggioli, "The Pastoral of the Self," *Daedalus* (Fall 1959); Poggioli, "Verso una pastorale dell'io," *Il Verri* 7, no. 11 (1963): 3–14; Poggioli, "Dante 'Poco Tempo Silvano': A Pastoral Oasis in the *Commedia*," *Eightieth Annual Report of the Dante Society* (1962).

tivists and naturalists, specifically by Montaigne, who favored Nature in opposition to reason.

Like Hiram Haydn, to whose "brilliant and controversial" (and irresponsible) *Counter-Renaissance* he cautiously acknowledges a debt, Tayler does not sufficiently differentiate the early Renaissance from the late. The distinction between right and wrong reason made by the ancients, recognized by the early humanists and used with large ease by Rabelais, became an urgent concern to the troubled generations after the Reformation. It is a concern that Spenser shared with Milton and Montaigne, however other causes may justify using the latter two thinkers as symbols of intellectual opposition. The late Renaissance way of handling the division of Nature and Art betrays the temper of the times in an emphasis on distinguishing between one kind of Art (or reason), which follows Nature, and the other kind, which perverts it.

To determine the full value of a thesis like Tayler's means to find out how much of the Renaissance it illuminates beyond the specific examples to which the author applies it. Tayler refers to the two most famous Italian pastoral plays of the sixteenth century, Tasso's *Aminta* and Guarini's *Pastor fido,* denoting their choruses on the Golden Age as examples respectively of Renaissance sexual naturalism and conservative morality. He quotes Tasso's "S'ei piace, ei lice" (I.2.681) and Guarini's "Piaccia se lice" (IV.9.1419), with a conclusion from J. B. Fletcher out of Haydn: for Tasso "what pleased was proper," whereas for Guarini "what was proper pleased." [4] Tayler also agrees with Samuel Wolff that the Italian pastorals lack the urban enveloping action that enlarges the scope of social and philosophical contrast in Elizabethan pastoral. [5] With this and a few more reiterations that Tasso is "naturalistic" and Guarini "more moral," Tayler dismisses the Italian pastoral. Presumably he does not disagree with Haydn's association of Guarini with orthodoxy, Stoicism, and Milton, or of Tasso with the "Counter-Renaissance," Epicureanism, and Montaigne—the latter all anti-intellectualistic and antimoralistic.

But in fact Tasso is not consistently pro or anti anything in *Aminta,* except love. He is for that, but he does not use the division of Nature and Art logically with regard to it. Guarini, on the other hand, is intel-

---

4. Tayler, *Nature and Art,* 54. In this article I quote *Aminta* in Bruno Maier's edition; Torquato Tasso, *Opere,* vol. 1 (Milan, 1963); and *Il pastor fido,* in Luigi Fassò's *Teatro del Seicento* (Milan and Naples, 1956).

5. Tayler, *Nature and Art,* 205 n. 15.

lectually consistent, employs the philosophical division, and makes the pastoral resonate with Christian allusions. *Il pastor fido* seems to belong exactly to the Renaissance tradition of Tayler's thesis and to gain meaning when reread in its light. Whether Guarini regarded Tasso's pastoral as a study in libertine naturalism or as a set of lyric variations on the theme of neoplatonic love, a stylistic tour de force of contrived simplicity, he found in *Aminta* suggestions that he adapted and worked into the more Aristotelian fabric of *Il pastor fido*.

In *Aminta* itself, however, these suggestions seem to occur helter-skelter, contradicting each other. How, for example, does Tasso use the theme of the Golden Age, which is central to the kind of pastoral examined by Tayler and which Guarini purposefully expands? Although the first-act chorus laments its passing, in the first scene of the same act Dafne, who is urging love and is therefore for the moment on the "right" side, derides the "mondo ancora semplice ed infante" (I.1.112) of the time when men were contented with water and nuts because they did not know how to make wine and bread.

Equally confusing is Tasso's stand on the controversy over city and country with which the division between Nature and Art was linked in the pastoral trope. In the prologue, Amore, representing the only unquestionably consistent force in the play, prefers the pastoral world to the court. Later, however, Tirsi announces that contrary to his expectations he has found the court full of noble spirits, a place of virtue and truth (I.2.565). Tirsi, we know, is Tasso himself, and this compliment to his Este patrons an example of the *drame à clef* element in *Aminta*. Still, the speech cannot be squared philosophically with Amore's, nor with characterization of Tasso as an anti-court, pro–green world naturalist.

More complicated is the satyr's denunciation of cities with the bitter charge that urban love of money has infected the pastoral world and made this age indeed "of gold." Even were this not contradicted by other speeches, it would be bewildering, for the satyr is on the "wrong" side: he is planning to ravish Aminta's Silvia. Moreover, he defends his intentions with the Aristotelian line mentioned by Tayler: because Nature made him "atto a far violenza," he feels justified in using his innate violence to take what he wants (II.1.803). On the one hand his conclusions might be interpreted as Tasso's attack on Art, that is, on reason understood as rationalization and sophistry. But it might as easily be an attack on the indulgence of Nature uncontrolled by Art or reason or law. This too would seem odd coming from the "naturalistic" Tasso.

The way Tasso uses *Natura* and *Arte* also leads in several directions.

Sometimes the terms seem to be set up in opposition, as in the famous chorus in which Honor is accused of tyrannizing over Nature:

> Tu prima, Onor, velasti
> La fonte de i diletti
> . . . .
> a i detti il fren ponesti, a i passi l'arte
> (I.2.695–96, 705)

It was you, Honor, who first veiled the source of delights . . . you imposed restraint in speaking and art in walking.

Here a "dura legge" (hard law) is set up in contrast to the "legge aurea e felice / che Natura scolpì: S'ei piace, ei lice" (679–681: happy golden law that Nature engraved: if it pleases, it is permitted). Honor is an enemy to Amore and Natura, but only in this passage is it associated with Art. Elsewhere Tirsi says that all girls have

> L'arte del parer bella e del piacere
> . . . .
> Benché, per dir il ver, non han bisogno
> Di maestro: maestro è la natura,
> Ma la madre e la balia anco v'han parte.
> (I.2.836, 847–49)

The art of appearing beautiful and pleasing . . . although, to tell the truth, they need no teacher; nature teaches Art, with some help from mothers and nurses.

In support of Aminta's instinctive respect for Silvia and his refusal to use ambush or violence like the satyr's, the chorus says that love is not learned from the schools of Athens but from Love itself. The term used in this endorsement of Nature is *arte*: Amore itself teaches the "arte d'amare" (II.3.1142). Love is both Nature and Art, and the enemies over which it triumphs are products of Art but also of Nature—lust, for instance.

The religious diction of Elpino's speech contains seeds of the *Pastor fido:*

> la legge con che Amore
> il suo imperio governa eternamente
> non è dura, né obliqua; e l'opre sue,

piene di providenza e di mistero,
altri a torto condanna. Oh con quant'arte,
e per che ignote strade egli conduce
l'uom ad esser beato

(V.1.1839–46)

the law by which Love governs his empire is not hard nor unjust; and his works full of providence and mystery are wrongly condemned. Oh, with what art and by what unknown ways he leads man to blessedness.

This and the second Intermedio, written later, which hails the "Sante leggi d'amore e di natura" (206: Holy laws of love and nature) leading to God, only add to the confusion. Tayler's "Christian landscape of the Renaissance pastoral" is not visible in *Aminta* except in short and inconsistent glimpses. Tasso's naturalism is not systematic, as his use of the terms in the philosophical controversy suggest. Nature and Art are used here in opposition, there in neutral division, again in complementary relationship, sometimes in utterly conventional and superficial ways, according to no plan. Although it sporadically reflects the interaction of the genre with the philosophical division discussed by Tayler, *Aminta* belongs to the other tradition of Renaissance pastoral.

But when Guarini borrowed pieces from *Aminta* and *Oedipus rex* and combined them in the intricately plotted *Pastor fido,* the result was something that should interest Tayler. Guarini's Arcadia is under a curse brought on by a nymph's infidelity to a shepherd. To remove the curse, the oracle says that two scions of divine stock must marry and a faithful shepherd must cancel out the old infidelity. The only scions known are Amarilli and Silvio, who do not love each other. Amarilli is loved by Mirtillo, and Silvio (Guarini's variation on Tasso's hard-hearted Silvia) by Dorinda. Through the machinations of Corisca, who lusts after Mirtillo and wants Amarilli out of the way, the lovers are brought close to death, but at last it is discovered that Mirtillo, the faithful shepherd, is the long-lost elder brother of Silvio, and through his marriage with Amarilli the oracle is fulfilled and the ancient curse removed.

Enormously successful and controversial, *Il pastor fido* has been both admired and attacked for the abstruse philosophical and moral reflections it contains. Common opinion among Italianists during the last century has had it that the work is essentially a piece of erotic escape literature, with grotesque graftings from Sophocles. Recently, however,

Nicolas Perella has put the Sophoclean irony back into its rightful place in interpreting the play, and though he agrees that *Il pastor fido* is escape literature, a "flight into an Arcadia of *volupté*," he declares that it is a deliberately ironic story of man's spiritual blindness to the transcendent (represented by Fate) and his inability to attain to natural truth accurately or to supernatural truth at all.[6]

From his analysis of Guarini's use of the motif of blindness, of optical imagery, and of patterns of illusion, until at last human "surrendering to blindness brings the truth to light," Perella concludes, "it is reason that is ultimately at fault if, in the cognitive process, reality is not seen for what it is."[7] In contrast to the early Italian Neoplatonists, who taught that the "higher" senses of sight and hearing might ultimately lead man to God, Guarini considered touch the least untrustworthy of the senses, useful in leading man to woman. *Il pastor fido* is thus interpreted as a lyric invitation to sensuality, its plot articulated to provide philosophical justification for naturalism. As for the "moral sentences," "The praise of *onestà* is a conventional pretext that is lost in the erotic world of the play, and fate is really subsumed into nature which ultimately reigns supreme as instinct and desire . . . fate is made to conform to nature."[8]

Perella's conclusion that *Il pastor fido* is programmatically naturalistic, that Guarini "removed his world from under a Christian sky" because he was a skeptic like Montaigne but without the deep moral vision of a Montaigne,[9] is a far cry from Tayler's easy notion of the "moral" Guarini. Yet it is Tayler who provides the means of moral rehabilitation for the *Pastor fido*, without disturbing any of the rich significance rediscovered by Perella. The key lies in such sentences as this: "To prefer Nature before Art in the Golden Age might be a plea for sexual 'naturalism' as in Tasso or an argument against the equation of Reason and Nature as in Montaigne. But the same preference in Eden is merely an acknowledgment of scriptural fact: unfallen Nature is by definition good and stands above 'Rule or Art.'"[10]

6. Nicolas J. Perella, "Fate, Blindness, and Illusion in the *Pastor Fido*," *Romanic Review* 49 (1958): 252–68.

7. Ibid., 255, 257.

8. Perella, "Amarilli's Dilemma: The *Pastor Fido* and Some English Authors," *Comparative Literature* 12 (1960): 359.

9. Perella "Fate, Blindness and Illusion," 265.

10. Tayler, *Nature and Art*, 100.

Many Italian Counter-Reformation pastorals were allegorical, but the *Pastor fido* was not one of them. Guarini added an ex post facto allegory in his *Annotazioni* (1602) to the play, deservedly dismissed by Perella as patently spurious. Like Marvell's "Mower" poems, however, *Il pastor fido* is redolent with meanings given off by symbolism inherent in the pastoral genre and its interaction with the controversy over Nature and Art. The terms themselves appear as variously as in *Aminta*, but without contradiction and always aimed in the same moral direction. *Natura* is used throughout as the touchstone of truth, but the less frequent use of *Arte* reveals more of Guarini's mind. Significantly, the word is most often on the lips of deceitful Corisca: from promiscuous women she has learned the "arte di ben amar," that is, to take lovers in quantity (I.3.652), and she phrases her predictable opinion of chastity thus: "altro alfin l'onestate / non è che un'arte di parere onesta" (III.5.619–20: chastity, after all, is nothing but the art of seeming chaste). Or the word is applied to her with the same meaning: after inveighing against feminine distortion of nature with cosmetics, the satyr complains of Corisca's deceitful manners: "son l'arti che fan sì crudo e sì perverso Amore" (I.5.1005–06: they are the arts that make Love so harsh and cruel); and of her wearing a wig he says it is "l'arte d'una impurissima e malvagia / incantatrice" (II.6.989–90: the art of a most unchaste and wicked enchantress). In the same spirit the corrupt contemporary world is accused in the fourth choral ode of thinking goodness an illusion and life an "arte" (IV.9.1443). The poet Carino, whose experience is just the opposite of Tirsi's in *Aminta*, having expected nobility at the court and found lies instead, characterizes it as a place of "arti" (V.1.164). But in the same speech he refers respectfully to "l'arte del poetar" (182: the art of making poetry), and elsewhere praise is accorded the art of medicine, manifest in the healing herb discovered through observing its use by a she-goat: "Essa a noi la mostrò, natura a lei" (V.7.1280: She showed it to us, nature to her).

Guarini twice uses the paired terms neutrally (IV.4.518; V.8.1428), and like Shakespeare he approves of fine art, an Art that is part of Nature. But most often *arte* is Guarini's word for the negative side of the moral controversy, composed of deceit, the false use of reason, and distortion of nature, connected with the city or court and with Arcadia after the Fall. *Natura* stands for the real, *Arte* for the apparent. Correlative to Art, human reason and resulting human law are also placed in opposition to Nature. But in keeping with the central theme of the play, antinatural reason and law are proved false; true reason and true law are found to be in accord with heaven, fate, and nature.

Although there is no urban enveloping action in the *Pastor fido*, the contrast of a decadent world with the green world exists doubly in the play. Carino's attack on urban society compares the city unfavorably with the Arcadia he remembers (V.1). Corisca, who like Longus's Lycainion has learned her bad *arti* in town, is now an Arcadian—but this contemporary Arcadia is corrupt and needs reform. The city is clearly less important than the antithesis of the two Arcadias, before and after the Fall. Amarilli compares her life with that of the "felice pastorella" who lives in and from nature a "vera vita, che non sa che sia / morire innanzi morte" (II.5.665: true life, not knowing what it is to die even before death). Amarilli is herself Arcadian, but she uses the condition of a more primitive Arcadian as a measure of her own, created by false reason that creates false laws, and suggests the larger comparison between the fallen Arcadia and the Arcadia of the Golden Age.

Like the pristine world of Marlowe's Mower or Spenser's Pastorella, Guarini's lost Arcadia is rich with the Eden allusion. Even more like *The Winter's Tale, Il pastor fido* shows Eden spoiled and a misinterpreted oracle fulfilled by the return of a missing babe, bringing man and Nature into harmony and restoring the Golden Age. No less than Perdita and Florizel, Amarilli and Mirtillo in love know naturally what false reasoning has obscured: they are by true law (germane to right reason and constructive Art) what they are by Nature (Gods' Art)—destined mates and restorers of Arcadia. Wrong reason tries to obey the gods but misinterprets their law and nearly destroys the natural savior. False postlapsarian Art corrupts Nature.

But Art and reason per se are not forbidden in Guarini's green world, nor even is speculation. The river god Alfeo's reminiscences about the Golden Age reveal the following:

> benché qui ciascuno
> abito e nome pastorale avesse,
> non fu però ciascuno
> né di pensier né di costumi rozzo,
> però ch'altri fu vago
> di spiar tra le stelle e gli elementi
> di natura e del ciel gli alti segreti;
> altri di seguir l'orme
> di fuggitiva fera

> . . . . . .
> La maggior parte amica
> fu de le sacre muse, amore e studio.
>> (Prologo, 58–66, 76–77)

though all here were shepherds in dress and name, no one was
rustic in thought or act, for some were eager to search the stars
and the elements to learn the high secrets of nature and heaven;
others to follow the tracks of wild beasts in flight . . . most were
friends of the sacred muses, of love and of learning.

Even such a champion of reason as Milton, whose angel advises Adam
to be "lowly wise," is stricter than this. When such intellectually ambitious undertakings as astronomy and geology are admired as suitable
activities in the ideal world of Nature, it becomes still clearer that
Guarini attacks only false reason and false art.

He pursues this end in the way he handles the traditional postures of
the Arcadian population. In the opening scene, which is indebted to
Aminta but honed to a philosophical edge, Silvio is warned:

> la gioventù d'amor nemica
> contrasta al Cielo e la natura offende.
>
> . . . .
>
> guarda
> che nel disumanarti
> non divenghi una fera, anzi che un dio.
>> (I.1.157–58, 207–09)

when youth is an enemy to love, it is a challenge to Heaven and an
offense to nature . . . have a care lest by dehumanizing yourself
you become not a god but a beast.

With this advice, reminiscent of Montaigne, Guarini enunciates a first
premise: Nature and Heaven are favorable to love.

But what kind of love? Not Corisca's "arte di ben amar," unfaithful
and therefore false love, yet based on natural instinct, as is the satyr's
lust. Hers leads to deceit, his to violence, which he attempts to justify,
like his prototype in *Aminta,* with a sophistical appeal to nature: "Amore
e la natura insegna . . . questa legge naturale e dritta" (I.5.1046, 1053:
Love and nature teach . . . this natural and right law). The villainess,

Corisca, says fidelity is an enemy to love—free love—but the hero, Mirtillo, answers that he will triumph over heavens, earth, and death by his
faith—faithful love (III.6.956–60). The authoritative chorus laments
infidelity as an offense to Love's holiest laws, which support faith as the
root of all virtue:

> Così di farci amanti, onde felice
> si fa la nostra natura,
> l'eterno amante ha cura.
>   (II.6.1019–21)

The eternal lover [God] takes care to make us love thus, whence
our nature is made happy.

It goes on to say that only the love that joins souls is real love. The love
favored by Nature is therefore true love, defined in obvious contrast to
the false. Both are "natural," that is, instinctive, but the satyr's violent
lust and Corisca's promiscuous appetite are accompanied by false reason and the latter is pointedly identified with a particular kind of *arte*.
While it is impossible to disagree with Perella that the erotic effect dominates in the *Pastor fido,* it is equally impossible to agree that the praise
of *onestà* is only a conventional pretext.

The distinction between right reason and wrong is emphasized again
in the conflict imagined between Nature (love) and law (reason, or Art's
interpretation of fate and heaven's will). We have seen the satyr invoking
the "natural law" to justify his violent inclinations. The well-intentioned
and chaste Amarilli gives an example of another kind of inadequate reasoning when she supposes her true love, which she correctly identifies
with Nature, to be forbidden by true law, which she confuses with false
law set up by wrong reason:

> Legge umana inumana,
> che dài per pena de l'amar la morte!
> Se 'l peccar è sì dolce
> e 'l non peccar sì necessario, oh troppo
> imperfetta natura
> che repugni a la legge;
> oh troppo dura legge
> che la natura offendi!
>
>   (III.4.522–29)

Inhuman law of man that punishes love with death! If sinning is so
sweet and not sinning so necessary, oh, too imperfect is the nature
that rejects the law; oh, too harsh the law that offends nature!

It has pleased generations of readers to take this passage out of context
as a statement of the human dilemma. In context, however, the effect is
one of dramatic irony: Amarilli is mistaken, for in fact there is no conflict between Nature and true law, as the sequel proves. But ever since
the original sin of infidelity disrupted the harmony of Arcadia, a curse
has lingered there and the oracle has been misunderstood by alienated
human reason. Instinct is right in Amarilli's and Mirtillo's case, because
their natures are noble and their instincts guided, his by *fede,* hers by
the feminine equivalent, *onestà.*

Corisca also separates Nature from morality. To the goddess Diana's
law against unchastity and infidelity, Corisca opposes the topos of love's
cosmic signory:

> Qual è tra noi più antica,
> la legge di Diana o pur d'Amore?
> Questa ne' nostri petti
> nasce, Amarilli, e con l'età s'avanza;
> né s'apprende o s'insegna,
> ma negli umani cuori,
> senza maestro, la natura stessa
> di propria man l'imprime;
> e dov'ella comanda,
> ubbidisce anco il Ciel, non che la terra.
>
> (III.5.592–601)

Which is the older law for us, Diana's or Love's? His is born in our
own breasts, Amarilli, and grows with age; it is not learned or
taught, but, without a teacher, is imprinted on human hearts by
nature's own hand; and where she commands, not only earth but
even Heaven obeys.

Corisca is at the center of the play, because she is artful and by false
reasoning tries to convince others that there is no value to right reason.
Her insincerity is revealed by the contradictory claim, in the same scene,
that the law is not made for the wise. Again she is wrong. In the philosophical context of the play, no one is above the law, but those who are
truly wise find their natures in harmony with law; unfallen instinct and

right reason go together. The law forbids Corisca's kind of natural love
but not Amarilli's.

This law of Diana does not command virginity but fidelity and the
chastity that belongs to it. The original sin in this Eden was infidelity,
the reestablishment of harmony in Arcadia will be effected by fidelity,
and the oracle that promises this reconciliation is an oracle of Diana. A
clue to the relation of law to instinct or of Art to Nature lies in the
prayer that the shepherds fervently but unreflectively chant, hailing
Diana the moon as complementary to Apollo the fecund sun:

> Tu, che col tuo vitale
> e temperato raggio
> scemi l'ardor de la fraterna luce,
> onde qua giù produce
> felicemente poi l'alma natura
> tutti i suoi parti, e fa d'erbe e di piante,
> d'uomini e d'animai ricca e feconda
> l'aria, la terra e l'onda;
> deh! sì come in altrui tempri l'arsura,
> così spegni in te l'ira
> ond'oggi Arcadia tua piagne e sospira.
>
> (V.3.376–86)

You who with your vital and tempered ray moderate the heat of
the fraternal light from which then great nature produces here below all her births, and makes the air, the earth and the waters rich
and fecund with grasses and plants, with men and animals and all
living things; ah! as in another you temper the burning, so may be
quenched in you the ire which makes your Arcadia today weep
and sigh.

Law that calls for control and right use of natural instinct is not in
conflict with the law of love, whatever Amarilli and the other benighted
Arcadians may think, and thereby hangs the irony.

The prime minister Nicandro formulates the laws of Nature and
those of man and heaven in opposition to each other:

> Contra la legge di natura forse
> non hai, ninfa, peccato: 'Ama, se piace';
> ma ben hai tu peccato incontra quella
> degli huomini e del Cielo: 'Ama, se lice.'
>
> (IV.5.620–23)

Nymph, perhaps you have not sinned against the law of nature: "Love, if you like"; but you surely have sinned against that of men and of Heaven: "Love, if it is lawful."

As regards the fallen Arcadia, he is not wrong. But the time of reconciliation is near with true love as its instrument, and in pristine Arcadia, which Amarilli and Mirtillo will restore, what pleases and what is proper are the same. There is harmony between man and Nature, as there has always been between God and Nature, though this truth has been lost sight of by fallen reason, that Art which opposes Nature.

Onestà and *fede* are part of Nature in the prelapsarian world. Fate seems to the Arcadians to stand with chastity and fidelity against Nature only because Fate's law is falsely interpreted in the postlapsarian world. We have Guarini's word for it that Fate is nothing more than Nature.[11] It is relevant that the campaign of the Counter-Reformation church against belief in Fate, magic, and divination was in full swing while Guarini was writing *Il pastor fido;* dramatists were encouraged to show up the so-called decrees of Fate as part of the Prime Mover's plan. Perella notes that Guarini disclaimed any attempt to account for divine Providence,[12] but disregards the first choral ode of the *Pastor fido* that hails a power higher than Fate (therefore higher than Nature too) and does so, moreover, in the vocabulary that had become standard for references to divine Providence:

> tu che stai sovra le stelle e 'l Fato,
> e con saver divino
> indi ne reggi, alto Motor del cielo
>
> (I.5.1139–41)

you who are above the stars and Fate, and with divine wisdom thence rule them, high Mover of heaven.

Without a view of the Christian landscape of Renaissance pastoral and the use in it of the division of Nature and Art to comment on pre- and postlapsarian nature, it would indeed seem that Guarini wanted no part of philosophical or theological controversy, preferring escape into naturalism, despite his orthodoxy in neutralizing Fate by identifying it with Nature and subordinating both to the Prime Mover. But Tayler's

11. "Annotazioni sopra il Pastor Fido," *Delle opere del cavalier Battista Guarini* (Verona, 1737), 1:28.

12. Perella, "Fate, Illusion, and Blindness," 267 n. 28.

study shows that for the Renaissance, "naturalism" in Arcadia could be
orthodox too, "merely an acknowledgment of scriptural fact." The conflict in the *Pastor fido* is the one that typically preoccupied the late Renaissance: not between Nature on one side and Art (including law and
reason) on the other, but between Nature and false art, false reason, bad
law—the Art that is opposed to Nature and perverts it. This Art is only
appearance; reality is Nature united with true honor, true love, true law
and right reason, the kind championed by Milton and Montaigne. Insofar as Art is right reason—as in the practice of medicine, which perfects,
cooperates with, and belongs to Nature—Guarini endorses Art. But
when Art is wrong reason, perverting instead of controlling Nature,
Guarini condemns it. His use of the terms and the pastoral genre consistently support this orthodox moral stand.

The celebrated exit in *The Winter's Tale* of Antigonus, "pursued by a
bear," and the Clown's pell-mell account of the poor gentleman's dismemberment in counterpoint with the likewise hilarious death of his
shipwrecked companions (III.3.58, 90–105), constitute a *locus difficilis*
of interpretation that even for late Shakespeare is unusually resistant to
realistic explanation. The jar between the subject of the narration and
its manner is after all not diminished by, for instance, J. H. P. Pafford's
able defense of both Antigonus's dream and his death as necessary to
unity and plausibility, which takes Shakespeare's addition of the character and scene to his major source as proof of an unwillingness to leave
Perdita's preservation as much to chance as Greene had done Fawnia's
in *Pandosto*, and explains the comic rhetoric as a means of excluding
pity and terror.[13]
The most enlightening readings are the most complex and the least
commonsensical ones: those, like that of S. L. Bethell,[14] which insist on
meanings elusive to tests of plausibility in the fable or of unmeditated
compassion in the reader. To these may be added a further complication
or two suggested by the status of animals in Italian stage pastoral, sup-
porting symbolic reading of Shakespeare with some practices of contemporary Italian comic drama, especially pastoral tragicomedy.
Shakespeare's bear has aroused a fair amount of debate as to both
provenance and species. J. M. Nosworthy attributes some influence to

13. William Shakespeare, *The Winter's Tale*, Arden ed., ed. J. H. P. Pafford
(London and Cambridge, Mass., 1965), lxiv, lix n. 4.
14. Samuel Leslie Bethell, *The Winter's Tale: A Study* (London, n.d. [1947]).

Mucedorus,[15] a dramatization of an episode in Sidney's *Arcadia* that includes from its source the heroine's rescue from a bear. Stage direction in the edition of 1598 runs as follows: "Enter Segasto running and Amadine after him, being persued with a beare," the last-named represented a few lines later by a severed bear's head.[16] A revised version of 1610 brings a whole, white-fronted she-bear onstage for encounter with Mouse the clown.[17] G. F. Reynolds surmises a particular tame bear, to which he attributes the extraordinary popularity of the revised *Mucedorus,*[18] perhaps the same bear conjectured by Quiller-Couch to have been hired by Shakespeare's company from the nearby Bear-Pit in Southwark.[19] Neville Coghill opts for a human bear.[20] Important as such speculations may be to the stage history of *The Winter's Tale,* however, they do not in the least clarify the bear's function in the play. Even James G. McManaway's persuasive suggestion that the idea came from the description of Barents's voyages, on which two men were torn to pieces by bears,[21] does not pretend to account for Shakespeare's oddly comic casting of the incident.

But if we think of *The Winter's Tale* as a dramatization of *Pandosto* in the manner of the Italian pastoral tragicomedy then fashionable throughout Europe (or at least as being as close to the manner as so freewheeling an assimilator and re-creator as Shakespeare was likely to come)[22] some of the ambiguities of the bear scene become understand-

15. William Shakespeare, *Cymbeline,* Arden ed., ed. J. M. Nosworthy (London, 1955), xxv.

16. *The Tudor Facsimile Texts,* ed. John S. Farmer (n.p. [London], 1910), A3r.

17. C. R. Baskervill, V. B. Heltzel, and A. H. Nethercot, eds., *Elizabethan and Stuart Plays,* (New York, 1934), scene 2.

18. G. F. Reynolds, "*Mucedorus,* Most Popular Elizabethan Play?" *Studies in the English Renaissance Drama in Memory of Karl Julius Holzknecht,* ed. Josephine Waters Bennett et al. (New York, 1959), 259–60.

19. William Shakespeare, *The Winter's Tale,* ed. Sir Arthur Quiller-Couch and John Dover Wilson (Cambridge, England, 1959), xx.

20. Pafford, ed., *The Winter's Tale,* 69 n. 58.

21. Ibid.

22. The pervasive contemporary admiration for Greek romance, and the reflection of Sidney's work in Shakespeare's observed by E. M. W. Tillyard (*Shakespeare's Last Plays* [London, 1954], 33), are also relevant to the genesis of *The Winter's Tale,* but the one had given early impetus to Italian drama, and the other might as easily be judged the result of Shakespeare's turning to romance as the cause.

able, though no less ambiguous. Pafford's down-to-earth challenge to Quiller-Couch, Leavis, Bethell, and others who emphasize the unreality and fantasy of *The Winter's Tale* denies kinship between the country-side of this play and the Forest of Arden, the wood near Athens, or any land of make-believe.[23] Yet if different in several particulars from the green worlds of *As You Like It, A Midsummer Night's Dream,* and *The Tempest,* the pastoral community near the seacoast in Bohemia is a type of Arcadia—the same type, in fact, that might be found as the sole set-ting for those contemporary Italian pastoral plays which followed the principles of verisimilitude elected by Tasso and Guarini. When Pafford lists those qualities shared by Shakespeare's last plays—elements of fairy tale and folklore, the supernatural, the dream, the masque, danc-ing, music and songs[24]—he is unwittingly listing the elements proper to the Italian genre and there employed in combinations determined by the dramatists's choice among the several flavors of stage pastoral currently being concocted by experimenters. For *The Winter's Tale* Shakespeare chose Guarini's verisimilitude, rationalizing the implausible features of the pastoral inheritance to leave only a reminder of sorcery and meta-morphoses in Paulina's statue trick, whereas in *A Midsummer Night's Dream* and *The Tempest* he eschewed the verisimilar for magic. Even the design repeated in his late plays of happiness broken by human evil, then restored by virtue and nature with divine help, is a pattern not only at work but often enunciated insistently in the mature Italian pastoral tragicomedy. An earlier tendency, visible in Tasso, consecrated the pas-toral elements to the sole service of love, but in the kind of pastoral drama of which Guarini's is the best example and the most influential model, reconciliation and divine providence emerge as theses. Rather than digress toward a larger subject to be treated elsewhere,[25] however, *revenons à notre ours* and its peculiar place among the beasts who in-habit or threaten the Arcadia of Italian Renaissance drama.

In that world, composed of *prato, grotta, tempio, fonte, selva,* and *capanne* amid *arbori, sassi, colli, montagne, herbe, fiori,* and *fontane,*[26]

23. Pafford, ed., *The Winter's Tale,* lxvii n. 3.
24. Ibid., xlix.
25. See chapter 6.
26. The field, cave, temple, spring, and wood common to the set are speci-fied in the stage directions of Alvise (Luigi) Pasqualigo in *Gl'intricati, pastorale* (Venice, 1581), A8; the huts, trees, rocks, hills, mountains, grass, flowers, and founts are in Sebastiano Serlio's description of the "Scena Satirica" from *Il secondo libro, di prospettiva* (1st ed., 1545), in *I sette libri dell'architettura* (Venice, 1584); facsimile repr. (Bologna, 1978), I. [49v–] 51.

sheep and other livestock are in a sense the least important of animals. Although spoken of continually, they are valued only as chattel. Not for them the comradeship of herds with shepherd that T. G. Rosenmeyer remarks in Theocritus's *Idylls*.[27] Rather, the sheep and goats of the pastoral play in numbers constitute wealth and individually serve as aids to dramaturgy. The need to tend the flock can cue exits and regroupings, and searching for a stray often leads the shepherd to dramatic discoveries, as in *The Winter's Tale* at the moment of old Antigonus's destruction and the infant Perdita's salvation, when the Clown meets with "things dying" and the Shepherd with "things new-born" (III.3.106–107).

Dogs, on the other hand, who likewise inhabit the pleasance where humans make their homes but also accompany their masters into the woods, are allowed some participation in the human drama. They too are denied the equality with humans enjoyed by Theocritan fauna, but often function as extensions of human feelings and desires or as instruments for comment on human action. Zinano's nymph Oristia has a dog with the Vergilian name of Licisca, whose stance as a defender of chastity is characteristic of canine benevolence in pastoral tragicomedy.[28] Lollio's shepherd Dameta also has a Licisca, typically cited for his aid in saving a lamb from a wolf.[29] Dogs are not benevolent to deer, of course, but only because their masters are not either. The praise that Lollio's nymphs Aretusa and Nisa give to each other's dogs, Lampuro and Melampo, for their action in hunting and killing a stag (II.1) are really praises at one remove of the nymphs themselves.

As companions to the lower-class members of Arcadia, the villani, pecorai, and caprai, dogs partake of their rustic masters' function as foils to the noble pastori. The nameless dog that Cresci's Corbaccio keeps by him,[30] silent sharer in the villani's crude song contest and coarse railing at love in parody of the refined transports of their betters, supports Cody's suggestion that Launce's dog Crab has a parodic function in *The Two Gentlemen of Verona*, which he links with Italian pastoral drama.[31]

Among the pastori, more seriously, dogs provide illuminating contrasts with humans. Silvio's Melampo, listed by Guarini among the

27. Thomas G. Rosenmeyer, *The Green Cabinet: Theocritus and the European Pastoral Lyric* (Berkeley and Los Angeles, 1969), 138.

28. Gabriele Zinano, *Il Caride, favola pastorale* (Reggio, 1590), II.3.

29. Alberto Lollio, *Arteusa, comedia pastorale* (Ferrara, 1564), III.2.

30. Pietro Cresci, *Tirena, favola pastorale* (Venice, 1584), II.3.

31. Richard Cody, *The Landscape of the Mind: Pastoralism and Platonic Theory in Tasso's "Aminta" and Shakespeare's Early Comedies* (Oxford, 1969), 100.

props required for *Il pastor fido* as "Un cane grande, bello domes-tico,"[32] accompanies his master in his passionate hunting, and as the major object of Silvio's affections he is one expression of the unawak-ened condition of the Adonis-like youth and his rejection of Dorinda's faithful love. Melampo's affection for her is made by Dorinda to point to the contrast between the relative humanity of the dog and the ferocity of his human master:

> Ecco il tuo cane,
> Silvio, che più di te cortese, . . .
>   . . . in queste braccia,
> che tanto sprezzi tu, venne a posarsi . . .
> · · · · · · · · · · · · · · ·
>   . . . cari avendo i miei baci e i miei sospiri.
>   (II.2.500–505)

Here is your dog, Silvio, who is more courteous than you, . . . in these arms that you so disdain, he came to nestle . . . welcoming my kisses and sighs.

Although not treated anthropomorphically, on the whole dogs are at least participants in the dramatic action and the movement of the forces of love constituting the essential fable of pastoral drama. The canine role is thoroughly comic, both in its natural association with the com-forts of life in the pleasance, with the feelings and laughter of the human society, and in belonging to the joy-bound action, that part of the tragi-comic movement which aids and supports, and tends toward the benefit and desires of human beings.

Another kind of animal inhabits the wild. Functioning as objects, a sort of undomesticated livestock, are the deer, natural prey of Diana's ninfe and pastori, who actually spend less time guarding flocks than in occupations befitting the courtiers they really are—making poetry, making love, and hunting the hart, which sport usually turns into hunt-ing the heart and the hunter into prey. The distance between Theocritan pastoral idyll and Renaissance pastoral play is nowhere more clearly seen than in the importance to the latter of the chase. The contradiction between herdsman and hunter in Theocritus noted by Rosenmeyer does not obtain in the drama.[33] Pastori all hunt, as do ninfe, who in this genre

32. Fassò, *Teatro del Seicento*, 323.
33. Rosenmeyer, *Green Cabinet*, 135.

are simply female counterparts of the shepherds. Their pursuit of game is ordinarily a sign of devotion to Diana, which in most cases is destined to be reconciled with the worship of Venus. Refusal to love is a challenge to the first principle and final cause of pastoral drama, in which the ideal state for Theocritus's shepherds, poise untroubled by amorous rapture, is treated as an adolescent condition to be cured. The action of hunting often expresses standard attitudes toward love, the major concern of pastoral tragicomedy, but the deer are given no character.

Carnivores fare differently. Although the lion is no more native to Italy than to Vergil's Arcadia or the Forest of Arden, where its presence has been much derided,[34] it belongs to Renaissance pastoral fauna not only by sanction of the *Bucolics* but also because of its role in the tale of Pyramus and Thisbe, Ovid's tutelary status rivaling Vergil's in pastoral tragicomedy of every type. When the lion is mentioned, it is usually in an action of straightforward violence. It inspires fear, but not that special horror, that sense of dismay, betrayal, and loathing that we feel when mortally threatened by animals we are accustomed to regard as familiars. The lion is the essence of an indifferent alien nature and the best of it. It is the natural enemy of the pastoral hunter; but it arouses no disgust. At worst it is cruel, but without rancor, and death at its paws is somehow clean, for the measure of its distance from the human is the manifest excellence of its kind; it connotes no perversion or baseness of humankind, but uncompromisingly signifies otherness.

The wolf, on the contrary, is the most hated of the predators, because it is a terrible dog and is associated with *insidias,* as in the *Bucolics* and the *Georgics.*[35] Its action is evil and pastoral dramatists use its dramatic possibilities in various ways. A wolf contributes to the plot and the moral of Guazzoni's *Andromeda* by stealing a child, then yielding to a miraculous prompting from the divine will to deliver it up unharmed.[36] Beccari's early and influential *Il sacrificio* ends with the classical metamorphosis into a wolf of the villain, a murderous, sly opponent of love and happiness.[37] Guarini's mendacious, town-bred disturber of pastoral peace, Corisca, is modeled after Longus's Lycainion, whose name shows her nature. When Guarini's Dorinda disguises herself, it is in the wolf-

34. William Shakespeare, *The Winter's Tale,* ed. Horace Howard Furness (1898), New Variorum ed. (New York, 1964), viii.

35. *Bucolica,* V.60, and *Georgicon,* III.537, in P. Vergili Maronis, *Opera,* ed. Frederic Arthur Hirtzel (Oxford, 1963).

36. Diomisso Guazzoni, *Andromeda, tragicomedia boscareccia* (Venice, 1587), I.6.

37. Agostino Beccari, *Il sacrificio, favola pastorale* (Ferrara, 1555), V.6.

skins of her capraio Lupino (IV.2). The act is not culpable, for Dorinda is a sympathetic character and her disguise, borrowed from the ancient herdsman's trick practiced by Longus's Dorco, is motivated by love-sickness; but it is nevertheless a deceit, potentially tragic, leading to bloodshed and expressing the corruption of an Arcadia in which human relations are suffused with falsehood.

More destructive but less sly is the boar, another nightmarish perversion of a domestic beast. A violent pig that acts in bestial rage, it is unlike the lion heavy with allusion to the story of Venus and Adonis and with associations to lust. It figures less as something alien to man than as the brute in human nature unbridled, even lower in the neoplatonic scale of love than the ordinary satiro. The boar in the *Pastor fido* is not only the dangerous prey that obsesses Silvio, blinding him to the self-sacrificing love of Dorinda; it is also a plague on all Arcadia, the scourge of a society needing redemption from original sin, the sin of infidelity in love. In short, Guarini's boar is associated with the forces that in human beings are manifest as the ireful and concupiscent passions, wrath and lust. In the line of the animal embodiments of the sexual force relegated to the periphery of the Theocritan pleasance, and of the boar image used to describe the garden-destroying, thwarted suitor in *Daphnis and Chloe,* the pastoral boar is everything suggested in *Cymbeline* by Post-humous's foul fantasies when he wrathfully conjectures of Iachimo, "Perchance he spoke not, but, / Like a full-acorn'd boar, a German one, / Cried 'O!' and mounted" (II.4.167–69).

Like the literary tragedy and comedy it was meant to fuse, Italian pastoral tragicomedy was confined by the principle of unity of place to a single set, but the set included pleasance and wood, places of comic and tragic action. The wood was to be extended by imagination far beyond its visible portion, and the most violent, potentially fatal actions happen in its unseen depths: there the boar attacks in the *Pastor fido* (IV.2); there bloody veils and the like grim tokens are discovered in *Aminta* (III.2) and countless other plays; there occurs the mass metamorphosis of nymphs fleeing the satyrs' violence in Giraldi's *Egle*.[38] The piece of forest onstage, however, also provides opportunity for actions that move away from that happiness which is the ideal in the pleasance, even the norm. Attempted suicides, flights from love, ambushings—the actions of hostility, opposition—in short, the tragic actions, like the beasts associated with them, belong to the forest. And they often occur and

38. G. B. Giraldi Cinzio, *Egle, satira* (n.p. [Ferrara], n.d. [1545–50?]), V.5.

almost always begin in the selva of the pastoral set, visibly the intermediate place between safety and danger, joy and sorrow. The "deserts
of Bohemia," where things dying and things newborn are met with, enjoy the same moral climate as the visible selva.

Uncommitted to unity of place, Shakespeare brings both court and
country onstage, but also shows an intermediate place between the
fallen world from which evil comes and the green one where the remedy
is cultivated, between woe and the turn toward a happy ending. His reversing of the places as he found them in *Pandosto*, which begins in
Bohemia, brings the action of *The Winter's Tale* closer to the kind of
unity expected in Italian pastoral plays. By transferring the tragic half of
the play to Sicily, the site of Vergil's Arcadia, and setting the overtly pastoral part in Bohemia, Shakespeare drew the whole within reach of the
pastoral world, and despite his English freedom with regard to time,
space, and decorum he accentuated the resemblance between his play
and Italian pastoral tragicomedy of the verisimilar sort, and specifically
Pescetti's *La regia pastorella*.[39]

The verisimilitude of the Italian dramatists did not of course demand
historical, geographical, or ecological accuracy, but rather adherence to
the possible in a fictional world of pastoral props and conventions, excluding only the magic permitted in the fantastic Ovidian pastoral
plays. The range of Italian pastoral drama was great, its approach to
"real" life sometimes close, and its borrowings from commedia erudita
numerous, but it never took on the aim of comedy to mirror custom. To
alter fact, to attribute a sea coast to Bohemia or lions to the Forest of
Arden, was to write as the pastoral demanded, confirming the freedom
from local habitation and name of the inner world, which with its fear
and fulfilment was the essential subject of the genre. The place and the
action performed there mean little in themselves, but they mean much
insofar as they express the alternation or juxtaposition of the tragic and
comic in human life; likewise, the animals are important primarily for
their relation to the human figures, a symbolic one revealed by what
they do and where they do it.

The bear in pastoral seems both more and less terrible than the other
wild beasts, because it is humanoid, capable of upright posture, ambiguous in reputation and habitat. From ancient times it was known for its
responsiveness to taming and its unreliability, the savage nature being
likely to break out without warning. If not completely at home in both

39. See chapter 6.

pleasance and wood, it nevertheless moves between the two more easily and plays more roles in the human stories than can the other animals. Although the bear had been sacred to Artemis, who was worshiped in its form in Arcadia,[40] it is less prominent in classical sources of Italian pastoral than might be expected. Slighted in the *Bucolics* and *Daphnis and Chloe* (which contrariwise is full of wolves), it is merely mentioned in the plural as *informes ursi* in the *Georgics*.[41] In *The Golden Ass* of Apuleius, however, which contains a variety of elements later found mixed in Italian drama (romance, rural life, metamorphosis, divine intervention), the two appearances of bears are arresting in the contrast they make: one emerges from a cave in the woods to dismember a boy; the second is dressed as a matron and carried through the city in a procession honoring Isis, goddess of all nature.[42]

Lack of a fixed character or, rather, inherent versatility of character is suitable in a creature described by Aristotle and Pliny as unformed at birth and requiring literally to be licked into shape by its mother.[43] Although the bear was relatively neglected in medieval bestiaries, perhaps owing to its omission from the Greek *Physiologus* and its earliest Latin continuations, the notion of its infantine shapelessness was perpetuated and strengthened by Isidore's derivation of *ursus* from *orsus* (beginning), because the cub is formed *ore* (with the mouth).[44] As a Vergilian metaphor of art, that is, of the imposition of form by a controlling mind, moreover, the bear's beginning was meditated in the Renaissance. In *La Chiappinaria*, a comedy of disguise and mistaken identity depending on a bear and a bearskin, Della Porta expands the literal and visual elements of the play into imagery by having Truffa, the manipulator, liken his plan, the intrigue and essence of the comedy itself, to the bear cub shaped by its mother.[45] Traditionally, as a fact of natural history, as a literary subject, and as simile, the bear is unformed and therefore poten-

40. August Friedrich von Pauly, *Real-Encyclopädie der klassischen Altertumswissenshaft*, ed. George Wissowa, II.2 (Stuttgart, 1896), 2761.

41. Vergil, III. 247.

42. Apuleius, *The Golden Ass*, trans. W. Adlington, rev. by Stephen Gaselee, Loeb Classical Library, (Cambridge, Mass., and London, 1915), VII.334, 338; XI.552.

43. Pauly, *Real-Encyclopädie*, 2759.

44. Florence McCulloch, *Mediaeval Latin and French Bestiaries* (Chapel Hill, rev. ed., 1962), 16–17, 26–27, 94.

45. Giambattista Della Porta, *La Chiappinaria, commedia* (Rome, 1609), I.5.

tially either tragic or comic; it must therefore have seemed almost emblematic of the tragicomic genre, which was primarily associated with the pastoral mode and was gradually formed and licked amid vivid controversy.

In the selva the theatrical bears may be harmful, as fatal to man as any lion or wolf, but even there without the uncompromising feral majesty of the one or the deceitful evil of the other. Sometimes they are simple predators, like the bear in the *Mucedorus* of 1598; in Pino's *Eunia* Nippio escapes from one such and Mindio is falsely reported to have been devoured by another, or perhaps by the same one.[46] The bear hunt, too, is a common activity for stage shepherds, as apparently it is for Bohemian rustics in *The Winter's Tale*.

But bears also function in Italian pastoral in ways unthinkable for other wild beasts. In Groto's *Pentimento amoroso* a shepherdess convicted of complicity in murder is condemned to be executed by being torn apart by a bear.[47] Here is a destructive bear for which destroying is a social function, a bear with a place within the human establishment, albeit a tragic one. It would be hard to imagine a wolf so employed; wolves are far more prominent in the pastoral, but not on the side of law and order any more than on the side of happiness.

In the pleasance the ursine character sometimes paradoxically becomes comic, appearing in the person of a bearish human, a clown made more ridiculous by virtue of identification with the beast. Cresci provides a striking case in Orsacchio, whose name probably comes from Sannazaro's Ursacchio, the hairy servant of Carino.[48] Cresci develops the possibilities dramatically, uniting with the name the qualities of the villano, whose function in pastoral plays is usually adapted from that of the commedia servo. Orsacchio counteracts the upward tendency of pastoral love by his grossness: his love is lust, his fidelity is promiscuity, his song is coarse, he drinks and urinates in public and is afraid of storms. He lives in the pleasance and serves the upper world of Arcadia, for which he is a foil and at which he pokes fun. He is both in it and against it, and stands in nature between the spiritual shepherds and

46. Bernardino Pino, *L'Eunia, ragionamenti pastorali* (Venice, 1582), IV.1, III.5.

47. Luigi Groto, *Il pentimento amoroso, nuova favola pastorale* (Venice, 1585), V.1.

48. Jacopo Sannazaro, *Arcadia*, VI.9, XI.29, in *Opere volgari*, ed. Alfredo Mauro (Bari, 1961).

the beasts, but unlike the satiro he is not of an order other than human. Cresci shows that the bear could belong to both prato and selva, to civilized and savage, to laughter and tears, as the other beasts could not. Dorinda's capraio Lupino in *Il pastor fido* is vestigially comic, it is true, but his dim ludicrousness (really simple cowardice) is not connected with his name, which merely indicates his possession of the garments evocative of Greek romance and necessary to Dorinda's disguise. The lupine element remains serious and sinister, for Dorinda's action is not comic. The wolfish deceit is directed to amatory purposes, but only in the tragic or potentially tragic phase of this love action. Even when it opposes love, whether by violence or by laughter, the ursine element, beast or clown, is not like other savage natures in the world, not like the domesticated animals who are mere conveniences and never willingly oppose humans; instead, it suggests human nature primitive but promising, somewhat amenable to refining influences.

For transitions especially the bear is a tragicomic beast par excellence. Often in Italian pastoral mistaken reports of dismemberment of pastori or ninfe by wild beasts are circulated on the evidence of bloody garments, so that a period of apparent tragedy ensues and must be ended by a complete reversal. The supposed disasters take place in the wilderness far offstage, where rage the forces of death, lust, or sin (depending on how deep into the inner life the dramatist intends to plunge). A remarkable fusing of tragedy and comedy is achieved by Vida in the last act of his bad play *Filliria*, as his love-scorning huntress makes an entrance as sensational as Antigonus's exit: "Filliria che vien fuggendo da un orso, & salisce sopra un Faggio" (Enter Filliria fleeing a bear and climbs a beech).[49] From its branches she watches the thwarted bear turn toward the deep wood where she has left her quiver and some clothing, and in a monologue she describes how he tears these to pieces in rage. At the very moment peril is averted its horror is evoked, while laughter is added to joy and terror in the spectacle of a half-dressed shepherdess discoursing in a treetop. Were lion, boar, or wolf substituted for bear, the effect would be unbalanced, weighted toward terror—more so, in fact, than if the bear were kept but Filliria's death were substituted for her escape. She does escape, unlike Antigonus, because Vida's symbolism is only sexual; his beast and intermediate place belong to a world in which virgin nymphs learn about love, whereas Shakespeare's seaside "desert" is a place where things dead and things newborn are found,

49. Gieronimo Vida, *Fillira, favola boscareccia* (Venice, 1587), V.1.

but not a place to live. The presence of the bear, however, makes either outcome possible and ensures the tempering of pain or laughter.

Although the mixture of tragedy and comedy that exercised late sixteenth-century Italian critics was tried by dramatists in various combinations from tragedia di fin lieto to commedia grave, the culmination of the movement was tragicommedia pastorale, itself a term not restricted to a single type. Although never so well formulated in England, a more than merely practical interest in mixture of dramatic genres existed there too, as even the primitive *Mucedorus* shows in the battle in its Induction between Comedy and Envy, who threatens to introduce tragedy into the action. The organization of *The Winter's Tale* and the materials selected for emphasis from Shakespeare's source declare his concern for shaping a clearly tragicomic form and enriching it through pastoral convention. He added to act 1 two happy scenes not found in Greene's *Pandosto*, to lighten the tragic first half of the story. He definitively transformed the ending to produce the general joy established by Italian experiment as the conclusion proper to the new genre of tragicomedy. For the latter alteration of his source he employed pastoral theatergrams made more plausible: the maga with her spells becomes Paulina, whose last speeches merely suggest incantations; the transformation to stone statue and back again, a favorite among Ovidian metamorphoses in Italian drama, becomes the staged effect of Hermione's return.

Shakespeare's major means of achieving formal tragicomedy, however, was his disposition of the third act. There have been many defenses of the achievement since Quiller-Couch's charge that tragedy and comedy in *The Winter's Tale* are not in fact interwoven.[50] Tillyard observes the deliberate exaggeration of dramatic devices and language in Antigonus's dream and death, which put an end to the tortured world of Leontes and save Perdita's joyful world from the appearance of slightness that might arise from directly juxtaposing the two.[51] Bethell sees the account of Antigonus's end as a presentation *sub specie aeternitatis*, revealing that death by shipwreck or by bear is less serious than we may think. He defines the viewpoint in general as comic, but with reversals of attitude, for example, toward tragic tempests and comic rustics. Fur-

50. Arthur Quiller-Couch and John Dover Wilson, eds., *The Works of Shakespeare*, vol. 32, *The Winter's Tale* (Cambridge, England, 1931, 2d repr. 1959), Introduction, xxv.

51. Tillyard, *Shakespeare's Last Plays*, 77–78.

ther, he regards the exit with bear, like Autolycus's later walking aside to urinate, as Shakespeare's deliberate return to outmoded dramatic machinery, calling attention to technique and thus distancing the story, so that the spectator may remain uninvolved with it and free to hear the higher (or deeper) statements.[52]

These and other recognitions of Shakespeare's techniques for balancing tragedy and comedy in act 3 seem to me to be true, but to overlook some of the specific loaded elements he uses to this purpose. The story, the dream, and the comic rustic are commonplaces of Italian pastoral tragicomedy, as is the ambiguous bear, the cooperation of which makes Antigonus's death and the description of its meaning fully two-sided, not merely double as Quiller-Couch would have it.[53] The scene occurs in the middle of the play, in a no man's land uninhabited even by the bear, between two worlds: one corresponds to the stage-set of Italian theatrical pastorals, the other to the court almost invariably mentioned in such plays but never seen, both part of the pastoral in the largest sense, which includes its own antithesis. Using more than a single setting, Shakespeare could make visible what in Italian plays could only be referred to (the court) or suggested by a border (the selva on the edge of the deeper forest). Every means linking the two worlds seems to have been pondered. Shakespeare may have been capable of extracting fun as well from the dismemberment of an old man by a wolf or a boar, but the effect would surely have been more strained and idiosyncratic. By choosing the bear he diminished the effort, so that like the beast itself the action could become more naturally tragicomic, and the tragicomedy more symbolic of the drama of human loss and recovery played out in the natural world.

52. Bethell, *Winter's Tale: A Study,* 64–65, 49ff.
53. Quiller-Couch and Wilson, *The Winter's Tale,* III.3.105–06.

CHAPTER SIX

The Third Genre:
Pastoral Hybrids

eginning with J. W. Lever's introduction to the Arden edition of *Measure for Measure* (1965), there have been signs in recent decades of a reappraisal of Elizabethan and Jacobean response to Italian drama.[1] The signs are heartening, despite a lack of consensus among the appraisers. If G. K. Hunter and Arthur Kirsch tacitly diverge from each other and from Lever in defining Italian tragicomedy, if Richard Cody and Jackson Cope reach no common ground while finding evidence of neo-platonic dramaturgy in Italy and England, and if Leo Salingar slights the late Cinquecento comedies nearest in time and importance to the Elizabethans in favor of those written before Elizabeth's birth,[2] these scholars, for all the distinctively original characters of their contributions, are

Parts of this chapter appeared in slightly different form in "La mimesi della realtà invisibile nel dramma pastorale italiano e inglese del tardo rinascimento," *Misure Critiche* 4, nos. 6–9 (1974): 65–92; and "Il teatro manieristico italiano e Shakespeare," in *Cultura e società nel rinascimento tra riforme e manierismi,* ed. Vittore Branca and Carlo Ossola (Florence, 1984), 427–48. Since 1974 valuable and sometimes related new perspectives on Italian pastoral drama have been published, especially in the works of Susanne Stamnitz, Marzia Pieri, Riccardo Bruscagli, Alain Godard, Luigia Zilli, and Jane Tylus referred to in the following notes.

1. William Shakespeare, *Measure for Measure,* ed. J. W. Lever (London and Cambridge, Mass., 1965). A powerful earlier impetus to reevaluation, but with delayed results, was given by Madeline Doran, *Endeavors of Art: A Study of Form in Elizabethan Drama* (Madison, 1954).

2. G. K. Hunter, "Italian Tragicomedy on the Engish Stage," *Renaissance Drama,* n.s. 6 (Evanston, Ill., 1975): 123–48; Arthur C. Kirsch, *Jacobean Dramatic Perspectives* (Charlottesville, 1972); Richard Cody, *The Landscape of the Mind: Pastoralism and Platonic Theory in Tasso's "Aminta" and Shakespeare's Early Comedies* (Oxford, 1969); Jackson I. Cope, *The Theater and the Dream: From Metaphor to Form in Renaissance Drama* (Baltimore, 1973); Leo Salingar, *Shakespeare and the Traditions of Comedy* (Cambridge, England, 1974).

cooperating to demonstrate the international nature of Renaissance drama and the scale on which Italian innovations infiltrated the English stage.

In the sixteenth-century exploration of theatrical materials and shapes there was a line of Italian experiments leading to important results that Shakespeareans have hardly noticed. Beginning in commedia erudita with the extension of the principle of contaminatio to include not only the fusion of two plots, as Terence had defended doing, or of three, as Caro announced for *Gli straccioni,* or even of as many as may be discerned in the multiple intrecci of Pino or of Castelletti, but also the conflation of theatergrams of action, character, and language from innumerable sources, experimentation finally arrived at a wholesale combining of generic elements and aims chosen for their presumed incompatability within the limits of the ideal forms of regular comedy and tragedy, then still in the process of practical definition for the vernacular theater. The playwrights' aim in this systematic transgression was to test the nascent rules and the possibility of inventing a regular genre corresponding to the third of the stage sets extrapolated from Vitruvius by Serlio as "Scena Comica . . . Scena Tragica . . . Scena Satirica,"[3] or to establish precedents for other generic mixtures; the products often seemed monstrous and sometimes still do. Relevant to such results is Thomas McFarland's comment on a late English experiment in this line: "In *Cymbeline,* where death does occur, the function of comedy is distorted and pushed beyond its limits, and comic symmetries dissolve into asymmetrical grotesqueries of locale, characterization, and time scheme. For example, a consul from antique Rome joins a Renaissance Italian Machiavel in leading an army at Milford Haven in Wales. In this play, indeed, it is as though the harmonies of *Così fan tutte* are threatened by the tormented strainings of *Wozzeck.*"[4]

The incongruity that McFarland evokes to communicate the force of Shakespeare's contaminatio was the danger feared but risked in more timid and less successful attempts at a noble hybrid by Italian dramatists of earlier date. If it produced no Italian Shakespeare, however, the search for mixed genres, conducted on the liberalized principle of contaminatio, had its successes. None had farther-reaching effects than the pastoral play with pretensions to regularity, and none has been more

3. Sebastiano Serlio, *Il secondo libro, di prospettiva* (1545), in *I sette libri dell'architettura* (Venice, 1584; facsimile repr. Bologna, 1978), I. [49v–] 51.

4. *Shakespeare's Pastoral Comedy* (Chapel Hill, 1972), 17.

Battista Guarini, *Il pastor fido, tragicomedia pastorale*, III (Venice, 1602).
Courtesy of the Folger Shakespeare Library

neglected as a genre. Although *Aminta* and *Il pastor fido* have always enjoyed secure places in the literary canon of the international Renaissance, and although Italianists know the satira of Giraldi Cinzio, the favole pastorali of Groto and Bonarelli, and the *pescatoria* of Ongaro, there are not many readers today of Cremonini's favola silvestre, Pona's pastorale,[5] or the more obscure members of their enormous family. Yet this genre, not adequately represented by *Aminta* or *Il pastor fido*, is uniquely revealing of the fermentation of Renaissance dramaturgy and of the influence of the Italian theater on the Elizabethan, a power traditionally underrated by those whose ideas of influences in drama go only as far as external resemblances and evidences of verbal borrowings from specific individual sources. As Greg informed our grandparents,[6] there was hardly any pastoral drama worth mentioning in England, if by pastoral drama is meant faithful rendering of plots, costumes, settings, and language of Italian favole boschereccie and tragicommedie pastorali. Lyly certainly knew the genre enough to make piecemeal appropriations from it, but Daniel's *Queen's Arcadia* and Fletcher's *Faithful Shepher-*

5. Giovanni Battista Giraldi, *Egle, satira* (n.p. [Ferrara], n.d. [1545–50?]); Luigi Groto, *Il pentimento amoroso, nuova favola pastorale* (Venice, 1585); Guidubaldo Bonarelli, *Filli di Sciro, favola pastorale* (Ferrara, 1607); Antonio Ongaro, *Alceo, favola pescatoria* (Venice, 1582); Cesare Cremonini, *Le pompe funebri, over Aminta e Clori, favola silvestre* (Ferrara, 1590); Giovanni Battista Pona, *Tirrheno, pastorale* (Verona, 1589). See chapter 4 for some aspects of the first four. Marzia Pieri's *La scena boschereccia nel rinascimento italiano* (Padua, 1983) provides the indispensable critical survey of a genre that is at last beginning to receive its due. Riccardo Bruscagli's reevaluation of Giraldi's theater, "La corte in scena. Genesi politica della tragedia ferrarese," and "G. B. Giraldi: comico, satirico, tragico," in *Stagioni della civiltà estense* (Pisa, 1983), 127–86, includes a new lease on the pastoral. In asking original questions about *Egle* in her "Purloined Passages: Giraldi, Tasso and the Pastoral Debate," *Modern Language Notes* 99, no. 1 (January 1984): 101–24, Jane Tylus signals the awakening of a new interest in the Italian pastoral on the part of American scholars. Among Italo-French comparative studies, Luigia Zilli's *La ricezione francese del "Pentimento Amoroso"* (Udine, 1984) brings Groto's pastoral to modern readers and illuminates it by the kind of analysis so successfully used by Daniela Dalla Valle in her study of the French reception of Guarini and his epigones, *Pastorale barocca. Forme e contenuti dal Pastor Fido al dramma pastorale francese* (Ravenna, 1973).

6. W. W. Greg, *Pastoral Poetry and Pastoral Drama: A Literary Inquiry, with Special Reference to the Pre-Restoration Stage in England* (London, 1906), esp. 262–63.

dess are among the very few plays that could be called English imitations of the Italian model (and even to the latter this provenance has sometimes been denied or at least minimized).[7]

More difficult to recognize are the resemblances under the surface between Italian pastorals and various kinds of English plays, and yet these are so numerous as to confirm the impression that English dramatists were aware not merely of one or another specific Italian play but rather of Italian theatrical fashion in general. That Elizabethan and Jacobean dramatists knew some plays from the early Cinquecento and many produced by contemporary Italians has been established by traditional source studies.[8] More significant for the question of Anglo-Italian rapport is the possibility that the genres, topics, and commonplaces of the Italian theater were known or known of in England without reference to any particular playwright or play. The evidence is especially important for doing justice to Shakespeare, whose work, albeit quintessentially English and with roots in medieval soil, demands recognition as avantgarde drama in which the latest theatrical fashions were appropriated in dazzlingly new combinations.

7. Greg, *Pastoral Poetry*, 262, grudgingly recognizes the "incentive" as Italian. And although Marco Mincoff objects to Eugene Waith's underestimating Guarini's influence on Fletcher's characterization, even he sees the influence as primarily external; see *"The Faithful Shepherdess:* a Fletcherian Experiment," *Renaissance Drama* 9 (1967): 177. In *Prettie Tales of Wolues and Sheepe: Tragikomik, Pastorale und Satire im Drama der englischen und italienischen Renaissance, 1550–1640* (Heidelberg, 1977), 22, Susanne Stamnitz affirms English familiarity with Italian drama and considers *The Queen's Arcadia* a milestone in seventeenth-century attempts at an independent English pastoral drama, following on preliminary combinations of Italian elements by Peele, Lyly, and Shakespeare.

8. The range of connections may be gauged by scanning the volumes of Geoffrey Bullough's *Narrative and Dramatic Sources of Shakespeare* (London, 1957–66). Among permanently useful contributions on Italian sources are those of O. J. Campbell and Daniel C. Boughner, and such basic reference works as F. S. Boas, *University Drama in the Tudor Age* (Oxford, 1914); G. C. Moore Smith, *College Plays Performed in the University of Cambridge* (Cambridge, 1923); M. A. Scott, *Elizabethan Translations from the Italian* (Boston, 1916); R. W. Bond, ed., *Early Plays from the Italian* (Oxford, 1911); Ferdinando Neri, *Scenari delle maschere in Arcadia* (Città di Castello, 1913; repr. Turin, 1961); K. M. Lea, *Italian Popular Comedy: A Study in the Commedia Dell'Arte, 1560–1620, with Special Reference to the English Stage*, 2 vols. (Oxford, 1934).

The single most innovative construction of Italian dramaturgy in this period was the pastoral drama. After many years during which shepherds had appeared onstage in one context or another (from the time of Poliziano's *Orfeo* in the preceding century onward), and amid critical debates about its admissibility to the pantheon of regular genres, the pastoral play finally achieved in the second half of the Cinquecento the status of drama worthy of being defended on the basis of literary criticism. In this long cultivation, the court of Ferrara enjoyed a nurturing eminence but other courts and academies also, in collaboration with the professional players, made flourish the pastoral and the experiments toward a third genre. Whether they were imposing *tragicommedie pastorali* full of intrigue plotting and movement like *Il pastor fido,* or *favole boschereccie* lyrical and slender like *Aminta,* or gallimaufries of fantasy and farce like Pasqualigo's *Intricati,* the Italian Arcadian plays, beginning with Giraldi's in the 1540s and Beccari's in the 1550s, constitute a canon from which criteria may be deduced and in which generic aims and practices may be discerned and abstracted to reveal kinship with developments in theater abroad.[9]

The inquiry is more profitably undertaken with the aid of conclusions shared by students of English pastoral, for with some exceptions Italian scholars have hardly taken seriously the content of their own pastoral drama, even those like Tasso's and Guarini's that are ranked high on stylistic grounds by expositors of mannerism and the baroque in literature.[10] Although it has long been remarked that the Renaissance

9. Alvise (Luigi) Pasqualigo, *Gl'intricati, pastorale* (Venice, 1581); Giraldi's *Egle,* performed in Ferrara, 1545; Agostino Beccari, *Il sacrificio, favola pastorale* (Ferrara, 1555). Primary bibliography of Italian pastorals is found in Carrara's panorama, in Raffaele De Bello's "Bibliografia della collana palatina delle pastorali," *Studi Secenteschi* 5 (1964): 161–74; 6 (1965): 285–98; 7 (1966): 145–54, and throughout Marzia Pieri's *La scena boschereccia.* Pieri traces the pastoral from the Quattrocento, and although not concerned to connect its vogue in the late Cinquecento with theoretical experimentation toward a third genre, she recognizes the second half of the century as its definitive phase and provides valuable material on the printed texts from that period.

10. Outstanding among Italianists' considerations of Guarini's content are Marziano Guglielminetti's "Introduzione," *Opere di Battista Guarini,* 2d ed. (Turin, 1971); Ferruccio Ulivi, "La poetica del Guarini e il *Pastor fido,*" *Humanitas* 6 (1951): 88–103; Nicolas J. Perella, "Fate, Blindness, and Illusion," and "Amarilli's Dilemma," quoted in chapter 5, above. See also *The Critical Fortunes of Battista Guarini's "Il Pastor Fido"* (Florence, 1973), and "Heroic

enthusiasm for pagan culture produced representations in the figurative arts, eventually including gardening and scene design, of an idyllic Ovidian and Arcadian world expressing the yearnings of the spirit,[11] generally absent from the Italian range of literary critical perspectives is the view of Renaissance pastoral as a form or vehicle for idea, be it the defense of contemplation or the debate between nature and art; or, however it is put (now more, now less philosophical in thrust), the pastoral as a landscape of the mind, as the heart's forest, as wish fulfillment, as you like it.[12]

Virtue and Love in the *Pastor Fido*," *Atti dell'Istituto Veneto di Scienze, lettere ed Arti* 132 (1974): 653–706; Roberto Alonge, "Appunti per il *Pastor fido*," *Lettere Italiane* 23 (1971): 381–87; Dalla Valle, *Pastorale barocca.* Such precedents, as well as the investigations fostered by the Centre Interuniversitaire de Recherche sur la Renaissance Italienne, which produces such volumes as *Ville et campagne dans la littérature italienne de la Renaissance*, vol 2, *Le courtisan travesti*, ed. André Rochon (Paris, 1977), have nourished the new awareness of the intellectual and cultural weight of the pastoral play. This is admirably represented by Gian Piero Maragoni, "Il carattere del genere drammatico pastorale e la *Filli di Sciro* di Guidubaldo Bonarelli," *Critica Letteraria* 8, no. 3 (1980): 559–80; and by Alain Godard, "La *Filli di Sciro* de Guidubaldo Bonarelli: précédents littéraires et nouveaux impératifs idéologiques," *Réécritures: Commentaires, parodies, variations dans la littérature italienne de la Renaissance* (Paris, 1984), 2: 141–225.

11. Pieri, *La scena boschereccia*, 185ff.

12. The decades following Bruno Snell's "Arkadien: Die Entdeckung einer geistigen Landschaft," *Antike und Abendland* 1 (Hamburg, 1945): 26–41, have produced most notably the following: Frank Kermode, introduction to his Arden ed. of *The Tempest* (London, 1954); Renato Poggioli, *The Oaten Flute: Essays on Pastoral Poetry and the Pastoral Ideal* (Cambridge, Mass., 1975); Paul J. Alpers, *The Singer of the Eclogues: A Study of the Virgilian Pastoral* (Berkeley, 1969); Edward Tayler, *Nature and Art in Renaissance Literature* (New York and London, 1964); Northrop Frye, *A Natural Perspective: The Development of Shakespearean Comedy and Romance* (New York, 1965); Cody, *The Landscape of the Mind;* McFarland, *Shakespeare's Pastoral Comedy;* David Young, *The Heart's Forest: A Study of Shakespeare's Pastoral Plays* (New Haven, 1972). A good sampling of major earlier work in this vein is Eleanor Terry Lincoln, *Pastoral and Romance: Modern Essays in Criticism* (Englewood Cliffs, N.J., 1969). Such recent criticism as William W. E. Slights, "Nature's Originals: Value in Shakespeare's Pastoral," *Shakespeare Survey* 37 (1982): 69–74 demonstrates that the rediscovery of the philosophical and psychological capacity of the pastoral mode in the Renaissance has produced in-

This significance has often been examined in English pastoral of all genres, but without adequate distinction among them; for the art of theatrical representation, for the Renaissance dramatist, the choice of the landscape of the mind as a setting presented challenges different from those facing narrative or lyric poets of the pastoral. To find precedents and pregnant analogies for the theatrical form given to the inner landscape and for Shakespeare's use of Arcadian elements, the place to look is in Italian pastoral drama of his time and of the generation just before his.

In the pastoral play is revealed with greatest clarity the intention that I propose as the most serious motivation of many late sixteenth-century Italian regular dramatists: that is, to give the comedy, tragedy, and calculated mixtures of the two a new object of imitation. Imitation of reality, the avowed aim for the burgeoning corpus of theater in search of theory in the first half of the Cinquecento, summed up for comedy in Donatus's much-quoted "imitation of life, mirror of custom, image of truth," remained an objective for the generations variously described as mannerist, prebaroque, and baroque. But these generations extended their range, not content to imitate only the reality of the physically visible world that the senses suffice to apprehend.

Theoreticians of drama obscured the new aim by harping on the *naturale* and the *verosimile* and debating the decorum of assigning polished speeches to the lips of shepherds. Critical formulation of the impulse to represent invisibile reality is to be found only indirectly, in the treatises on the principle of imitation as the aim of poetry, such as Fracastoro's dialogue on poetics, *Naugerius*, or Tasso's observations on the choice of subject for the epic in his *Discorsi del poema eroico.*[13]

---

struments, controversies, and perceptions that continue to prove illuminating for the study of Shakespeare. Directed to Italian literature, the perception of the immensely allusive power of the pastoral mode has produced seminal results in William J. Kennedy's *Jacopo Sannazaro and the Uses of Pastoral* (Hanover, N.H., and London, 1983); part of the harvest will appear in the field of drama.

13. Although controversies about history versus fiction as proper subjects and moral instruction versus pleasure as proper aim were staples of Renaissance treatises on drama, they contributed relatively little to the mass of critical writing on the idea of imitation, which has so richly furnished modern historians of literary theory: see for example Baxter Hathaway, *The Age of Criticism: The Late Renaissance in Italy* (Ithaca, 1962); Ferruccio Ulivi, *L'imitazione nella poetica del rinascimento* (Milan, 1959); and Riccardo Scrivano's review and ar-

The texts of Italian drama, however, and especially those of pastoral plays, manifest the aspiration toward a reality not directly accessible to the physical senses, a reality with two aspects. The more immediate of these was the interior world of emotion, particularly that of love and its related feelings, with a generous gamut of psychological refinements and variations. This was a reality always potentially important to Italian drama, and, as time passed, increasingly prominent in comedies and tragedies. But not even the gravest commedia grave or the most amatory tragedia di fin lieto of the Counter-Reformation period could fully satisfy the desire of dramatist and public to cultivate a regular genre that could concentrate on emotion without having to offer a mirror of custom, like comedy, or arouse terror and pity, like tragedy. A need was felt for a genre that would function as the vehicle of love, with love itself as protagonist, without the distraction of the social or political considerations held to be appropriate to the other two genres.

Although polemics about pastoral tragicomedy usually pivoted on the questions of mixing genres and of justifying within canons of verisimilitude and reason the civilizing depiction of country folk, critical observations on the subject let transpire the assumption that the pastoral world is the home of the naked heart. In the first defense of his controversial tragicomedy, Guarini finds in Arcadia "la nostra natura quasi vergine senza lisci, e senz'alcuno di quelli artifici, e di quelle finte apparenze che sono peccati propri della città" (our nature as if virgin, without embellishments, and without any of those artifices and false appearances which are the sins of the city). So too Leone De'Sommi, whose *Hirifile, pastorale* and dialogues on theatrical theory and practice probably antedate *Aminta*, says of pastoral eclogues: "Hanno per soggetto l'appresentare sotto abiti di pastori et di dei o dee, quella simplicità purità et piacevolezza de' primi secoli di che favolosamente si fa menzione da' nostri celebrati poeti" (they have for their subject the presentation, in the costumes of shepherds and of gods or goddesses, the

---

ticle of 1961 on the latter, reprinted in his *Cultura e letteratura nel Cinquecento* (Rome, 1966), 315–30. In "Purloined Passages," 18, Jane Tylus's comments on Giraldi's *Discorso* and his handling of characters as visual manifestations of the contrivances required to solve the pastoral's central problem of mediation between city and country give an exceptional view of a writer of both plays and treatises wrestling with one of the difficulties of attempting to represent the immaterial.

simplicity, purity and pleasure of primitive times fabled by our celebrated poets).[14]

The idea of an invisible reality was not, however, limited to the inner
reality of the heart but extended outward to a circumambient truth en-
visaged as giving form and meaning to human life and to multiple interwoven and tangled actions belonging to it. This was a reality of pure
idea or abstract pattern, to be seen only by the eyes of the mind, "gl'occhi dell'intelletto," the neoplatonic phrase reiterated and reflected in innumerable pastoral plays by the imagery of blindness and the choreo-
graphed confusion of intrigue plots, apparently chaotic except to the
enlightened spectator supposed capable of discerning in them a pattern
of higher meaning according with the providential plan of a divinity.
Only the mind's eye was expected to comprehend the totality of what to
the eyes of physical sense must appear to be a series of single moments;
the impression of jumble produced by this immediate physical reality is
revealed as mere appearance in contrast with that nonmaterial reality of
the landscape accessible to the intellect.

Given Shakespeare's use of pastoral elements in various ways less apparent than the outright presence of shepherds in *As You Like It* and
The Winter's Tale, and given too the ceaseless experimentation with generic mixtures in which he never simply repeated himself, a pastoral
genre cannot be isolated from the rest of the Shakespearean canon.
Turning from the obvious Arcadian elements infrequently present in
Shakespeare to some concerns equally obvious but very frequent will
bring us to the dual invisible realities relevant to the essential character
of Italian pastoral drama, as the external trappings of Arcadian decor
are not.

First is the deceptively simple fact that in comedy Shakespeare, like
Lyly, places the life of the heart at the center of the action and examines
love under various aspects, but deploys a broader range of character
types than does Lyly in plots that exhibit their diversity in love, without
confining the actuality of their dramatic life to the exigencies of debate.
In a peal of changes on the basic tones, *Two Gentlemen of Verona,*
Twelfth Night, A Midsummer Night's Dream, and *Much Ado about*

---

14. Battista Guarini, *Il Verato ovvero difesa di quanto ha scritto M. Giason
Denores contra le tragicomedie, e le pastorali, in un suo discorso di poesia* (Ferrara, 1588) [11v]; Leone De' Sommi, *Quattro dialoghi in materia di rappresentationi sceniche,* ed. Ferruccio Marotti (Milan, 1968), 34.

Nothing test the kinds and shifts of love and attest its primal force; in different keys *Cymbeline, The Winter's Tale,* and *The Tempest* exhibit the heart's truth in instinctive collaboration with the intellectually perceived truth of a reconciling, providential force that works redemption in a cursed and corrupt society.[15]

Equally relevant to these comparisons are Shakespeare's various probings in *As You Like It, The Winter's Tale,* and *Cymbeline* of the philosophical topic of nature versus art, not only by the literary means of debates and monologues but also by dramatic encounters between characters and in the disposition of plot lines. So too are his free use of expressionistic means and spectacular elements—plays within plays, dances, masquerades, and masques—to give physical confirmation to data of feeling or thought, and his occasional resorting to magic, demonic spirits, and metamorphoses (in *A Midsummer Night's Dream* openly, in *The Winter's Tale* rationalized in the name of versimilitude) to provide a theatrically visible image of psychological change, of an identity crisis symptomatic of inner illumination, or of the mysterious relation between human life and the powers shaping it. One such transcendent force is the providence that through vatic or unwitting agents executes designs invisible to the confused characters in *The Winter's Tale* and *The Tempest*. The power itself may be metamorphic, fre-

---

15. Although I attribute to Shakespeare a fuller and more direct knowledge of the Italian theater than he could have acquired solely by inheritance from Lyly, I do not wish the rapport with Italy that radiates from Shakespeare's work to diminish the importance of Lyly's previous reception of Italian fashions, or of his lesson to younger dramatists. The distance between Lyly's "theses" plays that are discussed by Joel Altman in *The Tudor Play of Mind: Rhetorical Inquiry and the Development of Elizabethan Drama* (Berkeley, Los Angeles, and London, 1978), 197 and chapter 7, and Shakespeare's theatrically vital and savvy representations of love and providence in action is the same distance as that between the didactic purposes of the humanist as courtier who wrote plays (G. K. Hunter, *John Lyly: The Humanist as Courtier* [London, 1962]) and that of the actor, playwright, and shareholder of a professional company that performed at court a range of successful plays with remotely humanistic origins. The cognitive striving that is foremost in the Tudor debate play and underlies the Terentian comedy concluded by providential *anagnorisis* (discriminatingly examined by Altman, 392–393) feeds the tradition that ultimately includes Lyly, Shakespeare, and the Italian third genre, but only the last two seem to inhabit contemporaneously the same theatrical universe.

quently appearing as a happily boomeranging sin or disaster, necessarily reminiscent of the Christian *felix culpa* evident also in other Shakespearean plays more remote from pastoral.[16]

Although his green worlds are called not Arcadia but variously the Forest of Arden, a wood near Athens, an island, a desert country near the sea in Bohemia, Windsor Park, the villa of Belmont, a forest outside Mantua, and the mountains of Wales, Shakespeare's penchant for sending his characters temporarily and symbolically to the country must be included among the fundamental principles share with Italian pastoral drama. For though the natural locus of the *favola boschereccia* is ordinarily not a place to be visited and left within the represented action—a restriction in observance of the unity of place generally accepted by mid-Cinquecento as a convention for the regular dramatic genres—the pastoral setting, whether *in villeggiatura* near Rome or Florence, or at "Arquadia," as in the Venetian pastoral honoring Petrarch's last home,[17] is like Shakespeare's wide range of green worlds in being a contemplative space where self-knowledge is acquired or a celestial design glimpsed, where the sick mind may be healed (perhaps by passing through madness, an illuminating furor), and where humanity may be put into harmony with all nature, including its own.[18]

Looking at Italian pastoral plays from the milestone of Beccari's *Il sacrificio* at the court of Ferrara in 1555 through Shakespeare's lifetime, we find common features proclaiming a conflict: between on the one hand, the dramatists' desire to imitate the invisible double reality of the human heart and of the superhuman design analogous to Shakespeare's objects of imitation, and on the other the inhibitions imposed on would-

16. Kirsch, *Jacobean Dramatic Perspectives,* and Hunter, "Italian Tragicomedy," attribute the presence of a providential pattern in the late plays to the influence of Guarini's tragicomedy, but Shakespeare had already used the pattern in *The Comedy of Errors,* having had some acquaintance with the practice of earlier commedie gravi; see chapters 2 and 3, above.

17. Francesco Contarini, *La fida ninfa, favola pastorale* (Venice, 1599).

18. This occurs for example in Cucchetti's *La pazzia* and Maddalena Campiglia's *Flori, favola boschereccia* (Vicenza, 1588). On the simultaneously liberating and paralyzing relation between the worlds convoked in Tasso's *Aminta* (that of the vision of love presented by a fictive scene, probably at a première performance on the Belvedere islet outside Ferrara, to an audience from the real world of the urban court), see Giovanni Da Pozzo, *L'ambigua armonia: Studio sull' "Aminta" del Tasso* (Florence, 1983).

be regular drama by the flourishing new science of literary criticism. How to give regular organic form and theatrical substance to the interior landscape, avoiding simultaneously all the defects of the predecessors who had brought shepherds onstage: the naive roughness of the Sienese artisans' Congrega dei Rozzi, the too-specific social and linguistic compass of the inimitable Paduan Ruzante, and the undramatic stasis of the pioneers Poliziano and Calmo?

The majority of the new pastoral playwrights chose with Beccari to adapt to their green worlds the generic units, groupings, and shape of city comedy. Consequently, intrigue plotting and differentiated social levels were established as proper to Arcadia. The egalitarian atmosphere of the Quattrocento and early Cinquecento farces or eclogues, in which classical shepherds, local Italian peasants, the urban middle class, magicians, and pagan gods freely met and parted, was replaced with a social structure, sometimes tending toward the bourgeois ethos of comedy and sometimes toward the courtliness of tragedy. Guazzoni's *Andromeda* offers the example of Panfila, labeled *serva* in the dramatis personae, who describes her own function to Andromeda as "d'esser di tua madre pastorella" (III.1) In *Il pastor fido* the goatherd Lupino, who functions as a kind of balio to Dorinda, and the distance that Amarilli measures between herself and the simple pastorella whose carefree state she envies (II.5.627), are tragicomic expressions of the social distinctions imported into the pastoral world with the intrigue plot structure of regular comedy.[19] One of Shakespeare's major additions to his dramatization of Lodge's narrative *Rosalynde* is the jester Touchstone, who dallies with inarticulate peasants while his patrons consort with eloquent classical shepherds and with disguised aristocrats like themselves. A cliché has it that the English pastoral world is more natural and vital than the Italian because it contains real rustics as well as literary types; the use of caprai or pecorai as comic foils for the upper-class *pastori* by scores of such Italian playwrights as Castelletti and Simonetti should nullify this notion.

If structures from the commedia erudita appear in the pastoral, however, Arcadia is nonetheless a landscape of the mind, and the transplanted auxiliary figures function accordingly, not merely as participants in the sexual, domestic, and economic struggle of comedy but as

19. Diomisso Guazzoni, *Andromeda, tragicomedia boscareccia* (Venice, 1587); references to *Il pastor fido* are to the edition of Luigi Fassò, *Teatro del Seicento* (Milan and Naples, 1956).

illustrations in the spectacle of love and providence. Characters are treated less as individuals than as forces of nature in its range from the bestial to the extremes of spiritual love. Touchstone, who takes loves easily and woos his country wench so as not to have to sleep alone, corresponds to many Italian underlings of pastoral drama, including Cresci's capraio Orsacchio, who says

> Un tempo già fui anch'io inamorato
> De la bella Smartilla [Amarilli], & a la fine,
> Per che ella non mi amava, io la lasciai.
>
>   (II.3.p. 23)

Me too, I used to love pretty Marilly [Amaryllis] but finally she didn't love me back, so I left her.

and Lollio's Menalca, who sings drunkenly

> O foss'io nudo
> In braccio a chi vorrei. Quella crudele
> Pur mi vuol mal; ma io n'ho tante, e tante,
> Ch'io mi satollerò.   (II.2)

Oh, to be naked in the arms of the one I want. But that cruel she doesn't want me. Well, I've got plenty of others to satisfy my need.[20]

They all partake of the servo-padrone relationship, but their pastoral theatrical task is not primarily to serve their masters nor even only to furnish a materialistic dimension to balance the noble lovers' extreme idealism (like Sancho Panza in another genre), but also to represent to the "eyes of the intellect" some of the forms that human nature assumes in love. Their presence allows the motions of the heart to be presented with a wide range of attitude, language, and tone and with the juxtaposed opposites of laughter and tears, refinement and coarseness, and also has a share in helping the action of an ordering superhuman power presiding over a human tangle to be made visible through the frantic but ultimately symbolic scurryings of the intrigue plot.

As the pastorals of Guidozzo, Pasqualigo, and commedia dell'arte

20. Pietro Cresci, *Tirena, favola pastorale* (Venice, 1584); Alberto Lollio, *Aretusa, comedia pastorale* (Ferrara, 1564).

demonstrate,[21] bringing visitors from different classes into Arcadia also contributes to dramatization of the debate about nature and art,[22] posed as country versus city or court, in encounters analogous to those of the Shepherd Clown with Autolycus in *The Winter's Tale* or of Caliban with Trinculo and Stephano in *The Tempest,* in which the materialistic country bumpkin is impressed and then disillusioned by the city sharper, equally materialistic but less simple. In *As You Like It,* the rustic William, bereft of Audrey by the courtly slicker Touchstone, and Audrey herself, her disillusionment merely postponed until after the play, are more distant variations on the gulled villano of Italian drama, who belongs both to the traditional popular farce and to the new polished pastoral.

Another way of exploring the fundamental pastoral antithesis of city and country by means of dramatic imitation is illustrated in the mediocre work of Orlando Pescetti, a prolific writer of critical treatises and plays whose name has been linked often but doubtfully with Shakespeare's through his tragedy *Il Cesare.*[23] In his *Difesa del Pastor fido* Pescetti conscientiously exhibits the preoccupation with Aristotle of the typical well-informed critic, while also revealing some assumptions about the seriousness of pastoral drama and the metaphysical reality it imitates. He never falters in support of verisimilitude and mentions neither symbols nor abstract significance enclosed in the metaphor of dramatic plot. But in justifying the harsh law of Diana governing Guarini's Arcadia, which had been attacked as incredible and unjust by Giovanni Pietro Malacreta, Pescetti slips almost absent-mindedly into a Christianized, neoclassical language that was one of the garden varieties of baroque style, in which imagery and literal assertion mingle evasively:

> I segreti di Dio sono imperscrutabili, ned è sicuro cer care quel,
> che nell'abisso si racchiude della sua eterna providenza; perche

21. Giacomo Guidozzo, *Il capriccio, favola boscareccia* (Venice, 1608); Pasqualigo, *Gl'intricati;* Neri, *Scenari delle maschere.*

22. The range of approaches to this issue, established as a required topic in any discussion of Renaissance pastoral, may be measured by the distance between Tayler's limited formulation in *Nature and Art* and Rosalie L. Colie's freestyle dash in *Shakespeare's Living Art* (Princeton, 1974), 248–53.

23. The arguments for connecting *Il Cesare, tragedia* (Verona, 1594) with *Julius Caesar* are retailed by Marvin T. Herrick, *Italian Tragedy in the Renaissance* (Urbana, Ill., 1965), 156–57.

bene spesso a' troppo curiosi avviene quel, che à Semele, & ad Icaro favoleggiono i poeti esser addivenuto. Molte cose a noi, che nell'invoglio siamo di queste terrene membra inviluppati, paiono ingiuste, che giustissime sono nel cospetto di Dio.

The secrets of God are inscrutable, nor is it safe to search what is enclosed in the abyss of His eternal providence; for those who are too curious often suffer the fate of Semele and of Icarus, as the poets fable. Many things seem unjust to us, wrapped in this mortal coil, which are most just in the sight of God.

He ends by quoting Dante's "Be satisfied, human kind, with God's *quia*," then, seemingly unaware of the approaching contradiction, and confident that false pagan myths must continue to express eternal Christian truth, even as the Counter-Reformation waxed strong, he adds:

Pure nel caso nostro non sarebbe forse molto difficile a chi cercar la volesse, il ritrovar la cagione del rigore, e della severità di Diana nel flagellare il popolo d'Arcadia: e forse è questa, che ella era Nume di sua natura sdegnosissimo, come da molti autori, e particolarmente da Orazio si può cavare.

Yet in the case at hand, for one willing to seek, it would not be too difficult to find the reason for Diana's harshness and severity in scourging the people of Arcadia: and perhaps it is this, that she was by nature a very angry goddess, as can be learned from many authors, especially from Horace.[24]

The unexplicated, though not inexplicable, fusion of rational verisimilitude, Horatian authority, and quasi-allegorical exegesis briefly juxtaposing an inscrutable Christian providence and an angry Diana, produces a flourishing specimen of Counter-Reformation neomedievalism.

In 1589 Pescetti published *La regia pastorella*,[25] defined as *comedia pastoral* in the prologue but exercising the prerogatives of tragedy in its chorus and royal characters; it is a play that repays observation with

---

24. *Difesa del Pastor Fido . . . da quanto gli è stato scritto contro da gli Eccellentiss. SS. Faustin Summo e Gio Pietro Malacreta* (Verona, 1601), 159–60.
25. *La regia pastorella, favola boschereccia* (Verona, 1589).

The Winter's Tale in mind. Pescetti assigns the prologue to Flora as the presiding goddess of spring, who comes to adorn the scene with flowers and addresses the feminine members of the audience, declaring that she too was once mortal, "fui, qual siete / Voi, belle spettatrici, donna." The royal shepherdess of the title is Partenia, princess of Caria, lost fifteen years before the play begins and reared in Lidia by a shepherd, whose daughter she believes herself to be. The crown prince of Lidia, Toante, comes to hunt in the country and falls in love with her. The ending of their story is a foregone conclusion, a structural commonplace of the genre.

What is interesting is the way Pescetti uses this story reminiscent of currently fashionable Greek romance to set up dramatic conflicts that give theatrical substance to the opposition of country to city, or nature to art. As in *The Winter's Tale*, the idea is examined in its aspect of birth versus breeding, or heredity versus environment. Partenia's beauty is such as to cause all who see her to think her divine: like many other interlocutors in Italian pastoral, Toante and a character called simply *lo Straniero* echo Aeneas's "Dea certe" on first seeing Partenia, both addressing her as a celestial being ("dea celeste," I.2; V.1). Her answer, "Io son, qual tu, mortal" (I.2.: I am, like you, mortal), echoes the goddess Flora's greeting. In *The Winter's Tale*, of course, the lost princess Perdita herself embodies both goddess and shepherdess. It is she who is arrayed as the presiding pastoral queen for a day, she who distributes flowers, she who is hailed as Flora by her princely lover Florizel, whose own name reveals his predestined devotion to her and to the idea she figures forth—*zelo di Flora*.

Pescetti's Partenia is interested in the topos of nature and art, aligning herself with nature, and during the coy phase of the five-act courtship adducing it as a reason for remaining a virgin. She declares that Nature made her free and vows to remain so ("Libera mi produsse la Natura / Libera viver voglio, e morir libera," II.4). Refusing to marry Toante and go to court, she ends her manifesto with a defense of the life of pastoral tranquility, contemplation, and virginity. Toante answers that as a beauty she has a double responsibility: to reproduce and so improve the appearance of the human race, and to direct her lover's mind platonically to contemplation of the divine idea and source of beauty, both of which duties she may fulfill by marrying him:

> Non spiega i raggi della sua bellezza
> Nelle cose create il gran' Iddio,

Perch'a gli occhi s'ascondan de' mortali,
Ma perchè percuotendo col lor lume
L'alme, le desti, e alla contemplazione
L'erga di se, che è il sommo, e vero bello
Fonte d'ogni bellezza, nel qual poi
Affissando lo sguardo, di fervente
Amor di lui s'accendan tutte.   (I.2)

The great God does not unfold the rays of his beauty throughout the created world in order to hide them from mortal eyes, but so as to strike souls with their light and thus arouse and lift them to contemplation of himself who is the highest and the true beauty, source of all beauty, on which thereupon fixing their regard, the souls may be ignited by fervent love of him.

Partenia's resistance is an element complicating the plot and her own mental processes, which are busy but not very clear. She says she is proud of being as nature made her; like Shakespeare's Perdita, she thinks the selfsame sun shines on her cottage as on the court. But as her heart warms to Toante, she worries about the inequality of their ranks; again like Perdita, she opposes unequal marriages, which unnaturally graft a highborn plant on a low one. She does not go in for the agricultural metaphor of Perdita's famous "gillyvor" speech, but "lo Straniero" does: like Shakespeare's Polixenes when he comes incognito to the country, the Stranger expresses wonder at encountering such exquisite beauty in the wilderness and issuing from a lowly shepherd. He asks if so noble a shoot may grow from so base a trunk, and concludes that it may, reminding himself that roses grow from thorny stems and lilies from fetid grasses:

Di ceppo cosi vil sì nobil germe?
Ma dalla spina ancor nasce la rosa,
E d'una fetid'erba nasce il giglio.
                                      (V.1)

He attaches greater importance to the result than to the source, and espouses the same argument favored by Polixenes: that both ends and means are decreed by nature.

At the denouement, when Partenia discovers that she is by birth (that is, by social rank) what she has always appeared to be by nature—princess, goddess, superior being—she shifts her ground and begins to worry instead that she lacks the nurture that would correspond to her nature and rank. She says she has been reared in the woods and has the manners of a crude mountain girl, not of a king's daughter:

> . . . . trà le selve
> Quantunque di real progenie, sono
> Stata nutrita; onde appellar mi posso
> Cittadina de' boschi; & hò creanze,
> Non da figlia real, ma da montana,
> E rozza villanella.   (V.5)

Partenia's declaration and condition are equally absurd if judged by principles of verisimilitude, considering that she has been observed onstage for five acts, holding her own in neoplatonic debates and roaming Arcadia elegantly dressed, as Toante describes her, in a green robe and white veil with sandals and matching accessories of gold. Her fears and Toante's reassurance bring the *Regia pastorella* startlingly close to *The Winter's Tale*. To her hope that she will not be a loss ("perdita" is her word) rather than an asset to her future husband, he answers, "O le perdite mie sien sempre tali" (V.5: Oh, may my losses ever be such!). More important than this coincidence of noun and name is the evidence that in dramatization of pastoral matter, whether by Italian poets or later by Shakespeare, the criterion of plausibility is not only neglected but challenged, whereas the topics proper to the pastoral tradition are given both expression in dialogue and as much physical theatrical reality as encounters between characters and turns of patterned plot allowed. The intention that transpires is that of persuading the spectators that although what is before them is no mirror of custom, it is yet an imitation of life and an image of truth, designed to make them think, to draw them by means of the senses into a world of ideas.

Another means employed by many Italian playwrights in developing a theatrical apparatus for Arcadia proved congenial to Shakespeare and Lyly for some versions of pastoral but was rejected by both Tasso and Guarini: the expressionistic use of fantastic actions, magic, and Ovidian metamorphosis among them, to make visible onstage a reality otherwise apprehensible only by the eyes of the intellect. A full-blown example of the magic favola boschereccia is offered by *Gl'intricati, pastorale,* written by the mysterious Count Luigi or Alvise Pasqualigo for performance at the Dalmatian court of Zara during the 1570s while

he was the Venetian commander there.[26] In his fashionable play appear
not only an early version of some structures and generic units that Lyly
later used in *Love's Metamorphosis* and Shakespeare in *A Midsummer
Night's Dream,* but also a demonstration of Italian interest in making
fantasy embody states of mind and abstract perceptions of being. Beginning with a love tangle borrowed from Montemayor's *Diana,* Pasqualigo sets up at the outset a basic pastoral complex of plot, topic, and
image. The nymph Selvaggia announces:

> Io per Alanio mi consumo, e moro.
> Alanio per Ismenia, ohimè, si strugge;
>
> . . . .
>
> Ismenia un tempo Alanio amar soleva
>
> . . . .
>
> Hor per Montano ell'arde.

I die for love of Alanio, he for Ismenia, who used to love him and
now adores Montano.

After setting forth other complications, she concludes:

> O inconstanza de l'humane cose,
> O disegni fallaci, o spemi incerte,
> O cieche menti nostre, inferme, e frali.
>   (I.2)

Oh, inconstancy of human things, oh erring designs and hopes, oh
how weak, infirm and blind our minds.

26. From Zara on Carnival Day, 1575, the author dedicated to Alvise
Georgio his comedy *Il fedele* (Venice, 1576), signing himself "Luigi Pasqualigo,
Conte." This was later adapted by Anthony Munday as *Fidele and Fortunio, the
Two Italian Gentlemen.* When Evangelista Ortense dedicated *Gl'intricati* in
1581 to Pietro Porto, prince of the Accademia degli Olimpici, he wrote that the
pastoral was written and performed while the late author was "in Reggimento a
Zara." See chapter 4, above, entry on "Pasqualigo," in *Italian Plays (1500–
1700) in the Folger Library* (Florence, 1968) and in Mauda Bregoli Russo,
*Renaissance Italian Theater: Joseph Regenstein Library of the University of
Chicago* (Florence, 1984); Richard Hosley, *A Critical Edition of Anthony Munday's Fedele and Fortunio* (New York, 1981); and Amedeo Quondam on Pasqualigo's *Lettere amorose,* in *Le 'carte messaggiere': Retorica e modelli di com-
unicazione espistolare* (Rome, 1981), 101–11.

The metaphor of blindness, and that contained in the later prayer addressed to Venus, "O mostrane la via, ch'uscir possiamo / Fuori di così oscuro labirinto" (IV.1: Oh, show us the way out of this dark labyrinth), state recurrent concepts—of sensory insufficiency, optical illusion, and the maze of error. These take on substance as theatergrams of action and place in the dramatized landscape of the mind.

The underside of love's spectacle is represented by the three buffoonish visitors to Arcadia, a villano from the Maremma and two raucous commedia dell'arte masks from the city. Unlike their opposite numbers in *A Midsummer Night's Dream*—Bully Bottom and his friends, who meet in the woods for the civic purpose, relevant to their social status and economic function, of rehearsing a competitive contribution to Duke Theseus's wedding festivities—the Maremmano, the Spanish braggart Calabaza, and the Bolognese Gracian are on a Saturnalian vacation, but they too take part in a theatrical venture, defining their low place in a neoplatonic plan of love by performing a kind of vaudeville turn in response to the shepherds' conventionally refined pastoral entertainment. The level of their amorous projects may be measured by the villano's brooding on the power of love:

> Gliè pur la strana bestia quest'Amore,
> Care madonne, e chi nol sa, nol dica.
> Io stò per spiritarmi da dovero,
> Quand'io ci penso, e ci ripenso bene:
> Non perdona nè a vecchie, nè a citelle
> Questo ribaldo, e tanto smania addosso
> El mette, che ne fa tutti [sic] strillare:
> Che cancar venga alla puttana vacca,
> Che partorì questa forfanteria.
> Ch'io son sì innamorato d'una Ninfa,
> Ch'adesso adesso m'è venuta in mente,
> Ch'io me n'arrabbio, mi dispero, e moro;
> Et ho tanto fraccasso in le budelle,
> Che par ch'io v'habbia un fatto d'arme dentro;
> O ch'egliè colpa di quest'amor ladro,
> O d'un caldaro di ricotta, ch'io
> Pensando a quest'amor tutto mangiai;
> Par c'habbia trenta Diavoi ne la panza.
> S'io non iscarco un po la frenesia
> Potrei creppar per quest'amor cagnaccio.
>
> (I.6)

This Love is a strange animal, dear ladies, and anyone who hasn't had it should shut up about it. I'll go right out of my mind if I think much about it: this scoundrel doesn't spare old women or young ones, and he puts such a craving in them all that they shriek; pox take the sluttish cow that gave birth to this roguery. For I'm so in love with a nymph—she just this minute came into my mind—that I'm going mad, I despair and die; and I've got so much rumbling in my guts that it's like a war going on inside; oh, this is either the fault of this thieving love or of a potful of curds that I gobbled up while thinking about it; it feels like thirty devils in my belly. If I don't relieve the frenzy a little, I could split apart on account of this cur love.

Here he makes an exit to answer the call of nature, for the moment triumphant over art.

The Maga who untangles the plot of *Gl'intricati* with aid from silent nocturnal spirits functions like Oberon in similar circumstances and is also accompanied by a talkative familiar, the puckish Lucifero. He fetches magic liquid from the distant fount of oblivion to make the lovers forget their misdirected desires, while the nightshades bring healing dreams from which all awake with truer knowledge of their own hearts. It is to provide an analogous experience for the three clowns, and to let them see themselves as they appear to the shepherdesses on whom they would force themselves, that the sorceress temporarily transforms their heads into those of beasts: a bull, a ram, and an ass. With a multiple wedding and general rejoicing at hand, the spokesman for all the Arcadians thanks Venus and Diana at the end, while the others join him in a ritual expressing the idea of reconciliation between the opposed concepts of love and chastity. The finale is a platonic emblem of *discordia concors,* that fundamental theme of regular pastoral dramas, of wedding feasts at which they were performed, and of course of *A Midsummer Night's Dream,* in which Diana is continually evoked by the imagery, the moonlight, and finally Starveling's lanthorn. Venus, played down here as in *The Tempest* with a genially subtle Shakespearean stroke, is also here, but considerably more than in *The Tempest,* the great silent dynamo moving the action.

Pasqualigo's play points to the range of the Italian pastoral and to that phase of its dramatization that Shakespeare repeats in his favola boschereccia without shepherds, *A Midsummer Night's Dream.* He uses an amalgam of magic, metamorphosis, dream, supernatural spirits, incorporeal voices, and unearthly music as theatrical means to express movement toward knowledge of the heart and to represent such abstract topics of debate as the power of the imagination and of art, the inexpressibility of truth, the blindness of the mortal mind, and the wise madness of love.[27]

The contrast between appearance and reality regarded as an axiomatic concern of late Renaissance dramatists in general is made as obvious as possible by the pastoralists, and is characteristically presented as a contrast between an apparent chaos visible to human beings and a real but invisible celestial order. The exclamation of Tasso's Arcadian spokesman that Amore's works, full of *provvidenza* and *mistero*, lead man to paradise by "ignote strade" (V.1.1841–47) when he thinks himself lost,[28] Pasqualigo's prayer to Venus to lead humans out of the "labirinto" of their "disegni fallaci" (IV.1), Guarini's comparison of the "fallaci" and "torti" paths by which the mortal mind tries to reach heaven and those "alti inaccessibili sentieri" (V.6.1207–11) by which grace travels from the eternal gods: all are typical references to an issue central to pastoral drama.

To see how issue interpenetrates with genre as the potentialities of the latter appear, it is instructive to observe the Italian dramatization of the two elements essential to this expression of the contrast between reality and appearance: first, a superhuman power (whether Love or an un-

27. Only in recent years has the presence of these topics in Italian pastoral drama begun to arouse scholarly interest corresponding to the attention long given to the thematics of *A Midsummer Night's Dream* by Shakespeareans; see for example Paul A. Olson, "*A Midsummer Night's Dream* and the Meaning of Court Marriage," *Journal of English Literary History* 24 (1957): 95–119; Thelma N. Greenfield, "*A Midsummer Night's Dream* and *The Praise of Folly*," *Comparative Literature* 20, no. 3 (Summer 1968): 236–44; David Young, *Something of Great Constancy: The Art of "A Midsummer Night's Dream"* (New Haven, 1966), esp. 81, 107, 113ff; Dennis J. Huston, "Bottom Waking: Shakespeare's 'Most Rare Vision,'" *Studies in English Literature* 13 (1973): 208–22; Marjorie B. Garber, *Dream in Shakespeare: From Metaphor to Metamorphosis* (New Haven, 1974), 59–87; David Marshall, "Exchanging Visions: Reading *A Midsummer Night's Dream*," *English Literary History* 49 (1982): 543–75. Slights, in "Nature's Originals," 70–71, interestingly finds *A Midsummer Night's Dream* disappointing to pastoral expectations, because it lacks a vision of the myth expounded by Kermode: recovery of the lost child and original virtue. A broadening of the formal definition of pastoral to include the theme of Love the tyrant and transformer and the Italian theater's range of experiments toward the third genre would offer means to compose such differences.

28. *Aminta*, ed. Giorgio Bàrberi Squarotti (Padua, 1968).

defined deity, or specifically Venus or Diana, or even the Christian God under pagan veils); and second, the human confusion compared with this power. The elements and the contrast produced by their juxtaposition were often stated through metaphors in the manner quoted above. But separately and together they were also represented dramatically. Shakespeare's use of micro-spectacle to symbolize and give visible substance to fundamental themes, as in the betrothal masque of *The Tempest,* the appearance of Hymen that ends *As You Like It,* or the dream of Posthumus in *Cymbeline* (not to mention the dreams and visions in some of the tragedies, or the unsupernatural but centrally symbolic harvest festival of *The Winter's Tale*), would seem to have been denied to Italian regular pastoral drama by the growing adherence in the Cinquecento to rules of unity and verisimilitude, relegating such spectacles to the intermedi. Certainly between-act entertainments were frequently defined as the proper vehicles for spectacular confirmation of the accompanying play's themes, especially the more abstract ones. The comments of De'Sommi and Bernardino Pino on the importance of a thematic link between intermedio and drama reveal this concern.[29] But in a surprisingly large number of pastoral plays microspectacles are employed within the acts, to dramatize one or both elements of the contrast between visible appearance and invisible reality, that is, between human confusion and superhuman control.

Angelo Ingegneri, director of courtly and academic theatrical productions and influential theorist of mixed genres, provides an example in *Danza di Venere, pastorale,* performed in 1583 for the Farnese court of Parma, long before he wrote the well-known treatise *Della poesia rappresentativa.*[30] Venus herself speaks the prologue, echoing the traditional angel of late medieval sacra rappresentazione as she announces the new miracle she will perform: restoring a man's wits by means of love, which so often steals them away. She is wiser than her antagonist Diana, who Venus says does not understand that if the universe is round, chastity at its extreme limit borders on its opposite, wantonness, into which the short distance makes it easy to slip:

> Miracol novo a fare hor m'apparecchio
> In quest'istesso loco. Il senno, il senno

29. De'Sommi, *Quattro dialoghi,* 68–69; Bernardino Pino, *Breve considerazione intorno al componimento de la comedia de' nostri tempi* (1572), in Bernard Weinberg, ed., *Trattati di poetica e retorica del Cinquecento,* vol. 2 (Bari, 1970): 642–43.

30. The play was printed in Vicenza, 1584, the treatise in Ferrara, 1598.

Ch'altri sovente, amando, perde; amando
Far ch'uom racquisti   .   .   .

.   .   .   .

Nè del suo vaneggiar [Diana] punto s'accorge,
Sciocca; nè sa, ch'un' honestate estrema
(Se l'Universo è pur rotondo)
Ad estrema lascivia è posta a canto;
Onde, per lieve sdrucciolar, si puote
Talhor cader.

Ingegneri's theme—harmony, platonic concord of discordant elements, paradoxically near and far, like and unlike at the same time—is illustrated in one way by the dramatic motion of the love madness, which restores to sanity a shepherd (formerly mad, but not for love) whom reason itself had failed to cure. But another kind of dramatic expression occurs in the middle of the central act (III.3), when a round dance is staged in which almost all of the heterodox dramatis personae join, singing and moving in patterns that present to the spectator's eyes and ears the circle and harmony of the concord that love forms out of discord. The microspectacle is made to fall in naturally with the plot, the forward movement of which also retrieves the characters from the emblematic set piece through its interruption by a disgruntled lover who abducts a nymph from the celebration. An episode of the plot, this *raptio* is in addition a phase of platonic motion and a demonstration that violence can never be permanently banished but only controlled, and will always erupt into discord unless maintained in difficult tension with its opposite. Thus Ingegneri represents visibly and dramatically the theme of divine (venereal) power, which in *Aminta* is expressed more exclusively by verbal lyricism.

In Pona's *Tirrheno*, one of the pastorals most admired by contemporaries,[31] a more fantastic microspectacle is even more intimately tied to the plot, in which the curse cannot be lifted from Arcadia until the waters of a fountain, which was once a nymph, are turned to flame. At the moment of resolving an exceptionally labyrinthine intrigue, full of sentences on the human blindness that requires direction from "la providentia eterna" (IV.2), Venus appears in person and orders Cupid to set the fountain on fire; he obeys, giving visible form also to their joint

31. Giovanni Battista Pona, *Tirrheno, pastorale* (Verona, 1589). In the *Difesa del Pastor Fido*, 115, Pescetti names as among the best examples of the genre *Tirrheno*, with *Aminta*, Bracciolini's *Amoroso sdegno*, Noci's *Cinthia*, Cremonini's *Pompe funebri*, and Ongaro's *Alceo*.

power and to the Petrarchan antitheses of fire and water, hot and cold, and so on, as well as giving emblematic substance to the essential theme of discordia concors.

Theatrical substance was required also for the unknown ways, the labyrinth, the twisted paths—for all the images corresponding to the venerable metaphor of journey and place that calls for a detached point of view enabling the spectator to see the design entire, as on a map. In the pastoral plays various means were tested for showing the whole labyrinth, so that the audience might distinguish right paths from wrong and see that what the characters took for wrong were in fact the unknown ways leading to the order and happiness decreed by the divinity. The freedom of Shakespeare's green world and the license to move in and out of it were not usually granted to regular Italian drama, but the generic pastoral set, because of its very stylization, offered a green space fit for habitation simultaneously by the spectator's mind and the Arcadian characters. The *locus amoenus* of the pleasance (called the *prato* in stage directions) and the nearby woods (*bosco* or *selva*), breathing anxiety, are universal places: the regulation hut or cottage is closer to the archetypal idea of a dwelling than are the Cinquecento houses of the regular commedia scene representing a street in a specific city, and the alter to Venus or Diana is a more generic representation of religious cult than some well-known real church in a piazza setting. In regular comedy as a generic commonplace and sometimes with symbolic intent, characters frequently exclaim "In che labirinto mi trovo!" (What a labyrinth I'm in!), but to have to say this on a stage set representing Piazza Farnese or the Grand Canal points up the discrepancy between the represented reality and the state of mind expressed. Not so in Arcadia. When Pasqualigo's prologue invites the spectators into the *intricata selva* of a pastoral play in which they will hear the prayer for deliverance from a labyrinth of misconceptions, the visible and invisible realities coalesce.

Supported by the universal nature of the standard scenery and props, the use of a complex plot, with a peripety arousing wonder, as a visual representation of the contrast between heavenly vision and human blindness and as a theatrical emblem of the providential pattern governing mortal confusion, could become even more effective in pastoral drama than in comedy, the genre in which intrigue structure had been evolved farthest. Although Tasso did not avail himself of this potential in his linear *Aminta*, many pastoral playwrights, while echoing his lines on the happily ironic contrast between the erring plans of blind humans and the unknown paths by which the heavenly power of love leads them to surprising joy, chose to associate the concept with the pastoral woods and the labyrinthine structure of the intrigue plot. The final peripeties of Cresci, Cucchetti, Pasqualigo, Ingegneri, and countless others resolve tangled plots so as to arouse wonder at the operation of love's power or indirectly of Christian providence; idea is made visible by means of the structural design, played out before the eyes of sense in a manner aimed at opening the eyes of the mind to the abstract whole. Shakespeare demonstrates his mastery of the technique in *A Midsummer Night's Dream* by intertwining the threads of the plot, syncopating the encounters and misunderstandings, and making them occur by night in a wood, the darkness of the one and the maziness of the other given as physical facts.

Just as Ingegneri's *Danza di Venere* contains a spectacle symbolic of Venus's power, other Italian pastorals may include visual confirmation of an already metaphoric plot structure in microspectacles, which yet again trace the operation of providence by unexpected means for the happiness of blind and confused mortals. Perhaps the most perfect and certainly the most famous is the game of blindman's buff in *Il pastor fido*, to which Guarini himself in his "Annotazioni" appended a simpering allegory: "La cieca fa la persona d'Amore, e quelle che gli scherzano intorno son come i cuori ch'egli cerca di prendere" (The blind girl who is "it" represents Love, and the nymphs who encircle her, teasingly keeping out of her reach, are the hearts which Love attempts to snatch).[32]

What Guarini does not say is more important: that this supposed allegory of Love is placed at the center of the play, well into the third of five acts; and that this scene is not merely a decorative pause but an essential section of the plot, inasmuch as Corisca, pretending to give Mirtillo opportunity to declare his love to Amarilli by introducing him into the girls' game while the blindfolded Amarilli is "it," really intends thus to implicate Amarilli in a love affair that seems to be forbidden by a divine oracle and would result in her execution, leaving Corisca a clear field with Mirtillo.[33] Corisca's plan is in itself an intrigue plot, and con-

32. "Annotazioni al Pastor fido," quoted by Fassò, *Teatro del Seicento*, 181 n. 92.

33. Dalla Valle's *Pastorale barocca* contains perceptive analyses of Guarini's structure, including a section on "La microstruttura della mosca cieca nel *Pastor Fido*," which puts forth observations akin to mine on the symbolic relation of this part to the whole. Although Dalla Valle is more concerned with Guarini's handling of the game as an example of baroque masked sensuality, our conclusions are ultimately compatible.

tradicting all expectations, it leads to a wedding between Amarilli and Mirtillo, which turns out to be precisely what the ill-interpreted oracle intended all along and results in the redemption of Arcadia. Corisca, wicked as she has been, is thanked at the end for having inadvertently contrived the universal happiness: "Destino t'usò per felicissimo strumento" (IV.10.1561: Destiny used you as a most felicitous instrument), Mirtillo tells her. The perfect reversal or peripety adds another example of the felix culpa: the deceiver is revealed as the agent of providence.

So too in the game of blindman's buff danced and sung in a theatrical spectacle: as Amarilli, blindfolded, tries to grasp one of the nymphs circling about her, she is possibly an allegorical figure of Love snatching at hearts, but she is necessarily a representation of human blindness, the reiterated theme of *Il pastor fido,* as of countless other Italian regular pastoral plays before and after it. By Corisca's machinations Amarilli's gropings end with her embracing Mirtillo: it seems a sin then and there and throughout most of the play, her love for Mirtillo appearing to be against the law that will be discovered to have been misunderstood by human reason unable to penetrate heavenly designs. In this oedipal plot with a happy ending, even the faithful shepherd himself is ignorant of being the lost child returned as a redeemer. The simple natural impulse that steers Amarilli to love him will prove consonant with the divine will; but only providence, operating by means of unconscious and unlikely agents, will be able to order and clarify all the complex motives. The game of blindman's buff, in the restricted space of a dance, is Guarini's means of theatrically representing in small and at the center of the play the emblem of the play itself, the tragicomedy of mortals in the labyrinth of their own blindness, directed to their proper happy end by a providence operating like a playwright skilled in producing dramatic peripeties.

The classification as "romances" of the group of late Shakespearean plays that includes *Pericles, The Winter's Tale, Cymbeline,* and *The Tempest* has never been quite adequate; the case for calling them "pastorals" is more convincing. But neither term communicates enough about the theatrical character of the works, about the vehicles and instruments that a fashionable experimenting playwright might have appropriated for representing elements quarried from narrative romance or from pastoral novels and eclogues. Because Shakespeare had been drawing on such materials as early as *The Comedy of Errors* and *A*

Midsummer Night's Dream, it is not in primary substances but in the intricacy of their combinations that we must look for the distinguishing style of his last phase. The late "romances" are strongly marked by an interest in mixing genres and pushing them to their limits, a zest for hybrids "pastoral-comical, historical-pastoral" and the like, as itemized by Polonius, structural variations in both content and disposition of the basic repertory of theatergrams, and the creatively transgressive method employed in their regard that makes it possible to associate Shakespeare's theater with Italian literary mannerism.[34] All are by some definition tragicomedies, each in its unique way continuing Shakespeare's exploration and testing of frontiers.

In Italy by this time, around the turn of the Seicento, the long, binary series of critical polemics and experiments toward a third regular genre had reaped a huge harvest of results. The most successful and fertile for theater in the rest of Europe was undoubtedly the pastoral play, but as we have seen, the charged simplicity of Tasso's bouquet of eclogues in *Aminta* and the complexity of Guarini's fusion of Sophocles, Aristotle, and commedia grave in *Il pastor fido* represent only the most esteemed portion of a large and varied pastoral production. Arcadian mixtures subtitled *favola pastorale-comica* or *tragica, boschereccia* or *marittima* (for piscatory variations substituting seaside for woodland settings), *satirica, grottesca,* and *allegorica* might combine comedy with pastoral satyrs, magic, and Ovidian transformations, or bring matters of state fit for tragedy to the country or coast in search of solutions to carry back to the court and the city. The raw materials of plot were often from romances, both from the Italian epic romanzi, especially the *Orlando furioso,* and from the Hellenistic narratives of Heliodorus and Achilles Tatius. More significant than the individual sources, however, was the general pressure toward commingling the three theatrical genres associated with court, city, and country, of sufficient force in some experiments even to countermand the rule of unity of place, and to warrant a brief use of the rural setting as a rest stop for characters in transit from tragedy to comedy.

An exceedingly successful example of theorizing transgression of genre boundaries was *Roselmina,* the *favola tragisatiricomica* of Giovanni Battista Leoni, a Venetian academician who wrote under the name Lauro Settizonio dal Castel Sambuco. The play was first per-

---

34. See my "Il teatro manieristico italiano e Shakespeare."

formed in 1595 by the Academy of the Pazzi Amorosi and was printed
in that year and many times afterward.[35] In our century *Roselmina* has
been adduced as a curious bit of Italian grotesquerie;[36] a closer look at
the phenomenon suggests that it belonged not to an eccentric eddy but
to the mainstream of the Italian theatrical wave that rolled to the coast
of England.

The playwright speaks in the prologue through a puckish "folletto,
spirito del Carnevale":

L'opera . . . è capricciosissima; è un composito di faceto, & di serio; di grave, & di giocoso; un mescuglio di Prencipi, & di gente
bassa, e mezzana, allegra, desperata, pazza e savia; un'intreccia-
mento di negotij grandi, & di burle giocondissime; & d'amori; ac-
comodati in modo, che nella loro discorde convenienza, fanno una
gentilissima, et harmonica compositione. Et perché sà l'Autore, si
come sò anch'io (& me ne rido) che qualche rigoroso literatone,
qualche sottile, & ostinato osservatore de i Dogmi Aristotelici dirà
con impeto d'iraconda litteratura, che questo è contra l'Arte, &
che non si può fare. Jo prima vi dico, che l'opera è fatta, & la sentirete con vostro molto piacere. Et se mi si dirà, che ciò non istà
bene in via di Aristotele; et io risponderò, che in via nostra la cosa
stà benissimo. Et se si replicarà che questo, è un Mostro ridico-
loso; et io confessandolo, dirò di haver ottenuto quanto si de-
sidera dall'Autore, che è di ridere, & far ridere con questa sua
compositione. Ben è vero, che l'ho sentito anco dire, che quello
ch'egli ha fatto, ha fatto con ragione, havendo mescolato le materie, & le persone con possibilità di accidenti, & verità di luoghi,
conforme à quello, che naturalmente si può verificare. Tenendo
egli per conclusione ferma, che i tempi siano padri de' precetti; &
che sia necessario di accommodar le compositioni à i tempi, &
non i tempi alle compositioni.

The work is very fanciful; it is a composite of joking and seriousness, of the grave and the gamesome; a mixture of princes

35. Elena Povoledo, "Una rappresentazione accademica a Venezia nel 1634,"
Studi sul teatro veneto fra rinascimento ed età barocca, ed. Maria Teresa
Muraro (Florence, 1971), 128, 132, 155.

36. Walter Bullock, "Tragical-satirical-comical: A Note on the History of
the Cinquecento 'Dramma Satiresco,'" *Italica* 15, no. 3 (September 1938):
163–74.

with folk of low and middle rank, happy, despairing, mad and wise; an intertwining of high affairs and most jocund jests; and of loves; so arranged that in their discordant coming together they make a noble and harmonious unity. And because the author knows (as do I and laugh at it) that some stern literary critic, some nitpicking and immovable upholder of Aristotelian Dogmas will burst into angry literary diatribe saying that this is against Art and cannot be done; I say first that it is done—the work is finished and you will hear it to your great pleasure. And if I am told that it would not sit well with Aristotle, I shall answer that it sits very well with us. And if anyone replies that this is a ridiculous Monster; admitting it, I shall say that it has accomplished the author's desire, which is to laugh and to amuse with this composition. Though it is true that I have also heard him say that what he did was done with reason, mixing plot matter and characters with concern for plausibility of circumstances and events and accuracy about places such as can be verified in nature. For he holds it as a firm conclusion that the time is father to the precept; and that compositions must be adapted to the times and not the times to compositions.[37]

Like the composition he boasts of, Leoni's declaration is very much of its time, manifesting the inevitable tropism toward Aristotelian and Horatian precepts by simultaneously challenging and using their terms, declaring independence from "Dogmi" in mixing *materie* and *persone* from different genres while defending the mixtures as reasoned choices intended to achieve a more expansive unity of action, decorum, and verisimilitude. Not a rejection of precepts, in short, but a characteristic late Cinquecento transgression of the "rules" in the dominant critical system by means of elements from the same system and leading to new precepts.

Like Leoni's later play *Florinda,* a grottesca drammatica, *Roselmina* carries political allegory on the wheels of a fictional plot, in this case from chivalric romance, with a dramatis personae, topics of discourse, and a disposition of events arranged for reference to the worlds and confines of the three theatrical genres and their canonical venues, as depicted in Serlio's stage sets for comedy, tragedy, and sylvan satyr play.

Both in content and in generic classification the principal action resembles Giraldi's tragedia di fin lieto, specifically *Arrenopia.* Its pro-

37. *Roselmina, favola tragisatiricomica* (Venice, 1595), 3v–4r.

tagonist is a Bradamantine British noblewoman roaming Ireland in knightly disguise in search of her lover, who is imprisoned and temporarily mad; in the course of this rescue mission she encounters the true heir to the usurped throne of England, and for helping to restore him is rewarded with the crown of Scotland. Along the way she meets an eloquent glutton, a macaronic pedant, and the braggart captain Fanfara Tiriparavampa, three typical denizens of comedy. Among the local Irish population appear satyrs and shepherds in whose woodland habitat are heard musings on the relative merits of court and country and on other conventional topics of pastoral drama. The mixture of tragic, comic, and pastoral matters is closely calculated, and the boundaries between the genres are crossed with such deliberation as to maintain relentlessly the promise in the subtitle: favola tragi-satiri-comica.

Although the raw materials of the plot are from traditional chivalric romance, the theatrical form of their representation is that of avant-garde mannerism: hybrid, stylistically self-aware, metaleptic, and with a sophisticated ingenuousness that invites symbolic interpretations. Were *Roselmina* really a unique phenomenon, were the prologue's claim to novelty a less fashionable gesture or the finished product one of exceptionally high quality, another example would serve better. As it is, however, *Roselmina* typifies for the late Cinquecento the continuing thrust of Italian dramaturgy toward the invention of a third genre and the critical justification of a range of tragicomic mixtures.

The professional awareness of the Continental theatrical movement visible in all phases of Shakespeare's career appears with special clarity in the mysterious and polysemous "romances." The most cherished of these, *The Tempest,* was shown by Ferdinando Neri more than seventy years ago to derive its island setting, major characters, and plot from one species of Arcadian scenario for improvised comedy circulating in the early Seicento both in plural manuscript versions and in performance.[38] Although Neri's demonstration has long been known to Shakespeareans, its implications have never been properly taken to heart and allowed to confirm the conscious kinship between Shakespeare and his Italian colleagues. Nor until recently has it led Italianists to a better definition of the complex relationship between the commedia dell'arte's mnemonic scenarios and the preceding texts of literary drama. Much close comparative reading will be needed for full clarification, but it is already apparent that in early seventeenth-century Italy

38. Neri, *Scenari della maschere in Arcadia.*

The Tempest could have been classified handily, according to the theatrical terminology expressing the transgressive manneristic principles then in fashion, as a *favola marittima tragicomica grottesca.*[39]

The Winter's Tale demonstrates another kind of experiment in the same theatrical laboratory; here even the smallest changes that Shakespeare introduced in tailoring the narration of Greene's *Pandosto* to the stage served to bring the play into the orbit of the measured design executed by Guarini in *Il pastor fido,* and of the triple tour de force of Flaminio Scala's ideal commedia dell'arte scenario, *Gli avvenimenti comici, pastorali e tragici, opera mista.*[40]

The first phase of *The Winter's Tale* is not merely inclined toward tragedy; it constitutes a fully rounded-off miniature of the genre, ending with the lament of King Leontes in half-crazed grief and remorse for the deaths of his wife and children. By rejecting the suicide that Greene decreed for the king at the end of *Pandosto* and by restoring not only the apparently dead daughter but the maligned wife as well, Shakespeare effects a substitution: a fully fused circle of the generic movements weal-

39. The virtue of such semitechnical classification is that it suggests Shakespeare's engagement in international theatrical trends, or at least nonisolation from them, without invalidating descriptions of the mixed nature of *The Tempest* that are based on its *dianoia:* "Revenge Comedy" is Elizabeth Freund's phrase in "The Wrath of Prospero," *Hebrew University Studies in Literature 6,* no. 2 (Autumn 1978): 194, a description seconded by James Black in "Shakespeare and the Comedy of Revenge," *Comparative Critical Approaches to Renaissance Comedy,* ed. Donald Beecher and Massimo Ciavolella (Ottawa, 1986), 137–51. Stephen Orgel observes that after the happy ending the tragic world awaits; see "New Uses of Adversity: Tragic Experience in *The Tempest,*" *In Defense of Reading,* ed. Reuben Brower and Richard Poirier (New York, 1963), 127, 131; Douglas L. Peterson concludes that "apparent tragedy is transformed into authentic comedy" in *Time, Tide, and Tempest: A Study of Shakespeare's Romances* (San Marino, Calif., 1973), 62. John B. Bender writes, "The play is a conspectus of theatrical forms and a commentary on the masque's limitations as a mirror of kingship"; see "*The Tempest* and the Court Masque Reconsidered" (paper delivered at the Renaissance Conference of Northern California, May 1974), 3. Later, demonstrating the universality of meaning attained by Shakespeare's integration of forms, Bender calls it "a dramatic *summa* of the rituals, ceremonials, festivities and emotions appropriate to its day and occasion" (Hallowmas at court, with reference to both Christian liturgy and archetypal pagan rites); see "The Day of the *Tempest,*" *English Literary History* 47 (1980): 253.

40. Flaminio Scala, *Il teatro delle favole rappresentative,* ed. Ferruccio Marotti (Milan, 1976), vol. 2, giornata 42, 433–46.

to-woe and woe-to-weal replaces the simpler two-way traffic in which Greene juxtaposes Pandosto's "tragedy" to his daughter Fawnia's "comedy."

The second phase not only takes its setting and thematics from the Arcadian world, but through Shakespeare's reversing of the geographical sites of Greene's plot to make Bohemia the pastoral locus and Sicily (alive with ancient pastoral connotations) the place of both the opening tragic and the closing comic actions, the middle of *The Winter's Tale* reinforces the idea of the pastoral play as the natural hinge between the other two genres, and of the resulting amalgam of tragedy and comedy as the instrument for representing psychological and intellectual realities in the theater.

Effecting the final healing of old tragic wounds in a broadly inclusive comic denouement of reconciliation and marriages, by means of the spectacular scene in which a preternaturally wise and powerful court-lady stages the lost queen's return as the awakening to life of a marble statue, Shakespeare makes his adaptation of one of the Ovidian animal, vegetable, or mineral transformations from the magic *favola pastorale* testify to a special blend of genres in this play. With the lost found, the dead brought to life, the tragedy turned to comedy through the re-vitalizing potential in the pastoral ethos, sin forgiven, prophecy fulfilled, and curse lifted, the final revelation of *The Winter's Tale* might suggest that Shakespeare was specifically imitating *Il pastor fido*, known to him at least since John Wolfe's London printing of 1591. The truth, however, is likely to be vaguer in outline and harder to document: once again Shakespeare was making an adventurous *contaminatio*, experimenting with mixtures of theatrical genres in high Italian fashion. He had made Polonius speak of a drama "tragical-pastoral-comical" and in *The Winter's Tale* brought it to the stage.

Finally, what is *Cymbeline*, oddest of the "romances"? Labeled *tragedie* in the First Folio, it is full of the dissonances that make McFarland think of an encounter between Mozart and Berg: a wicked stepmother out of a fairy tale, married to a pseudohistorical king, the legendary Briton Cymbeline; a princess who flees the court in male disguise to seek her exiled husband; an Italian intriguer who calumniates her in a maneuver familar to Italian comedy and originating in Boccaccio's *Decameron;* a lost heir to the throne found in pastoral retreat, and a royal family reunited in the British victory over the Romans at Milford Haven, the port to which in the distant fifteenth century the first of the Tudor kings would return from exile to found the dynasty that Shakespeare's history plays celebrate. The resemblance to *Roselmina* is obvious, more important for the conception of genre than for the details of plot and character. The family resemblance is what counts; *Cymbeline* is far closer to this kind of theatrical experiment than to any part of the mass of narrative designated by the term *romance*. Again it is Polonius, that up-to-date connoisseur of the drama, who provides the descriptive terms: tragical-comical-pastoral-historical.

In his edition of *Cymbeline*, J. M. Nosworthy writes that the play so fuses plurality into unity as to be "a vision of perfect tranquility, a partial comprehension of that Peace which passeth all understanding, and a contemplation of the indestructible essence in which Imogen, Iachimo, atonement, the national ideal have all ceased to have separate identity or individual meaning."[41] We need not accept so transcendental a reading to recognize that what Shakespeare wrought in *Cymbeline* invites a Pisgah view. The history of that achievement must include the long trials of genre mixing aimed at making visible the invisible in the Italian theater.

41. William Shakespeare, *Cymbeline*, Arden ed., ed. J. M. Nosworthy (London, 1955), Introduction, lxxxiii.

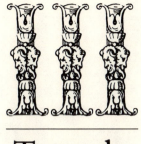

Tragedy

Serlio's "Scena Tragica"
"Le second livre de Perspective"
Il Primo Libro d'Architettura di Sebastiano Serlio, Bolognese (Paris, 1545).
By permission of the National Gallery of Art, Mark J. Millard Architectural
Collection (1983.49.106).

CHAPTER SEVEN

The Arts of Genre:
Torrismondo and *Hamlet*

n the part of the *Discorsi del poema eroico* where he discusses how to choose *materia* that permits admixture of poetic fiction without loss of *autorità,* by which he means truth or reality, Tasso recommends events occurring among faraway peoples in unknown lands and adds precise examples: "From the land of the Goths, from Norway and Sweden and Iceland, and from the East Indies and the newfound lands in the vast ocean beyond the Pillars of Hercules must the matter be taken." [1]

Tasso's theories of tragedy were closely intertwined with this discussion of epic, and his only tragedy is a story of melancholy Goths, Norwegians, and Swedes, *Il re Torrismondo,* issued by Italian presses in various cities ten times in its first year, 1587, and frequently afterward. His Scandinavian sources were the works of the brothers Magnus: Olaus's *Historia de gentibus septentrionalibus* (1555) for local color, weather, customs, and suggestions of incidents, and Johannes's *Gothorum Suenonumque historia* (1554) for names, situations, and historical details, which Tasso arbitrarily telescoped into his argument.[2]

Shakespeare's tragedy of a Danish prince, coming after the turn of the century, owes we know not how much to the mysterious Ur-*Hamlet,* which had reached London audiences by 1589. The choice of a Scandinavian past as a subject would obviously have meant something different to each of the two poets. In the Italian imagination the snowy and shadowy northern countries were Ultima Thule still, lands of romance,

This chapter appeared in slightly different form as "The Arts of Genre: *Torrismondo* and *Hamlet,*" *English Literary History* 47 (1980): 657–69. Copyright © 1980 by Johns Hopkins University Press.

1. *Discorsi,* 2: "Fra popoli lontani e ne' paesi incogniti finger molte cose di leggieri, senza togliere autorità a la favola. Però di Gotia e Norvegia e di Svezia e d'Islanda o de l'Indie Orientali o di paesi di nuovo ritrovati nel vastissimo oceano oltre le Colonne d'Ercole, si dee prender la materia." From Torquato Tasso, *Prose,* ed. Ettore Mazzali (Milan and Naples, 1959), 552–53.

2. See Jacques Goudet, "Johannes et Olaus Magnus et l'intrigue de *Il Re Torrismondo,*" *Revue des études italiennes,* n.s. 12, no. 1 (1966): 61–67.

indeed of romanzi.[3] For Shakespeare the distance to the Scandinavian north was both physically and spiritually shorter, the sense of its reality stronger, held by ethnic and historical ties. And the materia he took from the twelfth-century *Historia Danica* of Saxo Grammaticus, or a version of it in François de Belleforest's *Histoires tragiques* (1574), was more factual as well as more of a piece than were Tasso's levyings on the Magnuses.

But though poles apart, *Torrismondo* and *Hamlet* ask to be scrutinized together. Close enough in time to be called contemporary, they may tell us something about a theatrical context that was more international than has been properly acknowledged. Specifically, the choice of Scandinavian medieval chronicle history as plot, as foreground favola, may be demonstrated to have introduced into the two tragedies fashionable questions of dramatic theory, and to have functioned as a signal for attention to structures and procedures associated with what was to the Renaissance the supremely interesting issue of genre.

We may detect in *Torrismondo* and *Hamlet* a common concern for defining and expanding the genre of tragedy, and original responses to the generally felt challenge to earn a place in the great tradition by displaying mastery of the classical genres while surpassing the antique models—improving on them and satisfying the Renaissance craving for amplitude and for hybrid forms that might incorporate experience and art valued by the moderns and unknown to the ancients. This concern extended beyond innovation in practice; it included an aspiration to enlarge the body of ideas about genre, moreover about the mixing of genres, which was at the time a compelling question of which we often see the results without recognizing that the idea of mixing, of contamination, was not only a convenience for uninhibited, crowd-pleasing playwrights but also a vigorously debated aim of Cinquecento neoclassical criticism.

Tasso's involvement in the critical movement was intense, Shakespeare's all but imperceptible in comparison. Stephen Orgel, writing about Shakespeare and the kinds of drama, says that genre for Shake-

3. A vestige of that view surely contributed to Emilio Bertana's classifying *Torrismondo* primarily with the tragedies in his ill-sorted "romanzesco" group in *La tragedia* (Milan, n.d. [1905?]), 71, 101; and more recently, to Ettore Paratore's noting "the exotic suggestions of atmosphere surrounding the tragedy with its Nordic background," in "Nuove prospettive sull'influsso del teatro classico nel '500," *Il teatro classico italiano nel '500* (Rome, 1971), 64.

speare, as for Scaliger and Sidney, was a set of expectations and possibilities rather than a set of rules.[4] This might with equal truth be said for the better half of the Italian theoreticians, among them Tasso. I would go farther than Orgel does about Shakespeare. Shakespeare's canon shows him to have been knowledgeable about genre, both as theory and as practice, and continually interested in experimenting with the "expectations and possibilities," so much so that one may say he never repeated himself partly because of his interest in such experiments. In *Hamlet* this preoccupation can be recognized first in his choice of material.

On the subject of innovation, originality, and experiment Tasso was clear: innovation consists rather in form than in matter, for the poet enhances truth with fresh colors and makes new what is old. A poem cannot be called new merely because it has fictional names and characters, if its structure, complications, and resolution ("il nodo e lo scioglimento") are those already used in others' works; that, he adds, is what is wrong with some contemporary tragedies, which lack the authority of history and established fame on the one hand and the novelty of fiction or invention on the other.[5] What he thought significant about the choice of materia was therefore not the matter's absolute or innate novelty but rather the opportunity it afforded the dramatic poet of achieving new forma, of producing a structure that was at once new and proper to be contemplated alongside established forms or measured by them, and able to ignite critical comment on the subject of form, on genre.

Both Tasso and Shakespeare took as their arguments Scandinavian subjects from a new past (from the Middle Ages), and disposed them so as to make resonate a part of the old past that was common cultural heritage to the Renaissance (Greek myth); moreover, the two Greek myths they evoked were foremost in tragedy and were used as examples by Aristotle. The medieval foreign plots could be made to refer obliquely

4. Stephen Orgel, "Shakespeare and the Kinds of Drama," *Critical Inquiry* 6 (1979): 123.

5. Tasso, *Discorsi,* 2: "La novità del poema si considera più tosto a la forma che a la materia. A l'incontro non potrà dirsi nuovo quel poema in cui finti siano i nomi e le persone, là dove il poeta faccia il nodo e lo scioglimento fatto da gli altri; e tale è peraventura alcuna moderna tragedia, a cui manca l'autorità che porta seco l'istoria, e la fama e la novità de la finzione." *Prose,* ed. Mazzali, 532.

to the most famous tragic materie in a fashion denied to other commonly chosen subjects: by logic, Greek myth itself could not function thus; classical, contemporary, and national history and legend could do so only after modifications violating established knowledge and sentiment. The materials of *Torrismondo* and *Hamlet* allowed for a confrontation of ostensible history with undeclared myth in plots that silently claimed kinship with the very arguments cited by Aristotle. At the same time, the arguments from Scandinavian chronicle carried some weight of historical truth but were more hospitable to fiction than better-known history could be, freeing Tasso and Shakespeare to invent parallels with their own time and to annex whatever additional literary and theatrical matter would serve their plans for these specimens of the genus tragedy, in Tasso's estimation the only genre as fit as the epic to treat of "azioni illustri." [6]

Tasso's lyricism, mannerism, psychological subtleties, and blending of sadness and sensuality are usually so much more interesting to modern readers than anything else that the formal intentions he claimed as paramount are often acknowledged cursorily or dismissed as insignificant. Those structural specifications were, however, the first aspect of *Torrismondo* regarded by Tasso's contemporaries, and the degree to which they were realized was the first point of contention for polemicists. Tasso's defender Giulio Guastavini, the sponsor of the Genoa edition of 1587, pointed to the Aristotelian achievement of a plot not simple but complex, with recognition and reversal, the recognition or discovery arising inevitably from the argument in its skeletal reduction. The greatest merit that the admiring Guastavini sees in *Torrismondo* is that it is like Sophocles' *Oedipus rex,* which, he reminds the reader, everyone judges to be the best tragedy ever written in any language. [7]

6. Tasso, *Discorsi,* 2; *Prose,* ed. Mazzali, 543.

7. Giulio Guastavini: "Il riconoscimento è dei riconoscimenti di quella guisa che a tutte le altre maniere antepone Aristotele. Conciossiacosachè non per opra di segni ma necessariamente dalle cose poste innanzi si fa avvenire: da questo incontinente e senza indugio alcuno di tempo nasce la mutazione dello stato, e questo di felice in misero, che è il più proprio della tragedia. Tale appunto è il più proprio della tragedia. Tale appunto è la formazione della favola dell'*Edipo tiranno* di Sofocle, la qual tragedia fino a qui, per giudizio di ciascheduno, ha tenuto lo scettro di quante tragedie si son vedute scritte in qualsivoglia lingua. Ma questa del nostro Tasso, dopo tanti anni, se non glielo toglie, sì almeno al pari seco nell'istesso trono per ugual bellezza e maestà riguardevole s'asside." *Teatro di Torquato Tasso,* ed. Angelo Solerti (Bologna, 1895), 199.

At first the Gothic snowstorms of Tasso's plot veil without quite obscuring the familiar lineaments of the Greek myth, which become gradually clearer both in the fictional action and in the virtuoso form, *nodo* and *scioglimento,* demonstrating to a structure-wise audience the continued viability of the oedipal model. One of the results is meta-theatrical.[8] *Torrismondo* belongs to the art that calls attention to itself and to its achieving different ends simultaneously: one illusory, fictional, emotional, in a gloomy, romantic representation of dashed hopes, untimely death, and the vanity of human wishes; the other demonstrative, scientific, technical, in a display of dramatic construction with Sophoclean blueprints and more than Sophoclean materials.

The order of perceptions that I see projected by the election of arguments is the following: from history, to myth, to genre as idea, to genre as particular construction (by means of contaminatio and complication), to critical communication that takes the form in *Torrismondo* of a structure coexistent with the plot but ontologically different: a scene in which the discovery made by the protagonist is rigged to coincide with the audience's discovery of the governing structural principles.

Shakespeare's art is always so self-examining, the mantle of Prospero so often on him, that a long look is needed to see that in *Hamlet* he wears it with a difference. The difference begins with the choice of material. Whether the provenance was primarily the Ur-*Hamlet*, Saxo Grammaticus, or Belleforest is irrelevant; among Shakespeare's tragedies, only *Hamlet* has an argument from foreign medieval history. (The portion of French history that he uses elsewhere can hardly be considered foreign, proximate as it was to that of England.) It is an argument that thrusts up a pattern of a Greek myth that from Aristotle to André Green has ranked with the Oedipus story as an essential paradigm of tragedy: the myth of Orestes.[9] Obviously, neither the structural ideal of Sophocles' *Oedipus* nor the psychoanalytic potential of the oedipal myth can be ignored in relation to *Hamlet;* but at the same time, the story to

8. I use Lionel Abel's term (*Metatheatre: A New View of Dramatic Form,* New York, 1963) for a dramatic phenomenon that I view differently from the way he does, with regard to both historical context and significance.

9. However alien to Renaissance dramatic theory his reasons and applications may be, Green's basic statement coincides sweetly with sixteenth-century views: "Parmi toutes les situations tragiques celles de l'*Orestie* et de l'*Œdipodie* ont une valeur paradigmatique privilégiée," *Un œil en trop: Le complexe d'Œdipe dans la tragédie* (Paris, 1969), 53.

which the favola from Danish history directly points is that of the house of Atreus, specifically its Orestian revenge tragedy.[10]

As in *Torrismondo,* although ultimately with dissimilar results, the parallel between foreground plot and Greek myth directs attention to the genre of tragedy as idea, and to the expectations and possibilities created by a tradition in which the myth figures importantly. Next in the sequence of perceptions comes Shakespeare's particular construction, in which he baffles many of the expectations and expands the possibilities. Like Tasso, he makes a contamination with material from other genres; *Hamlet* includes at least token pieces from the principal dramatic kinds of Cinquecento drama. It takes up the commonplaces of Renaissance Senecan tragedy and lets them fall. It negatively confronts the Aristotelian model of complex tragedy of recognition and reversal. The protagonist's apparently inefficient improvised actions are repeated rejections of generic mechanisms, and the entire procedure is subjected to critical scrutiny from within. Hamlet the Orestian revenger and oedipal pursuer of truth is also Hamlet the patron, critic, and collaborator of acting companies. By the time he is consigned to the angels he has roved articulately over quite a range of structural formulas and devices. His discarding and perverting of them culminate in Shakespeare's winningly insolent critical communication.

Although the movements from history to myth to genre to criticism exist and follow the same order in *Hamlet* and *Torrismondo,* the individual structures and results are quite different. To reordered and elaborated fragments from the Magnuses' chronicles, Tasso added the conflict between love and friendship equally dear to the chivalric romance and to the novella tradition that underlay various dramatic versions of Boccaccio's tale of Tito and Gisippo. Tasso also added incest, of the fraternal sort, as in Speroni's *Canace,* but made it unwittingly committed and linked it with an old killing, as in *Oedipus rex.* As in Sophocles' tragedy the incest is again a given, a taboo, its prime power consisting in its being a mechanism or spring in the movement of a complex action. It must be brought to light for there to be a recognition from which the final peripety is inevitable. Sophocles' *Oedipus* functions tacitly in *Tor-*

10. In 1567 this subject had been treated in a manner faintly prophetic of *Hamlet,* in John Pickering's *Horestes, or an interlude of Vice,* ed. Daniel Seltzer, Malone Society Reprints (Oxford, 1962): after Horestes defeats his father's murderer, the usurper and kinsman Aegisthus, Nature counsels against killing his mother, Clytemnestra, but the Vice, whose name is Revenge, urges her death.

rismondo as a semiotic weight, which pulls the audience's consciousness toward the innovation constituted as the *Discorsi* demand by form, by the new tragic knot and denouement that Tasso gives to the old matter inherent in his new, ostensibly historical Scandinavian matter.

Briefly, the favola is that Torrismondo, king of the Goths, marries Alvida, princess of Norway, secretly regarding himself only as a proxy for his friend Germondo, king of Sweden. Germondo, having slain in battle years before the crown prince of Norway, would not be acceptable as a son-in-law to Alvida's vengeful royal father. On the voyage to the Gothic capital, where the unsuspecting princess is to be delivered to her Swedish husband, a storm creates the Vergilian occasion for Torrismondo, now helplessly in love with his supposed bride, to yield to temptation and take her virginity. All of the above is technically the antefatto, events preceding the crisis-structured played action. As the representation proper begins, Alvida cannot understand why her bridegroom has been avoiding her; Torrismondo, torn between love and duty to his friend, wonders if his sister Rosmonda might not be made an acceptable substitute for the bride whom Germondo expects. And Rosmonda argues against marriage in general, for several reasons that emerge at finely calculated intervals in the unfolding of the tragedy: she has a natural tendency toward a life of cloistered virginity, she is in love with her brother Torrismondo, and she knows that she is neither his true sister nor a princess but a nurse's child substituted for the king's daughter on account of a prophecy that Torrismondo's sister would bring grief on the dynasty and the nation. What no one knows until fate allows Torrismondo to deduce it in the fourth act, at last precipitating the recognition and reversal, is that the real Rosmonda is Alvida, who was taken long ago from her homeland to foil the curse, and was carried by fate's irony to Norway, where the king adopted her. The play and the dynasty end with a double suicide.

However trivial and like a soap opera this may sound compared with Sophocles' tragedy, we must note the similarity and greater complexity. By introducing the subplot involving Rosmonda in act 2, scene 3, Tasso puts the audience on notice that he is trying his hand at the formal expansion encouraged by his Ferrarese predecessor Giraldi Cinzio, of naturalizing the commedia love intrigue into tragedia; Tasso arouses expectations of a new virtuosity in construction to keep the multiple lines moving, artfully tangled and then ingeniously unknotted but without abandoning the single and uniform outcome of tragedy with an unhappy ending (in contrast to Giraldi's tragedia di fin lieto). He divides up the essential tragic data and keeps the secrets separate as long as possible. The secret kept from the spectators until late is how the dramatist will be able to make the tragic genre function ideally while leading it so far from Sophocles and amplifying it with comic design. Four events from the past, recent or remote, none known by more than two of the characters, create the pressure forcing the catastrophe: (1) the secret of Rosmonda's birth; (2) the secret of Alvida's birth; (3) the pact between Torrismondo and Germondo, necessitated by the killing of Alvida's supposed brother; and (4) the love and sexual union between Torrismondo and Alvida.

Marco Ariani has written that Tasso's dissolution of scenic diachronism displaced the cohesion of the Aristotelian system.[11] I think rather that the system was at least meant to be reaffirmed and surpassed by the mechanical means of synchronic redistribution. Tasso divides the oedipal function four ways. The fatal curse is not carried by Torrismondo, the protagonist who is impelled on the trajectory of purpose-passion-perception that has sometimes been defined as the oedipal idea of tragedy.[12] It is Alvida whose life is a time bomb; she is incestuous like Torrismondo (and with him), but her suffering comes not from gradually acquiring dreadful knowledge but from ignorance and despair at mistaken fear. Rosmonda, added to multiply the instances of false identity, is the substitute for the cursed Oedipus-child and is in the tragic dilemma of living a lie, a perilous but seemingly necessary one, with all the increasing complications attendant on that situation; she knows about her own birth, not about Alvida's. Torrismondo knows nothing about any births but is tormented by having betrayed his friend, and for three acts he thinks this sufficient cause for tragedy. The oedipal past action of killing a central, related figure is assigned to Germondo. The possibility of a happy resolution is kept alive as long as the incest is unknown. At the end of the third act, the chorus is still optimistically preaching about love and self-sacrifice, not yet aware that some things are beyond human control. The ultimate nature of the genre itself is so far held in suspense.

With the message in the fourth act that the king of Norway has died

11. Marco Ariani, ed., *La tragedia del Cinquecento* (Turin, 1977) vol. 1, Introduction, lvi. See also *Tra classicismo e manierismo* (Florence, 1974).

12. Adapted from Kenneth Burke by Francis Fergusson (*The Idea of a Theater* [Princeton, 1949], 18–32), the paradigm remains controversial, most convincing when applied to Renaissance imitations of *Oedipus rex*.

comes the last missing piece of information, in the manner of Sophocles: it is brought by the one figure from the past who can reveal that Alvida is Torrismondo's sister. When in the third scene of the fourth act Rosmonda reveals her identity to Torrismondo, the oedipal nature of the secondary action is clarified, immediately followed in the fourth scene by an encounter between Torrismondo and the Indovino, a Tiresias figure, and in the fifth between Torrismondo and Frontone, the Goth who originally took Alvida away. In this scenes the oedipal nature of the primary action is emphasized by structural paraphrasing of Sophocles. Main plot and subplots having come into conjunction, there lacks only the identification of the pirate who took the child from Frontone and carried her to Norway. The climax of the next scene (IV.6) reveals to Torrismondo the identity of Alvida, the irony of fate, and the end of his hopes of happiness—in short the tragic perception, which will be elaborated in the final choral lament on the insubstantiality of life's joys. To the audience it reveals what kind of tragedy Tasso has made; in offering a critical recognition of what he has achieved structurally in Torrismondo's oedipal recognition, Tasso is making a statement about genre. Tassisti are given to noting general parallels in the catastrophes of *Oedipus rex* and *Il re Torrismondo* and to comparing specifically the scene between Torrismondo and the Indovino with the one between Oedipus and Tiresias on which it is based (to the disadvantage of *Torrismondo*, naturally). After all, who would think that Tasso was better than Sophocles? Tasso would. Put crudely, that is the point of his structural demonstration, the two-layered recognition sequence. Tasso might have been pleased and perhaps surprised by the other reasons for which modern critics admire him, but he would certainly have wanted the innovation of his form to be understood as the achievement in genre that the recognition scene in *Torrismondo* proclaims.

To see the same order of perceptions at work in *Hamlet* means beginning at the beginning, in act 1, where the state of things in Denmark is announced as rotten. Simultaneously it is established by the tacit analogy between Hamlet-Gertrude-old Hamlet-Claudius and Orestes-Clytemnaestra-Agamemnon-Aegisthus as related to an illustrious action traditionally and currently regarded as the natural matter of the genus tragedy. A defining feature of the play is the contaminatio throughout with nontragic dramatic genres: not merely the general Shakespearean mixture of comedy with tragedy, but the particular introduction of the gravedigger, kin to hangmen and other officers of death in late commedia grave, the Pantalone side of Polonius, together with other graft-

ings from the commedia dell'arte, and the pastoral trappings and actions of the "nymph" Ophelia, whose watery death is a displacement of
the transformation of nymph into stream, a theatergram of action in the
neo-Ovidian favola pastorale,[13] employed like every other device in
Hamlet in hitherto unimagined ways.

More interesting with regard to the sequence of signals from history
to myth to genre is the theoretical game Shakespeare plays with the
standard expectations and possibilities of tragedy. The abrupt beginning
of *Torrismondo,* in a scene full of bewilderment and menace between
Alvida and her nurse, was for a knowledgeable audience a clue to
Tasso's having made a "Greek" choice, by which was understood a decision against employing the popular Giraldian version of the Senecan
ghost opening. In *Hamlet* an initial scene surpassing even Tasso's for
atmospheric pressure launches the play, with a thrust that leaves no time
to notice the absence of a first-act prologue, or of a detached ghost or
other supernatural being to speak it. Then, even before the antefatto is
broached, a fully assimilated ghost suddenly comes among the actors
and proceeds to suffuse the first act with the exposition, motivation, and
expectations proper to neo-Senecan revenge tragedy. The thwarting of
these expectations is, however, implicit in the manner of the ghost's
coming, and is gradually effected by the odd mixture of horror and hi-
larity with which his son treats him, preparing for the querulousness
that grows on the ghost together with his fading visibility later in the
play, until in the third act he ends as a dramatic dropout. He is "prologue to the omen" (I.1.123), as Horatio speculates such apparitions
may be;[14] indeed his whole scene is in matter and form a prologue to the
tragedy, but the tragedy is not the one the prologue heralds. For Hamlet, having been cast as the protagonist in an Orestian revenge action,
begins to behave as if the case might warrant an oedipal investigation,
which by virtue of the genre should culminate in a discovery and consequent reversal. What Ariani claims about *Torrismondo* is what occurs
later in *Hamlet:* the progression toward Aristotelian cohesion is dis-

13. See chapters 5 and 6, on the Ovidian pastoral plays. Versions of the
comic theatergram of the executioner and trafficker in corpses are the Boia in
Della Porta's *La turca, commedia* (Venice, 1606), Antonello in Oddi's *Prigione
d'amore, commedia* (Florence, 1590), and of course Abhorson in *Measure for
Measure.*

14. Shakespeare is quoted from *The Complete Works,* general ed. Alfred
Harbage, rev. ed. (New York, 1969), in which *Hamlet* is edited by Willard
Farnham.

rupted when Hamlet achieves his discovery at the end of the play within the play (II.2), to his own satisfaction at least, by recognizing Claudius's guilt. But it is not a new discovery, merely the confirmation of what the ghost has claimed in act 1, and instead of a decisive reversal, Shakespeare follows it immediately with a failure to act as an Aristotelian recognition would prescribe; by not killing Claudius at prayer (III.3) Hamlet is rejecting the Sophoclean sequence, although his mistaken assumption that the king's soul is in a state of grace equals Sophocles for irony.

The reversal, such as it is, comes when Hamlet seals his exile by blundering into bloodshed in the next scene (III.4), inconsequentially killing Polonius (an act as outrageous as shooting a fox, from the point of view of generic convention) and doing it behind the arras, as if taking literally Horace's injunction in the *Ars Poetica* to keep violent deeds behind the scene. On Hamlet's return from England, when he has assumed the stance of the comic improviser, readiness being all, he at last achieves the revenge, more by accident and impulse than by design. The design responsible for the carnage at the end is that of Claudius, gone wrong. The succession to the throne of Denmark is determined by default, making a pleasing, circular conclusion to the political state of things described in the first act, but it does not happen as a result of planning or of inexorable fate either. As for the illumination, the final, piercing perception that the tragic experience can bring to an Oedipus or a Theban chorus, Hamlet says "I could tell you" (V.2.324), but he does not do so. Horatio, under duress, assumes the generic function of epilogue and promises to give forma to the materia he lists in a fashion less Horatian than Aristotelian, though a compound of both:

> So shall you hear
> Of carnal, bloody, and unnatural acts,
> Of deaths put on by cunning and forced cause,
> And, in this upshot, purposes mistook
> Fall'n on th'inventors' heads.
>
> (V.2.369–74)

The catalogue's end sounds like a reference to Aristotle's approval, for dramatic purposes, of the end of the killer of Mitys, destroyed when a statue of Mitys fell on him (*Poetics* 9.52a5–10).

But if Hamlet cannot tell, and Horatio is simply the last of the generic structures demonstrated to be inadequate here, Shakespeare communicates what Hamlet does not: the irremediable, tragic fact of life and a glimpse of the power that permits it and abides. It is done in frank despite of the structures dismissed, and of the exaggerated awareness Hamlet displays of the craft of drama. Through the remarkable con-taminatio and the casting up and aside of conventions there runs an even more disjunctive discourse provided by Hamlet the dramaturge. Nowhere is Shakespeare more assiduous to display his familiarity with the terminology, issues, and models of dramatic criticism and theatrical practice. The description Polonius frames to interest Hamlet in the play-ers turns exclusively on the idea of genre and genre mixing: "tragical-comical-historical-pastoral" (for a fuller quotation see p. vi). Polonius cannot be safely underestimated. Susan Synder illustrates the impor-tance of his passage from a comic world to a tragic one,[15] and it should be emphasized further that his genesis was a fusion of the expected *con-sigliere* of tragedy with the unexpected *vecchio* of commedia erudita or Pantalone of commedia dell'arte. Just as he is not entirely comic, he is not entirely negligible but merely commonplace, a foil to the uncom-mon prince. Likewise, the authorities he cites and the dramatic genres, subgenres, and hybrids he lists in the players' repertory are common-places of critical discussion, descriptive of numerous Cinquecento mix-tures, ordinary, up-to-date theatrical issues to be caught up and spun around in Shakespeare's extraordinary work.

Hamlet's own vocabulary resounds with theater jargon; he is drawn continually to talk in echoes of dramatic theory, from the "vicious mole of nature" speech (I.4.23–38), a contemporary interpretation of the tragic flaw or error of the *Poetics,* to the advice he gives the players in an exhortation that not only reveals advanced ideas about acting, as might be expected, but also exploits the genre of "critical" Terentian prologue fashionable in Italy, from a Shakespearean angle that recasts Donatus's *imitatio vitae, speculum consuetudinis, imago veritatis* ("to hold, as 'twere, the mirror up to nature, to show virtue her own feature, scorn her own image, and the very age and body of the time his form and pres-sure," III.2.20–33) and foreshortens actors' and playwrights' doctrines into one. Hamlet himself is an amateur actor and playwright, ready to declaim and insert speeches into the standard repertory, to arrange pro-ductions, and to subscribe seriously to one of the standard Renaissance interpretations of the idea of catharsis ("The play's the thing / Wherein I'll catch the conscience," II.2.590–91).[16] This prince so conversant

15. Susan Snyder, *The Comic Matrix of Shakespeare's Tragedies: Romeo and Juliet, Hamlet, Othello, and King Lear* (Princeton, 1979), 110.

16. The "moral" variety is discussed in O. B. Hardison, "Three Types of Re-naissance Catharsis," *Renaissance Drama,* n.s. 2 (1969): 4–8.

with the theater, who dramatizes his own life, wears his mourning like a costume, soliloquizes like a one-man chorus, waits for cues, improvises scenes, jumping into graves or breaking into song or playing the madman, is the protagonist of a tragedy that is structurally a kind of tiring-room of generic parts, of theatergrams.

Far from suggesting that *Hamlet* is a parodic pastiche of tragic structures, however, I see it as a particular hybrid of dramatic generic possibilities in which Shakespeare plays with the expectations of tragedy; these constituted a fairly precise range for spectators who knew something about the way theory of drama and Continental practice had gone ever since Trissino's milestone tragedy, *Sofonisba*, in 1515. Shakespeare tries out, rejects, replaces, overturns, and presses to surprising but convincing conclusions a number of widely known structural possibilities—not to destroy but to make a tragedy, for *Hamlet* is a tragedy on its own terms, forged by testing and mixing the standard generic commonplaces and keeping up an unremitting stream of critical dramatic vocabulary and reference. Shakespeare's procedure is entirely different from Tasso's destruction of oedipal unity, effected in order to reconstruct a plot more complex than Sophocles' but with an equally catastrophic single recognition and reversal. In both *Torrismondo* and *Hamlet,* however, a preoccupation with genre, with experimental hybrids and structures, is made manifest by conducting a critical action simultaneously with a fictional dramatic fable, underlaid by a paradigmatic myth calling attention to genre. In both, the choice of Scandinavian medieval chronicle is the sign of the sequence of come: from history to myth to genre to critical contemplation of structure.

CONCILIO DI DEMONI CONTRO. S. ORSOLA
ATTO PRIMO

Alfonso Parigi · I ·

Andrea Salvadori, *La Regina Sant'Orsola, rappresentazione recitata in musica nel teatro del Serenissimo Gran Duca di Toscana,* I (Florence, 1625). Courtesy of the Fondazione Giorgio Cini, Venice.

CHAPTER EIGHT

The *Virgin Martyr* and the Tragedia Sacra

Pues ¿qué, si venimos a las comedias
divinas? ¡Qué de milagros falsos
fingen en ellas, qué de cosas
apócrifas y mal entendidas,
atribuyendo a un santo los milagros
de otro!

*El Ingenioso Hidalgo
Don Quijote de la Mancha*, I.48

hen it was printed in 1622, "The Virgin Mar-
tir, a Tragedie . . . by Phillip Messenger and
Thomas Dekker" had already "Bin Di-
vers times publickely Acted with Great Applause,"[1] and was destined to delight many
more audiences and bedevil generations of
scholars with doubts about its authorship,
date, source, and genre. Although *The Virgin Martyr* exhibits the characteristics common to a large number of Jacobean plays labeled "tragedy," its religious subject and a portion of the dramatis personae leave
something to be accounted for. The play has been described as Massinger's revival of "the spirit of the old Morality,"[2] and as Dekker's
modification of "an old type."[3] The vagueness of these phrases results
doubtless from the realization that *The Virgin Martyr* is after all neither
a morality nor a miracle play, whatever elements reminiscent of these
genres it may contain. For more than a century before *The Virgin Martyr* appeared, religious drama in England had consisted of plays on Old

---

This chapter appeared in slightly different form in *Renaissance Drama*, o.s. 7
(1964): 103–26. Reprinted by permission of Northwestern University Press.

1. *The Dramatic Works of Thomas Dekker*, ed. Fredson Bowers (Cambridge, England, 1958), 3: 365.
2. W. J. Courthope, *A History of English Poetry* (London, 1922), 4:352.
3. M. L. Hunt, *Thomas Dekker: A Study* (New York, 1911), 201.

Testament and New Testament subjects.[4] Post-Biblical saint's plays were almost nonexistent, except for fitful revivals of medieval miracles.[5] But on the Continent in the late sixteenth century the saint's play was established both in Latin and in the vernacular as a genre distinctly modern, a product of the Counter-Reformation. To this genre, specifically to the Italian form of it, *The Virgin Martyr* bears so striking a resemblance that it may properly be termed an English *tragedia sacra*.

Published now with the works of Massinger, now with those of Dekker, the tragedy poses a problem of attribution to which the most contradictory solutions have been proposed. To Fleay's notion that Massinger merely revised an early work of Dekker, recent scholars have preferred the assumption that the two playwrights collaborated.[6] The account of payment of Sir George Buc, master of the Revels, "For new reforming the Virgin-Martyr" on October 6, 1620,[7] provides the earliest date for the tragedy and raises the question of an even earlier date of composition. Bentley deduces from the size of the fee, however, that *The Virgin Martyr* was new in 1620, but required censoring and conse-

4. See C. H. Herford, *Studies in the Literary Relations of England and Germany in the Sixteenth Century* (Cambridge, England, 1886); Ruth Blackburn, *Tudor Biblical Drama* (diss., Columbia University, 1957); and especially Lily B. Campbell, *Divine Poetry and Drama in Sixteenth Century England* (Berkeley, 1959), pt. 2.

5. Alfred Harbage, *Annals of English Drama, 975–1700* (Philadelphia, 1940), lists lost plays of SS. Feliciana and Sabina (1516), St. Christina (1522), and St. Eustace (1539). These are neomiracles, like John Hobarde's *St. George* (1511), also lost. James Shirley's lost *Tragedy of St. Albans* (1638) and his *St. Patrick for Ireland* (printed 1640), described as a neomiracle but in fact a Counter-Reformation type, are rare exceptions. These were written later than *The Virgin Martyr*, however, and for an Irish audience. Campbell observes that despite opposition miracle plays were performed even in Shakespeare's day (*Divine Poetry*, 225), and notes H. C. Gardiner's statement that the disappearance of cycle plays was the result of political anti-Catholicism (*Mysteries' End: An Investigation of the Last Days of the Medieval Religious Stage* [New Haven, 1946], 142 n. 1).

6. See G. E. Bentley, *The Jacobean and Caroline Stage* (Oxford, 1956), 3: 263–66, for the fortunes of *The Virgin Martyr;* also M. T. Jones-Davies, *Un peintre de la vie londonienne Thomas Dekker (circa 1572–1632)* (Paris, 1958), 2: 391.

7. First quoted by W. Gifford, *The Plays of Philip Massinger . . . with Notes Critical and Explanatory,* 2d ed. (London, 1813), Introduction, lvii n. 7.

quently a second reading by Buc.[8] Demonstration of the kinship between this play and the tragedia sacra will cast one more vote for Massinger's reinstatement as a coauthor and for Bentley's dating.

The question of source has been studied more extensively. The martyrdom of SS. Dorothea and Theophilus was recorded as early as the sixth century and the details of their story in the seventh, but no one has succeeded in identifying the form in which the legend reached Dekker and Massinger. Some would have it that the immediate source was the lost play *Dioclesian* mentioned by Henslowe.[9] Others conjecture a Spanish *auto*,[10] or vaguely some medieval or foreign play,[11] or a combination of the version of the legend given by Laurentius Surius[12] with a variant version appended to the *Legenda Aurea* at some unspecified time and published in Graesse's edition.[13] Peterson notes that *The Virgin Martyr* also contains the original addition of material from the Agnes legend. Hunt assumes a hagiographical source and credits Dekker with inventing the love story and the supernatural and morality figures.[14]

The mold into which Dekker and Massinger poured these elements is one typical of the early seventeenth-century English stage, that of the five-act tragedy without chorus. It contains mixtures of blank verse with prose, of high seriousness with low comedy, and interwoven actions of love and state. But in this play the state action is not the restoration of a

8. Bentley, *Jacobean Stage*, 265–66.

9. F. G. Fleay, *A Biographical Chronicle of the English Drama, 1559–1642* (London, 1891), 1: 212–13.

10. A. W. Ward, *A History of English Dramatic Literature to the Death of Queen Anne* (London, 1875), 2: 270.

11. James Phelan, *On Philip Massinger* (Halle, 1878), 17.

12. *De probatis sanctorum historiis* . . . (Coloniae Agrippinae, 1576), 1: 896ff. This work is named in connection with *The Virgin Martyr* in Emil Koeppel, *Quellen-Studien zu den Dramen George Chapman's, Philip Massinger's und John Ford's* (Strassburg, 1897), 82.

13. Jacopo a Voragine, *Legenda Aurea*, ed. T. Graesse, 3d ed. (Vratislaviae, 1890), 910–11, called G-type in J. M. Peterson, *The Dorothea Legend: Its Earliest Records and Influence on Massinger's "Virgin Martyr"* (Heidelberg, 1910). Peterson does not investigate the martyrologies in which the G-type was available before 1620. It was the version used exclusively by Georg Witzel, *Hagiologium, seu De Sanctis Ecclesiae* . . . (Moguntiae, 1541), lxxxvii.

14. Hunt, *Thomas Dekker*, 56.

rightful heir or the overthrow of a usurper but (almost unique in English drama of the period) the Roman persecution of Christians, specifically though not solely of the virgin St. Dorothea. The forces of good, represented by this aristocratic heiress and her page, Angelo, who is literally what his name declares, are assailed on all sides. Their archenemy Theophilus is served by Harpax, a demon from Hell, and is such "a zealous Persecutor of Christians" that he has even caused his own beloved daughters to be tortured away from Christianity back into paganism. Dorothea is also persecuted by Sapritius, a governor of Caesaria, who uses her religion as an excuse to vent his anger at her unintentional thwarting of his paternal ambition. His son, the military hero Antoninus, persists in his rejected suit to Dorothea and refuses an opportunity to marry Artemia, daughter of Dioclesian. Both the emperor and his daughter are magnanimous figures. He, having just crushed rebellions in Pontus, Epire, and Macedon, frees the royal leaders in recognition of their bravery; she, conquering her passion and vengefulness, urges clemency for Antoninus and Dorothea and seconds his choice, provided that the virgin can be persuaded to abjure Christianity. Only in the matter of religion are Artemia and Dioclesian represented as being in the wrong.

Still another form of attack on Dorothea comes from within her own household, from the figures of fleshly vice Hircius and Spungius. Redeemed from prison by the saint's charity and converted to Christianity, they still long for women and wine, and are easily bribed by Harpax to betray their benefactress. Despite their grave moral function, Hircius and Spungius are technically the clowns of the piece and speak in a racy prose with a vocabulary that aroused disgust in more than one nineteenth-century reader.

The character of Dorothea is conceived as a spiritual triumph already completed, beyond doubt or conflict. Her exchanges with Angelo are dialogues between angels. Her invulnerability even to physical forces is sensed before it is demonstrated. When Sapritius, hoping to cure his son's mysterious illness, hands Dorothea over to be violated, it is a foregone conclusion that Antoninus will decide not to "Climbe that sweete Virgin tree . . . and pluck that fruit which none . . . ever tasted" (IV.1). His imagery foreshadows the culminating miracle of the heavenly fruit and flowers by which Dorothea converts Theophilus. The reiterated order for the rape merely provides the occasion for a stirring refusal by a noble-hearted British slave and for Dorothea's miraculous raising of Sapritius after Heaven has struck him down. Likewise it is no surprise that torture leaves the saint unhurt and lovelier than ever.

For conflict or moral progress, we must look to other characters: to Antoninus, whose martial valor requires the supplement of Dorothea's instruction in moral courage (II.3), and whose romantic love contains the seeds of his salvation; and to Theophilus, who progresses from temporal power under infernal auspices to the eternal crown of martyrdom. It is Theophilus who most nearly resembles a protagonist of classical tragedy. He opens the play, and his death is the final incident in it. He causes his own downfall from high wordly estate by mockingly requesting Dorothea to send him some of "that curious fruit" of Heaven. The answering miracle converts Theophilus and he dies a Christian martyr, cheered by visions of those who wait above: Angelo, Dorothea, Antoninus, and the daughters he executed after their reconversion. His downfall is his triumph—and Dorothea's. The power of the state, however, admits no defeat. Artemia is betrothed to her father's coemperor, Maximus, and the tragedy ends as Harpax sinks to Hell and Dioclesian proclaims defiantly, "I still stand unmov'd, and will go on, / The persecution that is here begun, / Through all the world with violence shall run" (V.2).

Such a combination of elements in such a form is very different from the saint's play of the Middle Ages and very like the saint's tragedy of the Counter-Reformation. The latter was however a literary descendant of the former. The medieval European tradition of the miracle play had in Italy culminated in the sacra rappresentazione, the spectacular dramatic form that attracted such poets as Feo Belcari, Lorenzo de' Medici (il Magnifico), Bernardo Pulci, and numerous anonymous writers of the fifteenth century, primarily but not exclusively in Tuscany. The subjects were derived from a wide range of sacred and profane sources, the Old and New Testaments, popular romances, official hagiography, and apocrypha: Abraham, Joseph, the life of Christ, and saints like Catherine, Lawrence, and Agnes were used as freely as Tobias, Uliva, and the Seven Sleepers. The conventions of the sacra rappresentazione included a preliminary announcement by an angel, the use of *ottava rima,* episodic movement unlimited as to time and space, elaborate scenic effects, bloody or edifying action onstage, freedom to mix comic realism with the supernatural. The size of the cast was determined by the author and by the munificence of the sponsoring confraternity.[15]

15. Early and late works on the sacra rappresentazione range from Alessandro D'Ancona, *Origini del teatro italiano . . . ,* 2d ed. (Turin, 1891), to Cesare Molinari, *Spettacoli fiorentini del Quattrocento: Contributi allo studio*

The many sixteenth-century editions, adaptations, and imitations of
the old sacre rappresentazioni demonstrate that useful movable parts
were transferred from one play to another. In *La devota rappresentazione di Joseph figliuolo di Jacob* and *La rappresentazione dell'Angelo Raffaello: e di Tobbia*,[16] for example, the first ottave are almost
identical, the second are the same except for their rhymes, and the
fourth are paraphrases of a common content. Commonplaces of situation were scattered about with equal freedom and often without hagiographical endorsement. The sacre rappresentazioni about virgin martyrs
specifically are marked by the repetition of elements that also appear in
Dekker's and Massinger's dramatization of Dorothea's story: beautiful
Christian virgins are loved by their pagan persecutors or by the persecutors' relatives (Theodora, Agnes, Dorothea, Domitilla, Apollonia,
Margherita, for example); after torture or starvation the virgin is either
untouched or, if harmed, miraculously restored (Catherine, Juliana,
Dorothea); a miracle prevents attacks on the virgin's chastity (Agnes,
Theodora, Colomba); Christian virgins are persecuted by their own fa-
thers or guardians (Christina, Margherita, Guglielma).[17]

---

delle sacra rappresentazioni (Venice, 1961). For bibliography see Paul Colomb
de Batines, *Bibliografia delle antiche rappresentazioni italiane sacre e profane
stampate nei secoli XV e XVI* (Florence, 1852) and Alfredo Cioni, *Bibliografia
delle sacre rappresentazioni* (Florence, 1961); for texts, D'Ancona, ed., *Sacre
rappresentazioni dei secoli XIV, XV and XVI* (Florence, 1872), 3 vols., and
Mario Bonfantini, ed., *Le sacre rappresentazioni italiane: Raccolta di testi dal
secolo XIII al secolo XVI* (Milan, 1942).

16. Respectively Florence, 1565, and Florence, n.d.

17. *La rappresentatione di Santa Teodora vergine: & martire* . . . (Siena,
n.d.); *Rappresentatione di Sancta Agnesa vergine et martyre* . . . (n.p., n.d.); *La
rappresentatione di Santa Dorotea vergine e martire* (Siena, 1610); *La rapresentatione di Santa Domitilla* (Florence, 1594); *La rappresentatione di Santa Apollonia vergine: & martire* (Siena, n.d.); *La rappresentatione et festa di Sa. Margherita vergine e martire* (Florence, 1557); *La devota rappresentatione di S.
Caterina vergine & martire* (Florence, 1561); *La rapresentatione di Santo Valentino, & di Santa Giuliana, e altri martiri* (Florence, 1554); *La rapresentatione di S. Colomba vergine martire composta nuovamente dal Desioso Insip-
ido Senese* (Siena, n.d.); *La rapresentatione di Santa Christina vergine et martire*
(Florence, 1555); *La rapresentation di Santa Guglielma* (Florence, 1557). These
and other editions are in the collection of the Biblioteca Nazionale of Florence.

Long after they had become old-fashioned, the sacre rappresentazioni were nostalgically beloved, reprinted and adapted even into the
seventeenth century, and still performed in convents or sometimes on
public occasions.[18] Meanwhile the virgin martyr was also kept on stage
by another form of drama, more modern and by sixteenth-century cultural standards more respectable. The movement for a "Christian Terence," begun by the publication of Hroswitha's long-lost comedies in
1501 and sped by the desire of humanistic pedagogues to teach Terentian style and form without corrupting their students' morals, produced
a line of five-act Latin comoediae on Christian subjects, occasionally
among them the lives of virgin martyrs.[19]

After the Reformation, although there was increased activity on the
part of Protestant Latin dramatists, only Catholics regularly wrote plays
about postbiblical saints. Latin religious plays began to serve purposes
beyond the pedagogical. Some of those written for the polemic war
could also be used as Latin school texts combining Christian substance
with Terentian form, but others—Kirchmayer's, for example—were totally deficient in the latter.

Among the types of religious drama related to the Christian Terence
movement but not part of it was the Latin drama of the Catholic
Counter-Reformation. Launched in Jesuit schools in Italy, these more or
less neoclassically constructed plays about Biblical characters, saints, or
allegorical figures were approved by the *Ratio Studiorum* in 1591 and
1599 as an aid to the study of Latin and oratory. But the prime purpose
of the genre was to reinvigorate the spirit of Catholic youth with orthodoxy and anti-Protestantism, and to communicate Church pronouncements on various questions to the adult members of the usually large

18. D'Ancona, *Origini del teatro italiano,* II.157, 186.

19. On the Christian Terence see Herford, *Studies in Literary Relations,* and
Marvin T. Herrick, *Tragicomedy: Its Origin and Development in Italy, France,
and England* (Urbana, Ill., 1955), chap. 2. The authors agree on the existence of
a later "Christian Seneca" movement after George Buchanan. It should be noted
that the earlier, "tragic" work of Giovanni Francesco Conti Stoa, *Tragedia de
passione Domini Jesu Christi: Que Theoandrathanatos* (Milan, 1508), is avow-
edly like the Christian Terence in purpose (see appendix, "Ad Lectorem"),
whereas that of Giano Anisio, *Protogonos, Tragoedia* (Naples, 1536), aims not
at substituting Christian content for pagan, but in a typically pre-Reformation,
humanist manner at identifying and merging the two, by means of mixed choruses of angels and nymphs and the like.

and aristocratic audience.[20] Before long this kind of Latin religious drama was flourishing in Europe wherever the Jesuits taught. In the wake of the Jesuit Latin plays came the vernacular religious drama, aimed not at the schoolboy but at the theatergoer. Orthodox and didactic but not pedagogical, this drama mirrored the hopes of the Council of Trent and the Church's decision to purge what could not be suppressed, by using the theater as a vehicle of orthodoxy.[21] Some spiritual leaders, like St. Carlo Borromeo, were altogether opposed to playacting. Many of them, however, were of the opinion of the Spanish Jesuit Juan Ferrer, who declared that *malas comedias* were a mortal sin for all who allowed, performed, and watched them, but that on the other hand, "las Comedias y representaciones de cosas santas, no solo no son malas, sino muy licitas, y provechosas" (comedies and representations of holy subjects are not only not evil but are highly permissible and useful). This was true only if the actors were virtuous people; otherwise there might be repetitions of the case of the respectable young girl of Barcelona, who on attending a performance of the farsa of the Magdalen's conversion fell in love with Jesus and ran away to live with the actor who played him.[22]

Encouraged by the Church throughout Europe with varying success, the writers of Counter-Reformation religious drama aimed at adapting their sacred subjects to the fashionable secular forms of the place and the moment. The results were sometimes neoclassical comedy or tragedy, sometimes very strange hybrid genres. In Italy one of these results was the flexible tragedia sacra.

Confusingly, there was no agreement about terminology. Although many playwrights chose to subtitle their works tragedia sacra or tragedia spirituale, there were as many who called them rappresentazione

20. On the origins of Jesuit drama in Italy see D'Ancona, *Origini del teatro italiano*, vol. 2; Mario Apollonio, *Storia del teatro italiano*, 2:2 (Florence, 1954), 267–75; and Benedetto Soldati, *Il Collegio mamertino e le origini del teatro gesuitico con l'aggiunta di notizie inedite sulla drammatica conventuale messinese nei secoli XVI, XVII, XVIII, e con la pubblicazione dalla Giuditta del P. Tuccio* (Turin, 1908).

21. On the general influence of the Council of Trent on drama see Apollonio, *Storia*, and Charles DeJob, *De l'influence du Concile de Trente* (Paris, 1884).

22. Juan Ferrer, *Tratado de las comedias en el qual se declara si son licitas, y si hablando en todo rigor sera pecado mortal el rapresentarlas, el verlas, y el consentirlas* (Barcelona, 1618; licensed in 1613 and published under the pseudonym Fructuoso Bisbe y Vidal), 81–82.

sacra, in the manner of the fifteenth century. But once past the title page there was no mistaking the difference. The tragedia sacra was distinctly a combination of religious content and up-to-date tragic form—that is, the neoclassical structure used by sixteenth-century Italian secular playwrights for audiences of tragedy, the literate upper classes who attended performances at court, in academies, or in private homes.

Although serious moral elements appeared in Italian drama even before the Council of Trent finally closed in 1563, there is no certain record of vernacular tragedia sacra before the *Saul* of 1566 and the *Martirio di Santa Caterina* of 1568 named by Soldati.[23] Giovanni Domenico di Lega's *Morte di Cristo, tragedia* (1549) may have been an earlier example.[24]

The subject matter of the tragedia sacra was in general of the same kind as that of the Jesuit Latin drama, biblical, hagiographical, historical, or allegorical. But the particular choices were often of figures from the Old and New Testaments and from lives of the saints already dramatized in the old sacre rappresentazioni: Adam and Eve, Esther (in one tragedy on the subject, with the significant substitution of Haman as a more classically tragic protagonist),[25] Susannah, the life of Christ, Judith, St. George, Mary Magdalen, and a high proportion of virgin martyrs, including Catherine of Alexandria, Justina, Agnes, Ursula, Dorothea, Cecilia, Christina, Theodora, Margherita, and Eugenia.

Heedful of orthodoxy, these Counter-Reformation playwrights seem to have checked their information against official sources, after choosing the subjects for their popularity from the sacre rappresentazioni. The spelling of Giambattista Della Porta's *Georgio, tragedia*,[26] indicates that the details of its story, which had already formed part of a widely known sacra rappresentazione, had been verified by the account of "Georgius" in the *Legenda Aurea*. The plot of Francesco Farina's *Dimne* must have been familiar to any audience as a variant on the rappresentazione story of Uliva, but the author emphatically retails his source: Surius, the authoritative Carthusian hagiographer, precursor of the Bollandists.[27] Having made these orthodox gestures, the writers of

23. Soldati, *Il Collegio mamertino*, 17.

24. Printed in Naples, 1549, and listed by Lione Allacci, *Drammaturgia . . . accresciuta e continuata fino all'anno MDCCLV* (Venice, 1775), 539.

25. *La rappresentatione di Aman* (Siena?, n.d.).

26. Naples, 1611.

27. *La Dimne: Rappresentatione spirituale cavata dal Surio . . .* (Venice, 1610).

tragedie sacre then treated their material as they chose. Caught between demands of fidelity to Church history and observance of neo-Aristotelian principles Bonaventura Morone chooses the latter, and apologizes for telescoping the chronology and geography of his story, explaining that only by so doing can he adhere to the unities of time and place.[28]

Some of the old sacre rappresentazioni bear traces of slight classical influence; but in the tragedie sacre the content had to be purged of paganism and then totally recast into some neoclassical shape, not only to keep religion free from falsehood and baseness, but also to keep in good repair the Church's reputation as the patron of intellectual and literary excellence, by following the latest critical definitions of classical form or some polemical departure from them. To the accompaniment of interpretations and misinterpretations of Aristotle, the series of experiments in tragedy beginning with Trissino's early in the sixteenth century had established a number of conventions for the genre in Italy, and the writers of sacred tragedy pursued these or departed from them just about as much and as often as did writers of secular tragedy. Sometimes they were the same writers.

One of the current conventions was the five-act structure developed by imitators of Seneca. Division into three acts was relatively rare, except in the Jesuit Latin drama. In the schools the length of the play was determined in part by the solemnity of the occasion; the grand end-of-the-year tragedy was always in five acts.[29] The vernacular playwrights, however, more closely followed the practice of the secular theater. Like the secular tragedies of Pomponio Torelli, sacred tragedy would revert exceptionally to the "Greek" style of Trissino and have no act division.[30] Morone's concern for the unities was shared by almost all his colleagues. Intent on unity of action, Della Porta constructed *Il Georgio* around a single incident in the saint's life, an incident that is but one of many in the best-known sacra rappresentazione about St. George.[31] In the tragedies about virgin martyrs, the usual pattern requires the saint to be accused of Christianity, exhorted to renounce her faith, and tortured re-

28. Bonaventura Morone, *La Giustina, tragedia spirituale* (Venice, 1617), A4.

29. Soldati, *Il Collegio mamertino,* 29.

30. For example, Giovanni Battista Liviera, *Giustina vergine, e martire santissima, hierotragedia* (Padua, 1593).

31. *La rappresentatione di Santo Giorgio cavaliere di Christo* (Siena, n.d.).

peatedly, to perform a miracle and at least one conversion, and to be executed—all in one busy day.

Violent action had been one of the drawing cards of the sacra rappresentazione in its heyday, and even in its Indian summer in the sixteenth century it was modified only when made necessary by limitations of stage facilities; in the tragedia sacra it was usually kept offstage. There were exceptions, of course: the same Morone who was so scrupulously respectful of the unities of time and place permits his virgin martyr and her companion to die in full view of the audience, explaining in his preface that he could not very well disappoint the public of a martyrdom when it came to see martyrs.[32]

In the Senecan manner there was usually a prologue. Sometimes, in a manner reminiscent of the sacra rappresentazione in which always "L'angelo annunzia," the tragedia sacra's prologue was spoken by an angel. The more self-consciously modern of the tragedie sacre, however, employed neoclassical or allegorical figures. In Pier Giovanni Brunetto's *David sconsolato* the prologue is spoken by the "Ombra del Figliuolo Adulterino di David" (the ghost of David's illegitimate son), who is suffering not in Hell but in Avernus.[33] Giovann'Agnolo Lottini calls all his tragedie sacre by the outmoded name sacra rappresentazione, but in his *San Lorenzo* the prologue is delivered by the "Chiesa Militante," and in *Santa Agnesa* by "Amor Celeste."[34] Riccardo Riccardi's *Maria Maddalena* is introduced by "Urania, Musa Celeste."[35]

When necessary, the saint's social position was raised to make him a suitably noble protagonist for tragedy. Virgin martyrs in tragedie sacre are invariably of high birth, though they are not all so in the Church calendars or in the sacre rappresentazioni.

A chorus was optional in these sacred tragedies and was used less often than in secular tragedy, but when used it followed the common secular practices: the playwright's choice was between using the chorus only at the ends of acts or using it also in the dialogue. It might be com-

---

32. Morone, *La Giustina,* A4.

33. Pier Giovanni Brunetto, *David sconsolato, tragedia spirituale* (Florence, 1586).

34. Giovanni Angelo Lottini, *Sacra rappresentazione di San Lorenzo* (Florence, 1592); *Sacra rappresentazione di Santa Agnesa* (Florence, 1592).

35. Riccardo Riccardi, *Conversione di Santa Maria Maddalena, ridotta in tragedia* (Florence, 1609).

posed of people or angels, or sometimes a chorus of one might supplement a semichorus of the other.

Prose became popular for tragedia sacra later in the seventeenth century, but before 1620 it was fairly rare, and *terza rima* rarer still. The ottava rima of the sacra rappresentazione was entirely discarded, and the usual line for tragedia sacra was that of secular tragedy since Trissino—*endecasillabo sciolto* (the line most nearly equivalent to English blank verse)—with a number of short lines interspersed increasingly as the lyric style of pastoral drama came to influence both secular and sacred tragedy.

After Guarini, the power of the pastoral was felt in many ways. The results in tragedia sacra were scenes like that in Morone's *Mortorio di Christo,* in which St. Peter retires to a sylvan glade to lament his betrayal of Jesus and is answered by Echo.[36] Touched by the same Arcadian breath, Farina's *Dimne* is set in "un luogo silvestre, con una chiesiola & Hostaria . . . tutti i personaggi vestiti da Campagna" (a woodland place, with a chapel and an inn, the characters all in country garb).[37]

In short, all the fashions in secular tragedy were made to work in the tragedia sacra *ad majorem Dei gloriam.* Only the most severely classical of the genre escaped the powerful influence of Giraldi Cinzio, whose preference for "she-tragedies" confirmed writers of sacred tragedy in their interest in female saints inherited from the sacre rappresentazioni, and whose defense of romantic fiction and double plots encouraged them to add love stories with complications to the lives of the saints, or to develop richly lyrical passion from a mere hint of lust.

The element of horror common in Italian secular tragedy from Rucellai's time, but most apparent after Giraldi, is fully represented in the tragedia sacra and in the same way (that is, usually offstage). The sacre rappresentazioni had provided the spectacle of tortures; the "neoclassical" tragedia sacra retained them all—burning, boiling, racking, beating, and mutilation—but in the form of a messenger's report. Oddly, the martyr tragedies were less ghastly than the secular ones. For sheer horror, Antonio Decio's *Acripanda* or Gabriele Zinano's *Almerigo* is unsurpassed—except by English tragedy.

---

36. Bonaventura Morone, *Il mortorio di Christo, tragedia spirituale* (Cremona, 1612), III.2. A similar duet occurs between the Prodigal Son and Echo in Orazio Persio, *Il figliuol prodigo, rappresentatione* (Naples, 1612), IV.6.

37. Farina, *La Dimne,* Prologue.

As the influence of the Cavalier Marino's lyric style grew, preciosity was joined to horror. Francesco Belli's graphic description of St. Catherine's decapitation concludes with the statement that the streams spurting from her jugular vein and carotid artery were one of blood and one of milk, like the symbolic rose and lily.[38]

Another sort of horror was furnished by the figures of the devil, who had appeared occasionally in the sacre rappresentazioni, but less frequently than in the tragedie sacre. Devils are absent from the very austere tragedies like those of Brunetto and Liviera, but they abound in others. Some of them have Dantesque names and shout "Papè Satàn aleppe!"; others are named for pagan or Old Testament figures—Asmodeo,[39] Belzebù,[40] and Aletto[41] are especially popular. In the martyr plays they function as aides to the persecutors, can change their shapes, and are usually pitted against angelic opponents.

The Counter-Reformation taste for allegory is sometimes represented in this timely genre by simple personification. In the virgin martyr tragedies, for example, appear La Castità and La Voluttà, Amor Celeste and Amor Lascivo.[42] In other plays the allegory is more sweeping or harder to find. Aside from those which were not sacred tragedies but outright allegorical plays, there were some intended for performance on one level and for meditation on another, the latter requiring instruction from the author. Andrea Perbenedetti and Morone respectively alert their readers to these potentialities in *Rappresentatione sacra della vita et martirio del glorioso S. Venantio* and *Mortorio di Christo*.[43]

---

38. Francesco Belli, *Catarina d'Alessandria, tragica rappresentatione* (Verona, 1621), V.3.

39. Asmodeo appears in Morone, *La Giustina*; and in Ambrogio Leoni, *La Taide convertita, rappresentatione spirituale* (Venice, 1599).

40. Belzebù is in Dionisio Rondinelli, *Rapresentatione del martorio de la vergine Margherita* (Verona, 1593); and in Morone, *Il mortorio di Christo*.

41. Aletto is in Andrea Perbenedetti, *Rappresentatione sacra della vita et martirio del glorioso S. Venantio da Camerino* (Camerino, 1617); and in Malatesta Porta, *I Santi Innocenti, tragedia* (Serravalle di Vinetia, 1605).

42. These personifications appear in Lottini, *Sacra rappresentatione di Santa Agnesa*; in Morone, *La Giustina*; and in Farina, *La Dimne*, in which La Virginità also figures.

43. Perbenedetti, *Rappresentatione sacra della vita et martirio del glorioso S. Venantio*, Dedication to the Priors and Citizens of Camerino; Morone, *Mortorio di Christo*, Preface to the members of his order, the Frati Minori Osservanti Riformati.

Another kind of allegory possible in tragedia sacra was the broad and unstated sort discerned by an audience accustomed to spying out hidden meanings. Counter-Reformation audiences were quick to draw parallels by spontaneous historical allegory. Soldati attributes the popularity of the story of Jezebel to the resemblance between the struggle of Elias and Jezebel to that between the papacy and the forces of the Reformation.[44] If this seems farfetched, it must be remembered that Buchanan pleaded before the Inquisition in Lisbon that his *Baptistes* was an allegory of the tyranny of Henry VIII against Thomas More, and his *Jephthes* an argument against Bucer's stand on vows.[45]

It cannot yet be determined how many tragedie sacre Italy produced in the late Cinquecento and early Seicento. Copies of them are not easy to obtain. Because tragedie sacre were often called sacre rappresentazioni and because the latter were reprinted decade after decade, they are often indistinguishable from one another in a nondescriptive bibliography like Allacci's, for example. Probably there were hundreds of them, all in one way or another seconding the double aim of the Church to reform both secular and religious drama by wedding the form of one to the content of the other. Antonio Ongaro's praise of Ploti for replacing heroines like Dido and Phaedra with Judith is typical of Catholic reaction, and Francesco Bozza's tribute to Liviera's *Giustina vergine* sums up a score of statements made regularly by admirers and writers of tragedia sacra: "Non può tragica scena à merto uguale / Salir, che Dio nel tuo bel dir accende / Nostr'alme erranti à sempiterni oggetti"[46] (The tragic stage cannot rise to such merit as that of your beautiful words inspired by God to direct our erring souls to eternal things).

As priests assumed mufti for travel, so instruction and edification were dressed up in the forms of secular drama and offered to European audiences. The Spanish drama was already developed beyond the need to import tragedia sacra; saints and other religious subjects were well-known in romantic holy comedias, farsas, and autos sacramentales. In France, however, the sacred tragedy gained a foothold in both Protestant and Catholic camps.

French Counter-Reformation vernacular sacred tragedy has some-

44. Soldati, *Il Collegio mamertino*, 83–84.

45. Campbell, *Divine Poetry*, 155.

46. Giovanni Andrea Ploti, *Giuditta rappresentata* (Piacenza, 1589), Antonio Ongaro's prefatory sonnet; Liviera, *Giustina vergine e martire santissima, hierotragedia*, Francesco Bozza's prefatory sonnet.

times been ignored or dismissed as a leftover from the Middle Ages.[47] Yet the author of *Achab* seems to be echoing Italian writers of tragedia sacra when he says his tragedy was drawn from "pancartes sacrées, recognoissant le debvoir d'un chrestien estre d'employer ses honestes loisirs, à traicter de la saincte Escripture, plustost que s'amuser et perdre le temps à representer des fables et histoires profanes" (sacred writings, recognizing it to be the duty of a Christian to use his virtuous leisure in treating of holy Scripture rather than in amusing himself and wasting time representing profane tales and stories).[48] Marcé's sacred tragedy is in five acts, beginning with a monologue by a ghost and ending with the lament of a soldiers' chorus. Jezebel's death is omitted, to avoid either altering the historical time sequence or destroying one of the unities. Dabney records ten other Biblical plays between 1589 and 1601, all in Senecan style with five acts and a chorus. There were also six plays about saints, of whom two are technically virgin martyrs—Cecilia and Jeanne d'Arc. Admittedly, the latter is not the traditional type of virgin martyr and is not treated as such in the tragedy, Jean de Virey's *Tragédie de Ieann D'Arques*,[49] which represents one way in which the Counter-Reformation tragedia sacra was Gallicized. Written in alexandrines with lyric variations for choruses at the ends of the five acts, this play is as much historical as religious. No supernatural characters are used, and the emphasis is less on sanctity than on *gloire;* Jeanne is likened to the Amazons and to Penthesilea, and behaves like the heroine of some romanesque Italian secular tragedy in the style of Francesco Bracciolini.

But the kinship of these French saints' plays with Italian tragedia sacra surfaces in Nicolas Romain's boast that his *Maurice* comes from Jesuit Latin tragedy and that his story is faithful to official Church history, specifically Nicephore's *Histoire ecclesiastique,* book 18.[50]

Whereas Jesuit Latin drama and vernacular saints' plays in some form or other were to be expected in Catholic countries, they were hardly the fashion in Protestant England. The only English Jesuit drama

47. H. C. Lancaster, *A History of French Dramatic Literature in the Seventeenth Century* (Baltimore, 1932), vol. 2, pt. 2, p. 656; Raymond Lebègue, *La tragédie religieuse en France: Les débuts (1514–1573)* (Paris, 1929), viii.

48. L. E. Dabney, *French Dramatic Literature in the Reign of Henri IV: A Study of the Extant Plays Composed in France between 1589 and 1610* (Austin, 1952), 4. Dabney attributes *Achab* to Rolland Marcé.

49. Jean de Virey, *Tragédie de Ieann D'Arques dite la Pucelle d'Orleans, native du village d'Epernay, pres Vaucouleur en Lorraine* (Rouen, 1603).

50. Dabney, *French Dramatic Literature,* 51 and n. 23.

was that produced across the Channel at the English College of St. Omers or by English Jesuits elsewhere in Catholic Europe.[51] And the only post-Reformation saint's play on the London stage before the theaters were closed in 1642 was *The Virgin Martyr*.

Two versions of the Dorothea legend are reflected in Dekker's and Massinger's work. The so-called G-type, which accompanies the *Legenda Aurea*, is set in the reign of Diocletian. The noblyborn Dorothea is loved by the prefect Fabritius, refuses to marry him or abjure her Christian faith, suffers torture, and reconverts her apostate sisters. The end of Theophilus is the same here as in all versions. In Surius's account, based on Aldhelm's, the prefect is the governor, Sapritius, and is not in love with Dorothea, nor are the apostates related to her; neither the reign of Diocletian nor Dorothea's high birth is mentioned. Koeppel and Peterson agree in supposing the immediate source of *The Virgin Martyr* to have been a martyrology in which the above two versions were combined.[52] This supposition is sound; the immediate sources of most tragedie sacre seem to have been martyrologies. But behind the immediate source lies the tradition of Dorothea's legend in Renaissance drama, largely ignored by students of Dekker's and Massinger's play.

The anonymous *Rappresentatione di Santa Dorotea vergine e martire* presents Dorothea as a heroine of the fifteenth-century sacra rappresentazione.[53] The G-type of the legend is used here exclusively. The structure is typically episodic and suitable to tableaux like that of Dorotea's visitation in prison by Christ and the angels. Characters are introduced when needed, not before: as in the nondramatic version, Teofilo appears only in time to ask his scornful question, and the boy angel is not seen until the moment of Dorotea's execution.

Like other sacre rappresentazioni, this one was reprinted in the sixteenth and seventeenth centuries. There are minor differences in spelling and even phrasing from edition to edition: the prefect's "Et che manc'egli à me?" of an early but undated Sienese edition becomes "E che mi

---

51. W. H. McCabe, "Notes on the St. Omers College Theatre," *Philological Quarterly* 17, no. 3 (July 1938): 225–39; McCabe, "The Play-List of the English College of St. Omers 1597–1762," *Revue de littérature comparée* 17 (1937): 355–75.

52. Koeppel, *Quellen-Studien,* 83; Peterson, *The Dorothea Legend,* 108. Peterson also notes that the legend had received literary treatment in England, though not in the drama. There exist five manuscript accounts of Dorothea's life, all in Middle English: three in prose, two in verse (p. 27).

53. The edition of Siena, 1610, is used here.

manca?" in the Florentine edition of 1617. Other saints, George for one, and sacred events were celebrated in more than one play in this genre, but apparently Dorothea was not; no other sacra rappresentazione about her is extant. The one we have is in twelve editions: one without place or date (probably very early sixteenth century, Florentine or Sienese); three published in Siena (two without date, one in 1610); and eight in Florence (1516, 1554, 1555, 1570, 1584, 1602, 1617, and 1648).[54]

By encouraging classical structure of sorts the Christian Terence movement brought the story of Dorothea closer to the form it would take in the later Renaissance, in Chilianus of Mellerstadt's comedy on the suffering and death of the virgin martyr Saint Dorothy.[55] The verse prologue to this prose play acknowledges its model: "Sacrimonialem secutus Rosphitam / Stilum que vortit in sacratos martires." Another prefatory poem contains the boast that nymphs, lovers, and corrupt servants are here banished from the stage to give place to a virgin martyr. This had been the boast of Hroswitha herself and would be made many more times in the sixteenth century. The G-type of the legend is employed here, as in the Italian sacra rappresentazione, and the action is only somewhat less episodic. An effect of greater structural unity is achieved by the division of the action into five Terentian acts, but with no attempt at unity of time or place. The general distribution of the action over the five acts is incidentally the same as that in *The Virgin Martyr*. This is neither surprising nor significant: nine out of ten dramatists would have made the same arrangement, given this material and a five-act structure to deal with. The most unifying effect of the Terentian influence is that it caused Chilianus to involve his characters in more of the action. The angel-child who appears at the end of he legend and of the sacra rappresentazione is here named Paranymphus and is with Dorothea from her first entrance. Dekker and Massinger were not the first to invent a demonic foil for this character: Chilianus provides not one but two devils, Pluto and Alecto, whose popular names look forward to the later Italian mixture of martyrs and neoclassical form.

Although Chilianus's comedia inspired the Danish translation of Christen Hansen,[56] there is no direct connection known between it and *The Virgin Martyr* or the Italian religious drama. Yet in the tragedia

54. Colomb de Batines, *Bibliografia*, 49–50.

55. Chilianus Mellerstatinus, *Comedia gloriose parthenices martiris Dorothee agoniam passionem depingens* (Leipzig, 1507).

56. Herford, *Studies in Literary Relations*, 403–04, quotes a fragment.

sacra Dorothea was to be a popular heroine, inherited from the sacra rappresentazione but treated more as she had been by the Christian Terence movement.

Three tragedie sacre about Dorothea are known by name, two of them earlier than *The Virgin Martyr*. The earliest is Della Porta's *Santa Dorotea*, written perhaps before 1591, the year in which one of his editors referred to an unspecified number of "Tragedie e martiri di Santi," and certainly before 1610, when another editor mentioned it by name.[57] This play was never printed, nor was its companion piece about the virgin martyr Saint Eugenia, but Della Porta's sole published sacred tragedy, *Il Georgio, tragedia,* provides an example of his handling of the genre. Doubtless his *Santa Dorotea* was in five acts of unrhymed hendecasyllables. Probably the love element in the G-type of the legend—the version well-known in Italy through the sacra rappresentazione—was developed in the romantic post-Giraldian manner. In *Il Georgio* Della Porta introduces without authority an elaborate love affair for the princess whom the saint rescues from the dragon. Other elements common to *Il Georgio* and most tragedie sacre may be expected to be found in *Santa Dorotea* if the manuscript is ever discovered: a chorus to sing lyric odes at the end of each act, and even to take part occasionally in the dialogue; action offstage reported by messengers; avoidance of the episodic effect by means of interweaving motives; and unity of time and place. Della Porta may even have done without unclassical angels and devils in *Santa Dorotea*.

The same style of speculation must be used on Orazio Persio's *Martirio di Santa Dorotea rappresentazione sacra,* published in Naples in 1610. Persio's *Figliuol prodigo* also is called rappresentazione, but its form is that of early Seicento commedia erudita with additions from tragic form, despite a prologue that denounces all the elements fashionable in the secular comedy of the Counter-Reformation. The story of the Prodigal Son demands comic rather than tragic form, but Persio handles it as tragically as possible by employing choral comment, endecasillabi sciolti, and a pair of devils. That Persio introduced a love story into *Il figliuol prodigo,* that in his prologue he blames his plot for forcing him to disregard the "precetti communi" of drama, that he wrote a strict but romantic tragedy on Pompey the Great and two romanesque pastoral

---

57. Giambattista Della Porta, *La Penelope, tragicomedia,* ed. Pompeo Barbarito (Naples, 1591), Dedication, A2–3; Della Porta, *Elementorum curvilineorum,* ed. Bartolomeo Zannetti (Rome, 1610), 99.

plays[58]—all suggest that his *Martirio di Santa Dorotea* was of the type represented by Morone's sacred tragedies, which are the standard variety: in conformity with Aristotelian precepts when convenient, but strong on love story, pastoral elements, and supernatural characters.

A third sacred tragedy, *La Dorotea vergine e martire, tragedia sacra*, published in Naples in 1642 by the secular priest Giovanni Leonardo Tristano of Isernia,[59] was too late to have influenced Dekker and Massinger, but its existence manifests the continued popularity of Dorothea as a heroine of the genre.

Failure to discover copies of these tragedie sacre about Dorothea frustrates one kind of conclusion but permits a larger speculation. If a close similarity were discovered between *The Virgin Martyr* and one of the lost plays, this investigation might end with the identification of a specific source. More rewarding to consider is the likelihood that *The Virgin Martyr* was planned primarily as an English tragedia sacra of the virgin martyr variety, and that in following the plan the playwrights chose the popular Dorothea from among the heroines traditional to the genre.

For the facts of the story, Dekker and Massinger may well have gone through the motions of Italian Counter-Reformation dramatists who chose their subjects from the tradition of sacred drama, next invoked the authority of an orthodox calendar of saints, and then infused as much fiction as pre-Reformation playwrights had done.

Although Koeppel and Peterson suggested that the source of *The Virgin Martyr* was an account of Dorothea's life in which the G-type and Surius's version were combined, neither was acquainted with any such combination. There was at least one available in print in Dekker's and Massinger's time, however: the work of Paolo Emilio Santori, at one time bishop of Cosenza, at another archbishop of Urbino. In 1597 he published with a dedication to the pope a Latin "zodiac" of twelve virgin martyrs: Thecla, Flavia Domitilla, Caecilia, Barbara, Agatha, Eugenia, Margarita, Dorothea, Agnes, Lucia, Catharina, and Ursula.[60] All

58. *Pompeo Magno, tragedia* (Naples, 1603); *Erminia pastorella* (Naples, 1629); *Armida infuriata* (Naples, 1629).

59. Listed in F. S. Quadrio, *Della storia e della ragione d'ogni poesia*, vol. 3 (Milan, 1743), 91.

60. *Pauli Aemilii Sanctorii Casertani. XII virginis et martyres* (Rome, 1597). The copy from the Vatican Library used here lacks the title page, but the *Catalogue géneral des livres imprimés de la Bibliothèque Nationale* (Paris, 1941), 162, supplies the title.

but Thecla were heroines of old sacre rappresentazioni and modern tragedie sacre.[61] Santori acknowledges his debt to Surius, among others, from whose account he takes the figure of Sapricius, governor of Caesaria. Sapricius does not love Dorothea, but he praises her beauty recommends marriage, preferably with a rich and distinguished Roman, and seems to take it personally when she rejects his advice. From the G-type Santori borrows the high birth of Dorothea and the time setting in Diocletian's reign. Moreover, he alone of the hagiographers includes details about the state of the Roman Empire at that period, with specific reference to rebellions in Britain and elsewhere put down by Diocletian and his coemperor, Maximianus Herculeus.

Santori's "zodiac" may have supplied the combination of Surius's account and the G-type employed by Dekker and Massinger, or it may simply represent the kind of source they used. After the Council of Trent closed, a great wave of hagiographies swept over Europe, and any playwright not averse to adapting Catholic material had an endless variety to choose from.

Whatever the source, *The Virgin Martyr* is like tragedia sacra in its theatrical departures from calendar accounts. And as in many tragedie sacre, it is not easy to distinguish original additions and variations from others that had become traditional. Peterson points to parts of *The Virgin Martyr* borrowed from the legend of St. Agnes: the change of the virgin's lover from the governor or prefect to the governor's son; the governor's order that the saint be ravished and the heavenly prevention of this; the illness, conversion, and death of the son.[62] Dekker and Massinger may have taken these elements directly from the legend of Agnes and grafted them onto Dorothea's plot, but it is worth mentioning that these were among the elements transferred from one saint's story to another in the sacre rappresentationi (and secularized in the romances that Shakespeare remembered in writing Marina's scenes of *Pericles*). For example, not only Agnes but Teodora and Colomba are victims of attempted rape. In the case of Colomba, a villain named Scialecqua attacks under orders, but when Colomba prays he becomes weak and falls prey to a passing bear, until the saint rescues and converts him. Just be-

61. Flavia Domitilla is celebrated in a sacra rappresentazione and in the Jesuit Bernardino Stefonio's *Flavia tragoedia* (Rome, 1621), but apparently not in any vernacular tragedia sacra.

62. Peterson, *The Dorothea Legend,* 53, 109. There are variations on the Agnes legend, however, in which the son himself attempts the rape and is struck dead, but is later resurrected and converted.

fore Colomba is beheaded, moreover, the voice of Christ is heard, inviting her to come as His bride to His "giardin celeste"—the destination
that Dorothea makes so much of in all versions of her story.[63] Teodora
responds to the Roman consul Quintiano's proposal of marriage by saying that her husband (Christ) is richer than he—exactly Dorothea's answer to the same proposal made by another Roman. Teodora even has a
pair of evil and treacherous friends, Daria and Clarizia, similar to the
vile Hircius and Spungius in *The Virgin Martyr*.[64]

These interchangeable elements reappear in the tragedie sacre about
virgin martyrs, often expanded for dramatic effect. In Morone's
Giustina the saint converts a pagan who was one of her erstwhile tor-
mentors and lovers, but instead of the quick account given to such
things in the sacre rappresentazioni there is an extended detailing of the
situation and the emotions involved, with great emphasis on the progress from earthly to heavenly love. In *The Virgin Martyr* Dorothea is
still harping of this theme as she dies, praying that Antoninus's love for
her will be purified and transformed, a prayer that is answered as her
head rolls and Antoninus drops dead (IV.3). In describing this scene
later, the converted Theophilus repeats a commonplace of the tragedia
sacra by comparing Dorothea with classical heroines, to the detriment
of the latter:

> They out of desperation,
> Or for vaine glory of an aftername
> Parted with life.   .   .   .
> .   .   .   she, vncompeld
> Chang'd this life for a better.
>
>   (V.2)

This proposal of kinship between *The Virgin Martyr* and a Counter-
Reformation genre is not intended to revive the question of Massinger's
Roman Catholicism, much less decide it. But for purposes of assigning
responsibility for the subject and plan of the play, it is useful to remem-
ber that Massinger's name, not Dekker's, has often been linked with
popery.

More than once before, Dekker had put a hand to religious drama,

63. *La rappresentatione di S. Colomba vergine martire* is a revival of the
old-fashioned sacra rappresentazione by Domenico Tregiano, prolific writer of
the 1570s and 1580s who published under his academic name, "Il Desioso" of
the Sienese Insipidi.

64. *La rappresentatione di Santa Teodora vergine & martire.*

but never of a kind to prepare the way for an English tragedia sacra. His
Jephthah, written in collaboration with Munday, is lost. Among Old
Testament subjects used in drama, this one was popular with Protestant
playwrights as well as Catholic ones. Dekker's *Whore of Babylon* also is
religious drama of sorts, but opposed to tragedia sacra on two counts:
unclassical structure, and anti-Catholic import. It is totally unlike anything produced by the Counter-Reformation, except perhaps for the
sympathetic glimpse it offers of Edmund Campion in the figure of Cam-
peius. Hunt speaks of Dekker's "profoundly religious nature" and sen-
sitivity to holiness and other beauty, whereas Jones-Davies calls him a
"sermonnaire laic," a laughing moralist, sympathetic to the oppressed,
generally tolerant and not usually given to polemic;[65] no one would
deny that he was temperamentally equipped to work on the subject of
the virgin martyr. But to judge from his other works, Dekker is not
likely to have thought of the subject to begin with. Massinger, on the
other hand, is very likely to have done so.

Dekker's brief picture of Campion shows him as a neglected scholar,
not as a Jesuit martyr, but in *The Renegado* Massinger paints a full-
length portrait of an ideal Jesuit. This play is very like Spanish Counter-
Reformation drama of the kind represented by Lope de Vega's *Comedia
de Santa Casilda*[66]—an adventurous tragicomedy involving the conversion of beautiful, high-born Moorish ladies by Christian captives, with
baptism and fairy-tale endings—while the character of Father Francisco
suggests the specifically Jesuit saints' plays, which were of course produced in Jesuit schools. The tortures inflicted on the priest's protégé,
Vitelli, are endured in the spirit of the martyr plays.

Massinger's play *Fair Anchoress of Pausillipo* is lost except for its
popish title, but *The Maid of Honour* reveals his deliberate use of elements favored by Counter-Reformation policy. To the story in his
sources—a combination of history with Boccaccio's "De Camiola sen-
ensi vidua" in *De claris mulieribus,* by way of Painter's *Palace of Pleasure*[67]—Massinger added the denouement in which Camiola enters a

65. Hunt, *Thomas Dekker,* 146; Jones-Davies, *Un peintre de la vie londonienne,* 2:76.

66. *Obras de Lope de Vega publicadas por la Real Academia Española:
Obras Dramáticas,* vol. 2 (Madrid, 1916). W. G. Rice, "The Sources of Massinger's *The Renegado,*" *Philological Quarterly* 11 (1932): 65–75, sums up the
scholarship on the specific sources of *The Renegado* and adds to it, but does not
take up the question of generic prototypes.

67. Philip Massinger, *The Maid of Honour* (London, 1927), ed. E. A. W.
Bryne, Introduction, ix n. 2, xxiii n. 1.

convent. Her conversion from earthly to heavenly love, entirely Massinger's invention, echoes the finale of many a tragedia sacra, and the substitution of the convent for the marriage bed is frequent in Counter-Reformation religious dramas that do not end in death, such as Giovanmaria Cappelletti's *Clesebia overo scorta alla religione, comedia spirituale* (Siena, 1616), Benvenuto Flori's *Teofilo, comedia spirituale* (Siena, 1625), and Ambrogio Leoni's *Taide convertita, rappresentatione spirituale* (Venice, 1599). Massinger here also lays great emphasis on fidelity to vows, in tacit agreement with the Catholic position on that hotly debated subject.[68]

Even Massinger's *Roman Actor* and *City Madam*, alien though both are to sacred tragedy, faintly echo Counter-Reformation themes. The former includes the character Paris, a figure reminiscent of Joseph and courted by his patron's wife, the smiling response to torture of heroic Junius Rusticus and Palphurnius Sura, and the evil counselor, given a name that was anathema to Counter-Reformation Italy—Aretinus. In the city comedy, Sir John Frugal pretends to enter a monastery at Louvain, and his wife and daughters are threatened with death as Christian sacrifices to an Indian devil cult in Virginia,[69] a topical motif to those who followed the activity of Jesuit missionaries in the New World.

But in *The Virgin Martyr* it is not the occasional reference or odd incident that betrays Counter-Reformation influence but the essence of the play. Of the kinds of tragedie sacre about virgin martyrs, Dekker's and Massinger's is closest to the type represented by Morone's works, in which are found free use of supernatural and allegorical characters and a well-developed love plot. The relative neglect of the unities of time and place and a freer use of comic elements in *The Virgin Martyr* are the results of its being in the tradition of English tragedy. A basic plank in the Counter-Reformation platform on drama was the importance of making whatever adaptations to local theatrical custom were necessary to attract the public.

The most recent scholarly opinions on the date of *The Virgin Martyr* support the theory of its Counter-Reformation origin and are supported by it. Jones-Davies agrees explicitly with half and tacitly with all of Bentley's idea that the "reforming" of 1620 was revision required by the

68. Noting Massinger's reputation for "earnest religious conviction," Bryne suggests that he contributed the religious element to Fletcher's *Knight of Malta* and *Lover's Progress,* specifically the emphasis on vows and joining religious orders (Massinger, *The Maid of Honour,* ed. Bryne, Introduction, xvii–xviii).

69. Massinger, *The Plays,* ed. W. Gifford, vol. 4, III.2 and V.1.

censors of a new play, not the recasting of an old one.[70] The censored material may have been religious or political in nature or both, the distinction being at the time not always easy to make. Quite possibly the revisions were aimed at rendering *The Virgin Martyr* "rather patristic than popish," as it seemed later to Hartley Coleridge.[71] Perhaps on first reading, the censor thought it the other way round. Even after revision, the very subject of the play would have smacked of popish idolatry to many of Dekker's and Massinger's contemporaries.

English censors were always on the watch for Catholic propaganda, and their allowing *The Virgin Martyr* to be licensed at all suggests either that they were unaware or unmindful of the Catholicism of the genre itself, or, as seems more likely, that censorship was less strict than usual at this time. I. J. Semper documents a lull in the persecution of Catholics in England between 1618 and 1625, because of the Spanish marriage proposed for Prince Charles. Even imprisoned Catholic priests were permitted to walk abroad during the day, and some of them used their freedom to go to the theater.[72] Without straining probability, one may imagine such priests attending the performances of *The Virgin Martyr* by the Servants of His Majesty's Revels, and with pleasure recognizing the tragedy as an English cousin to the familiar *tragedia sacra* of Rome.

Perhaps they and some others in the audience also recognized mildly allegorical possibilities in the plot. No outspoken popish propaganda would have escaped the censor's eye, but the unstated kind lurking in similiarities between dramatic situation and actuality had a chance of reaching the stage. Albright singles out Massinger as being "thoroughly aware of the value of drama as a means of forcing home a lesson by parallels which the conscience of the playgoer may make him see for himself," and points to Paris's speech in defense of actors (*Roman Actor*, I.3), which is really a defense of playwrights, as an open statement of this principle of instruction.[73] Massinger must therefore have realized that in England the central conflict of *The Virgin Martyr* would be apt for broad allegorical interpretation, as it could not be in Italy,

---

70. Jones-Davies, *Un peintre de la vie londonienne*, 2:391.

71. *The Dramatic Works of Massinger and Ford*, ed. H. Coleridge (London, 1839), Introduction, xxvii.

72. I. J. Semper, "The Jacobean Theater through the Eyes of Catholic Clerics," *Shakespeare Quarterly* 3 (1952): 46.

73. E. M. Albright, *Dramatic Publication in England 1580–1960: A Study of Conditions Affecting Content and Form of Drama* (New York, 1927), 45.

even though the virgin martyr type of tragedia sacra was there a favorite. Only in a Protestant country could the representation of struggle between a saint and the state religion suggest to a Roman Catholic mind the actual conflict of religious right and wrong; the Catholic in England was in the position of Dorothea in Roman Caesaria. The much-admired British slave, who refuses to rape Dorothea, saying

> is this your manly seruice,
> A Divell scorns to doo't, 'tis for a beast,
> A villaine, not a man.
>
> (IV.1)

might have been interpreted by Catholic sympathizers as a flattering or hopeful symbol of the average Englishman's opposition to persecution. Theophilus in his Roman fanatic phase, approvingly reading his agent's reports of Christians tortured for their faith in Britain (V.1), would have shadowed forth the excesses of anti-Catholic authority, and his conversion implied the change for which English Catholics never ceased to pray. The inconclusive issue of the dramatic conflict matched the unsatisfactory historical status quo; Dioclesian's determination to continue fighting Christianity must have seemed a reflection of official British policy toward Roman Catholicism.

Even for those spectators who drew no parallels between the play and contemporary affairs, *The Virgin Martyr* fulfilled the broadest aim of Counter-Reformation drama: to replace secular themes with sacred, specifically Catholic ones. And for the London playgoers who kept abreast of Continental fashions, the general and particular subjects, the use of them in tragic form, the mingling of romance with religion and of the supernatural with the historical, would have left no doubt that *The Virgin Martyr* was an imported tragedia sacra.

Carlo de' Dottori, *Aristodemo, tragedia* (Padua, 1657), frontispiece.
Courtesy of the Biblioteca Marciana, Venice.

CHAPTER NINE

Fate Is for Gentiles:
The Disclaimer in Baroque Tragedy

P art of the signifying apparatus of Della Porta's tragedy *Ulisse* of 1614 is a brief text perfectly representative of its miniature and marginal genre. It is labeled "Avvertimento a' lettori" and accordingly warns the readers: "La presente tragedia è rappresentata da persone gentili; e perciò se vi si trovano dentro queste parole: fato, destino, sorte, fortuna, forza e necessità di stelle, dèi ed altre simili, è stato fatto per conformarsi con gli antichi loro costumi et riti. Ma queste, conforme alla religione cattolica, sono tutte vanità, perché si ha da attribuire a Dio benedetto causa suprema ed universale, ogni effetto ed evenimento" (The present tragedy is enacted by Gentiles; and therefore if in it are to be found these terms—fate, destiny, chance, fortune, the power and coercion of the stars, gods and the like—they have been used to conform to their ancient customs and rites. But according to the Catholic religion, these words are but emptiness, for all consequences and all events are to be attributed to Blessed God, the supreme and universal cause).[1]

The function of formulaic disclaimers concerning "Gentili" (in some versions "Idolatri") ignorant of God's word is so much disregarded today that they are more often than not omitted from modern editions of Seicento plays or casually mistranslated.[2] Introduced in the late sixteenth century, the statement disclaiming belief in the gods, fate, and other concepts of predestination became a fairly standard accessory of tragedies about pagans. This category of drama was on the decline in the seventeenth century, but while memory remained of humanistic rivalry with the ancients it still inspired the most serious Italian attempts at high art in the theater. The argument that continued to be held the

---

1. Giambattista Della Porta, *Teatro,* ed. Raffaele Sirri, vol. 1, *Le tragedie* (Naples, 1978), 315.

2. Even so painstaking an Italianist as Marvin T. Herrick, when dealing with Della Porta's disclaimer, rendered "persone gentili" as "noble characters." *Italian Tragedy in the Renaissance* (Urbana, Ill., 1965), 290.

noblest for the genre was the tragic failure and irony of the human struggle against fate.

In relation to the text that it accompanies, a disclaimer may identify itself as a mere legal necessity, a requirement satisfied perfunctorily to obtain the imprimatur, like the "exorcising clue" appended half in jest by Francesco Andreini to his *Bravure,* forestalling objections by the Reverend Fathers of the Inquisition to his superabundantly mythical vocabulary.[3] The common purpose of disclaimers in general is to establish the author's orthodoxy, not his faith so much as the right reason or "erected wit" demonstrated in his ability to distinguish truth from falsehood, history from fiction. "Non conviene *Sacra profanis miscere*" (it is inappropriate to mix the sacred with the profane), G. B. Andreini tells the "benigno Lettore" of *Adamo,* his biblical rappresentazione, in which he carefully explains that a reference to the rainbow, called *iris* by the Church Fathers, must not be taken to mean "quella Iride favolosa" of pagan myth.[4] Whether the disclaimer informs the reader that "god" in a given play means "Jove," or that references to Jove or other gods do not question the status of the Christian Prime Mover as the only true ruler of the heavens, or that characters who speak of predestination are "Gentiles," the primary concern is invariably that truth and fiction not be confounded. A disclaimer presented as an afterthought, functioning

3. "E perché più facilmente potesse esser amessa questa mia fatica dalli Molti Reverendi Padri Inquisitori, sono andato scrivendo poeticamente, valendomi di quello che giornalmente si vede alle stampe, e con poetici scherzi, trattando di quelle Deità false e bugiarde de gli andati tempi, solo per dimostrare che sì come falsi e bugiardi erano tutti quei Numi, così falso bugiardo è tutto quello che di loro si ragiona e scrive." Quoted in Flaminia Scala, *Il teatro delle favole rappresentative,* ed. Ferruccio Marotti (Milan, 1976), vol. 1, app. 6, cviii. Lodovico Zorzi speaks of the "didascalie esorcizzanti" of the professional *comici* as camouflage from the censors' observation "La raccolta degli scenari italiani della commedia dell'arte." *Alle origini del teatro moderno,* ed. Luciano Mariti (Rome, 1980), 123.

4. Giovanni Battista Andreini, *L'Adamo, sacra rapresentatione* (Milan, 1613), second preface. As the play was written at the desire of Marie de' Medici and dedicated to her, the reference to the rainbow, established as a symbol of the alliance of Catholic powers achieved by her French marriage, was a compliment to the queen. Images of classical deities were used routinely in art to illustrate the idea (see Epilogue, n. 21); Andreini's disclaimer, like most others, does not reject pagan means of expression but differentiates between fictional image and true idea.

strictly post hoc, can be palinodic, rescinding the entire order announced by the work to which it is attached; a tragedy of fate will inevitably be cut adrift from its ostensible context by a codicil denying the very idea of fate. Or, if the dynamics and lexicon of the drama itself carry the seeds of self-contradictions, a disclaimer may function like the parodic formula in *A Midsummer Night's Dream* (II.2.26–41) by which Snout and Bottom propose to assure timorous ladies that the lion of their tragedy is in reality only Snug the joiner. More constructive than any of these possibilities is the relationship between preface and play obtaining in *Aristodemo,* the remarkable tragedy by the Paduan count Carlo de' Dottori.

Belonging to an external register and dispatched from a sender who is situated unequivocally beyond the limits of fiction, and who is therefore in a "real" space outside the drama and even outside prologues in the detached "Terentian" style often used by playwrights as vehicles for theorizing or critical apologies, disclaimers state that the cluster of forces central to the dramatic conflict does not exist except as a superstition held by the historically or geographically underprivileged, the invincibly ignorant races born too soon or too far away to know revealed truth. To the Seicento theater teeming with styles, means, and expectations, in simultaneously creative and frustrating tension with the classical tradition, and sensitive to contemporary philosophical issues, the formula offered an additional signifier, another of those speaking structures abounding in baroque art generously described (that is, an art that attempts universal, amalgamating monuments, poised and solid but asymmetrically tumescent from divergent inner pressures). The disclaimer had received its conventional shape, typified by Della Porta's "Avvertimento," in the decades before 1657, when Dottori published one in the first edition of his extraordinary work.

This masterpiece of the baroque, as Giovanni Getto called it years ago,[5] confirmed for contemporary readers by Antonio Daniele as the finest tragedy of Italian baroque theater,[6] was rediscovered in 1948 by Benedetto Croce, who praised it for not really being baroque. This view

5. Giovanni Getto, "L'*Aristodemo* capolavoro del barocco" *Nuova Antologia,* no. 1575 (1959): 455–72.

6. "Forse la più bella tragedia del teatro barocco." Antonio Daniele, "Note sull'*Aristodemo* di Carlo de' Dottori," *Cultura Neolatina: Istituto di Filologia Romanza dell'Università di Roma* 40 (1980): 373; repr. in Daniele's *Carlo De' Dottori. Lingua, cultura e aneddoti* (Padua, 1986).

is more or less shared by Claudio Varese when he characterizes Dottori as one who was of his time but far from baroque,[7] and by Franco Croce's searching study distinguishing in *Aristodemo* a firmness ("saldezza") unknown to writers who were more truly baroque.[8] These judgments are in turn modern versions of those expressed by eighteenth-century admirers, in whom there stirred nonetheless a tempering regret that Dottori too often used the florid style of his own century. Clearly, controversy here is less about *Aristodemo* than about the literary baroque, and anyone who has stepped into the thicket of critical debate on defining the term knows where the thorns are. Questions of terminology aside, the stuff of this tragedy and the tensions it lives by draw a great range of serious attention and have elicted Drost's discussion of Christian Stoicism in Seicento sensibility,[9] as well as Bella's almost existentialist reading[10] or Senardi's perception of an internal dialectic expressing the crisis of the aristocratic conscience.[11]

Aristodemo is generally acknowledged to be unique, "Un risultato a sé . . . una delle rare soluzioni interamente positive di quell'ansia barocca di grande e di fiorito altrove così costantemente deludente" (A result standing alone . . . one of the rare entirely positive solutions to that striving for grandeur and ornament so constantly disappointed elsewhere in baroque literature).[12] It is generally agreed to be superior to all Seicento tragedies except Federigo Della Valle's, and like Della Valle's it is considered different in kind from the other theatrical productions of the century—not only from pageants, music drama, romantic intrigue comedies, pastoral tragicomedy, and commedia dell'arte spectaculars, but also from the plays on subjects historical, novelistic, hagiographical, and allegorical that went by the name of tragedy.

7. Claudio Varese, "Il teatro del Seicento," repr. from *Storia della letteratura italiana,* ed. Emilio Cecchi and Natalino Sapegno, vol. 5 (Milan, 1967), 72.

8. Franco Croce, "L'*Aristodemo* e il barocco," *La critica stilistica e il barocco letterario: Atti del secondo congresso internazionale di studi italiani* (Florence, n.d. [1958]), 199.

9. Wolfgang Drost, "Carlo de' Dottoris Tragödie *Aristodemo,*" *Romanische Forschungen* 76 (1964).

10. Carla Bella, "'Le Dieu caché': L'*Aristodemo* di Carlo de' Dottori," *Paragone,* no. 340 (1978): 23–53.

11. Fulvio Senardi, "*Aristodemo* di Carlo de' Dottori: L'aristocrazia secentesca nello specchio del classicismo," *Tre studi sul teatro tragico italiano tra manierismo ed età dell'Arcadia* (Rome, 1982), 47; Senardi prefaces his interpretation with a valuable account of current scholarship.

12. Franco Croce, "L'*Aristodemo* e il barocco," 199.

Although the text had been neglected for a long time before Benedetto Croce's edition introduced it into modern anthologies, *Aristodemo* was no undiscovered masterpiece. Its fame began at home in
Padua with a first performance in 1654, and spread during the three
years in which Dottori revised it for publication, during which he corre-
sponded with Prince Leopoldo de' Medici and the Florentine literary establishment, aiming at the audiences of Cardinal Spada's Roman circle
and the Viennese imperial court of Eleonora Gonzaga, and buffing away
traces of supposed provincialism. At the time Padua was, in fact, a sophisticated theatrical center as well as an academic debating ground,
and not an unlikely place to form an intention to provide Italian literature with the noble tragedy that Dottori thought it lacked. From Paduan
presses issued the early editions, four of them by 1680, the year of the
author's death.[13]

A letter to Dottori's friend and Tuscan arbiter Ciro di Pers identifies
the sources: "Ho imitato Euripide nell'*Ifigenia*, Sofocle in qualche coro
e calcato per tutto Seneca, da me più inteso e goduto per la somiglianza
della lingua" (I have imitated Euripides' *Iphigenia*, Sophocles in some
choruses and throughout I have walked in the steps of Seneca, with
whom I feel most kinship and pleasure, owing to a similarity of style).[14]
In his preface to the "Courteous and Wise Reader," Dottori lists the
passages from Pausanias that constitute his argument, claiming both
historicism and freedom from it: "Io non hò osservata la Cronologia;
ma di questo non mi scuso punto, perche non m'hò preso a scriver' Istoria. Il Caso è fondato però tutto sù'l vero, come puossi veder da luoghi
ininterrotamente citati" (I have not kept the chronological order, for
which I make no excuse because I did not set out to write history. The
events are based on truth, however, as may be seen from passages quoted
in their entirety).[15]

When poets tell their sources they rarely tell all. Dottori's were far
more extensive than he reveals; his disposition of them (in which, for
him as for Tasso and other predecessors in the late Renaissance theatrical tradition, lay the originality and art of the enterprise) was as imagi-
native and scrupulously pondered as his language, which has received

13. For the evolution and history of the text see Antonio Daniele, "Note
sull'*Aristodemo*"; and Annalisa Marin, "Sul testo dell'*Aristodemo* di Carlo
Dottori," *Annali della Facoltà di Lettere e Filosofia dell'Università di Padova* 2
(1977): 187–232, repr. Florence, 1978.

14. Quoted in Franco Croce, "L'*Aristodemo* e il barocco," 179.

15. Carlo de' Dottori, *Aristodemo, tragedia* (Padua, 1657), 4v.

more attention.[16] What Dottori took from Euripides' *Iphigenia in Aulis* was an element of the plot: the sacrifice of a royal virgin required by the gods from a father whose ambition for power inclines him to obey, a classic situation of which variants were available in more than one of the favorite sources of Renaissance drama, and which held a rich potential for development as tragedy of *ragion di stato*.[17] Dottori's debt to Sophocles exceeded the declared borrowings from some choruses of *Oedipus rex*, and comprises in addition to other details of tragic data the central mechanism of a self-defeating challenge to fate. Aristodemo, princely aspirant to the throne of Messenia, is father to one of the two maidens eligible as a sacrifice that will placate the gods for an ancient outrage and thus save Messenia from the destruction threatened by Sparta. By lot the choice falls on the other virgin, but after her father, Licisco, first denies his paternity and then flees with her to Sparta when he is not believed, Aristodemo does not stay to know more of heaven's will, but sends archers in pursuit of them, and against his wife's protests urges the sacrifice of his own daughter, Merope. Her betrothed, Policare, tells Aristodemo with desperate mendacity that she is pregnant and therefore not fit to sacrifice, but the ruse misfires, the father vengefully slays his child, and in a last spasm of frustrated ambition he vainly tries to pass off the killing as ritual sacrifice. Finally he discovers that the maiden chosen by lot was his daughter also. She too is dead as a consequence of his action and Messenia is doomed. Before falling on his sword, Aristodemo recognizes the futility of opposing fate and learns a variation of the ironic oedipal lesson that things are never so bad that human beings cannot make them worse: thinking to outwit the powers above, he has merely seconded the unseen design and exacerbated its malignancy. The ironic pattern of self-thwarting by fighting against the apparent decrees of destiny is traced in subdued repetition by the experience of Licisco, the foster father who reveals the paternity of the chosen maiden and

16. See especially Marco Ariani, "Note sullo stile tragico dell'*Aristodemo* di Carlo de' Dottori," *Studi Secenteschi* 13 (1972): 163–79; Franco Croce, *Carlo de' Dottori* (Florence, 1957), 257ff; Croce, "L'*Aristodemo* e il barocco"; Antonio Daniele, *Carlo De' Dottori: Lingua, cultura e aneddoti.*

17. The conflict between the "reason of state" and private morality, central to a major body of late Cinquecento and Seicento tragedy, could be made to arise from many situations, but the royal father's dilemma was much favored as a point of departure. For the example of Della Porta's *Georgio, tragedia* see L. G. Clubb, "Ideologia e politica nel teatro dellaportiano," *Lettere Italiane* 39, no. 3 (1987): 329–45.

grieves that her death, like Merope's, has been useless, whereas either of the sacrifices, had it been carried out in a propitiatory spirit as the gods commanded, might have redeemed the nation.

At face value this is a pagan plot, a tragedy of fate for Gentiles. But of course the face value in baroque tragedy is only the first unit of a polyvalency. The play can be read as a study in Stoicism, on the Senecan model, with the types of innocent victim and overreaching tyrant represented in Merope and Aristodemo in a complementary relationship: Senardi takes this view and in the complex thematics of *Aristodemo* gives precedence to the idea of the inevitability of Fate. Although he sees an analogy between the Paduan tragedy and what Ezio Raimondi shows of a syncretic poetics held by poles of Stoic and Catholic principles in Seicento Roman Classicism, Senardi finds Dottori's characters ignorant of the value of resignation and unable to move beyond Stoic fatalism, alternating between attitudes of obedience and opposition to heaven.[18] The dynamics of the tragedy permit this interpretation, which leaves the conflict of ideas in unresolved tension and the concluding image as one of crisis. Some of the essence of *Aristodemo* eludes such a reading, however; the concluding mood is not ambivalent but charged with tragic certainty and acquiescence—in what? Neither bewilderment nor absurdity closes the desolated scene, but rather a sense, not of hope or redemption, but of rightness that in 1654 could not have issued from Stoicism alone. On the other hand, Senardi properly rejects both a devotional reading of *Aristodemo* as a tragedia sacra and Getto's more persuasive interpretation of the contrast between Merope and Aristodemo as a demonstration of the superiority of Christian ethics to Stoic.

Christian significance does hover about the drama, however, most immediately in the vicinity of the daughter in whom Aristodemo's highmindedness reappears as a will to self-immolation. Merope, resolute for death but in love with Policare and assailed by the force of his anguish, is a figure who has often distracted critics and encouraged them to read the play as her tragedy. The baroque aura of Christian resignation and sublimity about her does suggest the religious heroines of Della Valle and the virgin martyrs of the tragedia sacra. Dottori's allusion to this important contemporary subgenre surfaces in his treatment of Merope as an innocent although not passive sacrificial victim, who altruistically and with a sense of mission accepts the sentence of death; the genre of sacred tragedy is invoked also in specific relationships between inter-

18. Fulvio Senardi, "*Aristodemo* di Carlo de' Dottori," 46–47, 55–59.

locutors—Merope's last scene with the priest of Apollo (IV.3) is a collo-
quy between Christian martyr and father confessor—and in the growing perception of inner light that in this tragedy she alone experiences.

A stronger generic undercurrent is that of the pastoral drama. Although Merope resembles a virgin martyr of tragedia sacra, she and Policare belong also to the love stories of tragicommedia pastorale, the
genre rooted partly in commedia grave. The century and a half separating *Aristodemo* from the early models of Italian comedy do not obscure
the comic pattern plot of love opposed by parental interests. As Bella
has observed, the nurse's proposal of a sexual deceit to save Merope's
life is a suggestion appropriate to comedy, made in ignorance of the
tragic world she inhabits.[19] We recognize the familiar theatergram of the
balia when the nurse, repeating an old saw that had been essential to
commedia since the time of Bibbiena and Machiavelli, urges Policare to
action on the principle that fortune favors the bold (III.5). He takes up
the idea and develops it like a comic innamorato determined to act, then
goes on to assume the posture of a pastor *fido* of tragicommedia, consecrated to the service of love and praying to Venus:

> Bella dea, che mi reggi,
> santo amor, che mi guidi, ah sostenete
> il principio felice
> di sì gran mole. Oh ben gittate basi!
> Oh fondamenti validi e robusti
> d'una lodevol macchina d'inganno!
>
> . . . .
>
> La pia congiura
> guidi e protegga Amor
>   (IV.1.183–88, 194–95)

Beautiful goddess who rules me, holy love who guides me, ah aid
and further the happy beginning of so great a construction. Oh
solid grounds, justifying foundation of a pure and laudable plan to
deceive . . . may Love guide and protect our pious conspiracy.[20]

The deceit, which in the outcome procures rather than averts the catastrophe, boomerangs with the technical precision that had been trans-

19. Carla Bella, "'Le Dieu caché,'" 43.
20. This and succeeding quotations are from the edition of *Aristodemo* in
Luigi Fassò, ed., *Teatro del Seicento* (Milan, 1956; repr. Turin, 1976).

mitted by comic to pastoral dramatists. Following a structural design perfected by long experimentation, the irony of Policare's moment toward a result contrary to the one he aims at reiterates the principal action with which it is fused—that is, the action of Aristodemo, as he seeks to force heaven, giving the name of ritual sacrifice to murder. Similarly, Policare hopes that his lie will be redeemed by its happy result, "Cangerà nome / la colpa, e fatta industriosa frode / meriterà poi lode" (IV.2.198–200: The crime will change its name and, called a productive deception, will deserve praise), but his action too has been set on an unswervingly tragic course.

Features of the pastoral tragicomedy are visible in other aspects of *Aristodemo* as well, not least in the lyric, Petrarchan tone that scholarship has sometimes overemphasized, but more significantly in Dottori's recourse to the topos of the Golden Age, shimmering with connotations of an Arcadian paradise lost. Although the legendary Greek setting, by definition pastoral (like the fateful descendence of Messenia's royalty from Hercules on one side and from a princess of Arcadia on the other), is simply one of the trappings inherited from Pausanias, the thematics of Arcadia are a powerful steering force. The connection that Varese makes between the re-creation of a natural age in Tasso's *Aminta* and in Dottori's second and fourth choral odes is more than the individual debt he implies of Dottori to Tasso; it is evidence of new syntheses in dramatic form.

Although Tasso's famous "Age of Gold" chorus functions as an appeal to nature for freedom in love, the Tassoesque second ode in *Aristodemo* has a more sinister and Senecan philosophical context. Addressing Natura as the supreme force of the universe, "O sapienza eterna de Natura, / che dài legge alle stelle e che l'immensa / mole del ciel con certo moto aggiri" (II.7.407–09: Oh eternal wisdom of Nature, who decrees law to the stars and turns the vast firmament of heaven with sure motion), the chorus queries the right of Fortuna to disturb human life and describes the happy primitive time before her sway:

> Non fu così turbato
> certo l'umano stato
> quando era inerme e giovanetto il mondo,
> e dal regno non anco
> discacciato Saturno"
>
> (435–49)

. . . .

O felici quei primi uomini rozzi
a cui davano gli antri albergo e l'ombre,
facil bevanda il rio, cibi non compri
il pino, il sorbo, e lieta mensa il prato!
Il ciel non risplenda
d'immagini temute, il mar tacea,
stava chiuso l'inferno, e l'uomo in pace.
Nacquer odii e timori,
ambiziosi amori
quindi, e nacque Fortuna.

(435−49, 473−81)

Surely the human state was not thus disturbed when the world was young and harmless and when Saturn had not yet been driven from his reign . . . Oh happy those first rustic men to whom caves gave shelter and shade, the stream gave easy drink, the pine and berry food unbought, and the meadow gave happy board! The heavens did not shine with fearful sights, the sea was still, hellway was closed, and man in peace. Thereafter hates and fears and grasping loves were born, thereafter was born Fortune.

The fourth ode, following Aristodemo's decision to kill Merope, is a pendant to the second, continuing the topos in still darker tones still echoing Ovid's account of universal deterioration, lamenting the degeneration to the Age of Iron, the violation of Nature, and the perversion of her bounty into homicidal weapons:

Pèra chi prima
dalle segrete viscere de' monti
il già innocente ed or colpevol ferro,
e non senza rossor della Natura,
quel mostro palesò ch'ella copria
fra le cupe latebre della terra.
Ma vendicossi dell'umano oltraggio
Natura, e fu l'ingegno umano appunto
stromento alla vendetta,
che'l rigor dell'acciaro
domato da Vulcano
volse in usberghi, in aste,
e produsse la guerra

(IV.6.493−505)

Cursed be he who from the mountains' secret viscera, and not without Nature's blushes, first laid bare the then innocent and now guilty iron, that monster which she was wont to hide in the dark recesses of the earth. But Nature took revenge for that human outrage and the instrument of vengeance was human wit itself, which turned the power of steel harnessed by Vulcan's forge into hauberks and spears and so produced war.

The pastoral topos of lost innocence is announced, moreover, at the opening of the tragedy, in its brief moment of happy promise, by the intuitive character of Merope's mother, who functions throughout as a prophet of sorrow. Like the other evocations of the Golden Age, hers delicately avoids the obvious label, while employing the identifying terms of the return to the sinless world before the Iron Age:

> Io stessa della patria, e di noi degne
> qui sparger vo'le concepite preci.
> Rotin gli astri innocenti al mondo, e nutra
> alta pace le genti.
> Torni il ferro alla terra, onde fu tolto
>
> (I.2.186—90)

I shall send forth prayers worthy of our homeland and ourselves. May innocent benign stars turn again toward the world and may noble peace nourish the people. Let iron return to the earth from which it was taken.

The choruses in *Aristodemo* have an accumulative significance: the first prays optimistically for peace to the offended gods Castor and Pollux; the second muses ruefully on the last age of human infancy before the formation of society gave Fortune its power; the central, third chorus grieves for the approaching death of Merope but is moved by contemplation of her magnanimity and serenity to recognize the inwardness and spiritual nature of the sole happiness possible to mortals, and the enduring quality of virtue alone among human attributes; the fourth chorus has lost the sense of value inspired by Merope and despairs at the Age of Iron that has replaced the dream of the second chorus and violently rejected the prayer of the first.

In the manuscript of 1654 of the tragedy the chorus is heard again, in a medley of Senecan commonplaces as the fifth act ends:

> Così regnano i dei. Tanto lontano
> è l'uomo dalle stelle e sconosciute son da noi

quelle menti
che pensier temerario
d'interpretar s'ingegna.
Guarda le cose nostre ordine certo.
Fortuna è nome vano.
Ma la crea l'uomo insano
se, o diffidando o incerto
dell'alta Provvidenza,
oppone a'saggi dei folle prudenza.
Nasce dal suo delitto la sua pena
che cieca i ciechi
a precipizio mena.

Thus the gods rule. So far is man from the stars, so unknown to us are those minds which rash thought struggles to explain. Sure and certain order watches over our lives. Fortune is an empty name. But foolish man gives it substance if, challenging or doubting high providence, he opposes mad prudence to the wise gods. From his crime comes his punishment, the blind leading the blind headlong.[21]

As Franco Croce says, this choral ode is unnecessary; Dottori cut it from his revised text, recognizing that the characters and action alone so fully illustrate the truth of these concepts and the sweeping extent of the catastrophe that a final moralistic maxim could only diminish their effect. The events and the last, desolate words of Tisi, one of the few survivors, himself soon to be annihilated by the now inevitable victory of Sparta, are enough:

Ah, spettacolo indegno! In questa guisa
regni, infelice! In questo modo porgi
salute alla Messenia! O sfortunato,
o furioso Aristodemo! O quanto
sangue per una colpa ha sparso Itome!
Gran Dio, la cui sol man dà moto al tuono,
se siamo in odio al Ciel, s'agli occhi tuoi
spiace Messenia, e'l nome nostro abborri,
stendi le mura al pian d'Itome, abbatti
i tetti nostri, e giaccia
nel cener della patria

21. Quoted in Franco Croce, *Carlo de' Dottori* (Florence, 1957), 243–44.

il miserabil popolo sepolto;
O pur, se indegno è della man di Giove
folgore che punir debba i Messenii,
e pena più volgar riserba il Fato,
l'emula Sparta in questo giorno espugni
gli odiati rivali; alla ruina
l'invidia aggiunta. Più crudel ministro
dell'ira tua non troverai, che aggravi
con le vittorie sue le nostra pena
(V.8.670–89)

Ah miserable spectacle. Thus do you reign, oh luckless man! Thus do you heal Messenia! Oh unfortunate, oh mad Aristodemo! Oh how much blood has our city shed for one crime. Great God, whose hand alone moves the thunder, if we are hateful in Heaven's sight, if Messenia is displeasing to your eyes and our name abhorrent, raze to the plain Itome's walls, cast down our roofs and let our devastated people lie buried in the ashes of their homeland; or if unworthy that a bolt from Jove's hand punish the Messenians, if Fate reserves for them a baser stroke, let emulous Sparta now annihilate its hated rivals, joining envy to destruction. No crueler minister of your wrath will you find, whose victories make heavier our pain.[22]

The suppressed ode is the more expendable in that its statement receives supplementary expression by several means, including direct reference to a regression from the past Age of Gold and an indirect indication of possible progression toward a Christian application of the message by the instructed receiver. A late Renaissance acceptation of the topos of the Golden Age, with its generic bond to the pastoral and the hint of Eden inherent in its Arcadian ideal, encouraged this double movement of thought, without offense to either classical decorum or Catholic doctrine.[23]

By Dottori's time the pastoral play was more than a hundred years old. The capacity of the genetically engineered theatrical hybrid for

22. *Aristodemo,* ed. Fassò.

23. In these shifting suppositions Dottori employs for dramatic contrast several of the angles of vision on the topos assumed by predecessors and contemporaries. The range of Renaissance and earlier views is best surveyed by Gustavo Costa, *La leggenda dei secoli d'oro nella letteratura italiana* (Bari, 1972).

making visible the invisible, for staging visions of the heart and of the mind's eye, was by this time so securely established that its full range of significance could be invoked merely by reference. Whether called Arcadia or given a "real" name, the pastoral setting had come to be the emblem of a world of invisible truth, and the final peripety of a complex plot an emblem of the providential design governing ostensible confusion. After Guarini, countless imitations etched more deeply in the minds of playgoers and play readers the expectation of an appeal to the intellect to behold the labyrinth—a clear design viewed from the heavens, a dark maze to mortals who grope blindly within it. The pastoral play had itself become a metaphor, and its providential pattern was contiguous with the doctrine of Divine Providence and the mystery of its coexistence with human free will. The Counter-Reformation campaign against Protestant teachings on predestination had found its most congenial theatrical instrument. Tragicomedy of providence, made universal and classical by pastoral signs, offered a Catholic challenge to the tragedy of fate.

Still, the idea of an uncompromisingly tragic genre stirred the ambition of poets even in the 1650s; the belief that his native language needed a high tragedy could move Dottori to write. The critical investigation of *Aristodemo* that has forged superlative linguistic and philosophical instruments for a historical anatomy of Seicento thought and sensibility remains incomplete—if some consideration is not given to the persistence in theatrical composition of a magnetic field for the energies of classical genres and Counter-Reformed Christian "realities"; neither the interconnection of the vital systems of the play nor the tired question of its "baroqueness" can be comprehended until the tragedy is associated with the history of Italian Renaissance drama, seen as a long experiment in contaminatio of ancient forms for representing modern contents. In the wake of the *Pastor fido,* pastoral strains were regularly heard in tragedy, often announced in the descriptive, generic subtitle, as in Malmignati's *Clorindo, tragedia pastorale* (1604), Cortesi's *Orestilla, tragedia boschereccia* (1610), Bonifacio's *Nicasio, favola tragica* (1629), and Prospero Bonarelli's *Olmiro, regi-pastorale* (1655). Sometimes the effects were "baroque" in a thoroughly negative sense. But *Aristodemo,* which is as severely classical a play as it would have been possible for Italy to produce in the mid-seventeenth century, includes just as much of the pastoral drama as would suggest the universal Christian relevance with which the genre was charged.

It was to activate this charge that Dottori used the disclaimer. After discussing his classical sources in the preface, he concludes:

> Quello poi che si dice in questo Drama del Fato, degl'Iddij, delle Stelle, e di cose simili, si dice per bocca de Gentili, in secolo affatto lontano da questi, illustrati dalla misericordia di DIO Ottimo Massimo: detestando io tutte le superstizioni contrarie alla Religione Cattolica Cristiana, e valendomi di queste forme per esprimer gli affetti delle persone che parlono, e l'infelice genio dell'Etnica cecità."

> What is said in this drama about Fate . . . comes from the mouths of Gentiles, in a century far from these times enlightened by the mercy of great God on high: I detest all superstitions contrary to the Catholic Religion and I use these terms to express the feelings of the speakers and the hapless spirit of their ethnic blindness.[24]

To recognize the Catholic formula not only as the expression of a view of the universe that Dottori shared, but also as a means of transport to the outer orbit from which the metaphorical aspect of the plot can be perceived, offers a mediation among otherwise dissident critics who praise *Aristodemo* piecemeal, as well as a way of restoring the tragedy to its protagonist. Bella's interpretation of the tragic world as a closed machine for human destruction, lacking the hidden God even as a spectator, can be supported by the dramatic structure only if its nucleus is constituted in Merope, yielding to the oracular decrees of an authoritative system that she does not believe in. Readings of *Aristodemo* as a neo-Senecan tragedy of fate, or as a representation of unresolved conflict between Stoic and Christian principles, also are not interdicted by the denotative vocabulary of the text. But these readings question the trust in an unspecified supreme order communicated in overtones by continual modulations toward the forms of favola pastorale, commedia, and tragedia sacra, and negate the fervent intellectual coherence that characterizes Dottori's work from beginning to end.

The tragedy is named for Aristodemo, whose willfulness identifies him as the oedipal protagonist not only in his function as the *tyrannos* torn by inner conflict between the reason of state and personal ethics,

---

24. *Aristodemo, tragedia* (Padua, 1657), Dottori to the "Cortese, e Savio Lettore," [4v–] 5.

but also in another and still more universal function. Aristodemo is arguably a figure of absolutist power, and as such bears the political significance attached to the tragedy of Oedipus by Seicento thought, as it has been penetratingly revealed by Ossola.[25] On another plane, however, Aristodemo reiterates the ironic Sophoclean movement praised by Aristotle of the hubristic human challenge to the superhuman: to fate in a pagan world, to providence in a Christian one. And when the Christian world is Catholic, the challenger must have free will.

In the chorally punctuated passage from joy to misery in this tragedy, there is a pause for indicating a potentially Christian inward movement toward eternity, at the end of the third act when Merope's sacrifice is decided; this is the moment when Aristodemo's intentions begin to go disastrously wrong. The subsequent utterances of the chorus and Tisi mark stages of degeneration in the self-willed fall of a character increasingly deformed but always free. The Seicento intellectual and theatrical context in which the coexistence of providence and free will was dogma, mystery, and a challenge to the art of representation is missing from the text proper of the play. It is a context shared by Dottori with his spectators and his readers; the unstated opinions that arise from it are not the opinions of the chorus, but the disclaimer provides them, and with them a sign of that context, which is not ours either. Issued by the author, the disclaimer is no mere sop to the censors but a bridge between the otherwise closed machine and the reader, who is enabled by it to relate the train of events to Aristodemo at the center and to a Catholic world of spectators at the circumference. That *Aristodemo* came from a scrupulous, watchful, and intellectualizing environment and was intended for it is affirmed by everything that scholarship has established.

If the disclaimer did not function, the action could correspond to other levels of tragedy as classified by Aristotle: it would be a spectacle of great events; a representation of pathos, of the suffering of Merope and others; and a tragedy of ethos, of the moral character of Aristodemo. But Aristotle's "best" level, that of the complex plot with a reversal accompanied by a recognition, with a pattern of inexorable consequence, is present solely in the complete action of a protagonist self-destroyed by his attempt to outmaneuver destiny and bend fate to his will. This is the Oedipal pattern modernized, that is to say, Counter-Reformed, wedded to the doctrines of divine providence and free will, outlawing fate

---

25. Carlo Ossola, "'Edipo e ragion di Stato': mitologie comparate," *Lettere Italiane* 34, no. 4 (1982): 482–505.

and adding theological mystery to the already insoluble riddle of the classical sphinx. A fecund encounter of ideas to late Renaissance dramatists, its finest issue in the seventeenth century was Calderón's *La vida es sueño*.

The universally praised "saldezza" of *Aristodemo* begins with Dottori's firm concentration on a Sophoclean ideal of plot. To this he added mixed generic ingredients from a dramatic tradition that had long been "classical" while slowly assimilating modern transgression and significances, primarily the potential for Christian symbolism and the providential pattern of the pastoral tragicomedy. But the benignity of heaven thus injected into *Aristodemo* is only a hope circumvented by free will. Aristodemo's *culpa* is not *felix:* the consequences are not redirected by divine irony, the human agent is not let off from the results of trying to outwit the power above. This is a pagan tragedy made radically Christian, a tragedy of fate in which it is understood that there is no such thing as fate, really not even for the "Gentiles" who must be excused for believing in it. The Christian heirs of the Hebrews, the new "Jews" who possess as much of the truth as has been revealed, know that the power that truly rules the universe is that of Divine Providence. To know this is to know something, but not much, more. The new truth for Dottori's "times enlightened by the mercy of great God on high" is that man cannot know the whole truth; he is free to choose to act well or ill, but whichever he chooses, the outcome is already seen from above—as the disclaimer reminds the reader, discreetly preaching the paradoxical lesson of individual responsibility and quietism so often encountered in baroque literature, a freely willed receptivity that Milton a few years later called "lowly wise."

Isabella Andreini, *Rime d'Isabella Andreini Padovana, Comica Gelosa*
(Milan, 1601), frontispiece.
Courtesy of the Folger Shakespeare Library.

The Law of Writ and the Liberty:
Italian Professional Theater

The commedia dell'arte is usually supposed to be the most ephemeral as well as the most enduring product of the Italian Renaissance theater. More widely recognized by name than Machiavelli's *Mandragola*, Tasso's *Aminta*, or any other plays of famous authors, it is the first thing that comes to mind in connection with Italian drama. Everyone knows that professional troupes traveled through Europe, making household words of "pantaloon" and "zany," and that Harlequin and Punch and their fellows became staples of playmaking and universal receptacles for symbolizing. But the commedia dell'arte has long been thought also to be a theater too poor in texts ever to be known well and impossible to reconstruct, a shimmering world forever half-glimpsed of masks and scenarios, fixed roles and improvised recitations.

Although some of the best chapters on Italian theater history have been written in English, the distinction between literary drama and the commedia dell'arte, between erudition and entertainment, initially fostered by the professionals themselves and maintained by Italian criticism for historiographical purposes, has been allowed through long repetition in British and American studies to grow out of its usefulness and become most obfuscating where the linguistic distance is greatest. Even studies rich in corrective evidence sometimes repeat the misdirection through their titles, as does K. M. Lea's classic *Italian Popular Comedy*.[1] Among English readers there lurks a notion of commedia dell'arte

Part of this chapter appeared in "The State of the *arte* in the Andreini's Time," in *Studies in the Italian Renaissance: Essays in Memory of Arnolfo B. Ferruolo*, ed. G. P. Biasin, A. N. Mancini, and N. J. Perella (Naples, 1985), 263–81.

1. Kathleen M. Lea, *Italian Popular Comedy: A Study in the Commedia dell'Arte 1560–1620, with Special Reference to the English Stage*, 2 vols. (Oxford, 1934).

as a gestural and choreographing medium not only different from written drama but constitutionally antiliterary, and to judge from the average program notes, theatergoers sometimes even regard it as exclusively nonverbal and therefore quite irrecoverable.

Generations of scholars have combated the romantic fatalism of this view by recovering various kinds of documentation touching the contexts of the commedia dell'arte, but even scholarship has not been proof against the tendency to range it on one side of the cultural Great Divide in contrast to the premeditated or literary theater of humanistic origin. The uncertainty that attends any comparison of such different species of textual evidence reinforces the tendency, with the result that closely allied but different phenomena of the larger movement of Italian Renaissance theater have come to appear alien and inimical to each other.

My view of the combinatory principles and common repertory of theatergrams operating in Italy and wherever Italian fashions traveled in the Renaissance runs counter to the premise of an essential opposition between the commedia dell'arte and the literary drama. The other characteristics of Cinquecento theatrical texts to which the foregoing chapters give precedence—the simultaneous search for Aristotelian regularity and for mixed genres not in Aristotle's canon, for "perfect" Sophoclean structure that could represent invisible realities and express contemporary ideology—belonged to a theater also inhabited by the professional acting companies.

Just as the nineteenth-century reaction against neoclassicism obstructed a plain view of the sixteenth-century literary drama based on a rediscovery and emulation of classical forms and genres, the romantic view of the commedia dell'arte enshrined it as popular art and loaded it with folkloric significance while draining it of other weight, to impart a carefree, spur-of-the-moment image of lightning inspiration in dance and mime, presented as freedom and inventiveness in contrast with the slavery to authority and pedantry charged against regular drama.

With rather more justice, the declarations of Flaminio Scala and other articulate comici dell'arte extolling the acted play as greater than the written text are often read as absolute declarations of war on the literary intelligentsia, championing practice against theory; but like the contempt shown both by successful professionals and by private literary connoisseurs for the lowest kind of zannata, such displays of hostility belong to local infighting, which for all its undeniable significance was a minor division compared with the larger unity of a common theatrical culture. When Sidney contrasted the English drama of his day with that of Italy, observing that even the "ordinary players" there would not be guilty of the sprawling disunities of place and time common on the English stage, he recognized the existence of different levels within the Italian theater, but nevertheless saw a coherence in the character of the whole and a general superiority belonging in varying degrees to all its constituents.[2]

Fortunately, a powerful stream of attention is now being directed to the commedia dell'arte and an extraordinary amount of fresh information on the subject is being produced. Archival and critical scholarship, and the publication of related texts by Marotti, Taviani, Molinari, Ferrone, Tessari, Zorzi, Mariti, Mamone, and others, have built on the broad foundations laid by Adolfo Bartoli, Michele Scherillo, Alessandro D'Ancona, Benedetto Croce, Enzo Petraccone, Anton Giulio Bragaglia, Mario Apollonio, and Vito Pandolfi, as well as on the work of Constant Mic, Pierre-Louis Duchartre, Winifred Smith, Allardyce Nicoll, Kathleen Lea, and others outside Italy who in the past have contributed enduringly to the scholarly masonry.[3]

2. Philip Sidney, *The Defense of Poesie* (1583), 48, quoted in *Literary Criticism: Plato to Dryden,* ed. A. H. Gilbert (New York, 1940), 450.

3. Of especial importance are Ferruccio Marotti's editions of Leone De' Sommi, *Quattro dialoghi in materia di rappresentazioni sceniche* (Milan, 1968), and of Flaminio Scala, *Il teatro della favole rappresentative,* 2 vols. (Milan, 1976); Ferdinando Taviani's of Nicolò Barbieri, *La supplica, discorso famigliare . . . a quelli che trattano de' comici* (Milan, 1971); and Cesare Molinari's of Pier Maria Cecchini, *Le commedie: Un commediante e il suo mestiere* (Ferrara, 1983). Treatises, scenarios, and relevant documents in excerpt have also been published in Taviani, *La commedia dell'arte e la società barocca: La fascinazione del teatro* (Rome, 1970); Marotti, *Storia documentaria del teatro italiano: Lo spettacolo dall'Umanesimo al Manierismo: Teoria e tecnica* (Milan, 1974); Luciano Mariti, *La commedia ridicolosa: Comici di professione, dilettanti, editoria teatrale nel Seicento: Storia e testi* (Rome, 1978); Roberto Tessari, *Commedia dell'arte: La maschera e l'ombra* (Milan, 1981); texts of complete comedies are in Laura Falavolti, *Commedie dei comici dell'arte* (Turin, 1982) and Siro Ferrone, *Commedie dell'arte,* 2 vols. (Milan, 1985–86). Valuable material on particular contexts is in Ludovico Zorzi, *Il teatro e la città* (Turin, 1977), and essays by his colleagues are in *Il teatro dei Medici (Quaderni di Teatro)* 2, no. 7 (March 1980), Sara Mamone, *Il teatro nella Firenze medicea* (Milan, 1981), and Mamone, *Firenze e Parigi, due capitali dello spettacolo per una regina, Maria de' Medici* (Milan, 1987). In addition to the critical matrices of

The new abundance of materials and the historical contours they reveal have dispelled some myths. Taviani's salutary work, for instance, helps to weaken the crude notion of a recalcitrant antiliterary stance as the necessary basis for the professional players' self-assertive claims to equal dignity with academic dramatists. Emphasizing that the touring companies were for hire—hawking their versatility, ready to turn a hand to all kinds of theatrical work and to supply whatever was in demand—he shows the actors at the margin of mainstream culture, playing up to fashions originating in learned circles.[4] While they were perfecting the art of improvisation and excelling the dilettantes in all theatrical skills and techniques, the comici also collaborated in court and academic performances, and memorized plays and wrote them. Evidence of all this abounds in what they published, in what was published about them by their contemporaries, and in what modern historians have rescued from a "vast sea of lost manuscript papers."[5]

The sources include descriptions in diplomatic reports and private letters of court festivities in which plays figure. Massimo Troiano's printed account from imperial Munich in 1568 gives the first glimpse of an improvised *commedia all'italiana,* in which the composer Orlando di Lasso and other courtiers participated; professional actors are not mentioned, but their proficiency in extemporizing must already have been a model for the amateurs, and later descriptions of courtly spectacle amply confirm the collaboration of *dilettanti* with commercial troupes.

---

these works, major studies include Tessari, *La commedia dell'arte nel Seicento: "Industria" e "arte giocosa" della civiltà barocca* (Florence, 1969); Mariti, *Alle origini del teatro moderno: La commedia dell'arte* (Rome, 1980); Daniele Seragnoli, *Il teatro a Siena nel Cinquecento: "Progetto" e "modello" drammaturgico nell'Accademia degli Intronati* (Rome, 1980); Molinari, *La commedia dell'arte* (Milan, 1985); Taviani and Mirella Schino, *Il segreto della commedia dell'arte: La memoria delle compagnie italiane del XVI, XVII e XVIII secolo,* 2d ed. (Florence, 1986). Bibliographies are in Taviani and Schino, *Il segreto della commedia dell'arte;* Ferrone, *Commedie dell'arte,* vol. 1; and Thomas Heck, *The Commedia dell'Arte: A Research and Information Guide* (forthcoming). See also M. Pieri, *La nascita del teatro moderno in Italia tra XV e XVI secolo* (Turin, 1989).

4. Taviani and Schino, *Il segreto della commedia dell'arte,* 327–28, 354–55, 393–99.

5. Taviani and Schino, *Il segreto della commedia dell'arte,* 371: "Questo immenso mare di carte manoscritte scomparse, usate come segreto materiale di lavoro."

A few actors at their retirement published the dialogues, tirades, and poems they had used on stage, as Francesco Andreini did his own *Bravure,* or "ragionamenti," and his wife's *Rime* and "amorosi contrasti." Some practical and theoretical dialogues and treatises by such comici as Pier Maria Cecchini and Nicolò Barbieri began to be printed in the Seicento, but much more of such material remained in archives until our century.

The professional actors were reticent about publishing their scenarios, even in the Seicento, but at the end of the Cinquecento a number of regular plays by comici dell'arte had already gone into print.[6] In 1578 Adriano Valerini, an innamorato with a university education in the Gelosi company, published a neoclassical tragedy, *Afrodite.* Bernardino Lombardi, the "Comico Confidente" who may have been the Dottor Graziano of his troupe, published the full-text *L'alchimista, comedia* in 1583. Bartolomeo Rossi, known for playing the innamorato Orazio in the Confidenti company, gave his pastoral play *Fiammella* to the Parisian press of L'Angelier in 1584, and in the following year the same printer brought out *Angelica, comedia* by the Confidenti's popular Capitano Coccodrillo, Fabrizio Fornaris. Isabella Andreini's *Mirtilla, pastorale* was printed in 1588.

The existence of printed, full-text plays in five acts by actors better known for their professional skill in improvising suggests that Polonius's delineation of the ideal acting troupe, "the only men,"[7] would accurately describe a first-class company of comici, allowing only for one difference, the presence of actresses. These players were not mere purveyors of zannate but rather dealt in the genres most highly regarded in the academies—comedy, tragedy, pastoral, and history (in Italy more often sacred than civil)—and worked by contaminatio of theatergrams and genres to make dramas tragical-comical-historical-pastoral; they were knowledgeable about theoretical questions and could observe the unities of time and place to construct plays with "scene individable," or ignore them for the "poem unlimited"; they consulted classical models as needed, light Plautus for comedy and heavy Seneca for tragedy; they

---

6. Ferrone surveys the writings of the comici in *Commedie dell'arte,* 1: 45–53. The late Ludovico Zorzi's plan to publish the results of his équipe's research gives an idea of the dimensions of the submerged mass; see "La raccolta degli scenari italiani della commedia dell'arte," in *Alle origini del teatro moderno,* ed. Mariti, 104–15.

7. See p. vi for the passage from *Hamlet.*

could equally well perform a text word-for-word, according to "the law of writ," or improvise freely, using "the liberty."

One illustration of the versatility of the comici's modes of production is Fornaris's procedure with *Angelica,* which he adapted from Della Porta's regular comedy *Olimpia* for three-act improvisation by his troupe in Paris and then reexpanded into a five-act text for publication; another is Flaminio Scala's publishing *Il finto marito* (1619), like *Angelica* a five-act regular comedy with a fixed, polished text, a script to be performed as printed.[8] This demonstrates how a professional man of the theater moved as occasion demanded between literary and extempore presentations of the same material, for a three-act scenario of this plot, *Il marito,* had already appeared in 1611 in Scala's famous *Il teatro delle favole rappresentative,* the first collection of commedia dell'arte scenarios ever published.[9] The fifty "favole rappresentative" probably do not correspond to any specific scenarios used by a real troupe of players; more likely, they are ideal re-creations of typical plots as they would have been developed by the most famous actors of Scala's memory, including his friends Isabella and Francesco Andreini, had they all been brought together in one company. The scenarios contain descriptions and reductive summaries of each character's actions and words in every scene, and thus constitute something more detailed than the succinct *canovacci* used in performance, but much more schematic than a full-text script. A testimonial to the commedia dell'arte, Scala's *Teatro* was of practical value to organizers of amateur theatricals also interested in improvising.

Forty of the "favole" are labeled "comedia," combining, recombining, and varying the theatergrams familiar to the early Cinquecento

8. Carmine Jannaco analyzes the two prologues to *Il finto marito,* and gives a valuable account of Scala's method of defending improvisation and professional experience by displaying his ability to write regular comedy and theorize about it, in "Stesura e tendenze letterarie della commedia improvvisa in Due Prologhi di Flaminio Scala," *Studi Secenteschi* 1 (1961): 195–207. The comedy is reprinted in Falavolti's anthology *Commedie dei comici dell'Arte.*

9. The full title of the original on which Marotti's edition is based is *Il teatro delle favole rappresentative, overo La ricreatione comica, boscareccia, e tragica: Divisa in cinquanta giornate; composte da Flaminio Scala detto Flavio Comico del Sereniss. Sig. Duca di Mantova* (Venice, 1611). It was translated by Henry F. Salerno, with an appendix on English analogues, as *Scenarios of the Commedia dell'Arte: Flaminio Scala's Il teatro della favole rappresentative* (New York and London, 1967).

adapters of Plautus and Terence and to the audiences and readers of a century and more of commedia erudita, as even the titles tell: *Li duo vecchi gemelli* (giornata 1), *Le burle d'Isabella* (giornata 4), *Il vecchio geloso* (giornata 6), *La creduta morta* (giornata 7), *La finta pazza* (giornata 8), *Il pellegrino fido amante* (giornata 14), *La travagliata Isabella* (giornata 15), *Li duo capitani simili* (giornata 17), *Il finto negromante* (giornata 21), *Il creduto morto* (giornata 22), *Flavio finto negromante* (giornata 28), *Isabella astrologa* (giornata 36). Some correspond closely to the plots of well-known written comedies, thus starting up numerous scents for source hunters; the nearly tragic "comedia" *Li tragici successi* has been repeatedly compared with *Romeo and Juliet* and Borghini's *La donna costante*.[10]

Scala's last ten scenarios, from *La forsennata prencipessa, tragedia* (giornata 41), with some reminiscent theatergrams of *Hamlet*, to *La fortuna di Foresta prencipessa di Moscovia, opera regia* (giornata 50), resembling *The Winter's Tale* in minor details, constitute a small compendium of fashionable generic mixtures. *L'arbore incantato, pastorale* (giornata 49) includes all the elements of the Ovidian magic pastoral in the same combinations that may be observed in Pasqualigo's *Intricati*, Rossi's *Fiammella*, Castelletti's *Amarilli*, Neri's Arcadian scenarios, *A Midsummer Night's Dream*, and *The Tempest:* lovers and clowns; a sorcerer with book, staff, grotto, and familiar spirits; hallucinations, transformations, and spectacular apparitions; and elixirs of oblivion, with the enchantments, the madness, and the lovers' despair all shepherded toward pardons and weddings by providential supernatural power. Giornate 46, 47, and 48 constitute the three-part *Orseida, opera reale*, in which a divine oracle is fulfilled over a period of years by a bear's fathering on the daughter of Pan's high priest the hero Ulfone, destined to wed the princess Alvida and rule Arcadia, Algeria, and Denmark. To readers of *The Winter's Tale, Il re Torrismondo, Cymbeline*, or *Filli di Sciro* the dramatic texture is not unfamiliar.[11] In *Gli avveni-*

10. Marotti retails some old debates over precedence in his edition of Scala, *Il teatro delle favole rappresentative*, vol. 1, Introduction, xxvii–xxx.

11. Tasso's highly crafted and theorized contaminatio of dramatic and literary pre-texts was soon dismantled for retail use in improvised comedy too. As Marzia Pieri observes, "Anche una materia scenicamente inerte e usuratissima può essere riproposta con efficacia in varianti combinatorie nuove. Il *Torrismondo*, in effetti, rivela al proprio interno strutture molto tipiche, destinate di lì a poco a trapassare nei canovacci dell'Arte." "Interpretazione teatrale del *Torrismondo*," *La Rassegna della Letteratura Italiana* 90, no. 3 (1986): 411.

menti comici, pastorali e tragici, opera mista (giornata 42) one act is devoted to each genre, the setting moves from urban Sparta to "Arcadia Spartana" and back, and when all the kings have been killed at the end, Pantalone and Graziano discourse on "il volubil giro della Fortuna" and declare Sparta's return to a republic. It is obvious why Scala's compendium has so often been linked with Shakespeare and why Nicoll would rank its publication with that of the First Folio for importance to theater history. But although the commedia dell'arte and the firsthand acquaintance with it of his fellow actor Will Kempe may well have been Shakespeare's main source of information about the Italian theater,[12] his kinship with the comici was but one aspect of the more general kinship joining the commercial companies everywhere with the learned and courtly drama, a consanguinity of common aims and repertories of movable parts that was confirmed by a variety of texts, literary and subliterary.

Attempts to document the visible but opalescent affinity between Shakespeare and the Italian professionals have usually concentrated on the many parallels in his plots, groupings, characters, exchanges, and stage business with the scenarios, masks, and *lazzi* of the three-act, improvised commedie dell'arte as we know them from available scenarios and descriptions. On the whole Shakespeare's knowledge has been attributed to contacts developed from English tours by the comici, Kempe's visit to Italy, and travelers' accounts, as well as various sojourns of Italian musicians at Elizabeth's court. When the queen herself wanted to see an Italian comedy, she asked her resident composer Alfonso Ferrabosco to arrange it. Were we to go so far as to accept Rowse's identification of the Dark Lady of the *Sonnets* with Emilia Bassano, daughter of a later court musician, another kind of link between Shakespeare and Italian entertainers could be supposed.[13] In any case he had more than one means of acquaintance with the improvised comedy and its popular masks.

12. Louis Booker Wright, "Will Kemp and the *Commedia dell'Arte,*" *Modern Language Notes* 41 (1926): 516–20.

13. A. L. Rowse, *Shakespeare the Man* (New York, 1973). On Shakespeare and the commedia dell'arte see Winifred Smith, *The Commedia dell'Arte: A Study in Italian Popular Comedy* (New York, 1912); Allardyce Nicoll, *Masks, Mimes and Miracles: Studies in the Popular Theatre* (London, 1931) and *The World of Harlequin: A Critical Study of the Commedia dell'Arte* (Cambridge, England, 1963); K. M. Lea, *Italian Popular Comedy* and "Connections and Contrasts between the Commedia dell'arte and English Drama," *Rivista di studi teatrali* 9, no. 10 (1954): 114–26; Daniel C. Boughner, *The Braggart in Renais-*

But it is not merely the resemblance of Shylock and Brabantio to the "lean and slippered" mask of Pantalone, of Tranio and Grumio or the Dromios to a pair of zanni, of *The Tempest*'s plot to Rossi's *Fiammella* and the Arcadian scenarios published by Neri, of Don Armado to the mask of the Capitano, or of the lazzi and many references to plays performed according to "the liberty" that would have come to Shakespeare from his knowledge of the Italian professionals. What the comici had to transmit was more than the fruit of their famous improvising style. To know what they could do means to know what they met with; their repertory was the total of whatever was available in the theater, and it was this total that they offered to whoever met with them in turn.

Comparison with a contemporary Italian actor and writer can illustrate the broader basis of community. One often named in connection with Shakespeare is Isabella Andreini, born a year before him, whose success and versatility invite the comparison. Her career and those of her immediate family also bear witness against the persistent notion that the commedia dell'arte stage and the library were worlds apart, or that being popular meant being unlettered.

In 1607, three years after Isabella Andreini died at the age of forty-two, miscarrying what would have been her eighth child, her husband published a lament, calling her Fillide and himself Corinto, the names they assumed in pastoral roles:

Fillide, Anima cara e Consorte mia carissima, mentre che tu vivevi erano per me i giorni chiari e sereni, mille e mille amabili pensieri m'ingombravano la mente, la Fortuna dolce e propizia a i miei voti et il Cielo arrideva a' miei contenti. Ma ora, che tu se' rinchiusa dentro a freddo Sasso, avendo teco rinchiuse le Virtù tutte e le bell'opere, s'è talmente cangiato il mio Destino, ch'altro non mi

sance Comedy: A Study in Comparative Drama from Aristophanes to Shake-speare (Minneapolis, 1954); Henry Frank Salerno, "The Elizabethan Drama and the *Commedia dell'arte*" (diss., University of Illinois, 1956); Walter L. Barker, "Three English Pantalones: A Study in Relations between the *Commedia dell'Arte* and Elizabethan Drama" (diss., University of Connecticut, 1966); Eugene Steele, "Verbal *Lazzi* in Shakespeare's Plays," *Italica* 53, no. 2 (1976): 214–22; Ninian Mellamphy, "Pantaloons and Zanies: Shakespeare's 'Apprenticeship' to Italian Professional Comedy Troupes," in Maurice Charney, ed., *Shakespearean Comedy* (New York, 1980), 141–51.

rimane che la memoria d'averle vedute et amate. A Dio amara dipartenza, fiera messaggia di crudelissima Parca, tu non potevi venir meno del tuo tristissimo augurio, e non potevi errare, facendomi vedere l'amata mia Compagna, non dentro al letto maritale, ma sì bene dentro la funebre Bara della Morte. A Dio doni del Cielo, dal Cielo istesso a me rubbati e tolti; a Dio gravi ragionamenti, a Dio dolci et onesti diporti, a Dio Spirito nobile e peregrino, a Dio Divine grazie, voi mi serviste un tempo di vaghi et odorati fiori et ora (ahi lasso) mi servite di pungentissime spine. . . . O quanto volontieri, cara vittima, accompagnato avrei il suo dolore con le mie proprie essequie? O quanto volontieri averei le mie ossa con le sue ossa, la mia cenere con la sua cenere, rinchiuse in un medesmo tempo et in un medesmo sepolcro? Ma (lasso me) io me ne rimango dapoi di te, ributtato dal Destino, e l'anima tua seguitata da' miei desiri se ne vola al Cielo. Io qui rimango vedovo e solo, senza spirito e senza vita, facendo sacrificio de' miei sospiri infiammati, de' miei sospiri rinascenti, e delle mie strida seminate nell'Aria. Anima cara, amata mia Consorte, il coniugale Amore, che vive e sempre viverà nel mio petto mi sprona a seguitarte. Ma la pietà congiunta con l'amore de' nostri teneri Fanciulli e nostri communi Figli, mi ritiene il corso. Là onde qui me ne rimango combattuto giorno e notte da tanti dolori e da tanti tormenti, che tutte le lagrime delle umane luci non mi servirebbono, e non sarebbono a bastanza per piangere e lagrimare l'inaspettata et immatura tua morte.

. . . Ora a te mi rivolgo, o mia rustica e boscareccia Sampogna. Tu alla mia bocca e alle mie mani se' stata gran tempo piacevole essercizio, mentre me ne andava teco cantando ora il bel volto, ora il bel nome, et ora l'onesto e maritale Amore della mia vaga e graziosa Fillide. . . . Rimanti adunque per sempre appesa a questa verde et onorata Pianta, e teco rimanghino per sempre appesi, a questi verdi et onorati Tronchi, tutti gli altri miei pastorali stromenti solo invertiti a gloria e onor della mia cara Fillide.

Phyllis, my soul and dearest consort, while you lived my days were clear and serene, a thousand thousand delightful thoughts crowded my mind, sweet Fortune was propitious to my prayers and Heaven smiled on my contentment. But now that you are closed up in cold stone together with all your virtues and accomplishments, my lot is so changed that nothing remains to me but the memory of having seen and loved them. Adieu bitter parting, savage messenger of cruelest Fate, you could not fail of your most sad promise or stray from your task, showing me my beloved companion not in our marriage bed but, rather, on the funereal bier of Death. Adieu gifts of Heaven, by Heaven itself stolen away from me; Adieu grave colloquies, adieu sweet and blameless diversions, adieu rare and noble spirit, adieu divine graces; once you were to me lovely fragrant flowers and now, ah, alas, you are piercing thorns. . . . Oh, how willingly would I have shared the pain of the dear victim by my own funeral rites! How willingly enclosed my bones with hers, with hers my ashes, in a single moment and a single sepulchre! But, ah me! here I remain behind, rejected by Fate, while your soul flies to Heaven followed by my desire. I am left a widower and alone, without soul or life, offering up my burning sighs, sighs continually renewed, and my cries sowed in air. Dear soul, beloved consort, the conjugal love that lives and will forever live in my breast spurs me to follow you. But piety joined with love for our helpless little ones and children of our love, restrains me from that course. Wherefore I remain here buffeted day and night by such sufferings and such torment that not all the tears of all the eyes of mankind could aid me nor suffice to weep and lament your unforeseen and untimely death. . . . Now I address you, my rustic and sylvan pipe. You were long the delightful practice of my hands and lips, when with you I roamed singing the praises of the beautiful face, the glorious name and the chaste conjugal love of my charming Phyllis. . . . Hang, my pipe, forever on this honored verdant willow; and with you on these green trunks will evermore hang all my other shepherd's instruments, destined solely to celebrate the glory and the honor of my dear Phyllis.[14]

Through the bombast of Francesco Andreini's baroque evocation of Sannazaro's *Arcadia,* relentlessly histrionic and tumid with crocodile tears, those tuned to the history of this famous theatrical couple may hear the accents of genuine heartbreak. Like Shakespeare her contemporary, Isabella was called the wonder of her profession and her age, but

14. Francesco Andreini, *Le bravure del Capitano Spavento divise in molti ragionamenti in forma di dialogo: Di Francesco Andreini da Pistoia comico geloso* (Venice, 1607), repr. in Ferruccio Marotti, *La professione del teatro* (Rome, 1976), quoted in Marotti's edition of Scala, *Il teatro delle favole rappresentative,* vol. 1, app. 6, ci–civ.

unlike him she was called so in her own time by a vast international audience. Correspondence and printed encomia attest the regard she commanded from the Italian signories, the imperial court, French royalty, and (most gratifying to the Andreini and most telling for cultural history) the literary establishment. Tasso wrote verses on Isabella as an actress and poet, and after she took second place in a poetry contest that he won, the learned academy of the Intenti in Pavia elected her a member and crowned her effigy with laurel, proclaiming her Petrarch's heir and Tasso's rival.[15]

The grief literarily expressed by Isabella's husband in the accommodating pastoral mode familiar on public and private stages throughout Europe was felt for the rest of his life. He did hang up his pipe and never trod the boards again, but settled down in Mantua to write about her, edit her poetry and letters, and publish his own theatrical compositions with hers, wreathed always in loving celebrations of her fame. He survived her by twenty years. Their son Giovanni Battista was no less famous an actor, and a more prolific writer than either of his parents, composing a score of plays and a variety of other works. When he died in 1654 the commedia dell'arte had a long life ahead of it still (more than a century) but its brief golden age was over. The epoch in which professionals like the Andreini family were free to exercise their interpretive, improvisatory, and literary talents on a relatively open market in competition and collaboration with the dominant cultural elite had given way to the long and productive era of technical specialization in the *industria,* or trade, as described by Tessari, when the players lowered their sights to aspire modestly to a status of bourgeois respectability, in which the improvising actor would be guaranteed a dignity not different from that accorded other artisans.[16]

When the Andreini first made their mark, the phenomenon known as commedia dell'arte was established firmly, if only recently, as one kind of theatrical activity in Italy. The first documented evidence of profes-

15. For basic biographical and bibliographical information on the Andreini see Luigi Rasi, *I comici italiani: Biografia, bibliografia, iconografia,* vol. 1 (Florence, 1897); Achille Fiocco, "Andreini," *Enciclopedia dello spettacolo,* ed. Silvio D'Amico et al. (Rome, 1954); Franca Angelini, "Andreini," *Dizionario biografico degli italiani* (Rome, 1961); L. Pannella, "Canali, Isabella," *Dizionario biografico degli italiani* (Rome, 1974).

16. Roberto Tessari, *La commedia dell'arte nel Seicento: "Industria" e "arte giocosa" della civiltà barocca* (Florence, 1969), 69.

sional troupes is a contract dated 1545, binding eight men to play together under an actor-manager and to share the profits. In the 1560s there appeared companies that included women, although contemporary accounts refer also to professional performances of improvised comedy in which the female roles were played by men, as continued to be the case in the private amateur theater.

By this time the comici dell'arte manifested the traits most often associated with them, those that make the very term by which they are now identified a matter for debate as to whether *arte* is most precisely defined as *mestiere,* emphasizing professionalism, or as *tecnica,* underlining the codification of skill, talent, and means. The principal modern connotations of the label *commedia dell'arte* arise from features that became clear not long after the middle of the Cinquecento. As an institution commedia dell'arte is the complex of commercial companies that traveled about expressly to produce plays, as distinct from more general entertainment. Considered as a product, on the other hand, commedia dell'arte (in the Cinquecento called *commedia al soggetto, commedia improvvisa,* or simply *commedia all'italiana*) refers to one of the styles of acting cultivated by the professional players, exercising mnemonic verbal and gestural techniques to make a kind of drama related by plot and characters to the literary commedia regolare, but at one remove. Even at this early stage the commedia dell'arte was distinguished by improvisation on a minimal three-act scenario, or *soggetto,* in which fixed roles were taken repeatedly by actors specializing in them, each developing for his stage character or range of characters individual traits of appearance, gesture, and language within the limits of the types, one or more of which might become permanently associated with his name.

Francesco Andreini's preface to the repertory of dialogues, or *bravure,* which he published on retiring from his famous role of Capitan Spavento da Vall'Inferna, tells us that he began his stage career specializing in innamorato parts. These called for elegance of dress and carriage, a degree of proficiency in singing and accompanying oneself on a musical instrument, and a store of love-talk in the Petrarchan manner, with flights of lyric eloquence and various kinds of repartee delivered in cultivated Tuscan. The role of the lover "with a woeful ballad made to his mistress' eyebrow" was a far cry from that of the soldier "full of strange oaths and bearded like the pard," a type well established in commedia erudita as a sword-rattling liar on whose lips a word of Spanish never came amiss to the ears of Italian audiences all too familiar with Spanish political power. His speech jumbles outrageous exaggerations, ill-digested classical myths, and contemporary history with boasts of high lineage and prowess on the battlefield and in bed; his behavior, put to the test, often exposes him as low-born, cowardly, and sexually inept.

It was his version of this modern *miles gloriosus* that made Francesco Andreini's greatest fame, but he is said to have excelled also as the *Dottor siciliano*, a mask requiring dialectal parody of academic learning. He shone too as Falsirone the sorcerer, speaking a mélange of French, Spanish, Greek, Turkish, and "la schiava," or Dalmatian Slavonic, and he was sufficiently well known in his pastoral role of Corinto to warrant writing the elegy for Isabella in this guise.

Francesco and Isabella enter the history of the stage in 1578, already successful and just married, when their return to Italy after a tour in France was chronicled in Florence. She was sixteen and had been born in Padua to a Venetian family named Canali; he was a Pistoiese, about thirty, who had fought the Turks aboard one of the galleys of the Duke of Tuscany and once spent eight months as a prisoner of war. This adventurous hardship was probably the source of the Turkish and "Slovenian" patter he later put to theatrical use.

Isabella was considered a marvel of accomplishment from the beginning. Blessed with beauty of face and body, she deployed her natural endowments skillfully: even the crude woodcut portraits suggest how much charm must have lain in her expression and use of her features. The likeness printed in the edition of 1601 of her *Rime* shows her brows lifted in candid arcs of surprise; her large eyes glance sidelong knowingly and her mouth curves with mischief, as if about to utter a witticism.

She took the role of innamorata under her own name of Isabella, except in pastoral settings, when she became Fillide and wore the elegant wreathed, draped, and sandaled outfits depicted in illustrations of the most often-printed favole and tragicommedie pastorali. Whatever the costume, she always played the leading lady, not attempting a range of parts such as those her husband commanded; her fictive identity remained essentially that of the young and beautiful innamorata, graceful, accomplished, upper-class, chic, eloquent in pure Tuscan, and, most important, learned in literature. All of this she brought to each canovaccio for which she improvised the lines that gave body to the bare bones of plot, drawing her words and actions from the resources that study and exercise constantly reinvested in her role.

But the established features of the innamorata were hardly a straitjacket to her talents. Although she did not alternate between radically different basic roles, as Francesco did, Isabella found in the plots of the scenarios themselves justification for multiplying her characterizations. The perennial devices of disguise, mistaken identity, and madness offered opportunities for brilliant demonstrations of her versatility. A description by Giuseppe Pavoni, who beheld the famous entertainments accompanying the wedding in 1589 of Grand Duke Ferdinando de' Medici and his French bride, Christine de Lorraine, gives a glimpse of Isabella in one of her tours de force. In a command performance of what she herself regarded as one of her showpieces, Isabella dazzled the Florentines and their royal guests with a mad scene. Pavoni sketches the plot of *La pazzia d'Isabella,* from which the scene was taken, and recounts how on finding herself deserted and her honor compromised she abandoned herself to grief and passion, went out of her senses, and then

> come pazza se n'andava scorrendo per la Cittade, fermando hor questo, & hora quello, e parlando hora in Spagnuolo, hora in Greco, hora in Italiano, & molti altri inguaggi, ma tutti fuor di proposito: & tra le altre cose si mise à parlar Francese, & à cantar certe canzonette pure alla Francese, che diedero tanto diletto alla Sereniss. Sposa, che maggiore non si potria esprimere. Si mise poi ad imitare li linguaggi di tutti li suoi Comici, come del Pantalone, del Gratiano, del Zanni, del Pedrolino, del Francatrippa, del Burattino, del Capitan Cardone, & della Franceschina tanto naturalmente, & con tanti dispropositi, che non è possibile il poter con lingua narrare il valore, & la virtù di questa Donna. Finalmente per fintione d'arte Magica, con certe acque, che le furono data à bere, ritornò nel suo primo essere, & quivi con elegante, & dotto stile esplicando le passioni d'amore, & i travagli, che provano quelli, che si ritrovano in simil panie involti, si fece fine alla Commedia; mostrando nel recitar questa Pazzia il suo sano, e dotto intelletto; lasciando l'Isabella tal mormorio, & meraviglia ne gli ascoltatori, che mentre durerà il mondo, sempre sarà lodata la sua bella eloquenza, & valore.

like a mad creature roamed the city scene, stopping one passerby, then another, speaking now in Spanish, now in Greek, now in Italian and in many other languages, but always irrationally; and among other things she began to speak French and to sing French songs, which gave the most inexpressible pleasure to the bride, Her most Serene Highness. Then Isabella fell to imitating the manner of speech of all her fellow actors, [the Veneto dialect] of Pantalone, [the Emilian] of Gratiano, [the Bergamasque] of Zanni, and those of Pedrolino, Francatrippa, Burattino, Capitan Cardone and Franceschina, all so naturally and with such hilarious absurdities that it is impossible for tongue to tell the matchless worth and powers of this Woman. Finally, by the fiction of magic art and certain waters she was given to drink, Isabella was brought to her senses and here, with elegant and learned style explicating the passions and the ordeals suffered by those who fall into love's snares, she brought the comedy to its close, demonstrating by her acting of this madness the sound health and cultivation of her own intellect; leaving her audience in such murmuring of admiration and wonder that while the world lasts, the eloquence and inestimable worth of Isabella will ever be praised.[17]

The mad scene was a standard piece of stage action in the repertories of both the literary comedy, where it had originated and was continued, and the professional improvisers. Whether as a controlling theme, extended set-piece, or brief representation of a "fact" of the plot, and whether madness was feigned, like Hamlet's, or true, like Ophelia's, the theatergram of derangement attracted every kind of playwright, as the titles tell in such comedies as Grazzini's *La spiritata*, Sicinio's *La pazzia*, and Della Porta's *La furiosa*, and in pastorals like Cucchetti's *La pazzia di Fileno* and Totti's *Gli amanti furiosi*.[18] A contemporary French spectator of the Gelosi company's performances in the generation just before those of the Andreini observes that mad scenes were popular with the professionals because they gave actresses an excuse for ripping up their clothes to show off their breasts and the skillful undulations of their flesh. None of the accounts reveals how much of herself Isabella re-

17. Giuseppe Pavoni's diary is quoted in Marotti's edition of Scala, *Il teatro delle favole rappresentative*, vol. 1, app. 1, lxxv.

18. Antonfrancesco Grazzini, *La spiritata, commedia* (Florence, 1561), written before 1560; Cristoforo Sicinio, *La pazzia, comedia* (Orvieto, 1588), probably written in 1586; Giambattista Della Porta, *La furiosa, commedia* (Naples, 1609), written before 1603; Giovanni Donato Cucchetti, *La pazzia, favola pastorale* (Ferrara, 1581), later retitled *La pazzia di Fileno* (Venice, 1623); Ranieri Totti, *Gli amanti furiosi, favola boscareccia* (Venice, 1597). In M. Pieri, "Interpretazione teatrale del *Torrismondo*," 411, the author includes the psychic disassociations of Tasso's Torrismondo in this category of scene, calls Alvida in a state of hallucination a "high culture version of the various primadonnas who go mad onstage," and emphasizes Isabella Andreini's durable rapport with Tasso.

vealed, but as she was considered an uncommonly grand and moral sort of actress, it may be that she relied more on the talents for music, mimicry, and interpretation reported by Pavoni than on topless exhibitions.

Two scenarios containing mad scenes for Isabella, *La pazzia d'Isabella* and *La finta pazza,* both different from the plot summarized by Pavoni, appear in Scala's *Teatro.*[19] In *La finta pazza* it is merely noted that Isabella as well as Orazio "fa diverse pazzie," but in *La pazzia d'Isabella* are recorded snatches of fantastic ramblings such as those Isabella Andreini must have used: parodied bits of the imagery of love, food, war, obscenity, and classical learning plucked from the lexicons of the stock characters of comedy; and psychedelic conjunctions of visual metaphors, aural memories, and punning word associations, jumbling together Aristotle, harpsichords, butts of muscatel, and a "rainbow to give a clister to Isola of England, who couldn't piss."[20] This passage is probably an echo of Catholic, anti-Tudor calumny attributing by rumor various physical abnormalities to the Virgin Queen, and a hint at the marriage, politically menacing to Protestant England, of Henri IV with the Austro-Spanish powers represented by Maria de' Medici, whose symbolic association with the rainbow began during her wedding festivities in 1600 and continued for decades.[21]

From these fragments we can catch the tone of a movable mad scene and see the kind of reading drawn on for it, as well as the topical uses to which it could be put. Isabella's *Rime* and dialogues demonstrate her mastery of the Petrarchan register, and we may suppose that she could ring changes on it too for mad scenes, as Della Porta causes both of his young lovers in *La furiosa* to do with pathetic effect, wringing tears from the other characters. Angelini notes the resemblance between Isabella's mad scene and Ophelia's, while pointing to a fundamental difference created by the former's prose and the latter's singing;[22] but because Ophelia speaks as well as sings (and Pavoni testifies that Isabella also

19. Scala, *Il teatro delle favole rappresentative,* ed. Marotti, vol. 2, *La pazzia d'Isabella* (giornata 38), and vol. 1, *La finta pazza* (giornata 8).

20. "Anima secondo Aristotele è spirito, che si diffonde per le botte del moscatello di Monte Fiascone, e che per ciò fu veduto l'arco baleno far un serviziale all'Isola d'Inghilterra, che non poteva pisciare" (she puns on the Italian word for island, *isola,* and variant forms of the name Elizabeth, for example Isobel or Isabella). Scala, *Il teatro delle favole rappresentative,* ed. Marotti, 2:396.

21. Sara Mamone, *Firenze e Parigi,* 64.

22. Franca Angelini, "La pazzia di Isabella," *Letteratura italiana,* ed. Alberto Asor Rosa, vol. 6, *Teatri moderni* (Turin, 1986), 112–13.

did both in her excerpted scene for the Medici festivities), it is not incautious to recognize the family resemblance owed to the repertory that theatrical professionals shared, even if separated by the English Channel. The combinatory practice common to all produced any number of variants, including even Perdita's pastoral welcoming scene, in which the action of bestowing flowers chosen for each bystander, accompanied by appropriate comments, is a repetition of Ophelia's pathetic distribution of rue and rosemary, but with the madness omitted and the key changed.

The movable parts in another combination can be seen in the mad scenes of Fileno from the much-praised pastoral that Cucchetti wrote for Marfisa d'Este's wedding. Like Isabella and the lovers in *La furiosa,* the rejected shepherd babbles of love, death, souls, and heavenly spheres (III.2 and IV.4), and his mad talk, like Hamlet's, strikes his hearers as having some method in it: hearing Fileno wildly pun on "donna" and "danno," Metio comments; "Il ragionar non è da pazzo ancora / Che l'operation da pazzo sia." [23] The moon is often on the lips of theatrical lunatics: as the briefest of buzzwords for Bargagli's faking Lepida,[24] as the key signature of Lyly's *Woman in the Moon,*[25] as an evocative image in Isabella's "ballava il Canario con la Luna vestita di verde." [26] Reading the fragmentary records of her performances, we can see that Isabella's mad scene came to her from the common repertory, and can also see something of how she made it particularly her own.

Lacking the sound of her voice, the sight of her gestures and dancing, or any comprehensive description of them, we admittedly can never reconstruct entirely the art of Isabella, any more than we can that of other *commedianti.* But we have more of what Francesco Andreini called "fragmenti" than is generally supposed; pieced together, they produce an illuminating picture of the professional players' resources. More

23. "His talk isn't that of a madman, even though his behavior is." *La pazzia, favola pastorale* (IV.2).

24. In act 2, scene 2, of Girolamo Bargagli, *La pellegrina* (Siena, 1589), written ca. 1568, the comedy sumptuously performed as the centerpiece of the Medici wedding entertainment in which Isabella's troupe took part.

25. The "lunatic pastoral" (ca. 1593) that Maurice Charney finds charged with meaning discovered through madness in "Female Roles and the Children's Companies: Lyly's Pandora in *The Woman in the Moon,*" *Research Opportunities in Renaissance Drama* 22 (1979): 41.

26. Scala, *La pazzia d'Isabella,* in *Il teatro delle favole rappresentative,* 2:395.

complete than the speeches summarized in the scenarios above are the full-length dialogues or *contrasti scenici* published in Isabella's name by the grieving Francesco: whole scenes that she and her partners in the innamorato roles employed as movable blocks of theatrical material usable in any number of plays. Written by Isabella and Francesco for her use, they are on widely different subjects: the passions of love and hate, love and death, love and vows, marital love, tragedy, comedy, epic poetry, doctors and lawyers, and so on, and they always boil down at the end of the scene to lovers' compliments, pleas accepted or rejected, engagements, reconciliations, or adieux. In the process they display dexterity in appropriating all registers to the imagistic language of love.

The manneristic *ingenium* in Shakespeare's commandeering of musical, legal, and other terminology to make metaphors of the heart in his sonnets and plays is a superior exercising of the kind of wit that drives Isabella's successive (and ultimately mechanical) conversion of different lexicons to the same purpose. In her dialogues the vocabularies of law and medicine are made to express amorous desires, as theoretical literary terms also do when Diomede tells Ersilia in the "Contrasto scenico sopra la Comedia" that he wants to write a comedy entitled *Ersilia* in which the "Peripetia e Ricognitione dell'Amor mio" befall her. She advises him to call it *Diomede Out of Luck* (*Lo sventurato Diomede*) instead.[27] Each *contrasto* is assigned to a differently named pair, although Isabella would have kept her own stage name when she used these dialogues in improvised comedy. Their sexual game of parry and thrust, played with loosely grasped literary and philosophical weapons, is characterized in the amoroso contrasto on love's deaths, carried on by a pair named Eudosia and Manlio, though they might as easily be called Beatrice and Benedick, whose first encounter in *Much Ado About Nothing* begins thus:

> *Beatrice.*   I wonder that you will still be talking, Signior Benedick: nobody marks you.
> *Benedick.*   What! my dear Lady Disdain, are you yet living?
>
> (I.1.121–24)

Isabella's Eudosia opens the match with a move like Benedick's:

27. Isabella Andreini, *Fragmenti di alcune scritture della Signora Isabella Andreini Comica Gelosa, et Academica Intenta. Raccolti da Francesco Andreini Comico Geloso, detto il Capitano Spavento, e dati in luce da Flamminio Scala Comico, e da lui dedicati all'Illustrissimo Sig. Filippo Capponi* (Venice, 1620), 61.

Eudosia.	Signor Manlio, mi rallegro della vostra sanità, e che non siate morto, come publicamente si diceva.
Manlio.	Fù pur troppo vera la mia morte, & ancor semi-vivo mi trovo, anzi per dir meglio sono morto affatto.
Eudosia.	Voi mi fate venir voglia di ridere . . .
Manlio.	[launches into a series of paradoxes from love theory] Muore amando chiunque ama, perche il suo pensiero dimenticando se stesso, solo nella persona amata si rivolge, & vive.
Eudosia.	Questa è non meno ridicolosa della prima: . . .
	. . . .
	Ogni altra cosa mi sarei pensata in voi, eccetto che passione, & affetto amoroso . . .
	. . . .
	Et s'io vi tenessi sospeso, & in forse, che partito prendereste voi?
Manlio.	Viverei con speranza d'esser da voi col tempo riamato, perche la speranza gli amanti giamai non abbandona, sperando che l'amor nostro debba esser cambievole, ò per gli ascendenti, ò per i Pianeti benigni, ò per li Genij, ò per le complessioni tra di noi simili, e concordi.
Eudosia.	Or sù per terminar questo nostro ragionamento, e per mantenervi in qualche speranza, non essendo di dovuto, che in un subito io mi risolva, & all'improviso d'amarvi, ò di non amarvi, dicovi che in questo mentre, che voi anderete trovando la verità di queste vostre platoniche openioni [sic], che io parimente anderò pensando se debbo amarvi, ò nò.
Manlio.	Non occorrerà, che voi mettiate in dubbio quelle cose, che ci sforzeranno ad amarci cambievolmente.
Eudosia.	Signor Manlio, i Pianeti inclinano, ma non sfor zano.
Manlio.	Se non vi sforzeranno, vi sforzerò io.
Eudosia.	Me ne rido, perch'è passato il tempo de i Paladini, & voi non siete uno di quelli.
Eudosia.	Signor Manlio, I rejoice to see you in health and not dead, as rumor had it.
Manlio.	Alas, my death was true and I am still only half alive; no, in truth, it would be better to say that I'm altogether dead.

Eudosia.	You are making me laugh . . .
	. . . .
Manlio.	Truly he who loves dies by loving, for his mind deserts him to fix on the beloved, in whom alone it lives.
Eudosia.	This is no less ridiculous than your first claim.
	. . . .
	I would have expected anything from you but passion and amorous attachment.
	. . . .
	And if I were to keep you in suspense and doubt, what would you do?
Manlio.	I would live in hope of being loved by you in time, for lovers never cease hoping, hoping that our love would be made reciprocal, either by the ascendency of favorable stars or benign planets, or by natural inclinations of spirit or by similarity and compatibility of our humors.
Eudosia.	Well, to conclude this discussion and to give you some hope to go on with, though I am not required to make up my mind in an instant and decide suddenly to love you or love you not, I'll say that while you are searching out the truth of your platonic ideas, I shall likewise be thinking on whether or not I should love you.
Manlio.	There is no use your doubting those powers that will force us to love each other.
Eudosia.	Signor Manlio, the planets influence us but they can't force us.
Manlio.	If they don't force you, I shall force you myself.
Eudosia.	I laugh at the threat, for the time of knights in armor is long past, and you are hardly one of them.[28]

The tecnica of the best professional improvisers relied on judgement, exercise, timing, and memory; the sources they selected and memorized, as well as the models of organization, were largely literary. This has been obscured by the tendency to pit against each other the commedia dell'arte and written drama, the improvised and the preestablished, the spontaneous act and the fixed text, the natural and the artificial, the theatrical and the literary. As some literary dramatists affirmed the distance

28. Isabella Andreini, "Contrasto sopra le morti d'amore," *Fragmenti di alcune scritture*, 36–41.

between their plays and the improvised comedy, which they despised because at its worst it was often shapeless, slapstick, and obscene, so some
of the best professional comici, notably Francesco Andreini and his colleague Flaminio Scala, encouraged the polarization by emphasizing in
printed dedications and prologues the difference between the theatrical
works they published and the neoclassical literary drama of the intelligentsia. Actually, the contrast thus orchestrated by such actors arose
less from theoretical controversy than from a defensive promotion policy: it was a way of displaying the uniqueness of their wares, of justifying the unusual procedure of consigning improvising matter to definitive
printed form, and of disarming learned criticism.

Recent research on the commedia dell'arte, often directed toward
sociological and economic analysis of the genesis of modern show business, has emphasized the vulnerability to political and ecclesiastical
power of the professional actors, their outsiderly function with regard
to official culture, and the development of their survival skills. Such
studies frequently issue from lively, newly founded academic depart-
ments of theater history, where one might expect a vested lack of interest in attacking the idea of a fundamental opposition between the theatrical and the literary. The approaches taken by Taviani, Tessari, Zorzi,
and Ferrone, for example, are not incompatible with the idea, and yet
they lead to grounds on which challenge is possible. Tessari, concerned
with the total life span of the commedia dell'arte, observes it from its
vigorous but inchoate beginnings in the mid-sixteenth century to its period of widest dominance in the second half of the seventeenth, seeing
the latter-day commedia dell'arte as something like an industrial complex, with some companies receiving salaries from local governments
and incurring consequent political obligations. Tessari defines this period as one of limited range of content and high efficiency of technique,
when the commedia dell'arte became increasingly bureaucratic, expert,
and decadent, and he unfavorably compares this later time with the
phase of the *arte giocosa* in the late sixteenth century and the early seventeenth, when the Andreini were active and freedom, both artistic and
economic, was greatest. That this is also the era of the arte's closest association with written drama demonstrates the provisory rhetorical nature
of the traditional polarization of theater and literature. It is only a step
from acknowledging the vitality and breadth of the commedia dell'arte
at this time to interpreting these qualities as results of the link to literature, effects caused by a symbiotic relationship, not merely coinci-
dental with it.

That the commedia dell'arte appropriated the types and plots of the neoclassical comedy is an axiom of its history, as is the tardier occurrence of the writers of regular drama borrowing back from the comici the characteristics of their vivacious embellishments and modifications on what they had borrowed in the first place. The symbiosis was at its most active when the Andreini were at their most active. Five years before the names of Isabella and Francesco appear in theater history, their company, the Gelosi, had acted at the ducal court of Ferrara in the première performance of Tasso's *Aminta*. Such documented events can be multiplied by the score to demonstrate an underemphasized fact of commedia dell'arte life at the upper levels: that in addition to their popular specialty of improvising, troupes like the Gelosi and Confidenti continued the practice of learning and performing as written the prose and the verse plays of the literary establishment—the "recitar Comedie, Tragicomedie, Tragedie, Pastorali" that Francesco Andreini vaunted[29]—and that they took part in private productions, courtly and academic.

Isabella's career also illustrates the ambition and ability of the comici to write and publish plays. Although an inclination toward star turns and striking episodes at the expense of *durchkomponiert* structure in most of their texts hints to the practiced reader that they come from professional actors rather than from literary amateurs of the theater, the differences are subtle, and the formats and generic features precisely those of the literary avant-garde drama, chosen explicitly over those of the improvised comedy. This is the case of Isabella's verse play *Mirtilla, pastorale*, which appeared when imitation of *Aminta* and pursuit of the third genre were in full cry and just before the long-awaited *Il pastor fido* was published. Immediately sold out in its printing of 1588, Isabella's pastoral went into several editions.

Short on plot and long on Counter-Reformation moral attitudes with neoplatonic flavor, *Mirtilla* is derivative and preaching enough to bear out the claim made in the dedication to Isabella's *Lettere* (1607) that it was a work of her earliest youth, but it is also thoroughly and skillfully in the latest literary fashion. Beginning like Tasso with Amore's declaration of his power, Isabella straitlaces it into a didactic dialogue with Venere and sets out to exalt true or rational love leading to marriage, as opposed to mad furor, or what the Prologo calls "cieco error che la ragione uccide, e lascia al cieco senso il freno" (blind error that kills reason and leaves blind sense to curb itself).

Magic and metamorphosis are excluded from the plot, but Venere

---

29. Dedication to *Le bravure*, quoted by Marotti in Scala, *Il teatro delle favole rappresentative*, vol. 1, app. 6, cv.

quotes Ovidian examples of the harm Amore causes, beginning with that of Pyramus and Thisbe; he answers that it is furor's fault, not his, if these mortals be fools. Assuming the same providential position that Love or Venus or their deputy sorcerers take in pastorals like those of Tasso, Pasqualigo, Ingegneri, and Guazzoni, or that Oberon takes in *A Midsummer Night's Dream* and Prospero in *The Tempest,* Amore in *Mirtilla* watches unseen over lovers and designs for them heavenly lessons in self-knowledge. The strategies are necessarily complex, for the tangled emotions of the nymphs and shepherds in Isabella's wood are of the labyrinthine sort borrowed from the commedia regolare by many pastoral playwrights. They invite scenes of round-robin wooing and rejection: Mirtilla courts Uranio and he courts Ardelia, Ardelia spurns him and he spurns Mirtilla (II.3), in a pattern used by many contemporary dramatists and varied by Shakespeare in *As You Like It* (V.2) and *A Midsummer Night's Dream* (II.2).

Among other standard theatergrams of the literary pastoral that Isabella had already mastered are the lyric solo scene, written for her to sing as Fillide in duet with Echo (I.2), and the figure of the Satiro, who cites classical examples of hairy or horned creatures loved by beautiful female beings, human or divine (III.1). In his hopeful, complacent mood he is the precursor to Bottom, but when he attempts rape, as the satyrs of the favola pastorale ordinarily do, he foreshadows Caliban and so continues to do when he attaches himself in grateful admiration to the boozing glutton Gorgo and offers him rustic gifts (III.3). True to genre, all are finally reconciled in multiple weddings and thanksgiving to Amore, calling down blessings on the pastoral temple, dwellings, and landscape.

Three years before she died in Lyons while returning from the Gelosi's triumphal season at the court of Henri IV and Marie de' Medici, Isabella published her *Rime,* a collection of songs, sonnets, and other fashionable forms of occasional and lyric poetry in the latest manner cultivated within the Petrarchan tradition. Some of these poems she had probably used to good purpose in her improvising onstage; others were doubtless intended for purely literary purposes. The accomplishments for which poets like Tasso, Marino, Guarini, and Chiabrera celebrated her in verse were both histrionic and literary. They lauded now the one talent, now the other, but it is clear that the two functioned in her work by mutual stimulation. Just as Isabella and her colleagues were relatively free to choose how and for whom they would perform, not being on the steady payroll of any one ruling family or institution, so Isabella, her peers, and her son's generation enjoyed a social and intellectual mobility that brought them into contact with the world of letters and gave them cultural recognition and status as well as ideas and material to enrich the theater.

The comici of the great companies—the Gelosi, the Confidenti, the Uniti, the Desiosi, the Diana, the Accesi, the Fedeli—were in fact eager to exalt their achievements and distinguish them from those of the *cerretani*, the humbler troupes, the mountebanks and acrobats, the ragtag and bobtail of the profession who improvised farces in the piazzas. Like Tessari, Marotti recognizes in the publication of scenarios and dialogues used in acting an attempt to raise the status of this theatrical art to the level of high culture, of literature. Yet contrasts between the literature established as high art and the vital *arte giocosa* that for a time aspired to an equal status remain attractive as ideological or formal grids for historical reconstruction, and this still restrains some scholars from doing justice to the potency and influence of that literature on that art, an influence courted by the most gifted of the players.

During the Andreini years, the influence became so reciprocal that except in the rare, well-documented cases it would be impossible to state at any given moment in which direction it was moving. A single illustration of a common phenomenon is the topos trading apparent in contemporary texts of Francesco Andreini and Della Porta. Andreini's greatest role comes to life in his *Bravure del Capitano Spavento divise in molti ragionamenti*, fifty-five dialogues published in 1607, almost immediately translated into French in 1608, reprinted frequently, and enlarged by the author with new *bravure* and *ragionamenti fantastici*. In the thirty-sixth *ragionamento* Capitano Spavento swaggers and boasts to his straight man and valet Trappola about the duel he fought in an arena with Death herself:

La Morte da principio era grassa, colorita, e bella, come qual si voglia bella, e gratiosa Donna: E conoscendosi esser tale, divenne tanto altiera, e tanto orgogliosa, che fuora di tempo, & à voglia sua, uccideva questo e quello, non havendo riguardo nè à sesso, nè ad ordine, nè ad etate. . . . Veduta quella inhumanità che usava la Morte, vinto da giusto, e generoso sdegno, disfidai la Morte a combatter meco allo steccato; la Morte accettò la disfida, toccando ad ella l'elettione dell'Armi, & à me il ritrovare il Campo. . . . tolsi il Sole . . . e vedendo che la Morte dallo splendore de' suoi raggi rimaneva abbagliata, e più non scorgeva la strada del ferire; co-

minciai subito à stoccheggiarla, e malamente à ferirla. Durò l'ab-
battimento fiero insino al tramontar del Sole; là onde la Morte ve-
dendosi ridutta à mal partito . . . la svenai, lasciandole solamente i
nerbi, e l'ossa, come viene dipinta.

Death used to be plump, rosy, and pretty, like any good-looking
and charming woman. And because she knew it, it went to her
head and she became murderously proud and, whenever she chose,
she took to killing people off schedule and on whim, without regard to sex, or order or age. . . . When I saw how inhumanely
Death behaved, I was overcome by just and noble indignation and
I challenged her to combat in the arena. She accepted, and it fell to
her to choose the arms, to me to choose the field. . . . I took the
sun . . . and seeing Death dazzled by its rays, I began instantly to
batter and bruise her pitilessly. The fierce fight lasted until sun-
down; whereupon Death finding herself in bad shape, I deveined
her, leaving her with only sinews and bones, as she is usually
depicted.[30]

The Herculean feats of the bravure include Spavento's breaking
through the roof of the underworld by his dynamic dancing with Pro-
serpina, swallowing a hundred whole calves in an eating contest, and
playing ball against the gods with Death on his side:[31] all are given
bombastic descriptions punctuated by deflatingly literal questions and
straight-faced digs from Trappola, laughing up his sleeve. Exuberant
fantasizing belongs to the miles gloriosus as a type; and the elaboration
of grotesque episodes in baroque imagery, laced with classical allusions
and set off by the disingenuous underling, was the trademark of Andreini's handling of the role in improvisation.

In Della Porta's *Gli duoi fratelli rivali*, however, which is representative of the regular commedia grave as it was written in the late Cinquecento, there appears a version of the miles that suggests what give-

30. I quote from the second edition, *Le bravure del Capitano Spavento; divise in molti ragionamenti in forma di dialogo, di Francesco Andreini da Pistoia
Comico Geloso . . . Et in questa seconda impressione dal proprio autore ricor-
rette, & aggiuntovi molte cose curiose à discorso per discorso* (Venice, 1609),
92–93.

31. Ibid., "Del banchetto di Plutone" (ragionamento 37); "Della prove fatte
nel mangiare" (ragionamento 53); "Della partita al Pallone, fatta con diverse
Deità" (ragionamento 9).

and-take flourished between literary dramatists and the comici dell'arte. Della Porta's Capitano Martebellonio boasts to an incredulous and mocking glutton about a duel that he has fought with Death:

> Sappi che la Morte prima era viva, ed era suo ufficio ammazzar le genti con la falce. Ritrovandomi in Mauritania, stava alle strette con Atlante, il qual per esser oppresso dal peso nel mondo, era mal trattato da lei; io, che non posso soffrir vantaggi, li toglio il mondo da sopra le spalle, e me lo pongo su le mie . . . la disfido ad uccidersi meco; accettò l'invito, e perché avea l'elezion dell'armi, si volse giocar la vita al ballonetto. . . . Constituimmo per lo steccato tutto il mondo: ella n'andò in oriente, io in occidente. . . . che tema ho io del sole? Con una cera torta lo fo nascondere coperto d'una nube. . . . la presi per la gola con duo diti e l'uccisi come una quaglia. Talché non è più viva, ed io son rimasto nel suo ufficio.

> Know then, that Death used to be alive and it was her work to kill people with a scythe. Happening to be in Mauritania, I found her at odds with Atlas, whom she tormented while he bore the weight of the world. As I can't stand to see unfair advantage taken, I transferred the world from his shoulders to mine. . . . I challenged her to mortal combat; she accepted the invitation, and as she had the choice of arms, decided to play ball to the death. . . . For our playing field we designated the whole world: she went to the east, I to the west. . . . I fear the sun? With one scowl I make him take cover behind a cloud. . . . I took her by the throat with two fingers and I killed her like a quail. So she's no longer alive, and I am left in her place.[32]

The glutton counters by narrating his own defeat of Death in an eating match. *Fratelli rivali* went into print six years before Andreini's *Bravure,* but both the play, in manuscript, and the *ragionamenti,* in the mouth of Capitano Spavento onstage, had been around for years before the publication dates.[33] Whoever came first, playwright or actor, the

32. Giambattista Della Porta, *Gli duoi fratelli rivali/The Two Rival Brothers,* ed. and trans. L. G. Clubb (Berkeley, Los Angeles, and London, 1980), I.4.

33. Andreini's foreword presents the *Bravure* as a memorial of his acting, whereas Martebellonio of *Fratelli rivali* was mentioned in a Latin adaptation of another of Della Porta's comedies at Cambridge, possibly in 1598 and certainly by 1602; see L. G. Clubb, *Giambattista Della Porta, Dramatist* (Princeton, 1965), 275ff, and Clubb, ed., *Gli duoi fratelli rivali,* Introduction, 5.

conclusion to be drawn from the parallel is not that the other was a pla-
giarist but that the best efforts in literary and improvised comedy at this
time were in closer conjunction than they had been before or would be
later on.

The arte would be bureaucratized as it grew, its function would be
specified and classified, and at the end of the seventeenth century Andrea Perrucci would be able to categorize its proper style as the lowly
and its proper subject as the "urban ridiculous,"[34] that is, city farce exclusively. But before this era of consolidation and limitation set in, the
spectacular sunset of the commedia dell'arte's golden age was reflected
in the career of Francesco's and Isabella's eldest son, Giovanni Battista,
the only heir to their profession. His four sisters became nuns, one
brother a monk, and the other a captain in the ducal guard at Mantua.
Giambattista studied law at the University of Bologna for a time, but
before he was twenty he followed his parents into the Gelosi company
and quickly established himself as an innamorato under the name of
Lelio. If the illustrations are to be believed, he had the looks, the figure,
and the wardrobe for success in a role that demanded the presence of a
matinée idol and an abundance of embroidered silks and velvet cloaks,
as well as colored hose and good legs. Above all, he had a mind well
furnished with reading and a tongue and pen ready to use it.

When his mother died and his father retired, Giambattista formed
the company of the Fedeli; with them and sometimes with other groups
he traveled continually, to Prague, to the court of Emperor Ferdinand II at
Vienna, and at the invitation of Marie de Medici, now Queen Mother, to
France, where he returned often and lived for some years. He wrote
plays in many genres; some were starring vehicles for himself, such as
the comedies *Lelio bandito* and *Li duo Lelii simili;* the verse tragedy *La
Florinda* was written for his first wife, who became known from then on
as Florinda, though her real name was Virginia. He also wrote parts for
his second wife, another Virginia who took the stage name Lidia. In
short, in his theatrical career acting was linked from the beginning with
writing as well as with improvising, and eventually his literary production included a variety of works only indirectly connected with the theater. He was still writing when he died in 1654.

Giambattista Andreini's eighteen published plays attest large inges-
tion and assimilation of literature, and currency with the most up-to-
date literary fashion, but they are also innovative experiments in ba-

34. "Ridicolosità urbana," quoted in Tessari, *La commedia dell'arte nel Seicento*, 94.

roque theater, taking advantage of all the audio-visual and metaphoric potentialities of his medium. In *Le due comedie in comedia*,[35] a comedy about two comedies that an academy of amateurs and a troupe of comici dell'arte perform for each other, he uses the inevitably philosophical theatrical device of the play within the play to create mutually reflective realities, and to make capital of his critical view of the difference between private, literary comedy and professional, improvised comedy. Although its dialogue is written and requires the actors to stick to the script, such a play as this by its very nature leaves room for some of the lazzi and extemporizing of the commedia dell'arte stock types.

In other works Giambattista gave no occasion to himself for playing Lelio, nor to his colleagues for their improvisations, but instead called forth styles and characterizations illustrating the actors' range and versatility and Andreini's commitment to literary dramaturgy. The best-known of his dramas is the five-act sacred tragedy in verse *L'Adamo*,[36] made famous by Voltaire's declaring in the *Essai sur la poésie épique* that it was Milton's inspiration for *Paradise Lost*. The tragedy's setting in "Paradiso Terrestre," not masked by the name of Arcadia, is no place for Pantalone, Graziano, or Arlecchino, but it is hospitable to weightier roles: Adam and Eve, fallen and unfallen angels, virtues and vices, God the Father, the World, the Flesh, and the Serpent, who naturally has the best lines. Just as the Arcadia of ostensibly pagan pastoral plays is charged with Edenic potential, Andreini's Garden of Eden is enriched in reverse by the generic Arcadian promise of a happy ending, tacitly confirming the essentially tragicomic nature of the Christian doctrine of sin and redemption and insinuating the providential view that the Incarnation would make of Adam's tragedy a "fortunate fall."

One of Giambattista's greatest successes was on another sacred subject, that of Mary Magdalen, and demonstrates the experimentation with genre mixing carried to the brink of opera. Written originally at the command of the French queen, with music by a consortium of composers including Monteverdi, it was revised near the end of Andreini's life as *Maddalena lasciva e penitente* and later described by Rasi as a "bel pasticcio comico-drammatico-tragico-melodrammatico-mimo-danzante."[37] The polished baroque lyrics and verse dialogue are seam-

---

35. Venice, 1625, repr. in Ferrone, *Commedie dell'arte*, vol. 2.

36. *L'Adamo, sacra rapresentatione di Gio. Battista Andreino fiorentino. Alla m.tà christ.ma di Maria de Medici reina di Francia dedicata* (Milan, 1613).

37. *Maddalena lasciva e penitente, azione drammatica* (Milan, n.d. [1652]); Rasi, *I comici italiani*, 122.

lessly literary, without interstices for verbal improvisation, but the amalgam of genres and of music, miming, dance, spectacle, and scenic illusion offers great scope to theatrical art in general, as well as lures to individual performers. Surely no actress could resist the metamorphosis of the glittering, hard-hearted Maddalena "lasciva" into the haggard, conscience-stricken Maddalena "penitente" in sackcloth, carried fainting by two angels through the air from her sybaritic palace to the desert, where she is last seen weeping joyfully over a crucifix.

Like his parents before him, Giambattista Andreini hankered for aristocratic patronage, literary recognition, and moral respectability in a militantly religious era, and his ventures into sacred drama were dictated by all three of these goals. He also wrote treatises in defense of the theater as morally instructive and dedicated to Cardinal Richelieu a sonnet sequence entitled *Teatro celeste: Nel quale si rappresenta come la Divina bontà habbia chiamato al grado di Beatitudine e di Santità Comici Penitenti, e Martiri; con un poetico Esordio à Scenici Professori di far l'Arte virtuosamente, per lasciar in terra non solo nome famoso; ma per non chiudersi viziosoamente la via, che ne conduce al Paradiso.*[38] The sonnets treat of famous actors, beginning with their patron saint, Genesius, who was converted to Christianity by his own acting and martyred under Emperor Diocletian, followed by sonnets on some other canonized former actors, one on a certain Frate Giovanni who has left the stage for a monastery and is so holy that he lacks nothing of sainthood but death.

And then, touchingly, there is a sonnet on Isabella, of whose sanctity her son seems as certain as he is of her great art, in which he clearly regards acting and literature to have been equally blended. That was the art as he himself practiced it. When he too left the stage, that kind of art went with him, and the arte, the craft of the comici, then took a narrower path than the wide way it had followed with the Andreini family.

From the time of his first successes in the London theater world, when the dying and supplanted playwright Robert Greene attacked him as "an upstart crow, beautified with our feathers, that with his Tiger's

38. Paris, n.d. [1625]. Celestial Theater: In which is seen how the Divine Goodness has called Penitent and Martyred Actors to Beatitude and Sanctity, with an Exhortation to Stage Players to perform their Art virtuously so as not only to leave on earth a famous name but also not to close by vice the way that leads to Paradise.

heart wrapped in a player's hide, . . . being an absolute *Johannes fac totum,* is in his own conceit the only Shake-scene in a country," [39] Shakespeare was distinguished as a versatile assimilator of the latest fashions in dramaturgy. What Greene charged in his territorial resentment was plagiarism and presumption by a newcomer, a mere "puppet" actor, who wrote only by stealing; but even in 1592 the accusation was empty. To redispose existing material, to conceive and discourse intertextually, we know to be not only indivisible from the act of writing itself but also to have been the principal aim of literary composition recognized in Renaissance poetics. The contaminatio by which Italian drama was cultivated, and the staple elements that it accumulated into a great repertory, belonged to a theatrical mode of production and a mentality that penetrated European culture, enriching it with what is loosely but not wrongly classified as "Renaissance drama." Shakespeare's work from the beginning to the end of his career betrays acquaintance and skill with Italian theatergrams. He may have encountered them in literary plays, but it has yet to be established that he could read Italian easily or relied on his certain knowledge of Latin and probable grasp of French to make it out. If he read Italian at all, it could not have been done with depth or precision, to judge from his nonchalance about geography, customs, and spelling. Certainly he had access to Italian plays; some were performed at the universities and in London, translated for academic and town audiences, many were acquired for private libraries and consulted by John Florio for making the *Dictionarie* in which Elizabethans looked up Italian words, and a few were even printed in the original at John Wolfe's press in London.[40] But Shakespeare's main channel of information about European theatrical fashion, perhaps established by direct encounters but more probably by masses of secondhand accounts, were most likely to have been his Italian counterparts: the professionals, both Sidney's "ordinary players" and those who like

39. Quoted from Samuel Schoenbaum, "The Life of Shakespeare," in *A New Companion to Shakespeare Studies,* ed. Kenneth Muir and S. Schoenbaum (Cambridge, England, 1971), 5.

40. See John L. Lievsay, *The Englishman's Italian Books 1550–1700* (Philadelphia, 1969); Harry Sellers, "Italian Books Printed in England before 1640," *Library,* 4th ser. 5, no. 2 (September 1924): 105–28; repr. London, 1924; R. W. Bond, ed., *Early Plays from the Italian* (Oxford, 1911); F. S. Boas, *University Drama in the Tudor Age* (Oxford, 1914); M. A. Scott, *Elizabethan Translations from the Italian* (Boston, 1916); G. C. Moore Smith, *College Plays Performed in the University of Cambridge* (Cambridge, 1923).

Shakespeare himself, played to kings as well as groundlings and of whom he must have known much. These were the comici, sellers of theater.

What they sold was everything—whatever there was to play, as Taviani says. Polonius says so too. Beside the scenarios, the lazzi, and the masks of their three-act improvised plays, the Italian companies offered audiences their other assets, the memorized regular comedies, tragedies, and pastorals, the five-act format that they used in rote performances and for publication of their own literary plays, their avant-garde references to Aristotelian theory and interest in construction, their knowledgeable manipulation of genres and their dexterity with theatergrams from each kind: the wares of the theater vendors included the fruits of the fecundating rapport that they maintained with the literary sources of theatrical fashion.

These were not the wares that would be most in demand later, after the prolonged experience of the comici in France, when the image of the *comédie italienne* that eventually developed there would give it in the expectations of European audiences a more specialized, narrower, and less experimental character. In Shakespeare's time and for a little while afterward, however, this character was still unfixed. In the second half of the Cinquecento and the early decades of the Seicento, the commedia dell'arte came closer to *alta cultura* than it would ever again do.[41]

The English theater of the day differed from the Italian in its native antecedents, in having no room for women and little for improvising or the use of masks, but perhaps most of all in possessing what Taviani sees as principally lacking to the professional companies, the stability of a permanent theater in a central city. To the best English companies London offered both public theater buildings and aristocratic patronage; to Shakespeare's privileged corporation, holding a royal patent, it provided a degree of freedom, security, and stimulation such as Italian actors might well have envied. Ferrone compassionately defines the written plays of the comici in this era as the isolated offspring of a mismatch between actors in search of protection and writers in search of performers.[42] More abundant and validating progeny might be sought in a collateral branch of the international family of Renaissance drama—in the English companies, who also sold theater and played everything.

41. See Marotti's evaluation of Scala in this regard, in his edition of *Il teatro delle favole rappresentative*, Introduction, li.
42. "La Commedia dell'Arte era stata una *mesalliance*, un matrimonio di necessità tra diversi: tra istrioni in cerca di rifugio e letterati in cerca di compagnia." Ferrone, *Commedie dell'arte*, vol. 1, Introduction, 41.

Italian Plays

Acripanda (Decio), tragedy, 5 acts
Adamo, L' (G. B. Andreini), sacred tragedy, 5 acts
Afrodite, L' (Valerini), tragedy, 5 acts
Alceo (Ongaro), pastoral, 5 acts
Alchimista, L' (Lombardi), comedy, 5 acts
Alessandro, L' (Piccolomini), comedy, 5 acts
Almerigo, L' (Zinano), tragedy, 5 acts
Amante furioso, L' (Borghini), comedy, 5 acts
Amanti furiosi, Gli (Totti), pastoral, 5 acts
Amaranta (Casalio), pastoral, 5 acts
Amaranta (Simonetti), pastoral, 5 acts
Amarilli, L' (Castelletti), pastoral, 5 acts
Aminta (Tasso), pastoral, 5 acts
Amor costante, L' (Piccolomini), comedy, 5 acts
Amoroso sdegno, L' (Bracciolini), pastoral, 5 acts
Anconitana, L' (Ruzante), comedy, 5 acts
Andromeda (Guazzoni), pastoral, 5 acts
Angelica (Fornaris), comedy, 5 acts
Arbore incantato, L' (Scala), scenario, 3 acts
Aretusa (Lollio), pastoral, 5 acts
Aristodemo, L' (Dottori), tragedy, 5 acts
Armida infuriata (Persio), pastoral, 5 acts
Arrenopia (Giraldi), tragedy with happy ending, 5 acts
Astrologo, L' (Della Porta), comedy, 5 acts
Avvenimenti comici, pastorali e tragici, Li (Scala), scenario, 3 acts
Balia, La (Razzi), comedy, 5 acts
Barona, La, Il lamento del disgraziato pastore Clonico (Sabba da Castiglione), pastoral
    precursor, 1 act
Bernardi, I (D'Ambra), comedy, 5 acts
Burle d'Isabella, Le (Scala), scenario, 3 acts
Calandria, La (Bibbiena), comedy, 5 acts
Calisto, La (Groto), pastoral, 5 acts
Canace (Speroni), tragedy, 5 acts
Candelaio (Bruno), comedy, 5 acts
Cangiaria, La (Sacchi), comedy, 5 acts
Capriccio, Il (Guidozzo), pastoral, 5 acts
Caride, Il (Zinano), pastoral, 5 acts
Cassaria, La (Ariosto), comedy, 5 acts
Catarina d'Alessandria (Belli), sacred tragedy, 5 acts
Cecca, La (Razzi), comedy, 5 acts
Cesare, Il (Pescetti), tragedy, 5 acts

Chiappinaria, La (Della Porta), comedy, 5 acts

Cinthia, La (Noci), pastoral, 5 acts

Clesebia, overo Scorta alla religione (Cappelletti), sacred comedy, 5 acts

Clorindo, Il (Malmignati), pastoral tragedy, 5 acts

Conversione di Santa Maria Maddalena (Riccardi), sacred tragedy, 5 acts

Cortegiana, La (Aretino), comedy, 5 acts

Creduta morta, La (Scala), scenario, 3 acts

Creduto morto, Il (Scala), scenario, 3 acts

Danza di Venere (Ingegneri), pastoral, 5 acts

David sconsolato (Brunetto), sacred tragedy, 5 acts

Devota rappresentatione di Joseph figliuolo di Jacob, La (anonymous), sacred represen-
     tation, 1 act

Devota rappresentatione di S. Caterina vergine e martire (anonymous), sacred represen-
     tation, 1 act

Diana pietosa (Borghini), pastoral, 5 acts

Dimne, La (Farina), sacred tragedy, 5 acts

Diogene accusato, Il (Zoppio), comedy, 5 acts

Donna costante, La (Borghini), comedy, 5 acts

Dorotea vergine e martire, La (Tristano), sacred tragedy, 5 acts

Due comedie in comedia, Le (G. B. Andreini), comedy, 5 acts

Duoi fratelli rivali, Gli (Della Porta), comedy, 5 acts

Duo Lelii simili, Li (G. B. Andreini), comedy, 5 acts

Duo vecchi gemelli, Li (Scala), scenario, 3 acts

Egle (Giraldi), pastoral, 5 acts

Egloghe pastorali (Calmo), pastoral eclogues, 1 to 4 acts

Epitia (Giraldi), tragedy with happy ending, 5 acts

Erminia pastorella (Persio), pastoral, 5 acts

Erofilomachia, L' (Oddi), comedy, 5 acts

Erotodynastia, over Potenza d'amore, L' (Raimondi), comedy, 5 acts

Eunia, L' (Pino), pastoral, 5 acts

Fabritia (Dolce), comedy, 5 acts

Falsi sospetti, I (Pino), comedy, 5 acts

Fantesca, La (Della Porta), comedy, 5 acts

Fedele, Il (Pasqualigo), comedy, 5 acts

Fiammella, La (Rossi), pastoral, 5 acts

Fida ninfa, La (Contarini), pastoral, 5 acts

Figliuol prodigo, Il (Persio), sacred comedy, 5 acts

Fillide (Della Valle), pastoral, 5 acts

Filli di Sciro (G. Bonarelli Della Rovere), pastoral, 5 acts

Filliria (Vida), pastoral, 5 acts

Finta pazza, La (Scala), scenario, 3 acts

Finto marito, Il (Scala), scenario, 3 acts

Flavio finto negromante (Scala), scenario, 3 acts

Flori, La (Campiglia), pastoral, 5 acts

Florinda, La (G. B. Andreini), tragedy, 5 acts

Florinda (G. B. Leoni), hybrid, 5 acts

Forsennata prencipessa, La (Scala), scenario, 3 acts

Fortuna di Foresta prencipessa di Moscovia, La (Scala), scenario, 3 acts
Furbo, Il (Castelletti), comedy 5 acts
Furiosa, La (Della Porta), comedy, 5 acts
Furto, Il (D'Ambra), comedy, 5 acts
Gelosi amanti (C. Della Valle), pastoral, 5 acts
Geloso, Il (Bentivoglio), comedy, 5 acts
Georgio, Il (Della Porta), sacred tragedy, 5 acts
Giuditta (Ploti), sacred tragedy, 5 acts
Giustina, La (Morone), sacred tragedy, 5 acts
Giustina vergine e martire santissima (Liviera), sacred tragedy, 5 acts
Granchio, Il (Salviati), comedy, 5 acts
Guglielma, Rapresentatione di Santa (anonymous), sacred representation, l act
Hirifile, L' (De'Sommi), pastoral, 5 acts
Ingannati, Gl' (Intronati), comedy, 5 acts
Inganni, Gl' (Gonzaga), comedy, 5 acts
Inganni, Gl' (Secchi), comedy, 5 acts
Ingiusti sdegni, Gli (Pino), comedy, 5 acts
Intricati, Gl' (Pasqualigo), pastoral, 5 acts
Intrichi d'amore (Tasso?), comedy, 5 acts
Ipocrito, L' (Aretino), comedy, 5 acts
Isabella astrologa (Scala), scenario, 3 acts
Lelio bandito (G. B. Andreini), comedy, 5 acts
Lite amorosa (Contrini), pastoral, 5 acts
Maddalena lasciva e penitente (G. B. Andreini), sacred hybrid, 3 acts
Mandragola (Machiavelli), comedy, 5 acts
Marescalco, Il (Aretino), comedy, 5 acts
Marito, Il (Scala), scenario, 3 acts
Martia, La (Selvaggio de'Selvaggii), pastoral, 5 acts
Martirio di Santa Caterina, Il (anonymous), sacred tragedy, 5 acts
Martirio di Santa Dorotea, Il (Persio), sacred tragedy, 5 acts
Maschere, Le (Machiavelli), comedy
Mirtilla, La (I. Andreini), pastoral, 5 acts
Mirzia, La (Epicuro), pastoral, 5 acts
Moro, Il (Della Porta), comedy, 5 acts
Morte di Cristo, La (Lega), sacred tragedy, 5 acts
Morti vivi, I (Oddi), comedy, 5 acts
Mortorio di Cristo, Il (Morone), sacred tragedy, 5 acts
Moscheta (Ruzante), comedy, 5 acts
Negromante, Il (Ariosto), comedy, 5 acts
Nicasio (Bonifacio), pastoral tragedy, 5 acts
Olimpia, L' (Della Porta), comedy, 5 acts
Olmiro (P. Bonarelli Della Rovere), pastoral tragedy, 5 acts
Orestilla, L' (Cortesi), pastoral tragedy, 5 acts
Orfeo (Poliziano), pastoral precursor
Orseida, L' (Scala), scenario, 3 giornate, 3 acts each
Orsilia, L' (Percivallo), pastoral, 5 acts
Pastoral, La (Ruzante), pastoral

Pastor fido, Il (Guarini), pastoral, 5 acts

Pazzia, La (Cucchetti), pastoral, 5 acts

Pazzia, La (Sicinio), comedy, 5 acts

Pazzia d'Isabella, La (anonymous), scenario

Pazzia d'Isabella, La (Scala), scenario, 3 acts

Pellegrina, La (Bargagli), comedy, 5 acts

Pellegrino fido amante, Il (Scala), scenario, 3 acts

Penelope, La (Della Porta), tragicomedia, 5 acts

Pentimento amoroso, Il (Groto), pastoral, 5 acts

Pompe funebri, Le (Cremonini), pastoral, 5 acts

Pompeo Magno (Persio), tragedy, 5 acts

Prigione d'amore (Oddi), comedy, 5 acts

Protogonos (Anisio), tragedy, 5 acts

Rappresentatione di Aman, La (anonymous), sacred representation, 1 act

Rappresentatione di Sancta Agnesa vergine et martyre, La (anonymous), sacred representation, 1 act

Rappresentatione di Santa Apollonia, vergine e martire, La (anonymous), sacred representation, 1 act

Rappresentatione di Santa Dorotea vergine e martire, La (anonymous), sacred representation, 1 act

Rappresentatione di Santa Teodora vergine e martire, La (anonymous), sacred representation, 1 act

Rappresentatione di Santo Giorgio Cavaliere di Christo, La (anonymous), sacred representation, 1 act

Rappresentatione et festa di Sa. Margherita vergine e martire, La (anonymous), sacred representation, 1 act

Rappresentatione sacra della vita et martirio del glorioso S. Venantio Da Camerino, La (Perbenedetti), sacred tragedy, 5 acts

Rappresentazione dell'Angelo Raffaello e di Tobbia, La (anonymous), sacred representation, 1 act

Rapresentatione del martorio de la vergine Margherita, La (Rondinelli), sacred tragedy, 5 acts

Rapresentatione di Santa Christina vergine e martire (anonymous), sacred representation, 1 act

Rapresentatione di S. Colomba vergine e martire (Tregiano), sacred representation

Rapresentatione di Santa Domitilla, La (anonymous?), sacred representation, 1 act

Rapresentatione di Santo Valentino e di Santa Giuliana e altri martiri, La (anonymous), sacred representation, 1 act

Regia pastorella, La (Pescetti), pastoral, 5 acts

Re Torrismondo, Il (Tasso), tragedy, 5 acts

Roselmina (G. B. Leoni), hybrid, 5 acts

Sacra Rappresentazione di San Lorenzo (Lottini), sacred tragedy, 5 acts

Sacra Rappresentazione di Santa Agnesa (Lottini), sacred tragedy, 5 acts

Sacrificio, Il (Beccari), pastoral, 5 acts

Santa Dorotea (Della Porta), sacred tragedy

Santi Innocenti, I (Porta), sacred tragedy, 5 acts

Saul (anonymous), sacred tragedy, 5 acts

Schiava, La (Calderari), comedy, 5 acts
Sofonisba, La (Trissino), tragedy, no division into acts
Sorella, La (Della Porta), comedy, 5 acts
Sospetti, I (Lupi), pastoral, 5 acts
Spiritata, La (Grazzini), comedy, 5 acts
Sporta, La (Gelli), comedy, 5 acts
Straccioni, Gli (Caro), comedy, 5 acts
Stravaganze d'amore, Le (Castelletti), comedy, 5 acts
Suppositi, I (Ariosto), comedy, 5 acts
Taide convertita, La (A. Leoni), sacred comedy, 5 acts
Talanta, La (Aretino), comedy, 5 acts
Teofilo, Il (Flori), sacred comedy, 5 acts
Theodora, La (Maleguzzi), comedy, 5 acts
Tirena (Cresci), pastoral, 5 acts
Tirrheno (Pona), pastoral, 5 acts
Torti amorosi, I (Castelletti), comedy, 5 acts
Tragici successi, Li (Scala), scenario, 3 acts
Trappolaria, La (Della Porta), comedy, 5 acts
Travagliata Isabella, La (Scala), scenario, 3 acts
Tre tiranni, I (Ricchi), comedy, 5 acts
Turca, La (Della Porta), comedy, 5 acts
Ulisse (Della Porta), tragedy, 5 acts
Vecchio amoroso, Il (Giannotti), comedy, 5 acts
Venexiana, La (anonymous), comedy, 5 acts
Verginia, La (Gualterotti), pastoral, 5 acts
Virginia (Accolti), comedy, 5 acts

Index

DATE DUE			